A Handy Vocabulary

PREFACE.

This little volume is based on the Maclay-Baldwin Alphabetic Dictionary in the Foochow Dialect, first published in 1870 and again in 1897, but is now out of print.

The attempt has been made to get together into a small compact form, the most commonly used words of the Colloquial language. Many of the characters in the old Dictionary are now obsolete, while many others are seldom used. It has been the purpose to eliminate such. On the other hand the aim has been to bring the book up to date by the addition of new words and expressions. This has not been easy owing to the repeated transformation of the spoken language in conformity with the ever changing conditions. It is hoped however, that such additions as have been made, will prove helpful to beginners in the acquisition of a fully servicable and polished colloquial.

Because of the limited size of the book, a minimum number, and only the most common, English equivalents have been given to each character.

The phrases have also been omitted. Users of the book are reminded that this is by no means, a Dictionary of the Chinese language but rather a Colloquial Vocabulary and being such contains many characters not found in Chinese Dictionaries.

In spite of all the care taken, mistakes have crept in but it is hoped not so serious as to defeat the object for which the work was undertaken.

L. P. Peet.

Foochow, China,
January, 1928.

Stewart Peet Memorial Press
Foochow City
1928

A HANDY VOCABULARY.

Ă, 鴉 as in *ă-piéng* 鴉片 opium; *lō̤-(u) ă*, a crow.

Ă-*tàu*, 丫頭 A female slave.

Ă-*cì*, 阿猝 A locust, cicada.

Ā, 吓 The disjunctive *or*; a classifier; a connective or euphonic particle.

Ā, 啞 Mute, dumb, silent.

Ā-*siĕk*, 拗折 To break in two.

À, 吓 An interjectional, emphatic, and euphonic particle.

Â, 下 Below, down; next, future; a time, a while; a portion.

Â, 厦 as in *Â Muòng*, 厦門 Amoy.

Â-*iòng*, 挨延 To delay.

Ă̄, 矮 Short, low in stature.

À̤, 鞋 Shoes, slippers.

Â, 儢 Can, will; do, does; is; probably.

Aĕh, 唒 To belch.

Aéng, 甕 A jar, vase, pitcher, etc.

Áh ciā, 揖者 Salute!

Ăi, 哀 A motherless child.

Ăi căi! 哀哉 Alas!

Āi-ciā, 倚藉 To trust in.

Ai-sék, 愛惜 To prize.

Aik lŏh, 扼落 To press down.

Âing, 限 To limit.

Ák-giāng, 鴨仔 A young duck.

Ák-ciĕ, 壓制 To restrain.

Ăk, 匣 A box.

Ăng, 安 Still, settled, safe, calm, peaceful; rest.

Āng, 閤 To shut the door.

Āng-tŏng, 泔湯 Rice broth.

Ăng-sĭ, 按司 A Judge.

Ăng, 暗 Dark, as night.

Âng, 旱 Drought.

Âng: as in *âng báuk*, the embankment has burst.

Âng-lâiu, 銲料 Solder.

Ău, 凹 Used for coll. *náh* and

năh q. v.: indented, concave.

Āu-tó, 嘔吐 To vomit.

Áu, 後 After in time or place, behind: *áu chiŭ,* 後手 the left hand; *áu-nĭk* 後日 day after to-morrow; *áu-nièng,* 後年 year after next.

Áuk, 惡 Wicked.

Áuk-cháuk, 齷齪 Filthy.

Áung, 牧 To guard, watch, herd.

Áung, 篊 A pole.

Bā, 飽 Full, satisfied; over excess: *bā-bŏk,* 飽腹 A full stomach.

Bā, 把 A classifier.

Bá, 壩 A dam.

Bà, 抓 To climb, to clamber, to creep.

Bá, as in *bá-nā,* 爸奶 parents.

Bạ̄, 叭 An interrogative particle.

Bạ̀, 排 To arrange in order.

Báek, 北 The North.

Báh, 百 A hundred: *báh ngó,* 百

五 one hundred and five tens, i. e., 150; *báh nê,* 百二 120.

Báh, 伯 An uncle.

Báh, 擘 To break apart, to open; to skin, as an orange.

Băh, 白 White.

Bāi, 擺 A term for sedan men (when more than two—so as to take turns).

Bái, 拜 To bow to, to show honor to, to salute; it precedes the ordinal numbers for the days of the week after the Sabbath: *bái gŭi* 拜幾 what day of the week is it? *siŏh lā̤-bái,* 一禮拜 one week.

Báik, 八 Eight; the eighth: *Báik Ĭng,* 八音 the eight tones; the Eight Tone Book.

Báik, 佁 To be acquainted with.

Bāing, 辦 To prepare.

Băk, 鈸 A small bell; cymbals.

Băng, 班 A class.

Bàng, 平 Level, even, uniform; colloquial: *bàng-dĭk,* 平直 straight; *bàng-ciáng,* 平正 poor, inferior.

Bàng, as in *bēng-bàng,* 板棚 a board floor.

Báng, 病 Ill; sickness: *báng-cáung,* 病狀 symptoms; *báng-ā,* 病啞 dumb, silent.

Bău, 包 Bread.

Báuk, 剝 To burst, to break, as a boil.

Báuk-guá, 卜卦 To divine.

Báung, 謗 To slander.

Bé, 痺 Numbed.

Bék, 必 Certainly.

Bék, 筆 A pen, a pencil.

Bĕk, 拔 To pull; *bĕk ò,* 拔河 tug of war.

Bēng, 邊 Side, way, direction.

Bēng, as in *bēng-báik,* a corruption

of *báik ng báik,* 仈怀仈 acquainted with or not?

Bĕng, 板 A board, a plank, a page; to invert, to turn over.

Bèng, 丬 A side, a part.

Bèng, as in *bèng-iŭ,* 朋友 a friend, an acquaintance.

Bèng, as in *bèng-ngiè,* 便宜 cheap.

Bī, 比 To compare: *bī-ęu,* 比喻 for instance, to illustrate.

Biáh, 壁 A partition.

Biāng, 餅 A cake.

Biáng, 倂 To pour, to empty out.

Bié, 臂 The arm.

Biĕ, 避 To flee from.

Biék, 撇 To turn down, as a hem.

Biék, 憋 Lame, bent, wrenched.

Biĕk liè, 別離 To leave.

Biĕng, 邊 The side, the border; one of the 15 initials.

Biéng, 變 To change, to alter.

Bièng, 便 Convenient, proper;

ready, done, finished: *biêng-gek*, 便急 convenient, handy.

Biêu, 表 To manifest; to bring out, as an ailment, etc.; a watch.

Bĭk, 弼 To aid, to assist as statesmen do.

Bing, 兵 A soldier.

Bing, 冰 Ice.

Bing, 稟 A petition.

Bìng, 平 Tranquil, peaceful: *bìng-ăng*, 平安 well and happy, free from trouble, prosperous.

Bìng, 瓶 A vase.

Bìng, 憑 To obey, to follow.

Bó, 富 Rich.

Bô, 仅 Again.

Bŏ, as in *bŏ-là*, 坡璃 glass.

Bō, 保 or *bō-hô*, 保護 to preserve, to protect.

Bō-buói, 寶貝 Precious.

Bó, 報 or *bó-dák*, 報答 to recompense; a recompense.

Bò, as in *dà-bò*, 茶婆 A teapot.

Bò, 抱 To carry in the arms, to embrace.

Bò-ngiŏk, 暴虐 Oppressive.

Bói, 吠 To bark.

Bŏh, 泊 To anchor.

Bŏh, 薄 Thin.

Bók, 不 Not.

Bók-lō, 腹老 The abdomen.

Bŏng, 帮 To assist; a period of time.

Bōng, 榜 As in *bōng piéu*, 榜票 to kidnap for ransom.

Bóng, 放 To put down, to place; to loosen, to hold loosely: *bóng huōi*, 放火 to set fire to, incendiarism.

Bóng, 糞 Dung.

Bòng-biĕng, 傍邊 The side.

Bōng, 鈍 Read *dóng*, q. v.: dull, stupid.

Bŭ, 嗜 An interjectional particle.

Buâng

Bŭ-săk, 菩薩 Idol.

Buái, 簸 Read *bó* ; To winnow.

Buák, 撥 To distribute, to allot ; *buák - chă*, 撥差 to detach police; *buák-chāng*, 撥醒 to arouse.

Buăk, 跌 Read *diĕk;* to fall, as a person.

Buăk, 鈸 Read *băk* q. v. a kind of cymbal.

Buăng, 㨃 A sort, manner, kind.

Buăng, 班 also read *băng* q. v. an order, rank, a company.

Buăng, 搬 To remove.

Buáng, 半 A half: *buáng-làng-chiàng*, 半闌俄 half-done.

Buàng, 盤 A plate, a tray; *buàng-hié* 盤費 traveling expenses; *buàng-cŭ*; to copy a book ; *buàng-báuk*, to debate.

Buáng, 絆 To brush away, to strike with limber things;

to hamper to restrict; in the coll. to brush away; *dièng-buâng,* 縶絆 entangled, as by an obstruction; *met.* involved, obscure.

Buâng, 叛 To revolt, to rebel; *buâng-ngĭk,* 叛逆 rebellion.

Bùi, 肥 Read *pì*; fat; fertile; coll. word for which the last is used; leaven, yeast; *bău-bùi,* yeast.

Bŭk, 僕 to serve, a menial; *nù-bŭk,* 奴僕 a slave.

Bŭk, 瀑 a cascade; *bŭk-buó,* 瀑布 a cataract.

Bŭng, 崩 Read *bĕng*; to cave in; *bŭng-dō̤,* 崩倒 to fall as a wall. Read *bĕng* 崩 the demise of an emperor.

Bùng, 房 A room, a chamber.

Bùng, 嗙 To blow with the mouth, to inflate with air; *bùng guó,*

煬爲 to blow out (a lamp).

Buŏ, 哺 or màng-buŏ, 暝哺 night: siŏh-màng-buŏ, 一暝哺 last night; buáng-buŏ, 半哺 about 4 p. m; buŏ-sì-ṳ̄, 哺時雨 afternoon showers; more correctly, bók-sì-ṳ̄, 不時雨

Buŏ, 補 To mend, to repair, to recruit, as the body.

Buó 布 Cotton cloth.

Buó, 佈 To publish.

Buó, 播 Read bó, used for collbuó as in buó-chèng, 播田 to set out (rice plants) in the fields.

Buô, 步 A step: buô-hèng, 步行 to walk; buô-bĭng, 步兵 infantry.

Buô, 捕 To pursue and capture; buô-tiăng, 捕廳 subordinate officers who make arrests.

Buô, 部 A class, a bureau, a

Board; *cê-buô*, 字部 the radicals.

Buŏh, 剝 Read *báuk*: will, shall, about to; bent on; to strip off.

Buŏh, 縛 To tie up; *buŏh-sŏk*, 縛束 a binding rule.

Buói, 杯 A cup, a glass.

Buói, 背 The back, behind, rear; *buói-áu*, 背後 behind the back, i. e. secretly also read *buói* 背 q. v.

Buói, 褙 to mount maps and pictures; *buói-lièng*, —聯 to make scrolls; *buói-biáh*, —壁 to paper walls.

Buòi, 賠 To repay, to indemnify; *buòi-bŏk-sĕ*, 賠不是 to confess a wrong.

Buòi, 陪 To keep one company, as in sitting, laughing, or talking with him.

Buói, 倍 *gă-buói*, 加倍 To double.

că-giĕ, 齋規 the rules of a school; *că-sŭ*, 齋所 a study; *sṓi că*, 坐齋 to be a schoolteacher; *guŏng că muòng*, 關齋門 a private school; *siăh dòng că*, 貪長齋 a vegetarian.

Că, 齎 To present to, to despatch, as documents; *chĭng că*, 親齎 to deliver in person.

Că, 儕 A class, a company; *ngō̤-că*, 我儕 *ngù-că*, 吾儕 we, us; *dùng că*, 同儕 associates.

Cá, 濟 To cross over; to assist; able, clever; *cá-ìng*, 濟人 to ferry persons over; *sié-cá*, 施濟 to give alms.

Cá, 纃 A species of hemp; *cá-buó*, 一布 grass-cloth.

Cà, 齊 Even, level; to equalize; to respect; to arrange; quick, smart; good; together; at the same time; *cà lĭk*, 齊力 to work together; *cīng-cà,* 整齋 handsome; *cà ngiê,* 齊議 to consult together; *cà gă,* 齊家 to govern a family; *muôi cà,* 昧齊 not yet assembled as a company.

Cá, 劑 as *bău-cá,* 包劑 dough.

Câe, 助 Read *cô:* to assist; *bŏng-câe,* 帮助 to aid, to succor.

Cáh, 窄 Narrow; *cáh-géng,* 窄徑 a lane.

Cáh-siăng, 仄聲 Tones (p. 4)

Cáh 績 Read *cék:* as *cáh-siáng,* 績線 to join fibre.

Căi, 栽 To plant as *căi-céụng,* 栽種 *căi huă,* 栽花.

Căi, 災 Natural calamities; divine judgments, misfortunes.

Căi 齊 also read *cà* q. v. to restrain, to reverence.

Cāi, 宰 A ruler; to govern; *cāi-siŏng,* 宰相 a premier; *ciŏ-cāi,* că-giĕ, 齋規 the rules of a school; că-sū, 齋所 a study; sói că, 坐齋 to be a school-teacher; gŭong că mùong, 關齋門 a private school; siăh dòng că, 貪長齋 a vegetarian.

Că, 賫 To present to, to despatch, as documents; chĭng că, 親賫 to deliver in person.

Că, 儕 A class, a company; ngō̤-că, 我儕 ngù-că, 吾儕 we, us; dùng că, 同儕 associates.

Cá, 濟 To cross over; to assist; able, clever; cá-ìng, 濟人 to ferry persons over; sié-cá, 施濟 to give alms.

Cá, 纃 A species of hemp; cá-buó, —布 grass-cloth.

Cà, 齊 Even, level; to equalize; to respect; to arrange; quick, smart; good; together; at the same time; cà lĭk, 齊力 to work together; *cīng-cà*, 整齊 handsome; *cà ngiê*, 齊議 to consult together; *cà gă*, 齊家 to govern a family; *muôi cà*, 昧齊 not yet assembled as a company.

Cá, 劑 as *báu-cá*, 包劑 dough.

Câe, 助 Read *cô:* to assist; *bŏng-câe*, 帮助 to aid, to succor.

Cáh, 窄 Narrow; *cáh-géng*, 窄徑 a lane.

Cáh-siăng, 仄聲 Tones (p. 4)

Cáh 績 Read *cék:* as *cáh-siáng*, 績線 to join fibre.

Căi, 栽 To plant as *căi-céung*, 栽種 *căi huă*, 栽花.

Căi, 災 Natural calamities; divine judgments, misfortunes.

Căi 齊 also read *cà* q. v. to restrain, to reverence.

Cāi, 宰 A ruler; to govern; *cāi-siŏng*, 宰相 a premier; *ciŏ-cāi*,

眅鵁 to blow out (a lamp).

Buŏ, 晡 or *màng-buŏ,* 暝晡 night: *siŏh-màng-buŏ,* 一暝晡 last night; *buáng-buŏ,* 半晡 about 4 p. m; *buŏ-sì-ŭ,* 晡時雨 afternoon showers; more correctly, *bŏk-sì-ŭ,* 不時雨

Buó 補 To mend, to repair, to recruit, as the body.

Buó 布 Cotton cloth.

Buó, 佈 To publish.

Buó, 播 Read *bó,* used for coll- *buó* as in *buó-chèng,* 播田 to set out (rice plants) in the fields.

Buó, 步 A step: *buó-hèng,* 步行 to walk; *buó-bĭng,* 步兵 infantry.

Buó, 捕 To pursue and capture; *buó-tiăng,* 捕廳 subordinate officers who make arrests.

Buó, 部 A class, a bureau, a

Board; *cé-luó,* 字部 the radicals.

Buŏh, 剝 Read *báuk*: will, shall, about to; bent on; to strip off.

Buŏh, 縛 To tie up; *buŏh-sók,* 縛束 a binding rule.

Buói, 杯 A cup, a glass.

Buói, 背 The back, behind, rear; *buói-áu,* 背後 behind the back, i. e. secretly also read *buói* 背 q. v.

Buói, 褙 to mount maps and pictures; *buói-lièng,* —聯 to make scrolls; *buói-biáh,* —壁 to paper walls.

Buói, 賠 To repay, to indemnify; *buòi-bók-sé,* 賠不是 to confess a wrong.

Buói, 陪 To keep one company, as in sitting, laughing, or talking with him.

Buói, 倍 *gă-buói,* 加倍 To double.

că-giĕ, 齋規 the rules of a school; că-sṳ̆, 齋所 a study; sói că, 坐齋 to be a schoolteacher; guŏng că muòng, 關齋門 a private school; siăh dòng că, 貪長齋 a vegetarian.

Că, 齎 To present to, to despatch, as documents; chĭng că, 親齎 to deliver in person.

Că, 儕 A class, a company; ngō̤-că, 我儕 ngù-că, 吾儕 we, us; dùng că, 同儕 associates.

Cá, 濟 To cross over; to assist; able, clever; cá-ìng, 濟人 to ferry persons over; sié·cá, 施濟 to give alms.

Cá, 緕 A species of hemp; cá-buó, —布 grass-cloth.

Cà, 齊 Even, level; to equalize; to respect; to arrange; quick, smart; good; together; at the same time; cà lĭk, 齊力 to work together; *cīng-cà,* 整齊 handsome; *cà ngiê,* 齊議 to consult together; *cà gă,* 齊家 to govern a family; *muôi cà,* 昧齊 not yet assembled as a company.

Cá, 劑 as *băŭ-cá,* 包劑 dough.

Câe, 助 Read *cô*: to assist; *bŏng-câe,* 帮助 to aid, to succor.

Cáh, 窄 Narrow; *cáh-géng,* 窄徑 a lane.

Cáh-siăng, 仄聲 Tones (p. 4)

Cáh 績 Read *cék*: as *cáh-siáng,* 績線 to join fibre.

Căi, 栽 To plant as *căi-cęụng,* 栽種 *căi huă,* 栽花.

Căi, 災 Natural calamities; divine judgments, misfortunes.

Căi 齊 also read *cà* q. v. to restrain, to reverence.

Cāi, 宰 A ruler; to govern; *cāi-sióng,* 宰相 a premier; *ciŏ-cāi,*

主宰 the governing power, the mind.

Cāi, 指 Read *cī*: a finger, a toe.

Cāi, as in *mĕk-cāi* 目滓 tears.

Cāi, 紙 Read *cī*: Paper, a writing; *cāi bék*, 紙筆 stationery; *gĭng-cāi*, 京紙 common writing paper; *cāi bùng*, 一房 a paper manufactory or storing room.

Cāi, 載 also read *cái* q. v., a year, as in *nièng cāi*, 年載 a year; *siŏh nièng buáng cāi*, 一年半載 a year or half a year; *săng nièng ngū cāi*, 三年五載 from three to five years.

Cái, 載 to bear, to fulfill to adorn; recorded; *gé-cái*, 記載 to record.

Cái, 再 Again; then, further, continued; *cái gōng*, 再講 to explain again; *cái bái*, 再拜

repeated compliments; also regeneration.

Cái, 債 A debt; *cièng cái,* 錢債 money debts; *tọ̄ cái* 討債 to collect dues; *sùng cái,* 船債 fare, freight.

Cài, 才 Ability, talents; *kēu-cài,* 口才 eloquence; *cài-nèng,* 才能 or *cài-cìng,* 才情 talent, ability; *séu-cài,* 秀才 (*séu-còi,*) a Siutsai, a first degree graduate.

Cài, 材 Wood, timber, nature, qualities; *cài-láiu,* 材料 building materials, *met.* capability.

Cài, 財 Wealth, profits, money; *huó-cài,* 貨財 goods; *cièng-cài,* 錢財 wealth; *cài-bọ̄,* 財寶 riches; *huák-cài,* 發財 to become wealthy; *cài-ciō,* 財主 a man of wealth.

Cáing   19

Cái, 在 To be in; as, according to; *ù-bók-cái,* 無不在 omnipresent; *sū-cái,* 所在 a place; *cái nṳ,* 在汝 as you please.

Cái, 寨 also read *sái:* a stockade, a fortified place; *ngù-tàu-cái,* 牛頭寨 a ruin on Kuliang mountains, once a famous fortified retreat.

Cáik, 責 To blame; *cáik-bê,* 責備 to reprove; *cáik-sìng,* 責成 responsibility; *cáik-huăk,* 責罰 to punish, to fine.

Cáik, 汁 Gravy.

Cáik, 則 A rule; as *cūng-cáik,* 準則 a model.

Cáik, 節 read *ciék:* a joint, a festival.

Cáik-sĭng, 側身 read *cháik-sĭng:* sidewise.

Cáing, 諍 To reprove; also used

for *cěng* q. v. to wrangle.

Cáing, to revile; *càng-cáing*, 譏譖 to slander.

Cáing, 苫 A mat; mourning; *chāu-cáing*, 草苫 a straw mattress.

Cáing, 贈 To present, to give.

Cáiu 奏 To memorialize the throne; *cáiu siòng*, 湊上 to memorialize the emperor.

Cáiu, 皴 read *cĕu*: a scowl a frown; *cáiu-mì*, 皴眉 to frown; *puòi-cáiu*, 皮皴 wrinkled skin.

Cáiu-să, 縐紗 Crape.

Cáiu also read *cáiu* 驟 A fleet horse.

Cák, 匝 To go the rounds like a watchman; *cák-cák*, 匝匝 full, complete.

Cák, 紮 To bind, wrap.

Cák, 札 A letter, a document; *piĕ-cák*, 批扎 a dispatch.

Cák, 筒, also read *dák*, a contract; a reply from a higher officer; *cák-dăng*, 筒單 a purchase contract.

Cák, as in *ṳ̄ há siŏh cák*, 雨下一洓 a fall of rain.

Căk, 雜 Various, mixed; *căk cṳ̆*, 雜書 miscellaneous books; *căk-bà-dăng*, 雜排攤 stall for all sorts of wares; *căk-diō*, intersecting roads.

Căk, 柵 also read *cháik* q. v. and *chák*: a stockade, a palisade; *căk-lăk-muòng*, 柵拉門 street gates.

Căk as in *cūi căk*, 水閘 A sluice.

Căk, 卡 A military post.

Căk, 斲 Read *ciŏk*: to cut, mince.

Căng, 爭 Read *cĕng*: q. v. to quarrel.

Căng, 簪 A hairpin; *căng-giăng*, 簪仔 small hair-pins; *căng-*

huă, 簪花 to wear the golden flower as graduates do; căng-guá, 簪掛 to wear the silk scarf ditto.

Cāng, 井 Read cīng: q. v.: a well.

Cāng, 斬 To behead.

Cāng, as in ciū-cāng, 酒盞 A wine-cup.

Cáng, 讚 To come before an idol; to commend; cáng-mī, 讚美 to praise; chǐng-cáng, 稱讚 praise; cáng-lā̤, 讚禮 a master of ceremonies at sacrifices.

Càng, 巉 A high inaccessible peak; càng-ngàng, 巉巖 high rocks piled up; càng-ngiàng, 巉巖 overgrown.

Càng, 讒 as in càng-cáing 讒譖 to slander.

Càng, 殘 To destroy; càng-hái,

殘害 to injure; *càng-ŭng*, 殘忍 cruel.

Càng, 蠶 Silkworm; coll. *chèng*, q. v.

Cáng, 鏨 To chisel, cut.

Câng, 站 A stage, a journey; full amount; *iăh-câng*, 驛站 official post stations.

Càng-sì, 暫時 Briefly, a while.

Câng, 棧 a warehouse; palisades; *câng-bùng*, 棧房 a warehouse, a hong.

Cău, 燋 Charred; *chù-căo*, 柴— firebrands.

Cău póh, 糟粕 Lees, dregs.

Cău-cău-náung, Confused.

Cău, 爪 Nails, claws; the 87th radical; *căo-ngà*, 爪牙 nails and teeth; *met.*, servants, retainers.

Cāu, 走 Read *cēu*: q. v., to escape; to vary from.

Cāu, 找 To make change; *cāu cièng-muōi,* 找錢尾 to return a balance of money; *cāu diē,* 找裏 to receive a balance; *cāu chók,* 找出 to pay a balance.

Cāu, Read *cō*; as in *gā-cāu,* 咬蚤 a flea.

Cáu, 灶 A kitchen range; *cáu gŭng, cáu mā,* 灶君 灶媽 kitchen god and goddess; *cáu-sèng* 灶前 A kitchen.

Càu, 巢 A nest, a den; *mò̤ càu,* 毛巢 homeless.

Càu, 剿 To desolate; *càu-mìng,* 剿民 to exterminate people; *càu-miĕk,* 剿滅 to destroy utterly.

Cáuk, 作 To do, act; *cié-cáuk,* 制作 to invent, to discover; *cáuk-guái,* 作怪 strange, marvelous; *ciĕng-cáuk,* 賤作 rude, boisterous; *cáuk-gă*, 作佳 handsome, beautiful.

Cáuk, 剝 Read *cĕu* and *sáuk*; *cáuk dōng*, 剝斷 to sever.

Cáung, 壯 Healthy, strong; *cáung-cé*, 壯志 resolute; *cáung-nièng*, 壯年 a young man; *cáung sĭng*, 壯心 vigorous in mind; *cáung-giông*, 壯健 robust.

Cáung, 葬 To inter; *muài-cáung*, 埋葬 to bury; *sáeng-cáung*, 送葬 to attend a funeral; *cáung tù-diē*, 葬土裡 to hide in the ground.

Cáung, 錐 Read *chŭi*: An awl, a borer.

Cáung, 狀 Appearance, form, shape; *gó-cáung*, 告狀 to litigate; *cáung-nguòng*, 狀元 (coll. *cŏ-nguòng*,) the first of the Hanlin; *cáung-sṳ̆*, 狀師 a lawyer, a notary.

Câung, Sặ-câung, 西藏 Thibet.

Câung-hū, 臟腑 The viscera.

Cé, 至 To arrive at, to come; the summit, the end; very, most.

Cé, 誌 To remember; to record; annals, history.

Cé, 質 also read *cék* q. v. to testify; evidence, proof; *dó̤i cé,* 對質 to testify face to face.

Cé, 志 Resolution, intention; annals; *cé-ché̤u,* 志趣 the will, purpose; *iū cé,* 有志 a purpose, a design; *lĭk-cé,* 立志 to resolve; *lặ-cé,* to animate.

Cé siŏh lăk, 痣一粒 A body mole.

Cé, 字 A character, a letter; an epistle, a chit: *cé-tàu,* 字頭 initials; *cé-mō̤,* 字母 finals; *cé-diēng,* 字典 a dictionary; *cé-ngāng,* 字眼 set phrases; *cé-ngiĕ,* the literal meaning of

Cék 27

words; *chọ̆-cê*, 草字 running hand characters; *kāi-cé*, 楷字 elegant or pattern characters.

Cê, 自 (Read *cẹ̆u* q. v.) or *cê-gă*, 自家 self, one's self; *cẹ̆u-hái-cẹ̆u*, 自害自 to injure one's self.

Cè̤ guó, 擠過 To crowd by.

Céh, 泚 To spirt out.

Céh-céh-giéu, To squeal, as rats.

Cék, 跡 A footstep; vestiges; *sìng-cék*, 神跡 miracles; *hìng-cék*, 形跡 form.

Cék, 脊 Convergent, as ribs; ridge of a house; *piăng-cék-gáuk*, 背脊骨 the spine or backbone.

Cék, as in *Háiu-cék* 后稷 Harvest god.

Cék, 蹟 A foot mark; *gū-cék*, 古蹟 ancient signs.

Cék, 織 To weave; *cék buó*, 織布 to weave cloth.

Cék, 職 Tribute, to govern; to

record; title, office; *cék-hóng*, 職份 official duty.

Cék, 即 Now, forthwith; *cék-káik*, 即刻 instantly.

Cék-ngù, 鯽魚 A bream.

Cék, 喞 The hum of insects; *cék-ciák*, 喞吒 noise of lips in eating.

Cék, 執 To take in the hand; to keep; obstinate; *cék-sĕṳ*, 執事 committee; deacons.

Cék, 積 To hoard, to increase; *cék-héuk*, 積蓄 to accumulate.

Cĕk, 宅 Read *tĕk*, q. v.; as in *cĕk muòng*, 宅門 a door opening into the 2nd hall or private apartments of yamun.

Cĕk, 賊 coll. *chĕk* q. v., a thief, a bandit.

Cĕk, 鰂 The cuttle fish "*mĕk-ngù*". 墨魚.

Cĕk, 截 To cut, to divide, to

Céng 29

stop; *cĕk láng dū*, 截二堵 divided into two apartments.

Cĕng, 曾 To duplicate; a surname; one of the 15 initials; *cĕng-sŏng*, great grandsons.

Cĕng, 爭 coll. read *căng*, q. v.: to quarrel; to litigate; *cĕng-dáiu*, 爭鬥 to fight.

Cĕng, 針 A needle, a pin; a stitch: *cĕng-kă*, 針胶 a stitch.

Cĕng, 增 as in *gă-cĕng* 加增 to increase.

Cĕng gă, 僧家 Buddhist priests.

Cĕng-găng, 榛乾 Dried filberts.

Cēng, 剪 To cut with scissors, to clip even.

Céng, 浸 To soak.

Céng, 進 To advance; to promote; *céng-séu*, 進士 a Doctor of Laws, L. L. D.; *céng-sèng*, 進前 *céng-ĕk*, 進益 to advance; *īng-céng*, 引進 to introduce.

Céng, as in *báng-céng* 病症 Sickness.

Céng, 政 To rule, to govern; *guók-céng*, 國政 government.

Céng, 證 To bear witness; *céng-giéng*, 證見 to witness.

Cèng, 層 A story of a building; a shelf, a layer; a degree above.

Cèng as in *báik-cèng*, 仈曾 formerly; *muói-cèng*, 昧曾 never have.

Cěng, 盡 To exhaust; exhausted, finished; very, extremely, to the utmost degree.

Céng, 靜 Silent, quiet; to judge; *ăng-céng*, 安靜 peaceful.

Cěng, 棕 Read *cŭng*: as in *cěng-sǐ*, 棕絲 palm-fibre.

Cěng, 鬃 Read *cŭng*: mane, bristles.

Cēng, 鬃 Read *cŭng*; *cēng dáing*,

鬁店 a wig shop.

Cèng láng, Dash it wet.

Cēu, 走 To travel; coll. *cāu*, q. v.

Cēu, 鳥 Read *nēu*: a bird.

Céu̱, 蛀 Read *céu̱*: an insect that eats books; to decay; *céu̱-tèng*, 蛀蟲 a moth, bookworm.

Céu̱ má, 咒罵 To rail at.

Céu̱, 就 Then, immediately, soon; that is, just so: *céu̱ sê* 就是 that is, to wit, viz.

Céu̱, 注 To lead water into channels; *cūi céu̱*, 水注 water flowing in; *láng céu̱*, 濫注 to slough.

Céu̱, 厠 A filthy place; *céu̱-sū*, 厠所 a water closet.

Céu̱, as in *gă-céu̱-băo* a straw pouch or bag for cooking rice.

Céu̱, 駐 To stop a horse; *céu̱-cák*, 駐札 appointed to a post.

Céu, 漬 To soak; to dye; *céu láng*, 漬濫 soaked soft.

Céu, 自 Self: *cêu-iòng*, 自然 self-existent, of course; *cêu-mìng-cŭng*, 自鳴鐘 a clock; *cêu-lài cūi*, 自來水 water works; *cêu-lài cāng*, 自來井 an artesian well.

Cêu, 住 To live in.

Cêu-cĭk, 聚集 To assemble.

Cêu, 柱 coll. *têu*, q. v., a post, a pillar, a statesman.

Céuk, 足 The foot, the leg; full, sufficient, in full; *céuk é*, 足意 fully satisfied; *chŭng-céuk*, 充足 sufficient, ample.

Céuk, 粥 Congee.

Céuk, 燭 coll. read *cióh* q. v.; a candle; to shine.

Céuk, 叔 Read *séuk*; a father's younger brother; *céuk-báh*, 叔伯 paternal uncles.

Céuk, 囑 To order, to enjoin; céuk-táuk, 囑託 to commission.

Céuk, 祝 To pray; céuk-hók, 祝福 to bless, to bestow favors; céuk-siá, 祝謝 to return thanks; miéu-céuk, a temple keeper; buō˙ céuk, 補祝 to celebrate a birthday after its date; éu céuk, 預祝 to celebrate a birthday before its date.

Céung, 衆 A multitude, all, a concourse of at least three persons; gŭng-céng, the public.

Céung, 種 To plant, to sow; céung-dáu, 種痘 to vaccinate.

Céung, 縱 Remiss, careless, ùng-céung, 容縱 to allow, as to do wrong.

Céung, 從 Read cùng q. v. a clan, a family.

Cĭ, 之 Sign of the wen-li genitive, a personal pronoun.

Cĭ, 止 To stop, to rest; *cī tiáng*, 止痛 to soothe pain.

Cĭ, 子 Read *cū*, seeds; *guă-cī*, 瓜子 melon seeds.

Cĭ, 只 Only, merely; so much, thus much; here; this, this one: *cī-dòng*, 只長 just now, a moment ago; *cī-běng*, 只邊 this side; *miéh cī hŭ*, et cetera, *mò cī mò hŭ*, no trouble.

Cĭ, 枳 A numerative.

Cĭ, as in *cěng-cī*, 針帶 embroidery.

Cĭ, 旨 Intention; will, purpose; *cī-é*, 旨意 intention, will.

Cĭ, 指 A finger, a toe; *cī-diĕng*, 指點 to teach, point; *cī-sê*, 指示 to instruct.

Ci cūi, 焠水 To temper in water.

Ciă, 遮 To conceal, to screen; a

parasol; *ciă-ṳ̄*, 遮雨 a rain screen; *ciă-iēng*, 遮掩 to cover, hide.

Ciă 笊 Read *cāu*, or *cáu*; a cullender; *ciă-liè*, 笊籬 a ladle, a strainer.

Ciā, 姐 Read *cī* or *ciē*, an older sister.

Ciā, 者 It, this, that, these, those, he, she, who, etc.

Ciā, 嗻 A colloquial character used for the former; *ciā nèng*, 嗻仈 this person; *mò ciā sẹu*, or *mò ciā dài*, 毛嗻代, no such thing or matter.

Ciá, 樜 Sugar cane.

Ciá, 借 Also read *ciá:* to assist; to borrow, to lend: in coll. read *cióh* q. v.

Cià, 嗻 A euphonic and emphatic particle, this, &c.

Ciá, 藉 Also read *cĭk* to help;

to trust in, to rely or depend on; *cŭ ciá,* 資藉 to aid; *ciòng ciá,* 全藉 to trust wholly; *āi-ciá,* 倚藉 to trust in, by means of; *ciá sié,* 藉勢 to presume on one's influence.

Ciáh, 跡 Read *cék;* a track, trace, stain.

Ciáh, 雀 Read *chiók;* a wren, a small bird; *ciáh-giāng,* 雀仔 a sparrow.

Ciáh, 隻 One, single; a classifier of men, animals, birds etc; just, just now, then, just then; *cī ciáh,* 只隻 this one; *ciáh-ciáh,* 隻隻 singly; *cēu-ciáh,* 鳥隻 small birds. Also used for the coll. word meaning just, just now; *ciáh lì,* 隻來 has just come; *ká ciáh ká,* 快隻快 very quickly.

Ciák, 泎 Read *cáik;* to spill;

Ciâng 37

ciák uòng, 汖完 all spilled; *ciák muāng dê*, 汖滿地 spilled all around.

Ciăk, 吃 To smack the lips.

Ciăng, 正 Read *cĕng: ciăng nguŏk*, 正月 the first month of the year; *ciăng nguŏk chẹ̆*, 正月初 beginning of the first moon.

Ciăng 精 Read *cĕng:* form taken by spirits; *ciăng-guái*, 精怪 elves, sprites.

Ciăng, 鬹 Read *cāng:* fresh, not salt; insipid; *ciāng niă-nọ̆i*, somewhat fresh.

Ciáng, 正 Read *céng:* correct, straight, not awry; exactly; in the center; right; *ciáng-ùng*, 正文 written or classic style; *ciáng-ciáng-họ̆*, just the thing!

Ciáng, 淨 Read *cêng* and *ciáng:* clean, pure; to cleanse.

Ciĕ, 枝 A branch, twig; a classifier of slender things.

Ciĕ, 肢 The limbs of the body; *ciĕ-tā*, the whole body.

Ciĕ, 支 Posterity; *ciĕ-puái*, 支派 descendents; *ciĕ ciĕng* 支錢 to pay out money.

Ciĕ-muài, 芝蔴 Sesamum.

Ciĕ-cṳ̄, 梔子 The becho-nut, used in dyeing.

Ciē, 紫 A reddish, blue.

Cié 這 A demonstrative pronoun; *cié-iông*, 這樣 thus, so.

Cié, 祭 To sacrifice; *ciŏng-cié*, to present as an offering.

Cié, 制 To control, to endure, to bear up under; *Cié-dăi*, Viceroy.

Cié, 製 To cut out clothes; *cié-cáuk*, 製作 to make; *cié iŏh*, 製藥 to compound medicine.

Cié 際 To join, to cement, to

connect; *ng cié séu,* 怀際事 a trifling amount.

Ciék, 接 To receive, to go to bring back, as a sedan; *ciék-dâi,* 接待 to entertain a guest; *kó̤ ciék giêu,* 去接轎 to go and bring one back in a sedan; *ciék-chéu,* 接模 to graft trees.

Ciék, 節 coll. *cáik:* a festival; a verse; *ciŏng ciék,* 章節 chapter and verse; *ciék-ęung,* 節用 economy; *guăng-ciék,* 關節 a limit, a restraint; *ciék-háu-huŏng,* 節孝坊 honorary portals to virtuous widows.

Ciék, 折 To break off; *ciék-tàu,* 折頭 a discount, reduction.

Ciék, 摺 To fold; *ciék-liŏk,* 摺畧 a written digest or resumé.

Ciék-gŏng, 浙江 Chehkiang.

Ciĕk, 捷 To conquer; *ciĕk-kiēu* 捷巧 precocious, quick.

Ciĕng, 沾 To wash out, as a spot; to receive benefits; *ciĕng cā*, 沾早 to receive gratuitously; to receive as a gift.

Ciĕng, 毡 A woolen rug, carpet; *dê-ciĕng*, 地毡 a carpet, a rug.

Ciĕng, 煎 To fry, as pork; *ciĕng sŭ-sŭ*, 煎酥酥 to fry crisp.

Ciĕng, 尖 Sharp, pointed; clever; *ciĕng-lê* 尖利 sharp, grasping; *dĭng ciĕng*, 項尖 extreme, the best; *săng-gáek-ciĕng*, 三角尖 triangular; *gāng-lāng-ciĕng*, olive shaped.

Ciĕng, 尖 A wedge; to wedge, crowd in, add.

Ciĕng, 瞻 To revere; *ciĕng-uông*, 瞻望 to long for.

Ciĕng, 剪 coll. *cēng*; q. v. to cut, to kill; scissors.

Ciĕng, 踐 To tread upon.

Ciĕng, 菚 Young, fresh, unripe.

Ciĕng, 蝘 A house lizard.

Ciĕng, 枕 Read cīng: as ciĕng-tàu, 枕頭 a pillow.

Ciéng, 箭 As ciéng-chī, 箭矢 an arrow; siŏh ciéng, 射箭 to shoot arrows.

Ciéng, 僭 To usurp, to assume.

Ciéng, 佔 To trespass upon, to seize; ciéng dê, 佔地 to encroach on the land of another; kĕuk ĭ ciéng kó, 乞伊佔去 usurped by him.

Ciéng, 薦 Pasturage; to recommend; ciéng dê-huŏng, 薦地方 to recommend to a place; bō̤-ciéng, 保薦 to recommend and be security for; ciéng-cṳ̆, 薦書 a written recommendation.

Ciéng, 牮 A prop; to prop, to shore up.

Ciéng, 戰 To fight; timid, afraid; ciéng-dáiu, 戰鬪 to fight; gău-ciéng-daiu-gì = fighting fla *ciéng*, 交戰 to go to war; *dēu-dēu-ciéng*, 斗斗戰 to tremble; *ciéng iǎng*, 戰贏 a victory; *ciéng siŏ*, 戰輸 a defeat; *ciéng diòng*, 戰場 the field of battle; *ciéng-gū*, 戰鼓 drums sounding the charge.

Cièng, 前 Coll. *sèng*, q. v.; before, in time or place; in front of; to advance, to go forward; formerly; *cùng-cièng*, 從前 previously; *cièng hǎiu*, 前後 before and after; *cièng-buói*, 前輩 seniors, venerable sir! *bók cièng bók hǎiu*, 不前不後 just at the time.

Cièng, 鼶 Read *ièng*; *cièng-chū*, 鼶鼠 a ground mole.

Cièng, 錢 A copper coin, cash, money, property; a surname; *cièng-dáing*, 錢店 a bank; *cièng-piéu*, 錢票 bank note;

cièng-lé, 錢利 interest; *buōng-cièng,* 本錢 capital; *cièng dáung miâng,* 錢當命 money esteemed as life—excessively parsimonious; *cièng chiŏng běk mạ quó,* 錢穿拔賣過 "can't pull it through the cash hole;" *met.*, he is so stingy I can get no money out of him!

Ciêng, 賤 Worthless, mean, base, ignoble; cheap, low-priced; mischievous, restless, as children; *mì-ciêng,* 微賤 insignificant; *cêng ciêng,* 盡賤 very depraved, very mischievous.

Ciêng, 漸 To find its way in as water does; stealthily; to increase by degrees; *ciêng-ciêng,* 漸漸 slowly, gradually.

Ciĕu, 招 To invite, lead in; to beckon, to bring in, as converts; a hand bill, a sign or sign board; to raise, as troops; *ciĕu-ĭng*, 招引 to introduce; *ciĕu-bĭng*, 招兵 to recruit soldiers; *ciĕu-chĭng*, 招親 (coll. *ciĕu niè-sái*,) to invite one to be a son-in-law; *ciĕu-bặ*, 招牌 a sign, a sign-board; *ciĕu-cĭk*, 招集 to call together.

Ciĕu, 焦 Burned, scorched, vexed; *ciĕu-sọ́*, 焦燥 parched, feverish.

Ciĕu, 燋 To burn, to scorch; to sear, *ciĕu diŏh*, 燋着 burnt scorched.

Ciĕu, 纎 Raw hemp; *ciĕu ĭ*, 纎衣 yellow hempen clothes, worn in mourning for grandparents.

Ciĕu, 蕉 The banana or plantain tree; *bă-ciĕu*, 芭蕉 *bă-ciĕu-guō*, 芭蕉果 plantains.

Ciĕu, 椒 Pepper, peppery, hot;

hù-ciéu, 胡椒 common pepper; *huāng-ciéu,* 番椒 red pepper; *băh-ciéu,* 白椒 white pepper; *ciĕu-lâiu,* 椒料 spices.

Ciēu, 少 Read *siéu*: little, few, not much; briefly, less, seldom; *kák ciēu,* 太少 too few, too little; *dīng* or *cêng ciēu,* or *iā ciēu,* 忐少 very scarce, very little.

Ciéu, 照 or 炤 Light, according to; to shine on, brightness, to illuminate; to patronize, to care for: *ciéu-lùng,* 照輪 by turns, rotation; *ciéu méng,* 照面 or *ciéu giáng,* 照鏡 to look into a mirror; *ciéu-gó,* 照顧 or *ciéu-káng,* 照看 to oversee; *huāng - ciéu,* 返照 reflected light; *ciéu gêu,* 照舊 or *ciéu-siòng,* 照常 as heretofore; *ciéu-huói,* 照會 an official communication; *ciéu-lié,* 照例 according to custom or law; *ciéu sì-gá,* 照時價 according to current prices; *ciéu iông,* 照件 one by one, articles reckoned singly.

Ciéu, 詔 To proclaim; a proclamation, imperial rescript; *ciéu-cṷ,* 詔書 or *ngẹu ciéu,* 御詔 a royal mandate; *băng ciéu,* 頒詔 to promulgate the royal commands; *ẹng ciéu,* 紅詔 royal proclamation when an emperor ascends the throne; *băh ciéu,* 白詔 proclamation announcing the death of the emperor.

Ciéu, 醮 as in *cọ-ciéu,* 做醮 to sacrifice to ancestors.

Ciéu, 譙 To scold, to blame; *ciéu cáik,* 譙責 to rebuke; also read *ciéu,* 譙 a look-out tower, as *cièu-lèu*, the city loft where the "watches" are beat.

Ciéu, 呪 or 咒 Read *céu*; to curse, to imprecate; to recite spells; *ciéu-có*, 咒詛 to curse, rail at; *hù-ciéu*, 符咒 charms and spells; *náing ciéu*, 念咒 to repeat incantations.

Cièu, 憔 Lean, poor; *cièu-cói*, 憔悴 a lean, sallow look; *cièu-chó*, 憔燥 anxious.

Cièu, or *cièu* 嚼 noise of voices, read *ciéu*, to chew, to gnaw.

Cĭk, 集 To flock together, to congregate, to collect, to compile, a miscellany; *huôi-cĭk*, 會集 to assemble as by appointment.

Cĭk, 疾 Sudden disease; afflictions; to hate; sickness, calamities; *càng-cĭk*, 殘疾 maimed; *dáik-cĭk*, 得疾 to take a disease.

Cĭk, 嫉 Envy, jealousy; as *cĭk-dó*, 嫉妬 jealousy.

Cĭk, 寂 or 諔 Still, quiet as an empty house; *cĭk-lièu*, 寂寥 silent, solitary; *cĭk cêng*, 寂靜 a dead silence.

Cĭk, 藉 also read *ciá*, q. v.; *lòng-cĭk*, 狼藉 extravagant.

Cĭk, 籍 A book for records, a list, a register of the people; *děng cĭk*, 登籍 to take a census; *cái cĭk*, 載籍 to record; *nĭk-cĭk*, 匿籍 naturalized citizens; *mô-cĭk*, 冒籍 to assume falsely.

Cĭng, 眞 True, sincere; *cĭng hô*, 眞好 very good; *cĭng bók nê gá*, 眞不二價 positively not two prices—as on shop signs; *cĭng bók kăng*, 眞不堪 utterly unworthy; *cĭng-sĭk,* 眞實 true.

Cĭng, 睛 The eyeball, the pupil.

Cĭng 精 Fine, the best; the germinating principle in nature; in COLL. read *ciăng,* q. v.: *láung-cĭng,* 蛋精 the white of an egg; *cĭng-lìng,* 精靈 intelligence; *cĭng - tŭng,* 精通 well read.

Cĭng, 征 To go, to take, to subjugate; *cĭng-suói,* 征稅 to collect customs; *cĭng-liòng,* 征粮 to levy taxes; *chók-cĭng,* 出征 to go out to war.

Cĭng, 蒸 Vapor, mist; to cook by steaming; *cĭng nŭk,* 蒸肉 meat cooked moist; COLL. *cĭng làng,* 蒸濫 to boil soft; *cĭng-chói,* 蒸嘴 to kiss.

Cĭng, 斟 To lade out, lighten, adjust; a ladle, a spoon: *cĭng-ciók,* 斟酌 to deliberate.

to plan, to consider, to adjust.

Cīng, 津 A ford, a ferry; to moisten; *guăng-cīng*, 官津 an excise station; *Tiĕng-cīng*, 天津 Tientsin; *cīng-ĭk*, 津液 the secretions, as saliva.

Cīng, 晶 Luster; pure, clear; *háik-cīng*, 血晶 smoky quartz; *tàu-huók cīng*, 頭髮晶 moss-agate; *cūi-cīng*, 水晶 a crystal-quartz.

Cīng, 升 Read *sĭng;* COLL. *cĭng:* a Chinese pint measure and once made to hold a catty of rice.

Cīng, 侵 To usurp, to plunder.

Cīng, 枕 COLL. *ciĕng* q.v.: a pillow.

Cīng, 耽 as in *tàu-cīng*, 頭耽 back part of the head.

Cīng, 振 To stimulate; *cīng-dóng*, 振動 to shake, to rouse up; *cīng-hĭng*, 振興 to rise,

Cĭng 51

to flourish; *cĭng gèng,* 振高 to move up, as on a seat.

Cĭng, 拯 To rescue, to pull out, as from a well; *cĭng-géu,* 拯救 to save.

Cĭng, 賑 A bounty; to give relief; *cĭng-cạ,* 賑濟 to give aid.

Cĭng, 井 COLL. *căng,* q. v.: a well, a deep pit.

Cĭng, 整 To arrange, adjust, to trim up; *cĭng-dóng,* 整頓 to repair, to put in order, to improve, as a department of work; *cĭng-cạ,* in order; pretty, as a face or dress.

Cĭng, 鯖 The eggs of fish; the name of a fish.

Cĭng, 震 To shake, to quiver, to awe; *dê cĭng,* 地震 an earthquake.

Cĭng, 疹 Eruptions, pimples;

hŭng-cīng, 風疹 pustules from cold in the system.

Cìng, 秦 A kind of grain; *Sā̤-cìng,* 西秦 ancient feudal state (Shensi); *Cìng dièu,* 秦朝 the Tsin dynasty, B. C. 249—207; *Cìng-sṳ̄ huòng,* 秦始皇 first "Emperor" of Tsin dynasty, who consolidated the Chinese empire, B. C. 221.

Cìng, 情 The passions, feelings, desires; *gōng-cìng,* 講情 to act as a peacemaker; *cìng-hìng,* 情形 appearance, state of affairs; *ing-cìng,* 人情 money paid by guests invited to a feast; *tō̤-cìng,* 討情 to excite one's compassion; *cìng-iù,* 情由 the facts of a case.

Cìng, 晴 COLL. *sàng,* q. v.: the sky clearing up after a rain; the clear blue sky.

Ciŏ, 朱 A surname; ciŏ-dăng, 朱丹 vermillion.

Ciŏ, 茱 A warm peppery medicine; ciŏ-u̇, 茱黄 hellebore.

Ciŏ, 珠 A pearl, a bead; in the COLL. pox-pustules; cĭng-ciŏ, 眞珠 genuine pearl; chók-ciŏ, 出珠 small pox; cūi-ciŏ, 水珠 chicken pox.

Ciō, 主 Read cṳ̄; Lord, the chief, the head, a family; ciō-cāi, 主宰 a ruler; ciō-é, 主意 to control, to decide; ciō-sėu, 主事 a manager; guó-ciō, 過主 a transfer, as of property; mọ̇-ciō-é, 毛主意 no help for it! mạ̈ ciō dék é, 賣主的意 cannot control it; ŏng-ciō, 恩主 a benefactor; chió-ciō, 厝主 owner of the house; Géu-ciō, 救主 the Saviour.

Ció, 註 To define; annotations, a

commentary, notes; *ció cé,* 註字 comments.

Ció, 鑄 To melt, to cast, to coin; *ció cièng guŏh,* 鑄錢局 a mint; *ció tiĕk,* 鑄鐵 cast-iron.

Ció, 胙 Sacrificial flesh; to recompense.

Cióh, 燭 Read *céuk,* q. v.: a candle; *cióh-dāu,* 燭斗 a candle stick.

Cióh, 借 Read *ciá,* q. v.: to borrow, to lend; *cióh lì,* 借梨 to borrow, to beg of; *cióh kó,* 借去 to lend; *cióh muóng,* 借問 I beg to enquire; *siá cióh,* 謝借 thanks for the loan; *gâeng nṳ̄ cióh,* 共汝借, to borrow from you; *cióh-séuk,* 借宿 to beg a night's lodging.

Cióh, 嚼 Read *ciók,* q. v.: to chew, masticate; *gōng-uâ cióh-cióh,* 講話嚼嚼 to speak cautiously.

Ciŏk, 爵 A metallic wine cup; a degree of nobility, rank or station; used for *chiŏk*, small birds; *ciŏk-lŭk*, 爵祿 rank and income.

Ciŏk, 嚼 To eat, to craunch, to masticate, to ruminate; *cù-ciŏk*, 咀嚼 to chew.

Ciŏk, 酌 To pour out wine; a glass *met.*, a dinner, feast; to avail of; *cĭng-ciŏk*, 斟酌 to consider; *ciŏk diáng*, 酌定 to consider and settle.

Ciŏk, 着 COLL. *diŏh*, q. v.: to cause, to order; to be at, on, or in; *ciŏk ĭ sĭng-siông*, 着伊身上 to entrust to one; *ciŏk nṳ kó̤ báing*, 着汝去辦 I give you entire control of it.

Ciŏk, 絕 To renounce, to abjure, terminate; to exterminate, to destroy utterly; *ciŏk-uóng*,

絕望 to cut off hope, hopeless.

Ciŏng, 章 A chapter, a section; an essay; rules, laws; *ciŏng-tiàng*, 章程 regulations; *dù-ciŏng*, 圖章 a seal; *ciŏng-ciék* 章節 chapter and verse; *ùng-ciŏng*, 文章 an essay.

Ciŏng, 將 To take, to hold in the hand; sign of the future, shall, will, about to do; sign of ablative, by, with; used in COLL. as *kĕk* to mark the accusative; how, in what way? also read *cióng*, q. v.: *ciŏng-gŭng*, 將軍 a general, applied to Tartar General of the city; *ciŏng-uâng*, 將換 so, thus; *ciŏng-gì*, 將其 why? *ciŏng-lài*, 將來 hereafter; *ciŏng-buóh hŏ*, 將剝好 nearly well, almost finished; *ciŏng-iông*, 將樣 how; *dăng ciŏng-cŏ nĭ?* 伶將做呢

now how shall we manage it?

Ciŏng, 漿 Starch; to starch; pasty, thick; syrup, juice; *tù-ciŏng*, 土漿 mud, mire.

Ciŏng, 樟 The camphor; *ciŏng-nō̤*, 樟腦 gum-camphor.

Ciŏng, 專 or 耑 One, single, alone; to presume, to assume; *cĕu-ciŏng*, 自專 assuming; *ciŏng-é*, 專意 a single purpose.

Ciŏng, 磚 A brick, a tile; *ciŏng-nguâ*, 磚瓦 bricks and tiles.

Ciŏng, 掌 The palm of the hand; the paw or sole of animals; to grasp, to control, to rule; *chiū-ciŏng*, 手掌 the palm; *ciōng-gáu*, 掌教 to teach authoritatively; *ciōng-guāng*, 掌管 to control; *ciōng-só*, 掌數 to keep accounts.

Ciŏng, 獎 To exhort to animate; *ciŏng-lá*, 獎勵 to encourage.

Ciōng, 蔣 A surname; *ciōng-uāng,* thus, this.

Ciōng, 槳 An oar; *ciōng siŏh bā,* 槳一把 one oar.

Ciōng, 鞴 A kind of leather; *ciōng à,* 鞴鞋 to mend shoes.

Cióng, 醬 A sauce, pickle, condiment; *dáu-cióng,* 豆醬 a bean-relish.

Cióng,, 將 Read *ciòng,* q. v.: to take charge of troops; to act as a general; *cióng-gŭng,* 將軍 a general, the Tartar General.

Cióng, 障 A barricade; *bō-cióng,* 保障 to protect, a barrier.

Cióng, 瞕 A cataract growing over the eye.

Cióng, 瘴 Malaria, pestilential vapors; *cióng-ké,* 瘴氣 an epidemic; *cióng-!â,* 瘴癘 an epidemic a plague; *buóh cióng,* 剝瘴 an animal plague.

Ciòng, 全 All, complete, the whole; *ciòng-bê*, 全備 fully prepared; *sĕk-ciòng*, 十全 perfect, faultless; *bō-ciòng*, 保全 to guarantee; *ciòng-ciá*, 全藉 to trust wholly; *ciòng-nèng*, 全能 almighty; *sùng-ciòng*, 純全 pure and entire.

Ciòng, 泉 A fountain, a spring; *ciòng-cūi*, 泉水 spring-water.

Ciŭ, 周 Universal, complete, to environ; a famous dynasty of China B. C. 1122—250; *ciŭ-ciòng*, 周全 entire, complete; *ciŭ-ùi*, 周圍 to surround.

Ciŭ, 週 To revolve; *ciŭ-suói*, 週歲 a birthday anniversary; *ciŭ-ciòng*, 週全 all, complete.

Ciŭ, 州 A department less than a prefecture; *giŭ-ciŭ uáng-guók*, 九州萬國 the nine continents, the world.

Ciŭ, 洲 An island; a village; *Dŏng-ciŭ,* 中洲 island of Chung-chau between the bridges at Foochow; *ciŭ-chèng,* 洲田 alluvial fields.

Ciŭ, 舟 A boat, a junk; *lùng-ciŭ,* 龍舟 a dragon boat.

Ciŭ, 睭 as in *mĕk-ciŭ,* 目睭 the eye.

Ciū 酒 Wine, spirits, liquor; *met.,* a feast; *tiĕng ciū,* 天酒 dew; *ciū-sĭk,* 酒席 a feast; *ciū-kó,* 酒庫 a distillery; *ciū-cāng,* 酒盞 a small wine cup.

Có, 詛 To curse; *có-má,* 詛罵 to rail at; *có-chói,* 詛嘴 to swear

Cô, 助 COLL. *cáe;* to assist, to support; *hô-cô,* 護助 to succor.

Cọ̄, 遭 To encounter, to endure; *cọ̄-nāng,* 遭難 to meet trials; *cọ̄-huá,* 遭化 fortunately.

Cọ̄, 左 The left, the left hand;

a surname; *cō-bĕng,* 左邊 the left side.

Cō̤, 早 COLL. *cā,* q. v.; morning, early, soon, presently; *cō̤-huáng,* 早飯 breakfast.

Cō̤, 蚤 COLL. *cāu,* q. v.: a flea, sand flea.

Cō̤, 棗 The fruit of the jujube tree, dates; *mĭk-cō̤,* 蜜棗 sweet dates.

Có̤, 做 Read *cáuk* and *ùi,* to do, to act, to make, to build, to be: *có̤ cê,* 做字 to write an agreement; *có̤ tù,* 做土 a mason; *có̤ dó̤i,* 做對 to make couplets; *có̤-huá* 做化 fortunately.

Có̤, 佐 To assist, to help, to aid; a deputy, a substitute.

Có̤, 竈 COLL. *cáu* q. v.: a furnace, a place for cooking; a kitchen range.

Cồ, 曹 A sort of revising judge, a judge of appeals; *lệk cồ* 六曹 the six Boards; *tiếng cồ*, 天曹 Heaven.

Cồ, 嘈 Noise, an outcry; *lồ-cồ* 囉嘈 a clamor; *cồ-cồ-giếu*, 嘈嘈叫, a hubbub.

Cồ, 漕 A millrace, a canal; *cồ ồ*, 漕河 the Grain Canal.

Cộ, 坐 COLL. read *sội*, q. v.: to sit in judgment; in coll., to buy up goods; *cộ dòng*, 坐堂 in court, occupying the magistrate's bench; *cộ huố*, 坐貨 to buy up goods.

Cộ, 座 A seat, a throne; a classifier for temples, churches, towers, pagodas, etc., *cội-ồi*, 座位 a throne; a seat.

Cộ, 皂 Lictors, underlings; *cộ-lạ*, 皂隸 lictors, policemen; *ì-cộ*, 胰皂 soap.

Cội 63

Cộ, 造 Also read *chộ*, q. v.: to build, to erect, to create, to do, to record; *cháung-cộ,* 創造 to create; *cộ-huá,* 造化 to form, create.

Cộh, 倅 Read *cók*; *ngū-cộh,* 仵倅 coroners.

Cộh, 擲 Read *dĭk*, q. v.: to cast off; *cộh dái,* 擲投 to throw away.

Cói, 醉 Drunk, intoxicated.

Còi, 裁 To cut out garments, to trim; *còi cư̆,* 裁書 to trim off books, as in binding; *còi-dọ̆,* 裁刀 a paper knife; *còi-cēng,* 裁剪 to cut out.

Cợi, 最 To come together, to assemble; very, extremely; *cợi họ̄,* 最好 very good; *cợi bók-kăng,* 最不堪 utterly worthless; *cợi sèng,* 最前 anciently.

Cội, 晬 Read *cói*; A full year of

age—used in reference to children; *cói bā,* 晬把 or *cói-siông,* 晬上 over a year old.

Cói, 罪 Sin, breach of etiquette; *huáng cói,* 犯罪 to transgress, to sin; *nêng cói,* 認罪 to confess a fault; *sŭk cói,* 贖罪 to atone for sin; *hŭk cói,* 服罪 to confess and submit to punishment.

Cók, 卒 One who executes orders; to conclude, to finish; *bing-cók,* 兵卒 a soldier.

Cŏk, 濁 muddy, thick, impure; *iêng cŏk,* 艷濁 excessive.

Cŏk, 鑿 COLL. *chĕk,* q. v.: a chisel, a punch.

Cŏng, 尊 Honorable, eminent, respected, noble; *cŏng-chī,* 尊齒 and *cŏng gĕng,* 尊庚 (what is) your age? *cŏng hô,* 尊號 (what is) your honorable name; *cŏng-géng*, 尊敬 to revere; *cŏng-gá*, 尊駕 Sir, your honor; *lêng-cŏng*, 令尊 your father.

Cŏng, 遵 To obey, to comply with; *cŏng mêng*, 遵命 to obey commands.

Cŏng, 樽 As in *cáu-cŏng*, 酒樽 wine vase.

Cŏng, 妝 To adorn the head; to dress, to rouge; *cŏng-sók*, 妝束 to make the toilet.

Cŏng, 贓 Booty, stolen goods; *cŏng-ŭk*, 贓物 booty, plunder.

Cŏng, 裝 To store, to pack; *cŏng huó*, 裝貨 pack away goods; *cŏng muāng*, 裝滿 stowed full.

Cŏng, 莊 Sedate, serious; a surname.

Cŏng, 庄 Read *pàng*; a large shop, a store; *cŏng-gă*, 庄家 a customer.

Cŏng, 椿 Read *chŭng;* a sort, a kind; a classifier of affairs or incidents; *ciā cŏng,* 者椿 this kind; *cī siŏh cŏng gì dái,* 只一椿其代 this particular affair.

Cŏng, 鑽 Read *cuăng;* *cōng-bék,* 鑽筆 or *gĭng-gŏng-cōng,* 金鋼鑽 a small diamond for cutting glass.

Cóng, 俊 Fine, superior, eminent, excellent, exalted; *iā cóng,* 野俊 *cóng ciáh cóng,* 俊隻俊 fine, most splendid!

Cóng, 竣 To stop work, to complete; *bó-cóng,* 報竣 finished.

Còng, 藏 To store up, to hoard; to accumulate; *còng-cék,* 藏積 to hoard, lay by; *ŭng-còng,* 隱藏 concealed, secret.

Còng, 存 To remain, still on hand; to preserve, to lay by;

còng-áng, 存案 to reserve law-cases; *còng-é,* 存意 to intend; *ng còng-é,* 懷存意 unexpectedly, suddenly.

Cŭ, 租 Rent in kind, rental; to lease; tribute, taxes; *dê-cŭ,* 地租 land rent; *cŭ-bōng,* 租榜 a rent-contract, a lease; *cŭ chió,* 租厝 to rent a dwelling.

Cŭ, 只 as in *cŭ-uái,* 只塊 here; this many.

Cū, 祖 A grandfather; the founder of a family; *sṳ̄-cū,* 始祖 the first, as of a family; *cū-cŭng,* 祖宗 ancestors.

Cū, 阻 To hinder, to cause delay; to oppose; *làng-cū,* 攔阻 to oppose, to stop; *cū-cī,* 阻止 to hinder, to prevent.

Cū, 沮 To stop, to prohibit; *cū-cī,* 沮止 to quash, to intrigue against.

Cū, 咀 Read cù; to taste, to bite; cū-ciók, 咀嚼 to chew.

Cū, As in mò cū, not to know clearly or definitely.

Cù, 殂 To die; dead, gone! dead! cù kó, 殂去 dead, gone; ĭ cù kó lò, 伊殂去囉 he's dead!

Cŭ, 書 A book; a letter, a record, documents; cŭ-gĭng, 書經 the Shooking—Book of Records; séu-cŭ, 四書 the Four Books; gōng cŭ, 講書 to preach; cŭ-gá, 書架 book shelves; tŭng-cŭ, 通書 an almanac.

Cŭ, 資 Property, goods; a fee, guăng-cŭ, 關資 a teacher's salary; nguŏk-cŭ, 月資 the monthly pay (of employés); bék-cŭ, 筆資 the pay of a writer or physician; gĕng-cŭ, 工資 wages.

Cŭ, 諸 To discriminate, all, many,

Cū 69

every; *cŭ-nŏh*, 諸毛 all, everything; *cŭ-huàng*, 諸凡 all, every; *cŭ-hèu*, 諸侯 a feudal prince or viceroy; *cŭ ôi*, 諸位 all the persons, guests or places; *cŭ-niòng-nèng*, 諸娘人 a woman; *cŭ-niòng-giāng*, 諸娘仔 a daughter, a miss.

Cū, 齊 Read *cà*, and *cǎi*, q. v.: the lower part of one's garments.

Cū, 滋 Read *cù*, as *cŭ-é*, 滋味 a fine flavor.

Cū, 子 A son; an heir, posterity; *diōng-cū*, 轉子 the third watch —from 11 P. M. to 1. A. M.; *diōng-cū*, 長子 the eldest son; *cū-nŭ*, 子女 sons and daughters.

Cū, 煮 boil in water; *cū sŭk*, 煮熟 to cook thoroughly; *cū buóng*, 煮飯 to boil rice.

Cṳ, 主 COLL. ciō, q. v.: a ruler, a lord, cṳ-gŭng, 主君 or cṳ siông, 主上 your highness! my lord! the emperor; sìng-cṳ-bà, 神主牌 the ancestral tablet.

Cṳ̀, 慈 Love, kindness, mercy; a mother, gă-cṳ̀, 家慈 my mother; cṳ̀-pĭ 慈悲 compassionate.

Cṳ̀, 鷥 A kind of heron; lù-cṳ̀, 鷀鷥 the fishing cormorant; băh-lô, 白鷺 or lô-cṳ̀, 鷺鷥 a white egret, with pendant crest

Cṳ̀, 磁 The loadstone; china-ware; cṳ̀-ké, 磁器 crockery, fine pottery.

Cuă, 抓 Read cāu; to scratch, to tear with claws; to snatch.

Cuă, 搋 Read că; to take, to pull, to draw; cuă chók, 搋出 to pull out; cuă chiĕng, 搋籤 to draw lots.

Cuā, 爪 Read *cāu*, q. v.: claws, talons; an agent, a minion; *cuā ngà*, 爪牙 claws and teeth; *met.*, emissaries, assistants.

Cuăh, To vary from a model; *gáuk cuăh*, a bone displaced, sprained.

Cuăng, 鑽 An awl, a gimlet, to perforate; *cuăng lê*, 鑽利 avaricious.

Cuáng, 賺 Read *guāng*; to profit; *cuáng-lê*, 賺利 to make gains.

Cuáng, 饌 To eat, to drink; condiments, relishes; *ngàu-cuáng*, 殽饌 delicacies.

Cuăng, 撰 To regulate, to correct, to record; *ê - cuáng*, 異撰 strange, marvelous. Read *sáung*, to reckon. Read *sōng*, to select, to commission.

Cūi, 水 Water, fluids; clear, limpid; the tide; inundation; common, as water; *ṳ̄-cūi,* 雨水 rain water; *cūi duái,* 水大 spring tides; *cūi siĕu,* 水小 neap tides; *cūi káuk,* 水墢 a puddle; *cūi-ngṳ̀ng,* 水銀 quicksilver; *cūi-lṳ̀ng,* 水龍 a fire engine; *cūi dōng,* 水漲 flood tide; *cūi puóng,* 水汐 ebb tide.

Cŭk, 族 A clan, a tribe, a class; *cŭk-diōng,* 族長 the chief of a clan; *cŭk-puō,* 族譜 the genealogical register of the clan.

Cŭng, 宗 To honor, to reverence; the origin or source of; a clan; *cū-cŭng,* 宗祖 ancestors; *cŭng-sṳ̆,* 宗祠 an ancestral hall.

Cŭng, 踪 A vestige, a track; *cŭng-cék,* 踪跡 a foot print, a trace, a clue to.

Cŭng, 鬃 COLL *cĕng,* q. v.: a mane.

Cūng, 縱 Perpendicularly, a meridian line; the first also read cẹung, and the second chụng, cùng and cẹung, q. v.

Cūng, 棕 COLL. cęng, q. v.: a species of palm, whose bracts furnish coir for ropes, mats, etc.; a dark brown color, umber.

Cūng, 總 A generic term, generally, certainly; all, the whole; cūng-gŏng, 總綱 a summary, an outline; gẹung-cūng, 共總 the sum total; cūng-dók, 總督 a viceroy; lūng-cūng, 隴總 all, the whole.

Cūng, 準 Exact, right; a rule, a gauge; cūng-cáik, 準則 a rule, a model.

Cūng, 准 To hear or answer, as a prayer; to allow, to decide; bók cūng, 不準 (COLL. ng cūng,

怀準) not granted; *cūng gi-dọ̄*, 准祈禱 to answer prayer.

Cūng, 准 To guess; *cūng mê,* 准謎 to guess riddles.

Cùng, 崇 Noble, exalted, worthy of worship; to adore, to praise, to revere; *cùng dẹung,* 崇重 to respect profoundly; *cùng-bái,* 崇拜 to worship.

Cùng, 叢 A bushy place, crowded as trees; *cùng-lìng,* 叢林 a thicket.

Cŭng, 鐘 A bell, a clock; *cŭng-biĕu dáing,* 鐘表店 a clock and watch shop; *cẹ̄u-mìng-cŭng,* 自鳴鐘 a clock.

Cṳ̆ng, 舂 To pound, to pulverize; *cṳ̆ng mī,* 舂米 to pound or hull rice in a mortar; *cṳ̆ng kó̤,* 舂臼 a stone morter.

Cṳ̄ng, 終 The end, death; at length, finally; *lìng-cṳ̄ng,* 臨

終 near death; cŭng-giū, 終久 at last, finally; cŭng-sĭng, 終身 a lifetime.

Cŭng, 種 A seed, a germ; dìòng cūng, 傳種 to transmit; cŭng-cī, 種子 seed; iê cūng, 樸種 to sow, to plant.

Cŭng, 腫 To swell up; uòng cūng, 黄腫 jaundice; cūng kī, 瘇起 to swell, to bloat.

Cùng, 從 Also read chŭng and cêung, q. v.: to listen to, to follow; to agree; cùng cū- uái kī, 從只塊起 commencing from place of origin; cùng mêng, 從命 to obey orders; cùng biêng, 從便 at convenience; cùng-ciêng, 從前 formerly; cùng gū ī-lài, 從古以來 from former times to the present.

Cuòi, 贊 A demonstrative pronoun; ciā cuòi, 者嚊 this, this thing; cuòi dò kęuk ĭ, 嚊搉乞伊 give this thing to him.

Chă, 差 Also read *chặ* and *chĭ*, q. v.: a mistake, an error; *chă-bók-dŏ̤*, 差不多 nearly, almost; *chă dék huông*, 差的遠 a great difference.

Chă, 杈 An instrument for catching fish.

Chă, 叉 A fork in a road; *săng-chă diō*, 三叉路 three diverging roads; *chă-tiòng*, 叉杖 a pronged stick.

Chă, 瘥 Read *chŏ̤*: to recover from sickness; *sāu-chă*, 稍瘥 slightly better; *céng mạ giéng chă*, 症賣見瘥 no improvement in the disease.

Chā, 炒 To roast in a pan or boiler; to fry in oil; *chā-mī*, 炒米 roasted rice; *chā gă-bī*

炒菲菲 to roast coffee.

Chā, 吵 Read *chāu:* to annoy, to disturb; *chā ngū-hiă*, 吵五罅 to throw everything into confusion.

Chā, As *chā-sĕng*, 早先 a short time ago.

Chá. 鈔 Interchanged with *chău*, (to copy): a document; a banknote; paper money.

Chà, 柴 Fuel, brushwood; *tọ chà*, 討柴 to gather firewood; *chà-bā*, 柴把 bundles of wood; *chà-puói*, 柴柿 chips, shavings.

Chà, 孱 Thin, emaciated; *met.* vicious, depraved; *chà-bḗ*, 孱㾿 utterly vicious; *cọ̈ chà*, 坐孱 to degenerate.

Chă, 妻 A wife; *chéu chă*, 娶妻 to marry a wife; *chă-cū*, 妻子 wife and children.

Chă, 悽 Grieved, afflicted; *chă-*

chāng, 悽慘 pitiable, distressing.

Chạ, 凄 Intence cold, wintry, stormy; afflicted; chạ-liòng, or chạ-liòng chạ-chāng, 凄涼悽慘 pitiable, afflicted.

Chạ, 棲 To perch, to nestle; to sojourn; lodgings; câng chạ, 暫棲 temporary lodgings; chạ-sĭng, 棲身 a stopping place.

Chạ, 差 Read chăi: a messenger, an ambassador; also read chā, and chĭ, q. v.: kĭng-chạ, 欽差 an imperial commissioner; dŏng-chạ, 當差 to be a policeman; chạ-kiēng, 差遣 commission; chạ-sùng, 差船 revenue cutters; nguòng-chạ, 原差 (COLL. chạ-iăh, 差役) bailiffs; bĭ-chạ, 比差 to bamboo police men.

Chá, 糌 Flour made from rice.

Cháę, 葫 A kind of long gourd.

Cháę, 擦 Read *chák:* to rub with the hands or feet; *cháę kó̤,* 擦去 to rub off.

Cháę nèng, To scold people.

Cháęk, 軸 Read *dŭk:* a chart, map, hanging picture or drawing; *buôi cháęk,* 背軸 to make pasteboard for charts.

Cháęk, An intensive particle; *cháęk-cháęk-sĭng,* 軸軸新 span new.

Cháęng, 諍 Read *chăng:* to provoke; *cháęng kī-lì,* 諍起梨 to bristle.

Cháh, 冊 Read *cháik:* an inventory, a list, a census book; *cṳ̆ cháh,* 書冊 a register; *cháh guóng,* 冊卷 lawbooks; *gău-dâi cháh,* 交代冊 a transfer paper.

Cháh, 第 Read *cháik:* a book,

an essay; *cŭ-cháh,* 書第 books.

Chăi, 纔 Read *chài:* now, just now; the common colloquial is *ciáh* q. v.

Chăi, 猜 To guess, to conjecture; to fear; *chăi siōng,* 猜想 to suspect; *chăi mê,* 猜謎 to guess a riddle.

Chăi, 釵 Hairpins.

Chāi, 採 To select, to pluck, to choose; *chāi-mā,* 採買 to buy up for the government, as rice.

Chāi, 彩 Variegated, elegant, beautiful; *guŏng-chāi,* 光彩 glossy, brilliant; *chāi-sáik,* 彩色 variegated; *mĕk-chāi,* 目彩 discriminating taste.

Chāi, 綵 Variegated silks or satins; *chāi-diù,* 綵綢 red silk for festoons; *chāi buó,* 綵布 red cotton cloth; *chāi-gáik,*

綵結 festoons; *sáeng chāi,* 送綵 to send silks (to the betrothed.)

Chái, 菜 Vegetables, edible herbs; food, viands: *sŭ-chái,* 蔬菜 vegetables; *cău-chái,* 糟菜 pickled vegetables; *siǎh chái,* 儉菜 vegetarian; *chái-tàu,* 菜頭 the turnip radish; *băh-chái,* 白菜 cabbage.

Chái, 蠆 A bee; a kind of scorpion with a long tail; *pŭng-chái,* 蜂蠆 a bee; *chái mvōi,* 蠆尾 the sting of a bee.

Chài, 纔 COLL. read *chăi,* q. v.: an adverb of time; just now; presently, at once; *chài lài,* 纔來 just come; *chài kō̤,* 纔可 then it will do.

Chài, 才 Read *cài,* as *nù-chài,* 奴才 a slave, a bondman.

Chài, 豺 Read *cài:* a ravenous

beast, a wolf or lynx; *chài-lòng,* 豺狼 a wolf.

Chài, 材 Read *cài,* as *guăng-chài,* 棺材 a coffin.

Cháik, 側 COLL. *cáik,* q. v.: side, on the side, lateral; to incline, to bend; seditious; mean, perverted; *cháik mŭk,* 側目 to cast hateful glances at; *cháik ngĭ,* 側耳 to incline the ear; *huāng-cháik,* 反側 rebellious; *cháik sék,* 側室 a concubine.

Cháik, 測 To fathom, to estimate; *cháik-dŏk,* 測度 to investigate.

Cháik, 惻 Secret grief: distress, to pity, to sympathize; in the COLL. anger, envy; *kū-cháik,* 苦惻 grieved; *tiè cêng cháik,* 啼盡惻 to weep bitterly.

Cháik, 策 COLL. read *cháh,* q. v.: a bamboo slip, such as books were once engraved on; a writing, a book; a plan, a scheme; *giĕ-cháik*, 計策 a scheme, a contrivance; *cṳ̆-cháik*, 書策 books.

Cháik, 册 COLL. read *cháh*, q. v.: a list, an inventory, a register; *cṳ̆-cháik*, 書册 books; *sṳ̄-cháik*, 吏册 a historian.

Cháik, 柵 COLL. *căk*, q. v.: posts of a stockade, a railing; *cháik-muòng*, 柵門 street gates.

Cháik, 拆 To break up or open; to destroy, to take away; *cháik éng*, 拆印 to dismiss from office.

Cháing, 讖 To verify, to prove, to fulfill; an omen, a sign; *cháing-diêu*, 讖兆 a prophecy, an omen.

Cháing, 倩 COLL. *chiáng*, q. v.: beautiful, comely, fair; to serve an occasion; *cháing dái*, 倩代

to employ a substitute; *mī cháing*, 美倩 fine, beautiful.

Cháiu, 湊 to collect, to gather; a concurrence, as of circumstances; in the COLL. to add to, to increase, to supply a deficiency; *cháiu cièng*, 湊錢 to add more cash; *cháiu lā náung*, 湊禮亂 confusion worse confounded; *cháiu dáung*, 湊斷 to increase the mortgage and sell off.

Chák, 察 To examine, to judge, to observe closely; *că-chák*, 查察 to scrutinize; *sīng-chák*, 審察 to examine carefully; *chák cing*, 察情 to investigate the circumstances therof; *áng chák sī*, 按察司 Provincial Judge.

Chák, 插 To insert, to pierce; to transplant; to meddle, to help; *chák huă*, 插花 to in-

Chăng 85

sert flowers, as in a vase; *chák chói,* 插嘴 to interrupt, by talking; *chák běk-nèng dái,* 插別仈代 to meddle in other people's business; *kīng chák dái,* 肯插代 willing to help, as in lawsuits.

Chák, 礧 To pound off the husks of wheat; a pounder used in building earth walls.

Chăng, 叅 To advise; to blend; to have an audience; to depose; *guăng chăng,* 官叅 to depose from office; *chăng uòng,* 叅員 a degraded officer; *chăng cūi,* 叅水 to add water; *met.,* to talk covertly.

Chăng, 青 Read *chĭng:* the color of nature, as the azure sky, or the green of growing plants; a dark color; pale, sallow *duái chāng,* 大青 jet black;

tiék chăng, 鐵青 iron grey; *tiĕng chăng*, 天青 a reddish black; *chăng-gák*, 青蛤 a kind of green frog; *chăng-giăng*, 青仔 apricots; *chăng guŏ*, 青果 "the green fruit" — olives; *chăng-làng*, 青藍 dark blue; *chăng-buó*, 青布 black cotton cloth.

Chăng, 生 Read *sĕng*, q. v.: green, unripe; *met.*, ignorant, unskilled; *chăng-chék*, 生漆 raw varnish; *chăng siăh*, 生食 eaten raw; *buáng chăng sŭk*, 半生熟 half ripe, half raw or uncooked.

Chăng, 眚 Read *sĕng*: *chăng-màng*, 眚盲 blind.

Chăng, 慘 Cruel, inhuman, hardhearted; a superlative applied to sufferings; sad! lamentable! *chă-chāng*, 悽慘 most lamentable; *chă - liòng chă-chāng*, 凄凉悽慘 distressing, most pitiable; *chāng lŏ*, 慘囉 alas! *chāng mò̤ chāng*, 慘毛慘 is it not sad?

Chāng, 醒 Read *sĭng*: *chĭng-chāng*, 青醒 to awake from sleep or intoxication; *buák-chāng*, 撥醒 to arouse, to excite by appeal or instruction.

Chāng, as *chāng-chāng-sĭng*, just new; fresh and fine, as clothes.

Cháng, 燦 Bright, clear, resplendent: *cháng-láng*, 燦爛 brilliant, lustrous; *chăng-láng-guŏng*, 燦爛光 bright, luminous.

Chàng, Strong, rude, impetuous; *chàng dék hēng*, very strong and bold.

Chău, 抄 Also read *chá*, q. v.: to transcribe, to copy; to buy up, as forfeited goods; *chău că*, 抄書 to transcribe a book; *chău siā*, 抄寫 to copy; *chău cŏng*, 抄贓 to buy forfeited goods at pawnshops; *chău-gă*, 抄家 to confiscate household property.

Chău, 操 Read *chọ̤*: to practice, as troops; *chău-liêng*, 操練 or *tā-chău*, 體操 to drill; *káng chău*, 看操 to review troops; *cūi chău*, 水操 naval review.

Chău, 撈 Read *chĕu*: to hold up the dress in walking; to overhaul; *chiū-uōng chău gèng*, 手袖撈高 to push up the sleeves; *chău náung*, 撈亂 or *chău ngū-hiă*, 撈五罅 to throw into utter confusion by overhauling.

Chău, 草 Read *chọ̤*: grasses, herbs; plants in general; *chău ták*, 草榻 a straw bed;

Cháu 89

chāu-cháẹ, 草薊 coarse, badly done, as needlework, compositions, etc.; *chāu-lī-liák*, 草履韃 straw slippers without heels; *chāu-bău*, 草包 a straw pouch; *met.*, a simpleton; *chāu-à-mā*, 草鞋馬 foot travelers; *chāu-nèng-giāng*, 草仆仔 a straw image or scarecrow; *chāu-pī*, 草菲 grass.

Cháu, 吵 COLL. *chā* q. v.: to annoy, to disturb, to trouble; *chāu-iēu*, 吵擾 to annoy; *chāu-nâu*, 吵鬧 to make a disturbance.

Cháu, 臭 Read *chéu*: effluvia, bad odor, offensive to the smell; *cháu ké*, 臭氣 a stench; *cháu é*, 臭味 a putrid scent; *cháu-chŏ̤*, 臭鱢 a fishy smell; *cêng cháu*, 盡臭 an intolerable stench; *cháu huōi-ĭng*, 臭火烟

smoked, as in being cooked.

Cháuk, 錯 Also read *chó,* q. v.: to mistake, to err, as *cháuk-nguó,* 錯誤; *chă-cháuk,* 差錯 a mistake, an error.

Cháuk, 撮 A pinch; to snatch; *cháuk kī,* 撮起 to pluck up; *cháuk mọ̆,* 撮帽 to snatch off one's cap; *cháuk gĕng,* 撮工 to hire additional workmen; *cháuk siŏh guó,* 撮一句 to select a sentence; *cháuk să,* 撮疹 to pinch (the throat in order to cure) colic; *cháuk ciĕng,* 撮錢 to borrow money.

Cháung, 寸 The Chinese inch, regarded as long as the middle joint of the fingers, the tenth of a foot, and varies with the foot; *cháung-ék,* 寸一 one inch and a tenth; *cháung-siŏng,* 寸上 over an

Châung 91

inch; *cháung măh*, 寸脉 only an inch of pulse—near death; *cháung ĭng*, 寸陰 an inch of time.

Cháung, 創 To wound, in which sense also read *chŏng;* to invent, to create, to lay the foundation of; to reprove; *dĭng cháung*, 懲創 to blame; *cháung-cố*, 創造 to create; *cháung-sié*, 創世 to create the world; *cháung-sṳ̄* 創始 to begin; *cháung lié*, 創例 to establish a custom.

Cháung, 閂 Read *sŏng* or *suăng;* a crosspin, a bar, a bolt; *muòng cháung*, 門閂 a door bolt; *cháung muòng*, 閂門 to bolt the door.

Cháung, 闖 To bolt out, to appear suddenly.

Cháung, 闖 Read *cháung:* to bolt

ahead; *cháung diē*, or *chuáng diē kó*, 闖程去 to bolt into a place.

Ché, 伕 Read *chéu;* the bride's dowry, sent to the groom's house a few days before marriage; a corpse; *ngiàng ché*, 迎伕 to carry the dowry with a display; *ciek ché*, 接伕 to receive the dowry.

Ché, 飽 Read *dì:* to feed; *ché nèng*, 飽乳 to feed with milk; *ché niê-giàng*, 飽伲仔 to feed a child; *ché siŏh chói*, 飽一嘴 give him a mouthful; *ché miêng*, 飽麪 to offer vermicelli (to a corpse in a sitting posture.)

Ché, 試 Read *séu:* to experiment; to test, to compare and find out; *ché káng*, 試看 to test and see; *ché muóng*, 試問 to try with questions; *ché chiū-dáung*,

試手段 to test one's skill.

Ché, 嗏 Read *chŏi*: to taste; *ché siăh*, 嗏飡 to taste food; *ché siòng*, 嗏嘗 to test by tasting.

Ché, 市 A market place; to buy, to trade in the market; *ché uóng*, 市旺 prosperous trade; *chê bái*, 市敗 dull trade; *cūi-ché*, 水市 the tide *serving*.

Ché, 嚏 Read *dê*: as *hák ché*, 喝嚏 to sneeze.

Chẹ, 初 Read *chŭ*: the first, the beginning; incipient; *chẹ-ék*, 初一 the first day of the month; *nguŏk chẹ*, 月初 from the 1st to the 10th of the month; *chẹ sĕk diê*, 初十裡 before the 10th; *chẹ sĕk ngiê*, 初十外 just after the 10th; *chẹ-săng, chẹ-sé mì-mò nguŏk*, 初三初四眉毛月 on the 3rd and 4th it is eyebrow moon—

new moon; *chẹ gūi,* 初幾 what day of the first decade is it?

Chéh; As *chéh kọ́,* to go fast, to run away; *chì-chéh,* to rush past; *muāng-tiĕng-chéh,* a kind of rocket.

Chék, 七 Seven, the seventh; *chék-sĕk,* 七十 seventy; *chek ciáh,* 七隻 seven (persons or thing); *chék-chék,* 七七 the seven seventh—days of funeral rites for the dead; *chék iè, báik iè,* 七爺八爺 the tall and short devils—attendents of the *ngū dạ́,* 五帝

Chék, 叱 To scold, to cry out to; to mention; *chék mìng ông ăng,* 叱名問安 give my name and salutations—an epistolary phrase.

Chék, 尺 COLL. *chióh,* q. v.: a cubit or Chinese foot of 10

inches; *chék cháung,* 尺寸 regular, proportioned.

Chék, 拭 Read *sék:* to wipe, to rub with a dry cloth; *hók chek,* 拂拭 to dust and wipe; *chék táh,* 拭潔 to wipe clean.

Chék, 赤 COLL. *chiáh,* q. v.: carnation, flesh color; *chék sáik,* 赤色 carnation color; *chék dọ̆,* 赤道 the equator; *chék sĭng,* 赤身 sincere.

Chék, 漆 Varnish, lacquer; to paint, to varnish; *iù chék,* 油漆 paint and varnish; *chék să-hô,* 漆司父 a painter; *chăng chék,* 青漆 raw varnish; *kĕuk chék gá,* 乞漆咬 poisoned by lacquer; *chék siŏh guó,* 漆一過 to varnish one coat; *tŏi-guŏng chek,* 推光漆 highly polished varnishing.

Chék, 膝 The knee, the patella;

chék há, 膝下 at the knee; (*met.*, children)—an epistolary phrase; *kók chék*, 屈膝 to bend the knee.

Chĕk, 斥 To exclude, to expell, to send off; to scold at; to pry into; *mìng chék*, 明斥 to reprimand sternly; *cī chék*, 指斥 to point out one's faults; *miĕng chék*, 面斥 to rebuke one to his face.

Chĕk, 戚 To compassionate, to pity; near, related to; relatives; *chĭng-chék*, 親戚 kindred; *chĭng bèng chék iū*, 親朋戚友 kindred and friends; *chĭng-chék duái sạ*, 親戚大細 all of one's kindred.

Chĕk, 賊 Read *cĕk*: a thief, a robber, a highwayman; a term of reproach; *chĕk pī*, 賊匪 banditi; *chĕk dōng*, 賊黨 or

Chéng 97

chĕk-huō, a band of thieves; *chĕk-uŏ*, 賊窩 a den of thieves; *hāi-chĕk*, 海賊 a pirate.

Chĕk, 鑿 Read *cŏk*: a chisel, a punch; *chĕk giāng*, 鑿仔 a small chisel; *ièng chĕk*, 圓鑿 a gouge.

Chĕng, 撐 To prop, to shore up; a fulcrum, a prop.

Chĕng, 筅 Read *sièng*: a brush broom; *chēng-chiū*, 筅箒 a besom; *chēng-chiū-sĭng*, 筅箒星 a comet; *diāng-chēng*, 鼎筅 a brush to clean pots and pans.

Chéng, 秤 A steelyard; *guó-chéng*, 過秤 to weigh it; *chéng-guāng*, 秤管 a steelyard bar; *chéng huā*, 秤花 the notation of pounds and ounces on the bar; *chéng-tùi*, 秤錘 the poise; *chéng-gău*, 秤勾 the hook;

chéng-náu, the cord to hold by in weighing; *bàng-chéng*, 平秤 the common catty of 16 oz.; *duái chéng*, 大秤 the large catty of 18 or 20 oz; *ék-báik chéng*, 一八秤 a catty of 20 or 21 oz.

Chéng, 稱 Also read *chǐng*, q. v.: a steelyard; to weigh; suitable, corresponding to.

Chéng, 清 Cold, as weather, the person, things; *iĕk chéng*, 熱清 hot and cold; *ói chéng*, 畏清 (COLL. *giăng chéng*, 驚清) to fear the cold.

Chèng, 田 Read *dièng*: a field; land, plantation; *chèng dé*, 田地 cultivated lands; *chèng huòng*, 田園 fields and gardens; *chèng-chìng*, 田塍 dikes between fields; *chèng-cŭ*, 田租 the rent of fields; *chèng*-

Chéu   99

ciŏ, 田主 the owner of lands.

Chèng, 蠶 Read *càng*, q. v.: the silkworm, caterpillers, which weave cocoons; *chèng-gēng*, 蠶繭 the silkworm.

Chḙng, 葱 Read *chŭng*; onions ; *chḙng ciŏ*, 葱珠 onions cut up fine; *chḙng-tàu-dà*, 葱頭茶 a decoction of onions and tea, used in measles and colds.

Chḙng, 菖 Read *chiŏng*; *chḙng-buò*, 菖蒲 sweet flag, used on doors as a charm, on the 1st day of the 5th moon.

Chéu, 臭 COLL. *cháu*, q. v.: to track by the scent; smell, oder; a bad name, disreputable; *mì chéu uáng nièng*, 遺臭萬年 a bad name lasts forever.

Chéu, 糗 Roasted or parched or pounded wheat or rice; *chéu-*

né, 糗餌 parched rice cakes.

Chéu, 樸 Wood, a tree; timber, lumber; *chéu siŏh dău,* 樸一株 a tree; *chéu-mŭk,* 樸木 trees, woods; *ciék chéu,* 接樸 to graft a tree; *chŏi chéu,* 剉樸 to fell trees; *chéu lâiu,* 樸料 timber.

Chèu, 愁 mournful, sad; *chèu-kū,* 愁苦 grieved, distressed; *chèu-mô̤ng,* 愁悶 dispirited.

Chéu, 娶 or 取 A legal marriage; the 2nd also read *chū,* q. v.: *chéu chă,* 娶妻 to marry a wife.

Chéu, 趣 To run, to advance quickly; sprightly, playful; pleasing; *cī-chéu,* 旨趣 the purport of; *cé-chéu,* 志趣 desire, purpose; COLL. *ô chéu,* 務趣 remarkably amusing; *mò̤ chéu,* 毛趣 not worth seeing.

Chếu 101

Chếu, 覷 To spy, to look at; to reconnoiter; dối chếu, 對覷 to look at each other; chếu cỉnh, 覷眞 to see correctly; chếu bảnh, 覷病 to visit sick persons.

Chếu, 伙 COLL. ché, q. v.: light, nimble; to aid, to assist, to compare; chếu cố, 伙助 to aid, as by a gift of money.

Chếu, 次 Medium, inferior, to put in order; an inn, a stall; a mansion; a time, a place, chếu-sếu, 次序 order, arrangement; só-chếu, 數次 several times.

Chếu, 刺 A thorn, a sting, to pierce, to embroider; to stab, and kill; chếu-káik, 刺客 an assassin.

Chếu, 處 Read chū, q. v.: a place, a spot, a circumstance; hò-chéu, 何處 where? gáuk-chéu, 各處 or chéu-chéu, 處處 every where; séu-chéu, 四處 the four quarters; ôi-chéu, 位處 a place; chék chéu bié, 七處彎 to run all about.

Chéuk, 觸 To excite, to oppose: chéuk huâng, 觸犯 to incur anger; céng chéuk, 盡觸 greatly displeased at.

Chéuk, 歠 To be choked with anger, full of choler; chéuk sĩ, 歠死 angry to death.

Chéuk, 促 To constrain; urgent; páik chéuk, 迫促 very urgent.

Chéuk, 浞 To steep in water; dregs; COLL. scurf on the hands, incrustations.

Chéuk, 捉 To seize, to grip and hold: chéuk chěk, 捉賊 to catch thieves.

Chéuk, A coll. word, to chisel or

saw off; *chéuk dōi*, to shorten, to reduce the length.

Chéung, 銃 A gun, a pistol; *chiū-chéung*, 手銃 pistols; *bóng-chéung*, 放銃 to fire off guns.

Chéung, 辍 COLL. *chéung lā siăh*, 辍禮食 to invite one's self to eat; *chéung dóh*, 辍桌 to come unbidden.

Chéung, A coll. word: to insert; *chéung kă dóh*, a table with movable legs.

Chéung, A coll. word: *chéung diŏh*, to meet, to fall in with; *chéung ciā gīng*, to have met with this experience.

Chĭ, 癡 Stupid, dull; idiotic; wandering: *chĭ siōng*, 癡想 a silly thought; *chĭ háng*, 癡漢 a dolt.

Chĭ, 蚩 Ignorant, rustic; *chĭ màng*, 蚩氓 the uneducated people.

Chǐ, 雌 The female of birds; *chǐ hùng*, 雌雄 female and male; *met.*, a pair.

Chǐ, 笞 To punish with a bamboo; *biĕng chǐ*, 鞭笞 to flog.

Chǐ, 鴟 A kind of owl or hawk; *chǐ hiĕu*, 鴟鴞 the horned owl.

Chǐ, 差 Also read *chă* and *chă̤*, q. v.: uneven, projecting irregularly; *chăng chǐ*, 參差 uneven, irregular.

Chǐ : A coll. word: *chǐ chié-chié*, rough, uneven.

Chǐ : A coll. word: *ngù-chǐ*, the gills of a fish.

Chǐ, 齒 COLL. *ngāi* and *kī*, q. v. the teeth, age, years; *nièng-chǐ*, 年齒 or *chǐ só*, 齒數 age years old; *gǐng-nièng cŏng-chǐ* 今年尊齒 what is your age this year?

Chǐ, 矢 An arrow; swift as an

Chiă 105

arrow; direct, open; *gì dĭk ù chī*, 其直如矢 he is as straight as an arrow; i. e., blunt, honest; *ciéng-chī*, 箭矢 arrows.

Chiă, 奢 Wasteful, extravagant; *chiă huà*, 奢華 gay, wasteful.

Chiă, 車 Read *gŭ:* a chariot, vehicle of any kind; a machine for raising water into the fields; to screw in, to turn as in a lathe; *chiă hŭ*, 車夫 a charioteer; *cūi-chiă*, 水車 a machine for raising water; *dăk chiă*, 踏車 to work this machine with the feet; *huōi-lùng-chiă*, 火輪車 a railway train; *chiă dáing*, 車店 a turning shop; *tiĕng chiă*, 天車 an elevator.

Chiă, 蟶 As *chiă ngò*, 蟶螯 a large kind of mytilus; *chiă-ngò-chói*, 蟶螯嘴 mytilus mouthed—i. e., taciturn.

Chiā, 且 A conjunction; and, also; still, thus, so, yet, if, should; *hĕk-chiā,* 或且 if, perhaps; *huóng-chiā,* 況且 still more; *hĕk-chiā-iòng,* 或且然 possibly so.

Chiá, 斷 Diverging, criss-cross; *chiá ngāng,* 斷眼 cross-eyed, squinting.

Chiáh, 赤 Read *chék:* carnation, purplish, golden; color of any highly polished metal; *chiáh gĭng,* 赤金 burnished gold; *siáh chiáh,* 鑢赤 to shave and polish metal.

Chiáh, A coll. word: *chiáh cê,* words branded on the temples of banished criminals.

Chiák, 伋 Fearful, timid, palpitating; *gŭng á chiák,* 筋釁伋 the veins throb.

Chiāng

Chiák, A coll. word: to mince, to grate; *chiák chọ̈i,* to cut up fine; *chiák huăng-sụ̀,* to grate potatoes for drying; *huăng-sụ̀-chiák,* a potato grater.

Chiák, 泚 To rub, as in washing clothes; *chiák băh,* 泚白 to rub white.

Chiák, To pluck, to twitch, to pull at; *chiák dōng,* to break in twitching.

Chiăk, A coll. word: to tread on; *chiăk sī,* to trample to death.

Chiăng, A coll. word: a splinter, a sliver; *chiăng dọ̈h,* a sliver (in the hand).

Chiāng, 請 Read *chīng,* q. v.: to request, to invite, to bid; to beg, to confess; *chiāng ciū,* 請酒 to invite to a feast; *chiāng táik,* 請帖 invitation cards; *chiāng sọi*, 請坐 please sit; *chiāng dà*, 請茶 please take some tea; *chiāng ăng*, 請安 to salute; *chiāng cọi*, 請罪 to confess an error.

Chiāng, 癬 Read *siĕng*: ring-worm; *săng chiāng*, 生癬 to have a ring-worm.

Chiāng, 剗 Read *sāng*: to scoop, to lade up or out, as floor; *chiāng-gĭ*, 剗箕 a scoop.

Chiáng, 倩 Read *cháing*: to hire, to employ; *chiáng gĕng* or *chiáng giók*, 倩工 to hire workmen; *chiáng siēu-gĕng*, 倩小工 to hire for small jobs.

Chiàng, 成 Read *sìng*: to finish, to complete, as a job partly done; *cọ chiàng*, 做成 to finish; *buáng-làng-chiàng*, 半闌成 half finished.

Chiĕ, 呎 or 尺 Read *chĕk*: the

Chié 109

first also read *chá*: a note in music; also to scold, as *chiĕ-chiĕ-mō*, 叱叱母 a vixen; by *met.*, applied also to men.

Chiē, 侈 Extravagant, prodigal; *chiē dàng,* 侈談 extravagant talk; com. *chiă-chiē,* 奢侈 wasteful.

Chiē, 扯 Also read *chiā*: to tear open, to pull apart; *chiē pó,* 扯破 to tear asunder; COLL. *lă chiē,* to grasp, to embezzle. Used for *tiē.*

Chiē, 弛 To relax, to cast off; injured, spoiled; *chiē sáng,* 弛散 scattered; *hié-chiē,* 廢弛 obsolete, done away.

Chiē, A coll. word: to equalize.

Chiē, A coll. word: *chiē-tōi,* 弛腿 to half kneel, as in new year's salutations.

Chié, 幟 A flag, a pennon, long

and fringed; to signalize; *gì-chié,* 旂幟 flags; *séu chié,* 樹幟 to hoist a flag.

Chié, 熾 Flame, blaze, splendor: *chié-nié,* to spread, to catch as fire; *chié-huōi,* 熾火 to catch fire.

Chié, 翅翄 Wings, fins; *ngù-chié,* 魚翅 fins, the shark's fins.

Chié, 茨, 棘, 莿, The first read *cṳ̌,* the second *cháik,* the third *chéṳ*: thorns, briers, brambles; *chié-cháu,* 莿草 briers; *chié-bá-cháu,* 莿𦸐草 thorns; *chié-mà-dái,* 莿麻帶 a species of small prickly caterpillar; *met.,* a dangerous fellow.

Chié, 枕 Read *ciék* and *chéṳ*: *muòng-chié,* 門枕 the jams of a door; *huàng-chié,* 橫枕 the cross piece over the doorway; *dĭk-chié,* 直枕 the side pieces.

Chiék 111

Chiè, A coll. word: to move heavy articles; to shove, to veer, as the wind; *chiè ciáng*, to move till it stands squarely; as the sun approaching the summer solstice; *chiè uăi*, to move away; the sun approaching the winter solstice.

Chiê, A coll. word: same as *chiá;* transverse, diagonally; *chiê niă-nọ̆i*, somewhat diagonal.

Chiék, 竊 To steal, to take slyly; clandestine, privately; *tĕu chiék*, 偷竊 to steal; *chiék-chiéu*, 窺笑 to laugh at secretly.

Chiék, 切 To cut, to slice; to urge, to press; a superlative; eager, earnest; *chiék-chiék*, 切切 or *páik-chiék*, 追切 earnestly, pressingly; *kōng chiék gì-dọ̆*, 懇切祈禱 to pray fervently; *ék-chiék*, 壹切 the whole;

chiék-chī, 切齒 to gnash the teeth; *chiék cê*, 切字 to spell words.

Chiék, 妾 A concubine; a term by which ladies designate themselves; *chiék-sĭng*, 妾心 I, your handmaid; *ciêng chiék*, 賤妾 I, your lowly handmaid.

Chiék, 蠘 Read *cĕk:* a large crab.

Chiĕng, 千 A thousand; an indefinite number; *chiĕng-suói*, 千歲 (may the king live) a thousand years; your highness! *chiĕng-uâng*, 千萬 most certainly, by all means; *chiĕng-gĭng*, 千金 a thousand of gold, your daughter! *chiĕng-lī giáng*, 千里鏡 a telescope.

Chiĕng, 鮮 Read *siĕng:* fresh, raw, bright, new; *chiĕng-mìng*, 鮮明 fresh and bright; *chiĕng ngù*, 鮮魚 fresh fish; *chiĕng*

Chiĕng 113

huă, 鮮花 fresh flowers.

Chiĕng, 蟶, 虷 Used for COLL. chiĕng: chiĕng-găng, 虷乾 dried shrimps.

Chiĕng, 襈 A concealed stitch; chiĕng-cĕng, 襈針 the concealed fell stitch.

Chiĕng, 遷 To remove; to transpose, to banish; chiĕng-iè, 遷移 to move; chiĕng-gŭ, 遷居 to change one's residence.

Chiĕng, 僉 All, the whole; unanimous opinion; chiĕng gŭng-diàng, 僉公呈 a public document, announcing the settlement of an affair.

Chiĕng, 簽 To subscribe, to append a signature; chiĕng buô, 簽簿 a record of cases in court; chiĕng miàng, 簽名 to sign a a name to a paper.

Chiĕng, 籤 A slip, a warrant;

huōi chiěng, 火籤 an urgent warrant; chiěng buó, 籤譜 a record of taxes.

Chiěng, 箋 Memorandum tablets or slips; note paper: chiěng cāi, 箋紙 fancy note-paper.

Chièng, 戔 Used for chang: cruel; small, narrow, contracted, as one's mind.

Chiěng, 鋑 Also read cǐng and chǐng: to cut, to engrave; an engraver.

Chiěng, A coll. word: headlong; chiěng lŏh lì, to fall headlong.

Chiěng, 淺 Superficial light as colors; chiěng-sáik, 淺色 pale colors; chiěng-gău, 淺交 a slight acquaintance.

Chiěng, A coll. word: chiéng-chiéng, a few, just the proper amount.

Chièng, 揣 A fathom; to clutch

and pull recklessly.

Chiêu, 超 To excell, to surpass; *iā chiĕu*, 野超 excelling, very fine.

Chiêu, 釗 Also read *ciĕu*; in COLL. a probe for testing iron, sugar, etc.

Chiêu, A coll. word: to hem; *chiĕu cĕng*, the hemming stitch; *chiĕu ĭ-siòng*, to hem garments.

Chiêu, 俏 Handsome, pretty: *cóng chiĕu*, 俊俏 beautiful; *bók chiĕu*, 不俏 homely.

Chiêu, 笑 To laugh, to giggle; joyful, smiling; to laugh at, to ridicule; *chiéu méng*, 笑面 a laughing face; *màng-chiéu*, 玩笑 to jest, to make sport of; *hĭ-hĭ-chiéu*, 嘻嘻笑 to giggle.

Chiêu, A coll. word: to raise with a lever; *chiĕu sĕng*, to pry loose.

Chĭh, A coll. word: *chĭh cāu,* to run away, to abscond.

Chĭk, A coll. euphonic prefix, as in *chĭk-chĕk,* to chisel.

Chĭng, 青 COLL. *chăng,* q. v.: the color of nature; *chĭng-nièng,* 青年 youth, the time of youth.

Chĭng, 清 Pure, unsullied, clean; right principled; *chĭng-giék,* 清潔 pure; *chĭng-chū,* 清楚 plain, settled; *dèng chĭng,* 謄清 to make a final copy; *chĭng cŭ,* 清書 writers in yamens; *chĭng gŭk,* thin and thick, as fluids.

Chĭng, 深 Deep, profound; learned, very, extremely; *chĭng-chiēng,* 深淺 deep and shallow; *chĭng ó,* 深奧 abstruse; *chĭng háiu,* 深厚 extremely generous; *chĭng ciáh chĭng,* 深隻深 very deep or profound.

Ch'ing, 稱 Also read chéng, q. v.: to weigh, to designate, to compliment, to admire; *ch'ing hù*, 稱呼 to style; *cĕu ch'ing*, 自稱 to praise one's self; *kĕuk nèng ch'ing-cáng*, 乞仆稱讚 praised by others.

Ch'ing, 親 To love, near, intimate; belonging to one's self, myself; kith and kin; a wife; affianced; *ch'ing-chék*, 親戚 relatives; *ch'ing sŭ* or *sĕ*, 親疏 near and distant relationship; *ch'ing ái*, 親愛 to love; *ch'ing sĭng*, 親身 one's self; *léng ch'ing*, 令親 your relative; *siá-ch'ing*, 舍親 my relative; *có ch'ing*, 做親 to betroth; *tō ch'ing*, 討親 to marry a wife.

Ch'ing, A coll. word, as *ch'ing-cháng*, to awake from sleep.

Ch'ing, A coll. euphonic prefix, as

chĭng - chăng, to add more water.

Chĭng, 寢 To rest, to sleep; a bedchamber; a dwelling house; céu chĭng, 就寢 to go to sleep; chĭng sék, 寢室 a sleeping apartment.

Chĭng, 請 COLL. chiāng, q. v.: to request, to ask, as for orders; to invite; chĭng cŏi, 請罪 to apologize; géng-chĭng, 敬請 to invite respectfully.

Chĭng, A coll. word, as chĭng-chĭng, just so, exactly; chĭng-chĭng sṳ̆k, just cooked through.

Chĭng, A coll. euphonic prefix, as chĭng-chiāng, to invite, to request; chĭng chiāng, to lade out, as flour.

Chĭng, A coll. word: cṳ̄ kák chĭng, cooked too rare.

Chìng, 塍 A dike, a raised foot-

Chióh 119

path between fields: *tù chìng*, 土埕 an earthen dike.

Chiŏ, A coll. word: to turn, to screw; *chiŏ gīng*, screw it tight; *chiŏ ciáng*, to screw straight.

Chiŏ, A coll. word, as *chiŏ-ùng* or *chiŏ-ùng*, (reading form *iòng-muòi*,) the arbutus.

Chió, 厝 Read *cháuk* and *chó*: a house, a dwelling; *kī chió*, 起厝 to build a house; *gó chió*, 舊厝 a former residence; *chió cŭ*, 厝租 the rent of a house; *duái chió*, 大厝 a mansion; *chió-ciō*, 厝主 a house owner; *chió-diē*, 厝裡 in the house, a term for a wife; *siŏh chió nęng*, 一厝伙 a whole family.

Chióh, 粟 Read *séuk*: unhulled rice; paddy; *mī chióh*, 米粟 rice and paddy; *chió-diàng*,

粟埕 a threshing floor; *cā-chióh*, and *uòng ciĕng chióh*, 早粟黄占粟 the 1st and 2nd crops of rice.

Chióh, 尺 Read *chĕk:* a cubit, the Chinese foot of 10 inches; *chióh-cháung*, 尺寸 feet and inches — measured, proportioned; *bàng-chióh*, 平尺 the standard foot; *tiĕk chióh*, 鐵尺 an iron bar for beating thieves.

Chióh, 蓆 Read *sĭk:* a mat spread to sleep an; *chāu-chiŏh*, 草蓆 straw mats; *chiŏh siŏh liāng*, 蓆一町 one piece of matting: *chŭ chiŏh*, 舒蓆 to spread mats.

Chióh, A coll. word: to toss about clams in cooking (so as to diffuse the seasoning.

Chiók, 雀 COLL. *ciáh*, q. v.: a sparrow; a term for small

birds; *muòi-chiók,* 梅雀 almond trees and sparrows; *kūng-chiók,* 孔雀 a peacock.

Chiók, 鵲 A magpie; a jackdaw; *hī-chiók,* 喜鵲 (coll. *kă-chiók,*) a magpie; *ŭ-chiók,* 烏鵲 a raven.

Chiók, 妁 A go-between in making marriage contracts; a surname; *muòi-chiók,* 媒妁 a match maker.

Chiók, 芍 The peony, also the dahlia: *băh-chiók,* 白芍 the white peony.

Chiók, 灼 To burn, to singe, to cauterize with the moxa; *chiók ngái,* 灼艾 (COLL. *chiók ngié*) to burn the moxa.

Chiók, 綽 Large, ample; *iā chiók,* 野綽 or *chiók dék hēng,* 綽的很 very lively; pretentious.

Chiók, 啜 Read *ciók:* to drink,

to imbibe by mouthfuls; *duái chiók*, 大啜 a great drinker; *chióh siŏh chói*, 啜一嘴 to drink a mouthful.

Chiŏng, 昌 Light of the sun; elegant, prosperous; powerful: *chiŏng dái*, 昌大 prosperous and powerful; *chiŏng-séng*, 昌盛 flourishing.

Chiŏng, 鯧 As *chiŏng-ngù*, 鯧魚 the pomfret.

Chiŏng, 鎗 A spear, a lance; *chiŏng-huák*, 鎗法 the art of handling the spear.

Chiŏng, 菖 COLL. *chĕng*, q. v.: the flag; *chiŏng-buò*, 菖蒲 sweet flag:

Chiŏng, 川 Mountain streams; perennial brooks: *chiŏng-guŏng*, 川廣 the Szechuan and Canton provinces; *Chiŏng-siŏh*, 川石 Sharp Peak.

Chiōng, 穿 A hole, an opening; to bore through: in the COLL. to stretch out, to extend (the hand); *chiŏng-cĕng*, 穿針 to thread a needle; *chiū chiŏng dĭk*, 手穿直 to stretch out the arm; *chiŏng chiū muŏ tiĕng*, 穿手摸天 extend the hand and touch the sky—a vaulting ambition.

Chiōng, 搶 Read *chŏng:* to take, to extort, to rob, to snatch; *chiŏng-dŏk*, 搶奪 or *chiōng-giék*, 搶劫 to plunder.

Chiōng, 喘 Read *chuāng:* as *chiōng siŏng*, 喘上 to pant, to raise gas from the stomach.

Chiōng, 敞 A high terrace; displayed; *chiōng-liông*, 敞亮 a fine site; *kuăng-chiōng*, 寬敞 broad, spacious.

Chiōng, 廠 A shed or shanty for

a work-shop; *cièng-chiōng,* 錢廠 a mint; *sùng chiōng,* 船廠 a shipbuilder's work-shop; *kéuk-siăh chiōng,* 乞丐廠 a beggar's hovel.

Chióng, 唱 To sing, to cry out, to give the word; *chióng-dā,* 唱打 vocal and instrumental music; *chióng-gŏ,* 唱歌 to sing songs.

Chióng, 匠 A workman, a mechanic, an artizan of any kind; *kiēu chióng,* 巧匠 an expert workman; *mŭk-chióng,* 木匠 a carpenter; *tù-chióng,* 土匠 a mason.

Chióng, 倡 Also read *chiōng,* q. v.: to lead, to go before to induce, or seduce; a leader; *chióng sṳ̄,* 倡始 to take the lead; *chióng luāng,* 倡亂 to head a riot; *chióng chók lì,* 唱

Chiòng 125

出来 to lead, as in an enterprise.

Chiòng, 串 To string together, to connect; leagued or banded together: chióng-tŭng, 串通 in league with; chióng guó, 串過 to pass a string through.

Chiòng, 牆 A wall of bricks, stones or earth; a defense or wall; huōi chiòng, 火牆 a fire-proof wall; ùi-chiòng, 園牆 to inclose by a wall; kī chiòng, 起牆 to build walls of bricks or stone; huàng chiòng, 橫牆 a cross wall.

Chiòng, 薔 Also read sáik: a rose; chiòng mì huă, 薔薇花 a cinnamon rose.

Chiòng, 蹲 Read còng: to squat, to crouch, to sit on the heels; chiòng giá, 蹲下 to squat low; chiòng dê-dău, 蹲地兜 to squat on the ground.

Chiòng: A coll. word: to winnow, *chiòng chióh*, to winnow paddy.

Chiông, 象 An elephant, a figure, an image; imagination; *siōng chiông*, 想象 an idea, illustration; *chiông ngà*, 象牙 ivory; *huáng chiông*, 幻象 to imagine.

Chiông, 像 Like, similar; an idol, a statue; to imitate; *hìng-chiông*, 形像 an image, a form; *ngēu-chiông*, 偶像 an idol; *chiông-iông*, 像樣 right, excellent; *ng chiông nèng*, 伓像仒 unmanly; *chiông ciáh chiông*, 像隻像 very like to.

Chiông, 漎 Also read *dōng*: a swift current; *chiông cūi*, 漎水 to draw water.

Chiông, 鞝 Read *ciōng*: to insert; *chiông à*, 鞝鞋 to sole shoes.

Chiŭ 127

Chiông, A coll. word: as *chiông-tàu*, to dress the bride's hair.

Chiŭ, 秋 Autumn; the return of the year; a year; autumnal; *chiŭ-tiĕng*, 秋天 or *chiŭ-giè*, 秋季 autumn; *chiŭ-chiĕng*, 秋千 a swing, a seesaw.

Chiŭ, 輘 Traces of a carriage; *chiŭ-chiĕng*, 輘韆 a swing, a seesaw.

Chiŭ, 鰍 An eel; *nà-chiŭ*, 泥鰍 a fresh water eel; *hāi-chiŭ*, 海鰍 a sea-dragon; *met.*, a long narrow boat.

Chiŭ; A coll. word: whiskers, beard; *chói-chiŭ*, whiskers, mustaches.

Chiŭ, 手 The hand, the arm; *chiŭ-céuk*, 手足 the hands and feet, *met.*, brethren; *chiŭ-ciōng*, 手掌 the palm; *chiŭ-bié*, 手臂 the arm; *dó̤i-chiŭ*, 對手 to work together, to lend a hand; *chiū á*, 手下 under one's control; *chiū-cāi*, 手指 the fingers; *chiū-ták*, 手套 mittens.

Chiū, 醜 Ugly, deformed; disagreeable, shameful; *chiū-háing*, 醜行 disgraceful conduct; *chiū-lói*, 醜類 vagabonds.

Chiū, 箒 A besom, a broom; *sáu-chiū*, 掃箒 a broom; *chĕng-chiū*, 筅箒 a besom.

Chiù, 囚 To imprison, to handcuff; a felon; *chiù-huáng*, 囚犯 a criminal; *chiù-lèng*, 囚籠 a cage for carrying criminals.

Chiù, 揪 Read *chiū*: to pull towards one; *mŏh chiù nguāi*, 莫揪我 don't clutch me!

Chiù: A coll. word: thick, matted, disheveled hair.

Chiù: A coll. word: Wan, woe begone.

Chó, 醋 Vinegar, pickle; *chó-aeng,* 醋甕 a vinegar jar.

Chó, 錯 Also read *cháuk,* q. v.: to settle, to store up, to reject; *siā chó,* 捨錯 to throw aside.

Chŏ, 操 Also read *chău,* q. v.: to take; to drill; to restrain one's self; *chŏ-quòng,* 操權 to exercise authority.

Chŏ, 搓 To twist, to roll between the palms; *chŏ siáng,* 搓線 to twist thread; *chŏ ciā dái-giāng,* 搓苴帶仔 to adjust a difficulty.

Chŏ, 鱢 A fishy smell; strong, rank; lustful.

Chŏ, 草 Plants in general; the running hand; a rough copy; *chō-mŭk,* 草木 plants; *chō-cê,* 草字 the running hand; *chō gō,* 草稿 the first draft of a writing.

Chọ, 礤 Potash, saleratus; *chọ-cŭi,* 礤水 saleratus water.

Chọ́, 糙 Coarse rice; in the coll. unbleached; *chọ́ - mī,* 糙米 coarse or dark rice; *chọ́-băh,* 糙白 a darkish white.

Chọ́, 錯 Read *cháuk:* a fault, an error, a blunder; *nŭ ó chọ́,* 汝務錯 you err.

Chọ́, 造 Also read *cộ,* q. v.: to go, to complete; hurried; *chọ́ chéu,* 造次 agitated.

Chọ̆h, A coll. word: to stab, to pierce; *chọ̆h sī,* to stab to death; *chhĭh-chhĭh chọ̆h-chọ̆h,* to rush to and fro.

Chōi, 催 COLL. *chuōi,* q. v.: to urge, to press on; *chōi chéuk,* 催促 to urge.

Chōi, 髓 The marrow; *gáuk-chōi,* 骨髓 marrow.

Chōi, 揣 To estimate, to calculate; *chōi-mò*, 揣摩 to feel after; *chōi-dŏk*, 揣度 to investigate.

Chōi, A coll. word: a chain, as worn on the neck by a criminal.

Chói, 翠 The female of the kingfisher; *chói-mò*, 翠毛 kingfisher feathers.

Chói, 嘴 The mouth, the beak; a spout; the edge of a knife, etc.; *chói-siĕk*, 嘴舌 the tongue; *chói kák*, 嘴渴 thirsty; *chói-tàu uá*, 嘴頭話 slang.

Chọi, 碎 Bits, fragments, pieces; *chọi ęung*, 碎用 or *chọi sāi*, 碎駛 miscellaneous use; *páh-chọi*, 拍碎 to break to pieces.

Chọi, 剉 Read *chọ̈*: to cut, to chop, to fell trees; *chọi kọ̈*, 剉去 to cut off; *chọi chéu*, 剉橾 to fell trees.

Chŏi, 啳 COLL. *ché,* q. v.: to taste.

Chŏk, 出 Also read *chói:* to go out, to issue; to surpass: *chŏk sié,* 出世 to be born; *chŏk cièng,* 出錢 to pay money; *chŏk lì,* 出來 to come forth.

Chŏk, 焅 Read *ciók:* to scorch; to cauterize.

Chŏk, 擉 To take in the fingers, to take a pinch of; *chŏk siŏh chŏk,* 擉一擉 to take a pinch.

Chŏk, 獗 Read *dáuk:* small seals called *chŏk giăng,* 獗仔

Chŏng, 倉 A granary, a government store house for rice or salt as *mī chŏng,* 米倉 and *sièng chŏng,* 鹽倉

Chŏng, 蒼 Flourishing, prospering: *chŏng-sĕng,* 蒼生 living things, the people.

Chŏng, 瘡 A sore, an ulcer; an ulcerated wound; a bail.

Chŏng 133

Chŏng, 村 A hamlet, a village; *hiŏng-chŏng,* 鄉村 a village, the country.

Chŏng, 艙 Compartments in a boat or ship, called *chŏng dū,* 艙堵

Chŏng, 窓 A window; a school; a student; *chŏng-hâ,* 窓下 at school; *chŏng-iŭ,* 窓友 fellow students.

Chŏng, 鶬 A species of crane; *chŏng-gĕng,* 鶬鶊 mango bird.

Chōng, 忖 To guess; to surmise; to reflect on; *chōng-dŏk,* 忖度 to conjecture.

Chòng, 狀,床 A bedstead, a couch; *mìng-chòng,* 眠狀 a bedstead, a bed; *káung-chòng,* 匡狀 a couch, a settee.

Chòng, 鐘 Read *dùng:* to eat much; *duâi chòng,* 大鐘 a glutton; *chòng-cié,* 鐘祭 eat

134　　　　Chŭ

and stuff; *scil.*, and not work.

Chóng, A coll. word: to wring, to twist; to extort; *chóng ĭ-siòng*, to wring out clothes; *chóng cièng*, to extort money.

Chŭ, 初 COLL. *chĕ* q. v.: the first, the beginning; *sū-chŭ*, 始初 the beginning; *chŭ hŏk*, 初學 to commence study.

Chŭ, 粗 Coarse, uncleansed, rude, boisterous; *chŭ éu*, 粗幼 coarse and fine; *chŭ có̤*, 粗做 to do rough work.

Chū, 楚 A coppice, a thicket; well done, properly finished; *chĭng-chū*, 清楚 clear, complete, properly finished or settled.

Chŭ, 舒 To unroll; to spread out, to lie flat; *chŭ-puŏ*, 舒鋪 to spread the bed; *chŭ méng-siŏng*, 舒面上 to spread on top.

Chū, 此 A pronoun and adverb; bī-chū, 彼此 that and this; gó-chū, 故此 consequently; ĭng-chū, 因此 by, for, on account of; chū gĭng, 此景 this state.

Chū, 處 Also read chéu q. v.: to dwell; to judge and settle: gŭ-chū, 居處 to reside; chū dè, 處治 to adjust; dièu-chū, 調處 or chū huò, 處和 to settle a dispute.

Chū, 取 Also read chéu, q. v.: to take, to use, to assume; cêu-chū, 自取 to bring on one's self; chū-é, 取意 to prove; chū-bō, 取保 to get security.

Chū, 鼠 A rodent; met., timorous; thieving; a rascal; cūi-chū, 水鼠 a water rat; hiŏng-chū, 香鼠 a muskrat; lō-chū, 老鼠 a rat; hù-chū, 狐鼠 a squirrel.

Chù, 擄 Read *chū*: shoo! hoot!

Chuá, 篡 Read *chuáng*: to take away one's business, to scheme, to plot against.

Chuá: A coll. word; *chuá uăi*, distorted, awry.

Chuá: A coll. word: *chuá dộ*: to go the wrong road,—to become vicious.

Chuăng, 餐, 飡 A meal; to eat; the classifier of meals; *cō chuăng*, 早餐 breakfast; *uāng-chuăng*, 晚餐 supper.

Chuăng, 銓 To estimate the value of things; a carpenter's plane; *chuăng sōng*, 銓選 to select, as good officers.

Chuăng, 筌 A crab trap; *dáik ngù uòng chuăng*, 得魚忘筌 to take the fish and forget the net; *met.*, ungrateful.

Chuăng, 痊 Convalescent; *chuăng*

Chuǎng 137

ǜ, 痊愈 recovered from sickness.

Chuǎng, 喘 To pant, to gasp; breath, the life; *ké chuāng*, 氣喘 to wheeze.

Chuǎng, 饡 A mess, a table; to cook, to steam gently; *dùng chuáng*, 同饡 to eat at one table; *hǔng chuáng*, 分饡 to eat at separate tables.

Chuáng, 矡 Read *chuǎng*: a spear, a javelin.

Chuáng, 篡 COLL. *chuá*, q. v.: to seize violently, to usurp; *cháung ói*, 篡位 to usurp the throne.

Chǔi, 隹 Also read *cǔi*; short tail birds.

Chǔi, 雖 A dubitative particle; if, supposing, even if; *chǔi-iòng*, 雖然 although, albeit.

Chǔi, 錐 An awl, a borer;

trifling; *ù lĭk chŭi cĭ dê*, 無立錐之地 no place to stick an awl—wretchedly poor.

Chŭi, 推 To push away; to shirk, as responsibility; to refuse; to recommend; *chŭi-sù*, 推辭 to decline, to reject; *chŭi kiók*, 推却 to renounce, to refuse; *chŭi táuk*, 推托 to shift from one's self to another; *chŭi-gū*, 推舉 to recommend; *chŭi láung*, 推論 to reason out.

Chŭk: A coll. word: a superlative, as *ŭ chŭk-chŭk*, very dark, as at night.

Chŭk: A coll. word: to tread, to trample; *chŭk sī*, to trample to death; *chŭk dáing*, to trample down hard, as earth; *chŭk bàng dê*, to tread level with the earth.

Chŭng, 春 Spring, the beginning

Chŭng 139

of the year; *met.*, times, seasons, periods; COM. *chŭng tiĕng,* 春天 spring; *sĭng chŭng,* 新春 early spring; *máing chŭng,* 孟春 the first month.

Chŭng, 葱 COLL. *chĕng*, q. v.: an onion.

Chŭng, 聰 Astute, quick-witted; *chŭng-mìng,* 聰明 clever, intelligent.

Chŭng, 蠢 To crawl, to wriggle, as worms; to do stupidly; *ngù-chŭng,* 愚蠢 simple.

Chŭng, 瞲 Large eyes; in the COLL. drowsy, sleepy; *chŭng kó̤,* 瞲去 sleepy, dozing.

Chŭng, 冲 To mount upwards in the air; to dart, to strike against; in the COLL. to steep, to make an infusion; *chŭng tiĕng,* 冲天 to dart into the sky, as birds; *náu chŭng-*

tiĕng, 鬧冲天 the outcry pierces the sky; *chṳ̆ng dà*, 冲茶 to steep tea; *chṳ̆ng tŏng*, 冲湯 to pour on boiling water.

Chṳ̆ng, 种 Also read *tṳ̆ng*; small, delicate, as *éu chṳ̆ng*, 幼种

Chṳ̆ng, 盅 Also read *tṳ̆ng*: a cup or vessel, generally small and covered; *dà chṳ̆ng*, 茶盅 a covered cup.

Chṳ̆ng, 從 Also read *cŭng*, *cùng* and *cĕung*, q. v.: easy, complaisant, gentle; *chṳ̆ng-ṳ̀ng*, 從容 not hurried, repose of manner; *chṳ̆ng gūi nĭk*, 從幾日 to allow a few days longer.

Chṳ̆ng, 充 To fill, to satiate; sufficient: *chṳ̆ng-muāng*, 充滿 filled; *chṳ̆ng-céuk*, 充足 sufficient; *chṳ̆ng-gĭ*, 充饑 to satisfy hunger; COLL. *chṳ̆ng sioh miàng*, 充一名 to add another name, as of a partner.

Chŭng, 衝 A path, crossway; to rush against; *dái chŭng,* 大衝 a great road; *chŭng táu,* 衝透 to go fully up to, as a sedan bearer to the opposite side before turning.

Chṳ̀ng: A coll. word: to wrench, to sprain; *kă buăk chṳ̀ng,* the foot sprained by a fall.

Chuŏi, 炊 To cook: in the COLL. restricted to steaming: *chuŏi buóng,* 炊飯 to steam rice; *chuŏi bău,* 炊包 to steam bread; *chuŏi iĕk,* 炊熱 to heat by steaming; *chuŏi buáng-săng-sŭk,* 炊半生熟 steamed half done.

Chuŏi, 催 Read *chŏi:* to urge, to press; to dun for payment; *chuŏi páik,* 催迫 to urge greatly; *chuŏi tŏ,* 催討 to dun urgently; *chuŏi cièng-liòng*, 催錢糧 to dun for taxes.

Chuŏi, 吹 To blow, to whistle, to puff; a blast, a gust; to play on a wind instrument; *hŭng chuŏi*, 風吹 the wind blows; *chuŏi hŭng*, 吹風 exposure to wind—is bad for the sick; *chuŏi gĭng-gū*, 吹京鼓 to play on instruments; a band of musicians.

Chuói, 脆 Delicate, frail, brittle; in the COLL. quick, spry; foppish; *iù chuói*, 柔脆 pliant, flexible; *sōng-chuói*, 爽脆 quick, prompt; *ką́-chuói*, 快脆 soon done or affected; *chuói-diàng*, 脆腥 fluent, authoritative; *iā chuói*, 野脆 very finely dressed.

Chuòi, 箠 Read *sùi*: a bamboo switch; *chuòi-giāng*, 箠仔

small switches; *chuòi-tàu chók hō̤-giāng,* 箠頭出好仔 whipping makes a good child.

Dă: A coll. word: dry, not wet; *dă-sĕng,* very dry; *dă-só̤,* parched; *dă-dó̤,* the net profit.

Dā, 打 To strike, to beat; to cause to fight; an auxiliary, before verbs denotes present time, or simple action; also a preposition; *dā gĕng,* 打工 to job out work; *dā-siăh,* 打食 to do a job and board one's self; *dā-lăk,* 打獵 to hunt game; *dă-sáung,* or *dā-diēng,* 打算或打點 reckon, to calculate; *dā-huák,* 打發 to apportion; *dā-téng séng-sék,* 打偵信息 to go and learn the news; *dā-tiék,* 打鐵 wrought iron; *dā-làng-huàng,* 打攔橫 crosswise; *dā-sáu,* 打掃 to sweep; *dā iēu*, 打擾 have troubled you.

Dā, 蹕 Read *dō:* COLL. *dā-dā*, 蹕蹕 to toddle.

Dá, 醡 Read *cá*, q. v.: a wine or oil press; *ciū-dá*, 酒醡 a wine press; *dá-dôi*, 醡袋 a bag for expressing the juice.

Dá: A coll. word: to feign, to counterfeit; to pretend.

Dà, 茶 The infusion of tea; a tea, teas; *siăh dà*, 愈茶 to drink tea; *dà biāng*, 茶餅 tea pressed into cakes; *dà-biāng*, 茶餅 refreshments; *dà-òng*, 茶行 a tea hong; *dà-guāng-dáing*, 茶館店 a restaurant.

Dă, 低 Also read *dĭ:* cheap, low, humble; *gŏ dă*, 高低 high and low; *dă sĭng*, 低聲 in a low voice; *gá dă*, 價低 the price is cheap.

Dā, 底 Read *dĭ*: the base, the bottom; a copy, a first draft; *á-dā*, 下底 below, underneath; *gáu dā-dā*, 至底底 to the very bottom; *táu-dā*, 透底 to the very last, forever.

Dā, 抵 Read *dĭ*: to oppose, to ward off; *dā-dĭk*, 抵敵 to oppose, to meet a foe; *dā-dŏng*, 抵當 to bear a responsibility.

Dá, 帝 A ruler of the nations; *huòng-dá*, 皇帝 an emperor; *dá háiu*, 帝后 an empress; *huòng-dá ói*, 皇帝位 the imperial throne.

Dá, 諦 To examine, to judge; *sĭng dá*, 審諦 to examine and deside a case.

Dà, 蹄 A hoof, a leg; *met.*, horses.

Dà, 鵜 Read *tà*: *dà-hù*, 鵜鶘 a pelican.

Dà, 鞮 Also read *dă*: leathern shoes.

Dà, 題 A theme; a preface; to compose, to write; *dà-mĕk*, 題目 a theme, a text; *chŏk dà*, 出題 to give out themes; *dà cièng*, 題錢 to subscribe money; *dà-giòng*, 題捐 or *giòng-dà*, 捐題 to subscribe.

Dă, 弟 COLL. *diê*, q. v.: a younger brother; *nṳ dă*, 女弟 a younger sister; *hĭng-dă*, 兄弟 brothers; *dă-cṳ̄*, 弟子 pupils; *siá-dă*, 舍弟 my younger brother.

Dă, 娣 A younger sister.

Dă, 第 A series, an order, a rank; a literary degree; a mansion; *chéṳ-dă*, 次第 rank, order; *dă-tĕk*, 第宅 an officer's mansion; *dă-ĕk-hŏ*, 第一好 the best; *dă ngô buōng*, 第五本

the fifth volume; *dạ gūi,* 第幾 which order?

Dạ, 遞 To transmit, to send on; to hand up or in; *diòng dạ,* 傳遞 to send on, as by post; *dạ diàng,* 遞呈 to present an accusation.

Dạ, To screen, to cover, veil; *dạ hŭng,* to screen from the wind; *dạ ŭng-dìng,* to screen from the dust.

Dáe, 苧 Read *tŭ:* the grass cloth nettle.

Dáek, 觸 Read *chū* and *chéuk:* to gore, to push; to crush *dáek sī,* 觸死 to gore to death.

Dáek, 罩 Read *dáu:* a coop; to shut up; *dáek giĕ,* 罩鶏 to coop fowls; *diāng-dáek,* 鼎罩 a high pan cover.

Dáek: A coll. word similar to *ngêu* or *páung:* to meet with;

dáek dék diŏh, met him; *dáek mą̆ diŏh*, failed to meet him.

Dáeng, 凍 Read *dóng*: cold, as things; *dáeng nŏh*, 凍毛 cold things, as food; *liàng dáeng*, 凉凍 to cool by exposure to the air.

Dáeng, 棟 Read *dóng*: the main supports in houses; *dáeng-liòng*, or *dáeng àng*, 棟樑 beams, joists.

Dáeng, 重 Read *dę̆ung*: heavy, weighty; strong, as words; *dáeng dái*, 重代 hard work, toil; *dáeng uá*, 重話 harsh words; *ô niŏh dáeng*, 務箸重 how heavy is it? *káng-dáeng*, 看重 to view as important.

Dáeng, 動 Read *dóng*: to move; motion, action; *déng-dáeng*, 定動 to be agitated; *dê déng-dáeng*, 地定動 an earthquake;

kī-dâęng, 起動 thanks for your trouble! ng kī-dâęng, 伓起動 no thanks needed!

Dâęng, 洞 Read dông: a cave, a grotto; met., a delightful spot; dâęng-kāu, 洞口 a cave's mouth.

Dáh, 壓 Read ák: to press, to crush, to stake; dáh sī, 壓死 crushed to death; dáh giêu, 壓轎 to put additional weight on a sedan.

Dáh: A coll. word; to dishonor, to disgrace, as a wicked son does his parents.

Dăh, 擇 Read děk: to choose, as lucky days; dăh nĭk-cī, 擇日子 to choose a lucky day.

Dăh, 宅 Read těk: a village; săng-sěk-lěk dăh, 三十六宅 the 36 villages, known as Ŏng-ŏng-diĕ.

Dăh: A coll. word: to heat, to keep warm; dried; *dăh tŏng,* to heat water; *dăh buóng,* to keep the rice warm; *puóng dăh,* to ebb all dry (as the tide).

Dăi, 獃 Also read *ngài,* q. v.: stupid, ignorant, silly; slovenly; *cêng dăi,* 盡獃 excessively stupid; *dăi sióng,* 獃相 a stupid face.

Dăi: A coll. word: what? why? *dăi-sāi,* what need? *dăi-sāi ciŏng-uâng,* why so! why do so!

Dăi: A coll. word: a kind of millet.

Dāi, 歹 Bad, vicious, perverse; *bók dĭ họ̆ dāi,* 不知好歹 not know good from evil; *dāi sẹ̆u,* 歹事 a wicked act.

Dāi, 滓 Read *cāi;* refuse; dregs;

dāi-pŏh, 溠柏 refuse.

Dái, 帶 A girdle; a ribbon; bandage, a belt; a section of country; to guide, to conduct; uăk-dái, 襪帶 garters; kă-dái, 胶帶 bandages on ladies' feet; káiu-dái, 扣帶 to clasp a girdle; ék-dái, 一帶 the whole region of country; dái bĭng, 帶兵 to lead troops; dái lì, 帶來 to bring with one; dái lôi, 帶累 to implicate.

Dái, 戴 To carry or wear on the head; dái huă, 戴花 to wear flowers; dái mô, 戴帽 to put on a cap; dái há, 戴孝 to wear mourning; dái ngāng-giáng, 戴眼鏡 to wear spectacles.

Dái, 碓 A pestle; a foot pestle; chiă dái, 倕碓 pestles moved by water power; dái mī, 碓

米 to pound rice; Read *dŏi:* a bank, a heap: *tù-dŏi,* 土堆 a heap of earth.

Dài, 台 High, exalted, noble; your honor; *dài-gá,* 台駕 eminent sir! *hĭng-dài,* 兄台 noble brother! your honor!

Dài, 臺 A platform, a stage; a fort; a lookout; a title of officers; *hióng dài,* 憲台 a censor, magistrate; *dài-gá,* 臺駕 noble Sir! *cié-dài,* 制臺 *ū-dài,* 撫臺 *huăng-dài,* 官臺 *hŏk-dài,* 學臺 Viceroy, Governor, Treasurer and Literary Chancellor.

Dài, A coll. word as *dài-gă,* a husband's mother.

Dài, A coll. word: to patch, to mend; *dài-buō,* to patch.

Dài, 大 COLL. *duâi;* q. v., large, grand; extensive; as a superlative, very, much, *dâi chiểng*, 大千 the great thousand—the world; *dâi-gă*, 大家 all, we all, you all; *dâi-huàng*, 大凡 all, whoever, whatever; *dâi-liŏk*, 大畧 generally;

Dâi, 逮 An adverb of time, till, until; *dâi gĭk*, 逮及 even to; *dâi gĭng*, 逮今 until this time.

Dâi, 代 COLL. *dội*, q. v.: a generation, an age; a substitute; delegated, deputed; *sié-dâi*, 世代 an age; *lĭk dâi*, 歷代 successive generations or reigns; *dâi-tạ*, 代替 to act as a substitute; *dâi-bék*, 代筆 an amanuensis; *dâi-biểu*, 代表 a representative.

Dâi, 玳 Tortoise shell: COM. *dâi-nguôi* 玳瑁 the tortoise shell of commerce.

Dâi, 岱 A famous mountain

peak in Shangtung, also called *Tái-săng*, or Great Mountain.

Dái, 貸 To lend, to loan on interest, also to borrow; *ciòh dái*, 借貸 to borrow.

Dái, 袋 COLL. *dôi*, q. v.: a bag, a sack; a purse, a satchel.

Dái, 待 To wait upon, to treat, to behave to; *káng-dái*, 看待 to treat well or ill; *ciék éng dái káh*, 接應待客 to entertain guests; *dái nèng ngài*, 待伙呆 to treat persons ill.

Dái, 怠 Careless, remiss; lazy, wanting in courtesy; *hái-dái*, 懈怠 remiss; *dái-máng*, 怠慢 to treat disrespectfully.

Dái: A coll. word: to throw or cast away; to reject; *dái kó*, to throw away.

Dái: A coll. word: a matter, a business; *sié-nŏh dái-giè*, (or *ié*) what business ? what's the matter ? *có dâi*, to do work.

Dâi: A coll. word: as in *dâi-dŏng*, in the middle; *dâi dŏng-dŏng*, in the very center.

Dáik, 得 To get, to obtain, to acquire; to have, to be, to desire; used as *dĕk* in the coll. to express completion of action; *dáik bâng,* 得病 to be sick; *dáik-é,* 得意 pleased with; *dáik cŏi,* 得罪 to offend; *bók-dáik-ī,* 不得已 without remedy, must be so; *tău-dáik,* 偷得 secretly.

Dáik, 德 Virtue, moral excellence; *dáik-hâing,* 德行 virtuous actions; *mò dáik-hâing,* 毛德行 vicious, immoral, wicked.

Dáing, 店 A shop, an inn; *dáing-tàu,* 店頭 a shop; *káh-dáing,*

客店 a tavern; *mī-dáing*, 米店 a rice shop; *dáing-ciō*, 店主 a shop keeper; *buóng dáing*, 飯店 an eating house.

Dáing, 鐙 Also read *dâing*: com; *mā-dáing*, 馬鐙 stirrup.

Dáing, 殿 A lofty hall; a palace; a temple; *gĭng-luàng-dáing*, 金鑾殿 the audience chamber.

Dáing, 靛 Indigo; to dye blue.

Dáing, 墊 Read *diéng*: a cushion, a large mat; to wedge, to use blocking; *iē-dáing*, 椅墊 a chair cushion.

Dâing, 宸 Read *âing*: as in *muòng-dáing*, 門宸 the threshold.

Dáing, 有 A coll. character: solid, durable, hard; obtuse; *cêng dáing*, 盡有 very hard; *dáing chà*, 有柴 hard wood; *dáing-sĭng*, 有心 obtuse.

Dáiu 157

Dáiu, 鬭 COLL. read *dáu*, q. v.: to fight; to wrangle; to contest, to contend; *cĕng-dáiu*, 爭鬭 to fight; *dáiu-ké*, 鬭氣 pugnacious; *dáiu-chói*, 鬭嘴 to wrangle.

Dáiu, 吊 Read *diéu*: suspended; to lower by cords; *dáiu sī*, 吊死 to hang one's self.

Dáiu, 竇 A hole; a den, a burrow; a drain, an aqueduct; *gēu-dáiu*, 狗竇 a dog's kennel; *cūi-dáiu*, 水竇 a drain, or channel for water.

Dáiu, 豆 Beans, pulse; usually read *dáu*, q. v.: Read *dēu*: a peck, a measure.

Dáiu, 荳 Peas, beans; legumes; common term is *dáu*; *dáiu-káiu*, 荳蔻 a nutmeg.

Dáiu: A coll. word: to cast, to pitch, to throw down: *dáiu* má hiōng, throw it down, it does not ring, as a bad dollar.

Dák, 答 A bamboo rope; to reply; an answer; dák-éng, 答應 to reply.

Dák, 搭 To smite; to add to; to construct; dák-gá, 搭架 to erect a frame or stand; dák-sùng, 搭船 to take passage by boat; in the COLL.—dák-géu, 搭救 to save, to deliver.

Dák; A coll. word: to fit closely, to adjust; literal, exact; dák-dọi, cash bag; dák-gáng, to perspire thru one's clothes.

Dák, 組 Read déng: to baste, to sew slightly; dák-siáng, 組線 a basting thread; dák ĭ-siòng, 組衣裳 to baste clothes.

Dák, 錔 A hook, a grapnel; to hook; a clasp of a door; dák-gău, 錔鉤 a boat hook; muòng-

dák, 門鍚 a brass or iron door clasp; *mùong dák sĭŏh â,* 門鍚一下 just latch the door! *dák-cĕng,* 鍚針 a safety-pin.

Dák, 噠 Read *dăk: dák cṳ̄,* 噠子 name for the Tartars; *dák-bŏ̤-cŏng,* 噠婆裝 the Manchu female costume.

Dăk, 踏 To tread, to trample on; *ciēng-dăk,* 踐踏 to trample on; *dăk - dāu,* 踏斗 steps, stairs; *dăk mùong,* 踏門 to kick a door open.

Dăk, 達 COLL. *dák,* q. v.: intelligent; to permeate; to perceive clearly; *dăk ìng,* 達人 a shrewd man; *ciéng-dăk,* 薦達 to introduce; to recommend; COM. *tŭng-dăk,* 通達 to understand fully, intelligent; *huák-dăk,* 發達 rising, prosperous.

Dăk, 馨 The sound of a drum;

. dăk-dăk-gū, 馨馨鼓 a drum.

Dăng, 丹 A carnation color: *met.*, sincere; a medicine, a prescription; *ek piéng dăng sĭng*, 一片丹心 devoted, loyal, sincere; *dăng să*, 丹沙 vermillion.

Dăng, 珊 Also read *săng*, q. v.: coral; *dăng-hù*, 珊瑚 coral; *dăng-hù-ciŏ*, 珊瑚珠 coral beads; *dăng hù dīng*, 珊瑚頂 a red coral button—the highest in rank.

Dăng, 蹣 Read *săng*, q. v.: to hobble, to halt; *dĭ-dĭ dă-dăng*, to stagger.

Dăng, 聃 A man's name; *Lō-dăng*, or *Lō-cū̆*, 老聃 or 老子 the founder of Tauism.

Dăng, 單 Also read *siéng*, q. v.: single, alone, a single garment; a bill, a receipt; a check; *dăng-dăng*, 單單 single; *dăng-tṳ̀ng*, 單重 a single thickness; *dăng chiū*, 單手 single handed; *dăng-sĭng-gṍ*, 單身哥 a bachelor; *khŭi dăng*, 開單 to make out a bill; *dĭ-dăng*, 知單 a circular; *siā-dăng*, 謝單 a note of thanks; *dăng-dó*, 單倒 reversely, wrongly.

Dăng, 殫 Also read *dāng*: to carry to the utmost; the extreme, exhausted; *dăng lĭk*, 殫力 the whole strength.

Dăng, 襌 A single unlined garment; *dăng ĭ*, 襌衣 a single inner garment.

Dăng, 擔担 Also read *dáng*, q. v.: to carry across the shoulder on the ends of a stick; to be responsible or security for; *dăng-dăng*, 擔担 to carry a load; *bĕng-dăng,* 板擔 a carrying stick or yoke; *dăng gĕng,* 擔工 cooliage; *dăng iŭ,* 擔憂 solicitious; *dăng-dŏng,* 擔當 responsible for; *ó dăng-dŏng,* 務擔當 and *mò dăng-dŏng,* 毛擔當 can and cannot; *dănggŏh,* 擔擱 delayed; Read *siêng:* to borrow; pretending.

Dăng, 儋 To bear, to carry; a load of two piculs of grain.

Dăng, 伶 A coll. character: now, the present time; *dăng céu kó,* 伶就去 to go immediately; *gáu dăng,* 至伶 till now; *dăng gì nĕng,* 伶其仫 the men of the present time.

Dăng: A coll. word: on the contrary; reversely, backwards; *dăng kó,* on the contrary, wrongly; *dăng dó có,* to do the wrong thing first; *dăng-dó-*

Dăng 163

tàu, the wrong end first.

Dăng: A coll. word, as *chiū-dăng*, the elbow; *kă-áu-dăng*, the heel; *chiū-dăng dŭng*, to knock the elbow.

Dāng, 膽, 胆 The gall, the gall bladder; courage, fortitude; *găng-dāng*, 肝膽 the liver and gall; *met.*, the very heart; very intimate; *duâi dāng*, 大膽 great courage; *dāng kè*, 膽氣 a courageous spirit; *dāng sièu*, 膽小 cowardly, timid: COLL. *giăng puái dāng*, 驚破膽 scared enough to split his gall bladder! very frightened.

Dāng, 瘴 Also read *dáng*: disease from overwork; erysipelas; *uòng-dāng*, 黃瘴 jaundice.

Dāng: A coll. word; often, frequently; *dāng - dāng ciŏng-*

uâng, repeatedly so; dāng-dāng chéng, constantly cold, as the weather.

Dáng, 但 But, only, simply; as soon as; kī-dáng, 豈但 how only; lók dáng, 不但 not simply; dáng nguông, 但願 only wish that! would that!

Dáng, 旦 Sun rising, the morning, dawn: clear, bright; dáng-sĭk. 旦夕 morning and evening; nguòng-dáng, 元旦 new year's day; sáuk-dáng, 朔旦 the 1st day of the month.

Dáng, 筦 Also read dāng: a small basket; to brush away; bamboo mats for roof.

Dáng, 擔担 A burden, a picul; also read dăng, q. v.: dáeng-dáng, 重担 a heavy load; ciek-dáng, 接担 to go and relieve one of his load.

Dáng, 誕, 謊 To boast, to brag; *huóng dáng,* 放誕 to lie, to brag.

Dáng, 蛋 Read *láung,* q. v.: an egg.

Dáng: A coll. word: to force, to strain.

Dáng: A coll. word: to spread, to extend; a copy slip called *cê-dáng; dáng těng-táu,* it has wet through.

Dàng, 談 To converse; to dispute; to discuss: *hàng-dàng,* 閑談 chitchat; *gōng chiéu-dàng,* 講笑談 to laugh and chat; *dàng-láung,* 談論 to discourse.

Dàng, 壇 An alter of sacrifice; a public hall.

Dàng, 彈 Also read *dâng,* q. v.: to play on stringed instruments; *dàng-kìng,* 彈琴 to play on lutes, etc; *dàng miêng,*

彈綿 to bow cotton; *dàng-ák*, to subdue.

Dâng, 彈 Also read *dàng*, q. v.: a ball, a pellet; *dâng uòng*, 彈丸 a pellet; *dâng-cī*, 彈子 a pellet.

Dâng, 鄭 COM. *dâng-dë̤ung*, 鄭重 earnest, respectful.

Dâng, 啖 To eat, to masticate; a bite, a morsel.

Dâng, 淡澹 Fresh, tasteless; thin, weak, as tea; the opposite of *nùng*; heartless, distant, as a friend; *dâng sáik*, 淡色 a light color; *lēng-dâng*, 冷淡 indifferent to; *dà kák dâng*, 茶太淡 the tea is too weak.

Dâng: A coll. word: to err; an error; *mò dâng*, right, no error; *nṳ̄ ô dâng*, you are in fault; *dâng diô*, the wrong road.

Dău, 兜 Also read děu: a helmet, or helmet-shaped; in the COLL. at, by, in time or place; cáik-dău, 節兜 near the time of a festival; nàng-mùòng-dău, 南門兜 at the South Gate.

Dău, 攬 Also read děu: to grasp, to seize; to monopolize; in the COLL. to befriend, to care for; dău sĭng-biĕng, 攬身邊 to befriend, as an orphan; pŭôi dău diē, 被攬裡 to tuck the quilt under; dău-liāng, 攬領 to monopolize, as trade.

Dău, 株 Read tŭ: a classifier of pillars, posts, etc.; chéu siŏh dău, 樸一株 a tree; têu siŏh dău, 柱一株 a post.

Dāu, 斗 Read děu: a dry measure of 10 cĭng or pints; mī dāu, 米斗 the common rice peck; dāu-lĭk, 斗笠 a coolie's rain hat; *dăk-dāu,* 踏斗 steps, stairs; in the COLL. *sèng-dāu,* 前斗 or *sèng-dāu-sié,* 前斗勢 before, in front; *á-dāu,* 後斗 behind, in the rear; *ók-dāu,* 熨斗 a smoothing iron.

Dāu, A coll. word: to shake, as clothes; to count, to reckon up; *dāu-dāu,* shake it; *dāu ŭng-dìng,* to shake out the dust; *dāu só,* to reckon the day's accounts.

Dáu, 罩 A cover, a shade; to cover; *giêu-dáu,* 轎罩 a sedan cover; *giĕ-lèng-dáu,* 鷄籠罩 a movable chicken coop; *dáu guó tàu,* 罩過頭 to cover the head with the bedding.

Dáu, 鬥 Read *dáiu*; to strive, to compete; *dáu ká,* 鬥快 to compete in speed; *dáu-ké,* 鬥氣 the spirit of competition.

Dáu: A coll. word: midday, noon, *mct.*, dinner; *nĭk-tàu dáu*, 12 m.; *sióng-dáu*, and *á-dáu*, forenoon and afternoon; *puái-dáu*, midday; *dáu siăh lāu*, have eaten dinner.

Dàu, 骰 As *dàu-cī*, 骰子 dice.

Dàu, 投 Read *dèu*: to throw one's self unto another as *dàu ĭ lā*, 投伊禮; *dàu-bŏh*, 投泊 to cleave, to depend upon as an orphan does; *dàu hòng*, 投降 to submit; *dàu iùng*, 投營 enlist.

Dâu, 豆 Also read *dáiu*, q. v.: beans, peas, legumes; *gĭng-dâu*, 金豆 peas; *dâu-giék*, 豆莢 string beans; *dâu-guăng*, 豆乾 cakes of bean curd; *dâu-ngà*, 豆芽 bean sprouts.

Dàu, 痘 The small pox; *céung-dáu*, 種痘 to inoculate; *dáu*

ciòng, 痘漿 foreign vaccine virus.

Dáu, 胭 Read dáiu: as dáu-gáuk, 胭骨 the neck; dâu-liāng, 胭領 the neck of a garment.

Dáuk, 啄 To peck, to eat as fowls do; dáuk céu, 啄蛀 to peck through the shell, as chicks.

Dáuk, 琢 To work gems; děu-dáuk, 雕琢 to cut and dress gems.

Dáuk, 揬 To strike; to push; to carve, as letters.

Dáuk, 卓 Read dọ́h, q. v.: high, eminent.

Dáuk, 踔 Read dáu: to tread on; to jump over; unusual.

Dáuk: A coll. word: to lift, to carry with both hands; dáuk kī, to take it up; dáuk iĕ, to carry a chair; dáuk ciáng, to take and place properly.

Dáung, 當 Also read dŏng, q. v.: to pawn; to regard as; for, instead of; *dáung dáing,* 當店 a pawnshop; *dáung ĭ-siòng,* 當衣裳 to pawn clothes; *dáung dà,* 當茶 in the place of tea; *ūng-dáung,* 穩當 safe; *có dáung,* 做當 a guarantee; *ng dáung có séu,* 怀當做事 do not regard it; no matter!

Dáung, 擋 To jolt, to jounce; to impede.

Dáung, 頓 Read *dŏng:* a meal, a repast; *met.,* a spell, a while; *siŏh nĭk săng dáung,* 一日三頓 three meals a day.

Dáung, 段 A piece, a section, a numerative of pieces, plats etc.; a piece of silk; skill; *siŏh dáung dê,* 一段地 a plat of ground; *hō chiū-dáung,* 好手

段 good workmanship.

Dáung, 緞 Glossy silk; satin; *diù-dáung,* 綢緞 silks and satins; *huă-dáung,* 花緞 brocade; *guŏng-dáung,* 光緞 plain satins; *góng-dáung* 貢緞 best quality satins.

Dáung, 遁遯 To run away; to retire, as into privacy; *ŭng-dáung,* 隱遁 to retire to private life.

Dáung, 撞 Read *dùng* and *dông:* to pound; to dash against; to intrude; *met.,* to swindle: *dáung diē,* 撞入 to intrude.

Dáung, 斷 Read *duăng:* to stop, to break off; free from; *dáung òng,* 斷晌 long discontinued; *dáung ké,* 斷氣 to die; *dáung nèng,* 斷朧 to wean.

Dáung, 盪 To miss, to err; to fall; to let fall; to rain;

dâung kó, 遏去 dropped; dâung mò, 遏毛 lost; páh-dâung, 拍遏 to let fall; dâung ṳ̄, 遏雨 to rain; dâung buŏ-sì-ṳ̄, 遏嚗時雨 a summer shower; dâung lŏ̤h lì, 遏落來 to fall down, as things.

Dâung, 蕩 Vast, magnificent; extravagant; huŏng-dâung, 敨蕩 careless, profligate; dâung-dâung, 蕩蕩 vast and deep.

Dâung, 盪 Also read táung, q. v.: a washing tub; disturbed; tiéu-dâung, 跳盪 in a panic; sā-dâung, 洗盪 to wash and rinse; gò-dâung, (or lâung, to 高盪 to rinse.

Dâung, 丈 Read diông: ten Chinese feet, equal to 117½ English inches; dâung siŏng, 丈上 o-ver ten feet; dâung-gŏ̤, 丈篙 a 10 foot pole.

Dé, 蔕蒂 The stalks of flowers; the stems of leaves or fruit; COLL *dì-dé,* 蔕蒂 stem; *siâng-dé,* 緒蔕 remnants of thread left in sewing.

Dé, 智, 知 The second read *dì,* q. v.: wisdom, understanding; intelligent; *dé-hiê,* 智慧 wisdom; *dé ngù,* 智愚 clever and stupid; *ciòng dé,* 全智 all wise.

Dé, 緻 As *biĕu-dé,* 標緻 fine, pretty.

Dé, 致 A causative before verbs; to order, to manage; the form, appearance of; that, in order to; *ī-dé,* 以致 so that; *dé-é,* 致意 to bow slightly.

Dé, 置 To establish, to place; to purchase; *dé-huó,* 置貨 to lay in a fresh stock of goods.

Dé, A coll. word: to raise, as with the head and hands; *dé* má kī, can't raise it, as a heavy article.

Dê, 地 The earth, the ground; earthy; the first color in painting; only; merely; *dê-tū*, 地土 the soil; *dê ciō*, 地主 a landlord; *buōng-dê*, 本地 native; *dê-â*, 地下 or *dê-dău*, 地兜 on the ground; *dê-lī*, 地理 geography; *páh dê*, 拍地 to prime.

Dê, 治 To rule, to govern; good government; *bìng dê*, 平治 general tranquility; *dê cŏi*, 治罪 to inflict punishment; *ĭ-dê*, 醫治 to cure; *dê-báng*, 治病 to heal a sickness.

Dê, 稺稚 Small; tender, delicate; *dùng-dê*, 童稺 a youngster, a boy.

Dê, 雉 Pheasants, as *dê-giĕ*, 雉雞.

Dê, A coll. euphonic prefix, as

in *dé-dái*, to throw away; *dé-dậ*, to screen.

Dệ: A coll. word: used for *sī*, to die.

Dệ: A coll. word: an exclamation, There! there it is!

Dék, 的 After nouns a sign of the possessive; after adjectives denotes comparison; after verbs denotes completion of action; in the coll. must, positively, certainly; *dék nèng tiáng*, 的仈愛 esteemed by others; *hō dék sậ*, 好的倆 much better; *dék sè*, 的是 it certainly is; *dék-dék ó*, 的的務 must be or have; *dék diŏh*, 的着 must; *ậ hiĕu-dék*, 儹曉的 to know it; *gōng dék ká*, 講的快 to speak rapidly.

Dék, 嫡 The first wife; *dék cṳ̄*, 嫡子 children of the wife.

Dék, 滴 A drop, *met.*, a very little; *sióh dék-giāng*, 一滴仔 a little; *sióh dék dŭ mò̤*, 一滴都毛 not a bit.

Dék, A coll. euphonic prefix, as *dék-dák*, to baste; *dék-dáuk*, to carry with both hands; *dék-dók*, to punctuate.

Dĕk, 值 Read *sĭk* and *dĭk*; the price; to be worth; *dĕk cièng*, 值錢 it is worth money,— dear; *dĕk niŏh-uái*, 值箸壞 what is it worth?

Dĕk, 擇 COLL. *dăh*, *q. v.*; to choose, to prefer; *gēng-dĕk*, 揀擇 to select; *dĕk gău*, 擇交 to select associates.

Dĕk, 澤 A marsh, a fen; to enrich, to fertilize; to favor, to benefit; also a noun; *ŏng-dĕk*, 恩澤 favor, beneficence; *éung-dĕk*, 潤澤 to enrich.

Děk, A coll. word: to drain, to filter; *děk dă*, drained dry.

Děk, 特 Single, solitary; only, specially; *děk ện*, 特諭 a a special edict; *děk-é*, 特意 or *děk-dĭk*, 特直 with special design or purpose.

Děk, 毒 Read *dŭk*; a poison; cruel; to hate; *chói děk*, 嘴毒 malicious talk; *děk sĭng*, 毒心 cruel; *kện dŭk siá*, 去毒社 anti-opium society.

Děng, 登 To advance, to ascend; to gain a degree; to record, at once; *děng děng*, 登登 responsive, as voices; *děng cĭk*, 登籍 to take a census; *děng gŭk*, 登極 to ascend the throne; *děng-gĭ*, 登基 the time appointed to ascend the throne.

Děng, 燈 COLL. *dĭng* and *diĕng* q. v.: a lamp, a lantern; *met.*, moral light; *děng ngò,* 燈蛾 a moth.

Děng: A coll. word: to prick, to bruise; *děng-dŏh,* to bruise, as the feet.

Dēng, 等 COLL. *dĭng,* q. v.; a class, a species; a grade, a rank; a sign of the plural; to compare; *dēng-lôi,* 等類 sorts, classes; *dēng-dēng,* 等等 et cetera; *siông, dựng, hâ, săng dēng,* 上中下三等 the three classes, upper, middle, lower.

Dēng, 點 Read *diēng:* a dot, a black spot; an hour; to reckon; to call a roll; *dēng-ó,* 點污 a stain; *gūi dēng,* 幾點 what o'clock is it? *gūi dēng cụng,* 幾點鐘 how many hours? *dēng guó,* 點過 to count over; *dēng miàng,* 點名 to call the roll.

Dēng, 典 Read *diēng;* a mortgage; *dēng ngiĕk,* 典業 to mortgage property; *dēng kié,* 典契 a mortgage; *dēng ciō,* 典主 the mortgagee.

Déng, 碇矴 Ballast; an anchor; *pă déng,* 抛矴 to cast anchor; *kī déng,* 起矴 to weigh anchor; *páh déng,* 拍矴 to moor.

Déng, 定額 The forehead. (see *dêng.*)

Déng, 鎮 To quell, to protect; a mart: *déng ák,* 鎮壓 to quell disturbances; *chê déng,* 市鎮 busy mart; *déng-dài,* a brigadier.

Déng, 釘 Also read *dĭng,* q. v.: to fasten with nails; to bind, as books; in the coll. to sting, as bees; *déng dĭng,* 釘釘 to drive a nail; *déng cŭ,* 釘書 to bind books; *déng bēng-bàng,* 釘

Déng 181

板棚 to lay a floor; *pŭng déng,*
蜂釘 the bee stings.

Déng: A coll. word; to stitch; *déng à,* 釘鞋 to stitch shoes.

Déng, 訂 To make an agreement, as *déng iók,* 訂約

Déng: A coll. word: strong, as infusions: *dà kák déng,* the tea is too strong.

Déng: A coll. euphonic prefix, as *déng-dáung,* to pawn.

Dèng, 澄 Still water; clear; *dèng chĭng,* 澄清 very limpid.

Dèng, 謄 To copy, to transcribe; *dèng-liŏh,* 謄錄 to copy out.

Dèng, 墥 Also read *dièng,* q. v.: to make up a deficiency. Read *dĭng:* to fix, to settle. Read *dìng:* a long time. Read *diēng:* exhausted; liberal.

Dèng, 還 To cancel a debt; to restore a borrowed article;

dèng-cái, 還債 to pay a debt; dèng gá, 還價 to offer a lower price; dèng só, 還數 to settle an account.

Dēng, 定 Also read déng: COLL. diáng q. v.: fixed, secure; surely, positively; to adjust; ék-dēng, 一定 positively; dēng cṳ̆, 定書 to recite by reading.

Dēng, 阵, 陳 The second also read dìng, a surname: a rank, squad, a battalion; a company, a gust; buó dēng, 布陣 to marshal columns; cọ̆ dēng, 做陣 to bear one company.

Dēng: A coll. word: dēng-dáeng, to set in water to cool.

Dẹng, 冬 The winter season as dẹng-gié, 冬季; dẹng-cáik, 冬至 festival at the winter solstice; dẹng-cĭ, 冬只 chilblains.

Dẹng, 東 Read dŭng, the east,

met., this, this one, here; *dẹ̌ng báck,* 東北 north east.

Dẹ̌ng: A coll. word: where? how? *dẹ̌ng-nẹ̄ nẹ̀ng,* whence is he?

Dẹ̀ng, 同 Read *dùng:* the same, alike, a fellow; *dẹ̀ng huói,* 同歲 of the some age.

Dẹ̀ng, 筒 Read *dùng:* a tube, pipe; a cup, a flue; *iĕng-dẹ̀ng,* 烟筒 a chimney; *hŏng-dẹ̀ng,* 煙筒 a tobacco pipe; *huă-dẹ̀ng,* 花筒 a kaleidascope.

Dẹ̀ng, 銅 Read *dùng:* copper; *báh-dẹ̀ng,* 白銅 white copper, tutenag; *uòng-dẹ̀ng,* 黃銅 brass; *dẹ̀ng-cièng,* 銅錢 cash.

Dẹ̀ng, 僮 Read *dùng:* as *dẹ̀ng-cī,* 僮子 a medium.

Dĕu, 簋 Also read *dău:* a trough; a light mountain sedan, as *dĕu-giêu,* 簋轎; *dĕu-hŭ,* 簋夫 the bearers.

Dĕu, 雕 To engrave, to cut characters; *dĕu-káik*, 雕刻 to carve.

Dĕu: A coll. word: bitter, harsh in taste.

Dĕu, 斗 COLL. *dāu*, q. v.: a peck; *dĕu-dāng* 斗胆 Presumption!

Dĕu, 陡 Suddenly; *dĕu-iòng-gāng*, 陡然間 unexpectedly.

Dĕu: A coll. word: to strike, to whip, to lash; pendent; *dĕu mạ diŏh*, failed to hit it.

Dĕu: A coll. word: to tremble, to quake; *dĕu-dĕu-ciéng*, in a tremor.

Dēu 投 COLL. *dàu*, q. v.

Dèu, 條 A classifier for long things; COM. *giĕ-dèu*, 規條 regulations; *dèu-lī*, 條理 reasonable; *huák-dèu*, 法條 the mainspring of a watch.

Dèu, 調 Read *dièu*: to mix in,

Déu 185

to spice; *dèu sièng*, 調鹽 to season with salt.

Dèu: A coll. word: to whip, as *dèu hēng-hēng*, to whip severely.

Déu, 稻 Rice in the ear, the ripe grain; rent, taxes; *déu sŭk*, 稻熟 rice ripened; *dêu-gō*, 稻稿 rice stalks; *gák déu*, 割稻 to harvest rice.

Déu: 蹛 A coll. word: to dwell, to reside, to live in or at; *dêu chió*, 蹛厝 to live in a house; *děng-nē déu*, 冬那蹛 where do you reside? *dŏng mặ dêu*, 當儕蹛 intolerable; *guāng ặ dêu*, manageable.

Déu, 著 Also read *ciŏk*, q. v.; to manifest; to narrate, to compose and publish books; *déu cṳ̄ lĭk siŏk*, 著書立說 to compose a book.

186　　　Déuk

Dèu, 箸 Chopsticks; *dêu dèng*, 箸筒 a cup for holding chopsticks; *ngà dêu*, 牙箸 ivory chopsticks.

Dêu: A coll. word, used in the sense of *diòh*: to be at, or in a place; *dêu mò dêu*, is he present or not?

Déuk, 竹 The bamboo; *déuk sūng*, 竹笋 bamboo sprouts; *déuk-piĕ*, 竹披 a bamboo stick for punishing offenders.

Déuk, 竺 A species of bamboo: *Tiĕng-déuk guók*, 天竺國 India.

Déuk, 築 To beat earth solid: COM. *déuk chiòng*, 築牆 to make an earth wall; COLL. *déuk săng-gák tù*, 築三夾土 to make a cement pavement; *déuk-chū*, 築杵 a pounder used in making mud walls.

Déuk: A coll. word: to sum up mentally; *chói déuk,* to reckon with the mouth.

Déung, 中 Also read *dŭng,* q. v.: to accomplish; fit, suitable; *déung-é,* 中意 pleased with; *déung siăh,* 中食 fit to eat; *déung éung,* 中用 (COLL. *déung sāi,* 中駛) fit for use; COLL. *ng déung dĭh,* 怀中值 not desirable.

Déung, 仲 The second month of a season; *déung há,* 仲夏 the 5th month.

Déung, 重 Also read *dùng:* COLL. *dâeng* and *tŭng,* q. v.: *cĕu déung,* 自重 self respect; *déung éung,* 重用 to employ one in weighty matters; *ūng déung,* 穩重 steady, trusty.

Dĭ, 知 Also read *dé,* q. v.: to know, to understand; knowledge, prudence; *ŭ dĭ,* 無知 ignorant; *dĭ-séh,* 知識 knowledge; *dĭ-gáuk,* 知覺 to perceive; *tŭng-dĭ,* 通知 to inform; *dĭ-céuk,* 知足 contented; *dĭ-sĭng,* 知心 intimate; *dĭ-dăng,* 知單 an invitation list?

Dĭ, 胝 Also read *ciĕ:* to grow callous; corns on the feet.

Dĭ: A coll. word: hanging, suspended; *dĭ-dĭ dŭ-dŭ,* hanging all about.

Dĭ: A coll. word: a corruption *diê,* which? what? *dĭ siŏh ciáh,* which one?

Dĭ: A coll. word, as *siŏh dĭ-dĭ,* a mere mite, a very little.

Dĭ, 邸 A lodging, a lodging house; a royal residence; *Tĭ-sì dĭ* cottage at Kuliang.

Dĭ, 抵 In the coll. read *dă,* q. v.: to oppose, to ward off; to bear the blame; *dái-dĭ,* 大抵 for the most part; COM. *dĭ-dŏng,* 抵當 to bear the blame of; *dói-dĭ,* 對抵 to barter; COLL. *dĭ dék dĭk,* 抵的直 to make ends meet.

Dĭ, 砥 A grindstone as *dĭ-lả,* 砥礪 *met.,* to reform one's self.

Dĭ, 底 COLL. *dả,* q. v.: the bottom, foundation, menial; but, only; *ừ-dĭ,* 無底 bottomless; *dĭ-cĭ,* 底止 antecedents of; *mò dĭ-cĭ,* 毛底止 no clue to.

Dĭ, 禠 To take away insignia; *dĭ-gáik,* 禠革 to degrade.

Dì, 遲 To delay; slow, tardy: also read *dé:* to wait for.

Dì, 馳 Also read *tì:* to gallop.

Diă, 爹 A father; *diă nă,* 爹奶 father and mother; *lọ̆-diă,* 老爹 his Honor, the officer: coll. *ĭ-diă,* 阿爹 papa!

Dià: A coll. word: weak, drooping, as eyes.

Diáh, 摘 Read *cáik:* to pluck, to cull, to nip; *diáh huā,* 摘花 to pluck flowers.

Diăh, 糴 Read *dĭk:* to purchase; *diăh mī,* 糴米 to buy rice.

Diăh: A coll. word: to throw dice as *diăh dàu.*

Diăk: A coll. word: *diăk guó chiū,* to cheat.

Diăk: A coll. word: to expose to, borne by the wind; *diăk pé,* to scent it.

Diāng, 偵 Read *dīng:* to spy, to lie in wait for; *diāng chĕk,* 偵賊 to lie in wait for thieves.

Diāng, 鼎 Read *tīng,* a frying pan; the rice pan; *diāng cáu,* 鼎灶 pans and furnaces.

Diáng: A coll. word: intensely fragrant.

Diâng 191

Diàng, 呈 Read *tìng*, q. v.: also spoken *tiàng*: a statement, a plea; to petition; *dạ diàng*, 遞呈 to present a petition.

Diàng, 埕 A space before a house; *kĕng diàng*, 空埕 a plat; *bóng-dọ́ diàng*, 糞倒埕 a compost heap.

Diàng: A coll. word: to crush; to pour in; to give a hint; to splash; *diàng sī*, crushed to death; *diàng cūi*, to add water.

Diàng: A coll. word: a peg, a nail for hanging things on.

Diàng, 定 Read *dêng*: steady, fixed; to settle, to adjust; *mọ̀ diáng-diŏh*, 毛定着 uncertain; *diàng cièng*, 定錢 bargain money; *diâng-tẹng*, 定蟲 a lazy lout; *diàng cọ́*, 定做 to engage to do.

Diăng, 錠 Read dêng: an ingot, bullion; nguòng-bō-diáng, 元寶錠 an ingot of sycee.

Diē, 入 Read ik: to enter; entrance; diē kó, 入去 to go in; diē chók, 入出 ingress and egress; diē siàng, 入城 to go into the city.

Diē, 裎, 裏 Read li: within; inside; nearly related; diē diē 裡裏 within; chió-diē, 厝裎 in the house; a term for wife.

Diè, 池 A pool, a pond, a tank; dŭng diè, 中池 the heart. Read dò: diverging streams.

Diè, 弟 Read dá, a younger brother; hiăng-diè, 兄弟 brothers; sá-diè, 細弟 a lad; i-diè, 阿弟 my lad! my boy!

Diē, 佃 A COLL. character; which, what, whoever; preceded by kŏ why, wherefore; diē-nèng

Dick 193

俤仈 what person? *kŏ-diê*, or *kŏ-diê dái*, wherefore? why thus?

Diê, 蠣 Read *lá*, an oyster; *diê-buò*, 蠣房 oyster, in the shell.

Diê: A coll. word: an interrogative pronoun (*see above*), *diê-nèng*, who? *diê-nèng diē*, at whose house?

Diê: A coll. corruption of *dé* (ground) as *diê-dău*, on the ground.

Diék, 哲 Wise, intelligent.

Diék: A coll. word: disgraced; *diék-gū*, to disgrace one.

Diék, 秩 Also read *dĭk*: order, succession, a decenninm; *ngó diĕk*, 五秩 five tens or decades; fifty years; *lŭk-diĕk*, 祿秩 official salary.

Diĕk, 疊 COLL *tăk*, q. v., to pile up, to make a heap.

194 Diĕng

Diĕk, 碟 A small plate; *diĕk-giāng*, 碟仔 a saucer; *sĕk-nê diĕk*, 十二碟 the twelve small plates for the first course at feasts.

Diĕk, 蝶 As *hù-diĕk*, 蝴蝶 a butterfly.

Diĕk, 跌 COLL. *tiĕk*, and *buăk*, q. v.: to kick out, to slip, to stumble and fall.

Diĕng, 甜, 餂 Sweet in taste; pleasant, agreeable.

Diĕng, 癲 Deranged, insane, mad; *diĕng-guòng*, 癲狂 raving mad.

Diĕng, 頇 The top, the apex; to upset; to subvert; *diĕng-dŏ*, 頇倒 inverted, turned upside down.

Diĕng, 巔 The summits of hills; the highest peak of a mountain.

Diěng, 燈 Read děng: diěng-sǐng, 燈心 a wick.

Diěng, 典 COLL. děng, q. v.: a classic, a standard work; cë-diēng, 字典 dictionary; gū-diēng, 古典 ancient records; ŏng-diēng, 恩典 favor, grace.

Diěng, 點 COLL. děng, q. v.: a spot, a stain; the stroke of a clock; to count; cī-diēng, 指點 to direct, to show to one; diēng-sǐng, 點心 a light luncheon; diēng-huōi, 點火 to light a fire.

Diěng, 展 To arrange and examine; COM. diěng áing, 展限 to extend the time.

Diěng, 輾 To roll, to turn over half way; diěng-diōng, 輾轉 to go to and fro.

Diěng, 玷 A flaw, or defect, in a gem.

Dièng, 田 COLL. *chèng*, q. v.: a field, cultivated lands; to cultivate; *sĭng-dièng*, 心田 mind, disposition.

Dièng, 塡 Commonly read *dèng*: to fill up or in; to pay; to forfeit, as life.

Dièng, 廛 A shop; *dièng-chê*, 廛市 a bazaar.

Dièng, 纒 To bind, to wrap, to bandage; *dièng-kă*, 纒胶 compressed feet; *dièng-buáng*, 纒絆 caught, involved.

Dièng, 躔 An orbit, a course; *dièng-dô*, 躔度 an orbit.

Dièng, 佃 Also read *dièng*: to farm on shares; *diêng-hŭ* 佃夫 a husbandman; *diêng-hô*, 佃戶 a plowman, one who farms on shares.

Dièng 鈿 Also read *dièng*: *ièng guāng diéng*, 圓管鈿 bracelets

Diĕu 197

having a round surface.

Diéng, 奠 *diéng-ciŭ,* 奠酒 libations.

Diêng, 電 Lightning, electricity; *lòi-diêng,* 雷電 thunder and lightning; *siĕng-diêng,* (COLL. *niák-niáng,*) 閃電 a flash of lightning, *diàng diêng,* 呈電 "respectfully presented to your glance"—an epistolary phrase.

Diêng: A coll. word: full; up to the brim; *diêng-diêng,* 囝囝 brimful; *kák diêng ặ păk,* too full, it will overflow.

Dĭĕu, 刁 Read *tiĕu:* perverse, rebellious; *dĭĕu-nguàng,* 刁頑 perverse.

Dĭĕu, 雕 COLL. *dĕu,* q. v.: *dĭĕu-káik,* 雕刻 to engrave.

Dĭĕu, 鵰 A species of eagle.

Dĭĕu, 朝 Also read *diêu,* q. v.:

the dawn; early; *diĕu-diĕu*, 朝朝 every morning.

Diĕu, 貂 The marten or sable, called *diĕu-chŭ*, 貂鼠.

Diĕu: A coll. word: as *diĕu-miĕu*, lively, playful.

Diéu, 吊 COLL. *dáiu*, q. v.: to suspend; *diéu áng*, 吊案 to order a second trial.

Diéu, 弔 To condole with mourners; condolence; *diéu sŏng*, 弔喪 or *câuk diéu* to wail over the dead; *iè diéu*, loose, as a tooth or nail.

Diéu, To draw, as plasters; *diéu-gŏ*, a drawing plaster.

Diéu, 晝 A day, daytime; *diéu iâ*, 晝夜 day and night, incessantly.

Diéu, 釣 To angle, to fish; *diéu né*, 釣餌 a bait; *diéu-ngù*, 釣魚 to angle for fish.

Diêu   199

Diêu: A coll. word, used for *chiĕng*, a thousand cash.

Dièu, 朝 Also read *diĕu,* q. v.: an audience; to go to court; *dièu-dìng,* 朝廷 the court; His Majesty; *dièu-dội,* 朝代 a dynasty; in the coll.: fronting, facing; *dièu nàng,* 朝南 facing south; *dièu chók,* 朝出 facing outward; *dièu siōng,* 朝上 facing upward; *dièu ōng,* 朝影 shaded.

Dièu, 潮 The morning tide; *sông dièu,* 順潮 to go with the tide; *dièu duái,* 潮大 spring tides; *dièu dōng cūi,* 潮漲水 the flood tide.

Dièu, 調 Also read *diĕu,* q. v.: to harmonize, to blend; to season, to spice; to regulate; *dièu chiéu,* 調笑 to ridicule; *dièu ĭng,* 調音 to harmonize sounds; *dièu é,* 調味 to spice; *dièu-tióng,* 調暢 happy, joyously; *dièu-chṳ̄,* 調處 to settle, as lawsuits; *dièu-dĭk,* 調直 straight, honest.

Dièu, 調 Also read *dièu,* q. v.: a tune, a ballad; *kiŏng-dièu,* 腔調 a ditty.

Dièu, 召 Also read *sièu,* q. v.: to summon, to order one to come; to send; *dièu giéng,* 召見 to call to court.

Dièu, 兆 An omen; one million; *é-dièu,* 億兆 myriads; *dièu mìng,* 兆民 millions of men, the people; *gék dièu,* 吉兆 a lucky omen; *hṳ̆ng dièu,* 凶兆 unpropitious sign.

Dĭh, 值 Read *sĭk* and *dĭk*; to wish, to desire; *dĭh ng dĭh,* 怀值 wish it or not? *nguāi buóh dĭh,* 我剝值 I desire it;

dĭh sié-ngh, 值世毛 what do you wish?

Dĭh: A coll. word: same as *cĭh,* to stammer, to stutter.

Dĭk, 直 Straight, honest, upright; exact; to go direct; but, only, COM. *dĕk-dĭk,* 特直 purposely; *dĭk nęng,* 直仈 a blunt, honest man; *dĭk táu,* 直透 straight through; *ék-dĭh,* 一直 straight ahead.

Dĭk, 值 Also read *sĭk;* COLL. *dĕk* and *dĭh:* to hold; to manage; value, worth; *dĭk dòng,* 值堂 those who serve in turn in yamens.

Dĭk, 姪, 侄 A brother's children: COM. *dĭk ì,* 姪兒 a nephew; *dĭk-nṳ̄,* 姪女 a niece.

Dĭk, 擲 Same as *cȯh,* and *dái,* q. v.: to reject, to waste, as one's time.

Dĭk, 敵 COLL. *tĭk*, q. v.: a foe; to oppose; to contest; *dĭk guók*, 敵國 rival nations; *siù-dĭk*, 仇敵 an enemy; *dā-dĭk*, 抵敵 to oppose.

Dĭk: 笛 A flagelet; a flute

Dĭk: A coll. enphonic prefix as *dĭk-dŏk*, to snatch.

Dĭng, 丁 An adult, *dĭng-hiŏng*, 丁香 cloves.

Dĭng, 叮 To bid, to charge one; to enjoin.

Dĭng, 燈 Read *dĕng*, a lamp, a lantern; *dĭng-mā*, 燈馬 a lamp; *dĭng-lèng*, 燈籠 a lantern; *dĭng-mā siŏh cāng*, 燈馬一盞 one lamp.

Dĭng, 珍 Read *cĭng*: precious; rare, noble; to esteem; *dĭng-bō̤*, 珍寶 precious; *dĭng* (or *cĭng*) *ciŏ* 珍珠 pearls; *dĭng-dêung*, 珍重 to esteem.

Dĭng, 釘 Also read déng, q. v.: a nail, a pin, a peg; COM. tiĕk-dĭng, 鉄釘 iron nails.

Dĭng, 疔 Ulcer, pimples; tetter.

Dĭng, 徵 To summon, as dĭng-diêu, 徵召; dĭng-bĭng, 徵兵 to enlist troops.

Dĭng, 窨 A coll. character: dĭng chió, 窨厝 a deadhouse for depositing coffins.

Dĭng, 貞 Virtuous, pure: dĭng-nṳ̂, 貞女 a chaste maiden.

Dĭng: A coll. word: as dĭng-bēng, a kitchen chopping block.

Dĭng, 頂 COLL. tĭng, q. v.: the top; to carry on the head or top of; a superlative, very, extremely: dĭng bók-kăng, 項不堪 very unworthy.

Dĭng, 等 Read dēng q. v.: to wait, to delay; dĭng siŏh siáh gū, wait a while.

Dìng, 亭 A portico, a pavilion; dà-dìng, 茶亭 a tea pavilion.

Dìng, 停 COLL. tìng, q. v.: to rest, to delay; COM. dìng buó, 停步 to stop walking; dìng gĕng, 停工 to stop work; dìng siŏh á, 停一下 wait a little.

Dìng, 埕 An amphora: COLL. dìng, păng, buák, áeng, four kinds of earthern jars.

Dìng, 塵 Dust, molecules; met., the world, its customs and vices: COLL. ŭng-dìng, 氳塵 dust.

Dìng, 澄 Read dèng: dìng chĭng, 澄清 settled, limpid.

Dìng, 廷 A court, an audience hall; dièu-dìng, 朝廷 the Court; met., His Majesty, the Emperor.

Dìng, 蜓 The dragon-fly called chĭng-dìng, 蜻蜓; COLL. mà-hù, 蟆蛛 q. v.:

Dìng, 霆 The sound of thunder, as lòi-dìng, 雷霆.

Dìng, 籐 Read dèng: rattan; dìng-bà, 籐牌 a rattan shield; dìng-chòng-kuŏng, 籐床匡 a rattan bed-bottom.

Dìng, 藤 Read dèng: creepers, trailing plants.

Dìng, 陳 A surname; to arrange; set in order also read dêng, q. v.

Dìng, 蔯 An herb, as ĭng-dìng, 茵蔯 wormwood.

Diō, 躱 To conceal one's self; diō-biê, 躱避 to evade.

Diō, 貯 Read tŭ: to contain, to hold; diō cūi, 貯水 to hold water.

Diò, 屠 To butcher animals; diò-hó, 屠戶 a butcher.

Diò, 廚 A kitchen, as diò-bùng, 廚房; cọ diò, 做廚 to be a cook.

Diò, 路 Read lô: a road, a path,

a course; *diô-dŏng,* 路中 on the road; *ciòh-muóng diô,* 借個路 to inquire the way; *sông diô,* 順路 on the way.

Diô: 躲 A coll. wood to shirk; *diô gĕng,* 躲工 to shirk work.

Diŏh, 貯 Read *tṳ̄:* to cause to contain; *diŏh diéng,* 貯甸 fill it up.

Diŏh 灼 Read *chiŏk:* to kindle, kindled; as *diŏh kī lì,* 灼起梨 *huōi mặ diŏh,* 火賣灼 the fire will not kindle.

Diŏh, 着 Read *ciŏk:* to be in or at, to be present; ought, must; *diŏh mò diŏh,* 着毛着 is he here or not? *diŏh chió diē,* 着厝裡 in the house; *diŏh tĕk,* 着踢 to stumble; *dĕk-diŏh,* 的着 must, positively.

Diŏh: A coll. word: to be seized

Diŏng 207

with; *diŏh să,* 着痧 seized with colic.

Diŏng, 張 To grow, to increase; a classifier of chairs, tables, paper, for which the coll. is *tiōng,* q. v.: *mò ciō-diōng,* 毛主張 no way to manage it.

Diŏng, 轉 To turn, to return: to do by proxy; to pass over to another; *diōng gié,* 轉寄 to transmit at second hand; *diōng uăng,* 轉彎 to turn a corner; *diōng chió,* 轉厝 to return home; *diōng dáu,* 轉罩 to go home to dinner.

Diŏng, 長 Also read *diòng,* q. v.: senior; *diōng-cṳ̄,* 長子 the oldest son; *diōng-lọ̄,* 長老 elders; *săng-diōng,* 山長 the president of a college; *diōng-duâi,* 長大 to grow in age and size.

Diŏng, 丈 Read *diông:* COLL.

diòng, q. v.: diōng-nā̤, 丈奶 a wife's mother; diōng-nè̤ng, 丈仈 a wife's father.

Dióng, 帳 A curtain, a screen; an awning: COM. dióng-bùng, 帳房 (COLL. dióng-pùng,) a military tent.

Dióng, 賬 An account; dióng-bùng, 賬房 a counting room.

Dióng, 脹 To swell, dropsical; dióng hŭng, 脹風 flatulency.

Dióng: A coll. word: to alter, change; dióng sáik, to change color.

Diòng, 塲 An area; gă-diòng, 較塲 a parade ground; ciĕk siŏh diòng, to get a job of work.

Diòng, 腸 COLL. dòng, q. v.: the intestines; met., the feelings, affections.

Diòng, 長 COLL. also read diōng and dòng, q. v.: long in time or distance, *diòng-giŭ*, 長久 a long time, lasting.

Diòng, 傳 Also read *diông,* q. v.: to transmit, to perpetuate; to publish, to narrate; COM. *diòng-dô,* 傳道 to publish a doctrine; *diòng-niĕng,* 傳染 infectious; *diòng uă,* 傳話 to interpret; *iòng-diòng,* 揚傳 to publish.

Diòng: A coll. word: used for *uōng,* past, former; *diòng-nĭk,* former days.

Diông, 傳 Also read *diòng,* q. v.: narratives, traditions: in the COLL. to move, to stir, to pass things; *diông chók,* 傳出 to pass things out.

Diông, 篆 A kind of ancient character; *diòng cê,* 篆字 seal characters.

Diông: A coll. word: remainder,

balance; *gó ô diông*, 故務剩 there is still some left.

Diŭ, 丟 COLL *liŭ*, q. v.: to reject, to cast off; *diŭ-sáek*, 丟摔 to dash it down.

Diū, 肘 A coll. word: to prop, to shore; a support, a prop; to place by; up to; to meet; to answer; *diū-biáh*, 肘壁 to prop partitions.

Diū: A coll. word: to happen; just at the time of; *diū-diū hō̤*, happens just right.

Diù, 榻 Used in COLL. for closet; *hâng diù*, 餡榻 a cupboard; *cŭ diù*, 書榻 a book case.

Diù, 綢 Silk in general; pongee; *diù-dâung*, 綢緞 silk and satins; *nìng-diù*, 寧綢 fine pongee.

Dó, 妒 Jealous, envious, as *dó-yê*, 妒忌.

Dó, 旺 Read *cū*: *dó-dó*, 旺旺 to call fowls.

Dó, 肚 COLL. *dū*, q. v.: the stomach, the belly; *dṳ́ dó*, 猪肚 the pig's stomach.

Dó, 度 Also read *dŏk*, q. v.: a rule, regulation; endurance; *ṳ́ dó*, 無度 unlimited; *puō-dó*, 普度 rites; *huák-dó*, 法度 methods, regulations; *dô miâng*, 度命 to gain a livelihood.

Dó, 渡 To ford, to cross a stream; a ferry; *dô gĕng*, 渡江 to cross a river; *dô sùng*, 渡船 a ferry boat.

Dó, 鍍 To gild, to wash with gold; *dô gĭng*, 鍍金 to plate with gold.

Dó: A coll. word: as *dó-dáing*, a lizard.

Dŏ, 刀 A knife, dagger, a canoe; a classifier of quires of paper of various sizes, which in the COLL. is *tŏ*, q. v.: *tié-dŏ*, 剃刀 a razor; *chái dŏ*, 菜刀 a cleaver; COLL. *dŏ-giāng*, 刀仔 a penknife; *dŏ siŏh bā*, 刀一把 one knife.

Dŏ, 多 Many, much; a superlative: very, too much; to admire, to praise; *gĭ-dŏ* 幾多 how many? COM. *dŏ-lę̆u*, 多慮 very anxious; *dŏ-ngì*, 多疑 suspicious; *dŏ sę̆u*, 多事 much trouble; *dŏ-siá*, 多謝 many thanks! *dŏ gōng*, 多講 to say too much; *dŏ ù*, 多餘 excessive; COLL. *dŏ-dék-dŏ*, 多的多 for the most part; *dŏ-dòng*, dear, expensive, extravagant.

Dŏ, 島 An island, as *hāi-dŏ*, 海島.

Dŏ, 禱 To pray, to supplicate the gods: *gì-dŏ*, 祈禱 to pray; *dŏ-gó*, 禱告 to inform (the gods).

Dọ̄ 213

Dọ̄, 倒 COLL. dọ́, q. v.: a fall; to fall, to lie down; diĕng-dọ̄, 顛倒 deranged; COLL. páh-dọ̄, 拍倒 knocked over, fallen; dọ̄-huái, 倒壞 ruined.

Dọ́, 倒 Read dọ̄: to empty, to throw out; reversed; dăng-dọ́, 單倒 on the contrary; dăng-dọ́-tàu, 單倒頭 the wrong end first; dọ́-tọ̣i, 倒退 to recede; dọ́ iâ sê, 倒也是 after all it is so.

Dọ́, 到 Sign of the past tense; complete; on the contrary; dọ́-dā̤, 到底 after all, at last; dọ́-chéu, 到處 everywhere.

Dọ̀, 駝 A camel, as lŏk-dọ̀, 駱駝 COLL. ūng-dọ̀-piăng, 隱駝背 humpbacked.

Dọ̀, 舵, 柂 Also read dọ̄: a helm a rudder; in coll. read duái, q. v.

Dò, 萄 The vine: COM. *buò-dò*, 葡萄 grapes.

Dò, 逃 To flee, to abscond; *guāi-dò*, 拐逃 to kidnap; COM. *dò-cāu*, 逃走 to run away; *dò-biê*, 逃避 to elude.

Dò, 鎞 A term for a kind of scales; *tiĕng-bàng-dò*, 天平鎞 large scales for weighing silver.

Dò, 掏 Used for the COLL. *dò*, to take in the hand, to carry; *dò lì*, 掏梨 to bring; *dò kó̤*, 掏去 to take away.

Dò, 道 Read *dô̤*: as *dò-dái*, 道大 Tauist priests.

Dò, A coll. word: as *dò-dĕk*, to injure, to tease, to annoy; *dò-dĕk ciā guŏng-gĭng*, to ruin one's prospects.

Dò, 道 COLL. *dò*, q. v.: a path, road, way; doctrine; *dò-tàu* 道頭 a wharf, a landing, a jetty; *dô̤-lī,* 道理 doctrine, reason; *dô̤-gáu,* 道教 Taoism; *dô̤-bò̤,* 道袍 a surplice; *dô̤-dáik,* 道德 virtue.

Dô̤, 導 To lead, to teach, to direct; *īng-dô̤,* 引導 to guide, to instruct.

Dô̤, 惰 Indolent, spiritless; *lāng-dô̤,* 懶惰 lazy, loitering.

Dô̤, 盜 To take by fraud or force; *dô̤-chĕk,* 盜賊 a robber, a thief.

Dŏ̤h, 卓 A surname; also read *dáuk,* q. v.

Dŏ̤h, 棹 Read *dáuk:* a table, a stand; *dŏ̤h-giāng,* 棹仔 a small table; *nguŏk-dŏ̤h,* 月棹 round tables; *dŏ̤h-dáu,* 棹罩 a table cover; *dŏ̤h siŏh tiŏng,* 桌一張 one table.

Dŏ̤h: A coll. word: to prick, nip off, as leaves.

Dŏi: 堆 A multitude, a mass,

pile: *tù-dŏi,* 土堆 a heap of earth; *dŏi-săng,* a large quantity.

Dŏi: A coll. word; where? how? *dŏi kọ́,* where go? *dŏi hiĕu,* how know?

Dōi, 短 Read *duāng*: short (in length), contracted: *dòng dōi,* 長短 long and short.

Dŏi: A coll. word: as *dŏi-dĭk,* specially, purposely—the same as *dĕk-dĭk,* 特直 q. v.

Dói, 墜 To let down by a cord; to mark; *dói lŏh kọ́,* 墜落去 to let it down.

Dói, 隊 A rank, a company; *dói-ngŭ,* 隊伍 files, platoons.

Dói, 縋 A cord, a rope; *dói lŏh,* 縋落 to let down, as into a well.

Dói, 對 To answer, to suit, to pair, to match, to compare;

Dók, 217

dọ̆i chiū, 對手 to assist; *dọ̆i méng*, 對面 opposite; *dọ̆i bèng*, 對半 into parts or halves; *cūi-tū mạ dọ̆i*, 水土賣對 the climate unsuitable.

Dọ̆i. 塊 Read *kuāi* and *kuái*: a piece, a place, a dollar; *gò-lòng-dọ̆i*, 囫圇塊 a whole piece; *muāng-dọ̆i*, 滿塊 everywhere.

Dọ̆i, 兌 To exchange, to barter; *dọ̆i uâng*, 兌換 to exchange, as jewels or coin.

Dọ̆i, 代 Read *dái*: a generation, an age; *dọ̆i-dọ̆i*, 代代 or *siè-dọ̆i*, 世代 successive generations; *hâiu dọ̆i* 後代 posterity.

Dọ̆i, 袋 Read *dái*: a bag, a sack, a pocket; *dọ̆i-dọ̆i*, 袋袋 a bag.

Dók, 督 To lead, to command, to oversee; a general; *cūng-dók*,

總督 the Viceroy; *gáng-dók*, 監督 an overseer, a bishop; *dók-gĕng*, 督工 to oversee work.

Dók: A coll. word: to mark, to punctuate; to prick in, to dip in, to light; *dók siŏh dók*, to make a dot; *dók siŏh ciáh*, to light one, as a match or lamp.

Dŏk, 凸 Used for the COLL. *tū* q. v.: protuberant, convex.

Dŏk, 突 Abruptly, to rush out; *dŏk-iòng-găng*, 突然間 suddenly.

Dŏk, 奪 Read *duăk*: to rob, to snatch, to plunder; *chiōng-dŏk*, 搶奪 to rob.

Dŏk, 度 Also read *dó*, q. v.: *chăi-dŏk*, 猜度 to guess; *chōi-dŏk*, 忖度 to conceive; *dŏk kī lì*, 度起理 an initial phrase in talking.

Dŏng 219

Dŏng, 當 Also read dáung, q. v.: suitable, proper; to bear the responsibility; to be, to endure; when; COM. găi-dŏng, 該當 ought; nàng-dŏng, 難當 hard to bear; dŏng-sì, 當時 at that time, when; dŏng-méng, 當面 in the presence of; COLL. dŏng mḁ́ dêu, 當賣住 can't endure it, as pain; ḁ́ or mḁ́ dŏng dék dêu, 徛, 賣當的住.

Dŏng, 鈍 Read dóng, q. v.: dull, as a knife; dŏng dék hēng, 鈍的很 very dull.

Dŏng, 中 Read dŭng: the middle, the center; the heart, the core; dâi-dŏng, 大中 in the middle; dâi-dŏng-dŏng, 大中中 in the very midst.

Dŏng, 墩 Read dŭng: a prop; a numerative of villages; siŏh dŏng, 一墩 a village.

Dŏng: A coll. word: to sweep up and throw away, as *dŏng kó dó*.

Dŏng: A coll. word: to geld, to castrate.

Dŏng: 擋 A coll. word: to trap, snare, catch, as *dŏng ngṳ̀*, 擋魚 to catch fish; *dŏng lō̤-chṳ̄*, 擋老鼠 to trap rats.

Dŏng: A coll. word: to pick, to renew with the chisel; *dŏng mó̤*, to pick millstones.

Dŏng: A coll. word: to take turns, rotation.

Dōng, 砧 Read *tĭng*: a block, an anvil, as *tiék-dōng*, 鉄砧; *siŏh dōng*, 石砧 a stone seat, a stone pillar or base.

Dōng, 黨 A faction, a gang; *pī-dōng*, 匪黨 banditti; *giék dōng*, 結黨 to form a cabal.

Dōng, 斷 Read *duáng:* to snap,

Dóng　221

to break in two; *páh dōng,* 拍斷 snapped in two.

Dōng: 漲 A coll. word: the rising of the tide; *cūi dōng,* 水漲 the flood tide; *dōng báik,* 漲八 the tide risen eight tenths; *dōng diéng,* 漲匀 full tide.

Dōng: A coll. word; to gain, to increase; to indulge one, as *dōng ĭ.*

Dōng: A coll. word: to purchase cotton cloth, as *dōng buó.*

Dóng, 凍 COLL. *dáeng,* q. v.: cold, freezing; to cool; *bŭ-sŭng-dóng,* 拳鬆凍 a shiver, a chill.

Dóng, 囤 A large hamper; *dòng-cék,* 囤積 to hoard grain.

Dóng, 頓 COLL. *dáung,* q. v.: to salute respectfully; to adjust; to reject; *dóng siū bái,* 頓首拜 with respectful salutations; *cīng-dóng,* 整頓 to adjust;

dóng siöh á, 頓一下 to pause, to rest the voice on.

Dòng, 唐 To boast, bragging; the name of a dynasty; *Dòng diêu,* 唐朝 the Tang dynasty; *huòng-dòng,* 謊唐 exaggeration; COLL. *dòng-buŏ,* 唐哺 a male, a husband; *dòng-buŏ-nèng,* 唐哺伙 a man; *dòng-buŏ-giāng,* 唐哺仔 a male child, a boy, a son; *dòng-nèng,* 唐伙 a Chinese.

Dòng, 螳 A mantis; *dòng-lòng,* 螳螂 the praying mantis.

Dòng, 堂 A hall, temple, court room; a classifier of trials; a session of court; *hŏk-dòng,* 學堂 a school; *lěng-dòng,* 令堂 your mother—a polite term; *tiĕng-dòng,* 天堂 heaven, paradise.

Dòng, 膛 Fat, fleshy; COM. *hŭng-*

dòng, 胸膛 the breast, as of a fowl.

Dòng, 腸 Read *diòng* q. v.: the intestines; *dòng-dó*, 腸肚 the bowels; *duái dòng*, 大腸 and *siēu dòng*, 小腸 the large and small intestines.

Dòng, 長 Read *diòng* and *diōng* q. v.: long in time or measure; more, exceeding; *buáng-dòng*, 半長 a half length; *dòng-miáng*, 長命 long life; *dòng dōi*, 長短 long and short; *dòng-gĕng*, 長工 steady employment; *dòng-giū*, 長久 a long time, lasting.

Dòng: A coll. word: to stamp with the foot.

Dŏng, 動 COLL. *dáeng*, q. v.: to excite, to agitate; to begin; to influence the mind; *dŏng-sĭng*, 動身 agitated in mind: COM.

hèng-dóng gū-cī, 行動舉止 actions and conduct; gāng-dóng, 感動 to influence, as the spirit does.

Dóng, 炖 Read dŭng; to cook in a double boiler; dông buông, 炖飯 to cook rice; dông lâng, 炖爛 to cook soft.

Dóng, 鈍 COLL. dŏng, and bông, q. v.: blunt, dull; witless, stupid.

Dông, 鼕 A coll. character; dông dông, 鼕鼕 the noise of drums.

Dŭ, 都 Tax districts; COLL. all, altogether, wholly; dŭ-dók, 都督 a commander of an army; dŭ-tūng, 都統 a major general of the Tartars; dŭ-sṳ̆, 都司 a military officer of the 5th rank; COLL. dŭ-sìng, 都成 a carpenter; dŭ hŏ, 都好 all good; dŭ mò, 都毛 none at all; *dŭ sāi dék*, 都駛的 any way will answer.

Dŭ: A coll. word: *dŭ-dŭ-dáiu*, suspended, as from the ceiling.

Dŭ, 堵 A section, a panel, a compartment, an apartment; *cĕk có lâng dū*, 截做二堵 to divide into two apartments.

Dŭ, 賭 To gamble, to wager; *dū báuk*, 賭博 gaming; *dū-ciĕng-diòng*, 賭錢塲 a gambling place.

Dū, 肚 Read *dô*: *dū-bèng*, 肚并 a sort of half vest, worn in front and fastened about the neck.

Dū, 蠹 Read *dó*: *dū-ngù*, 蠹魚 the tinea or book worm.

Dū: A coll. word: to happen, to chance; *dū-dū-hŏ*, to happen exactly right.

Dù, 圖 A map, chart, diagram;

to plan, to plot, to intrigue, as *dù-mèu*, 圖謀; *dê-lī-dù*, 地理圖 geographical maps; *dù-lái*, 圖賴 to charge unjustly.

Dù, 徒 To go afoot; a disciple; only, simply, barely; *dù-dà*, 徒弟 a learner, an apprentice; *muóng-dù*, 徜徒 to exile for three years; *dù cŏi*, 徒罪 exiled for crime.

Dù, 塗 Mud, clay; to daub, to plaster; to erase; *dù-muák*, 塗抹 to blot out; *dù iŏh*, 塗藥 to rub on ointment; *dù-huŏi*, 塗灰 to plaster with lime.

Dù, 途 A road, a path; *met.*, a pursuit, a mode; COM. *buáng dù ì hié*, 半途而廢 to stop half way, to give up a pursuit.

Dù, 梌 A variety of pine: COM. *dù chà*, 梌柴 a fine hard pine, used in furniture.

Dù, 茶 A bitter herb; *met.*, wretched, miserable; *dù-dŭk*, 茶毒 bitter trials.

Dù, 薔 A rose: also read *chiòng*, q. v.: COM. *dù-mì*, 薔薇 the cinnamon rose.

Dŭ, 猪 A hog, a swine; COM. *dŭ-mō*, 猪牳 a sow: *met.*, large, coarse; *dŭ-tàu-ciŏng*, 猪頭瘴 the mumps.

Dù, 除 To exclude, to reject; to deduct, to divide; *dù-miĕk.*, 除滅 to destroy, to exterminate; COLL. *dù táh-táh*, 除净净 to make a clean sweep of.

Duà: A coll. word: to shake about; *duà mī*, to sift rice.

Duái, 大 Read *dái*: large, great; old, the eldest; a superlative, very, much: full and quick, as the pulse; *duái-iè*, 大爺 official attendants in a yamun; *duái* giāng, 大仔 the oldest son.

Duái, 舵 Read dọ̀, and dọ: a rudder, called muōi-duái, 尾舵; duái gŭng, 舵公 a helmsman; buăng duái! 搬舵 to put the helm to starboard; ă duái! 挨舵 port the helm!

Duăk, 奪 Coll. dŏk, q. v.: to seize, to rob; to deprive of rank; to criticise.

Duăng, 端 Straight, proper; the origin; a numerative of matters, subjects, and pieces of silk; duăng ngà, 端倪 the beginning; duăng-cŏng, 端聳 correct, decorous; duăng-ciáng, 端正 upright, proper.

Duăng, 短 COLL. dōi, q. v.: short, shortcomings, faults; as duăng chéu, 短處; duăng ciĕu, 短少 still owing, in arrears.

Duáng, 斷 Also read duăng, q.

v.; to decide, to settle; to give an opinion; surely, decidedly, positively; COM. *duáng áng*, 斷案 to decide a lawsuit; *giók-duáng*, 決斷 to decide, to resolve upon a method; COLL. *duáng-duáng ng kīng*, 斷斷怀肯 decidedly unwilling.

Duáng, 斷 A'so read *duáng;* COLL. *dâung* and *dōng*, q. v.: to divide, to cut asunder; cut, broken, snapped; *duáng kié*, 斷契 final deed of sale, an unredeemable bond.

Dŭh, 揪 Read *tŭk:* to stab; *dŭk těng-táu*, 揪通透 to perforate;

Dŭi, 追 To pursue, to overtake, to reflect on; to dun; *dŭi bĭng*, 追兵 soldiers in pursuit; *dŭi cái*, 追債 to dun; *dŭi mặ diŏh*, 追賣着 cannot overtake him; *dŭi dộ huôi*, 追悼會 a memorial service, or services.

Dùi, 搥 Also read *tùi*, q. v.: to beat, to pound, to hammer out.

Dŭk, 毒 Coll. *dĕk*, q. v.: a poison: to poison; noxious, injurious; *dŭk iŏh*, 毒藥 a poison; *dŭk-ké*, 毒氣 noxious vapors.

Dŭk, 纛 Read *dọ*: a standard; COM. *dŭk-gì*, 纛旗 the main standard of an army.

Dŭk: 獨 Alone, single, only; *dŭk cṳ̄*, 獨子 an only child; COM. *dŭk ék*, 獨一 one only; *dŭk-lĭk*, 獨立 independent.

Dŭk, 瀆 A sluice, a drain; to profane, to insult; COM. *siék-dŭk*, 褻瀆 to blaspheme.

Dŭk, 軸 The ends of an axle; the roller of a map; a picture, or map; scrolls; *lièng-dŭk*, 聯軸 narrow and wide scrolls;

COLL. *dŭk siòh hók,* 軸一幅 one map or scroll.

Dŭk, 逐 To expel, to drive out; sincere, earnest; *dŭk gūi,* 逐鬼 to exorcise demons; *dŭk-nĭk,* 逐日 day by day, daily; *mâ dŭk dék diŏh,* 賣逐的着 cannot overtake him.

Dŭng, 東 COLL. *dĕng,* q. v.: the east; the place of honor; the host; a master, a friend; *dŭng-gă,* 東家 the host.

Dŭng, 墼 COLL. *dŏng,* q. v.: a heap, a mound.

Dŭng: A coll. word; to knock, to strike against; *dŭng-dọ̄* to knock over.

Dŭng, 董 To rule correctly; to manage; to hold firmly; *dŭng-sḙu,* 董事 to rule, as a committee does; *gū-dŭng,* 古董 curiosities, antiques.

Dùng, 同, 仝 COLL. *dẹng,* q. v.: together, alike; with, and; in or of the same, as class, place, time, etc.; to harmonize, to assemble; *dùng-gŭ,* 同居 living in the same house; *dùng cé,* 同志 of the same aim; *bók dùng,* 不同 different; *dùng sĭng hăk é,* 同心合意 to agree in mind; *dùng bàu,* 同胞 of the same parents; *dùng cŭk,* 同籍 to assemble.

Dùng, 洞 Read *dông*: *dùng bùng,* 洞房 a bridal chamber.

Dùng, 筒 COLL. *dẹng,* q. v.: a tube, a hollow cylinder, a pipe.

Dùng, 童 A boy, a lad; a bachelor; *dùng-sĕng,* 童生 a student; *dùng-nàng* 童男 or *dùng-nàng-giāng,* 童男仔 a bachelor.

Dựng, 中 Also read dểụng, and in the COLL. dồng, q. v.: the middle, the center; medium; in, within; complete, right; COM. Dựng-quốk, 中國 China; dựng-găng, 中間 inside, in the midst of; dựng-niềng, 中年 middle aged, about 40; dựng-bộ, 中保 a mediator—applied to Christ.

Dựng, 忠 Faithful, loyal, devoted; sincere; dựng-hấiu lộ-sửk, 忠厚老實 sincere and honest.

Dừng, 重 Also read dểụng and in the COLL. từng, and dấeng, q. v.: to add; to repeat; to pile up; dừng-cửng, 重整 to remodel.

Dừng: A coll. word: used in the sense of cừng, from, whence, commencing from; dừng chừ, from this time; dừng dạ gấu méng, 從底至面 from bottom to top.

É, 意 The intention, will, purpose wish; thoughts; inclination, opinion; COM. é-séu, 意思 idea, purport of; sĭng-é, 心意 intention, will; é-giéng, 意見 opinion; kēu-é, 口意 purport of one's remarks; iū é, 有意 intentionally; dáik é, 得意 gratified; COLL. ng còng-é, 怀存意 unexpected.

É, 薏 Barley; COM. é mī, 薏米 pearl barley; é-mī-tŏng, 薏米湯 barley broth.

É, 憶 To recall, to recollect; huòi é, 回憶 to bring to mind.

É, 億 Ten myriads, a lac, a hundred thousand; innumerable; é-diéu cī céung, 億兆之衆 multitudes of people, all mankind.

Ḕ, 衣 To clothe, to put on clothing; also read *ĭ* q. v.

Ḕ, 矣 A final euphonic particle, denoting completion of sense; *i-i-ḕ,* 而已矣 finished, just that and nothing more.

Ḕ, 未 Not yet, not now; time from 1—3 P. M.; *ḕ bék iòng,* 未必然 probably not.

Ḕ, 味 Taste, flavor, relish; to relish; *kēu ḕ,* 口味 taste of the mouth; *met.,* good to eat; *kĭ ḕ,* 氣味 the natural flavor; *met.,* feelings.

Ḕ, 易 Also read *ĭk,* q. v.: Easy, simple, readily accomplished; *ùng-ḕ,* 容易 easy, not difficult.

Ḕ, 異 Separated, foreign; heterodox; to oppose; *ḕ-bǎng,* 異邦 foreign countries; *ḕ-duǎng,* 異端 heterodox; *ḕ-cṳ̆ng,* 異種 foreign kinds, as of plants.

Ê: A coll. word: dirty, filthy; *dê á iā ê*, the ground is very dirty.

Ê 肄 To practice; *é ngiĕk* 肄業 a resident graduate.

È 呃 Read *ì*: *è láeh*, a hiccough.

Ék, 一, 壹 COLL. *siŏh*, q. v.: one, the first, the whole; *dặ-ek*, 第一 the first; *ék-kái*, 一概 all, the whole, wholly; *dŭk-ék*, 獨一 the only one; *ék-dêng*, 一定 certain, settled; *ék-dĭk*, 一直 direct; *hŭng-hŭng bŏk-ék*, 紛紛不一 confused, as talkers.

Ék, 乙 Bent, curved; second year in the cycle of 60 years; *gák ék*, 甲乙 the first and 2nd of the 10 stems; *met.*, this and that.

Ék, 揖 A bow *a la Chinoise*; a salutation; *sāng ék*, 三揖 three bows; *cáuk ék*, 作揖 to salute.

Ék, 益 COLL. *iáh*, q. v.: to benefit, to prosper; more, in a higher degree; *cĕng ék*, 增益 to add to; *céng-ék*, 進益 to advance and prosper; *ù ék*, 無益 profitless.

Ék, 邑 A city, a domain; a district or its walled city; *siū-ék*, 首邑 the chief district of a prefecture.

Ék: A coll. euphonic prefix, as in *ék-ók*, to bend; *ék-ák*, to repress, as quarrels.

Ĕng, 鶯 The nightingale; *chŭng ĕng*, 春鶯 the vernal thrush, poetical for *uòng ĕng*, 黃鶯 the mango bird.

Ĕng, A coll. word; *ĕng-sĕuk huă*, 鶯粟花 poppy flowers.

Ĕng, 嬰 Also read *ĭng*; an infant, a babe; *ṳ̆k-ĕng-dòng* 育嬰堂 an orphan asylum; *ĕng-ì*, 嬰兒 a suckling.

Éng, 櫻 A cherry; *ĕng-tò*, 櫻桃 a red cherry.

Éng, 鸚 A parrot; COLL. *ĕng-gŏ*, 鸚鵡 the parrot.

Éng, 薨 The death of a prince; to die.

Éng, 安 Read *ăng*: to place, to put; to lay down or on; *ĕng giâ*, 安下 to place low; *ĕng nŏh*, 安毛 to set things; *ĕng ciáng*, 安正 place it straight; *ĕng ci diĕ*, 安只裡 set it in here.

Éng, 陰 Read *ĭng*; as in *ĕng-ŭ-tiĕng*, 陰烏天 a dark, muggy atmosphere.

Éng, A coll. word: to touch, as *ĕng siŏh â*, to give a touch.

Éng, 印 A seal, a stamp; to stamp, to print; *kăi éng*, 開印 to open the seals; *hŭng éng*, 封印 to close the seals;

ciĕk éng, 接印 to enter upon office; *éng cṳ̆*, 印書 to print books.

Éng, 應 Also read *ĭng*, q. v.: proper and right, ought, should be; to answer; to fulfill; proportionate; *éng dó̤i*, 應對 a reply; *dák éng*, 答應 to respond; *ciĕk éng*, 接應 to entertain guests; *éng-hṳ̄*, 應許 also *éng-sìng*, 應承 to promise; *éng gōng*, 應講 answered; *éng-ngiêng*, 應驗 fulfilled prediction; *éng-gāi*, 應該 ought.

Éng, 蔭 To protect, to shelter, as *éng-bé*, 蔭庇.

Éng: A coll. euphonic prefix; *éng-ŏng*, to dip; *éng-áung*, to watch.

Èng, 閒 Read *hàng*; leisure, repose; idle, unoccupied, as a place; *mò̤ èng*, 毛閒 no leisure, busy; *èng-nèng,* 閒伏 idle persons.

Éng, 任 Sincere, sure; trusted, a reponsibility; to undertake; COM. *càik èng,* 責任 a trust, a charge; *èng-é,* 任意 according to one's wish; *dó-èng,* 到任 to assume office.

Êng, 妊 孕 As *huài èng,* 懷孕 pregnant.

Êng: A coll. euphonic prefix; *èng-uâng,* to change, to exchange.

Ẹng: A coll. word: as *ẹng-ngiè,* ants; *ẹng-ẹng,* a centipede.

Ẹng, 紅 Read *hùng:* a red color; reddish; *duài ẹng,* 大紅 a deep red; *ngùng ẹng,* 銀紅 a pale red; *càu ẹng,* 糟紅 a dull red.

Eǔ, 甌 A bowl, a cup; a surname; *dǔng ĕu,* 東甌 ancient

name of Fukien; COM. *dà ĕu*, 茶甌 a tea cup; *ĕu buáng*, 甌半 a cup and a half; COLL. *chṳ̆ng-ĕu*, 冲甌 a covered tea cup.

Eü, 鷗 A gull; *gùng-ĕu*, 羣鷗 a flock of gulls.

Eŭ: A coll. word: hungry, as *bók-lṓ ĕu*, the stomach empty.

Ĕu, 謳 A chant, a ballad; *ĕu gǫ̆*, 謳歌 to sing songs.

Ĕu, 歐 To sing; a surname; *Ĕu-lṑ-bă*, 歐羅巴 Europe.¹

Eū, 嘔 COLL. *āu*, q. v.: also read *ĕu*; to vomit; *ĕu háik*, 嘔血 to spit blood; *ĕu tó*, 嘔吐 to vomit.

Eū, 毆 To strike, to beat with a stick; COM. *ēu chă*, 毆差 to beat the police.

Eŭ, 幼 Young, tender; fine, as workmanship; *nièng ĕu*, 年幼

juvenile; *éu-dùng*, 幼童 a lad; *éu-dê huòng*, 幼稚園 a kindergarten; COLL. *éu náung*, 幼嫩 sleek, velvety.

Eû, 又 A conjunction: more, also, moreover, and, and then, *éu giĕng*, 又兼 additional.

Eû, 右 The right hand; to honor; honorable; *cō̤ éu*, 座右 "to the right of your seat"— your honor! an epistolary phrase; *êu chiū*, 右手 the right hand.

Eû, 佑 祐 To aid, to succor; assistance; *bō̤ éu*, 保佑 to protect, to defend; *éu cô*, 佑助 to aid.

Eû, 囿 A park, a menagerie; *huòng êu*, 園囿 gardens and parks.

Eû, A coll. word: to glaze; *puák êu*, to put on glazing.

Êu, A coll. word: on fire; *éu diŏh*, on fire, is burning.

Êu, 預 To prepare, already; to confer with; *éu ngiòng*, 預言 a prediction; *éu-gĭ*, 預期 to long for; *éu-bé*, (or *báing*,) 預俻 to get ready beforehand.

Êu, 與 Also read *ū* and *ù*, q. v: together with; interested in; *éu mèu*, 與謀 to consult with; *găng-éu*, 干與 to interfere in, meddling; *hò-éu*, 何與 what connection with? COM. *éu hông*, 與份 to have a share.

Êu, 譽 To praise, to extol; to flatter; *séu éu*, 受譽 to receive praise; COM. *mìng-éu*, 名譽 fame, reputation.

Êu, 裕 To enrich; plenty; liberal; *chŭng éu*, 充裕 in abundance.

Éu, 喻 To know, to manifest; to teach; instruction; *hiĕu-éu,* 曉喻 to cause to know; *pī-éu,* COLL. *bī-éu* 譬喻 to compare; a parable.

Éu, 諭 Orders, edicts; to proclaim; *siông éu,* 上諭 the emperor's command; COM. *hiĕu-éu,* 曉諭 to proclaim.

Éu: A coll. word: to wear away; *éu kó,* worn, attrite.

Éuh, 嘟 Read *éuk*; a sound in the throat; *éuh-éuh-giéu,* 嘟嘟叫 grunting.

Éung, 湧 Read *ūng*; bubbling, as a spring; *éung chók,* 湧出 water gushing forth.

Éung, 擁 To gather round, as a crowd; *éung cā,* 擁擠 to press, crowding.

Éung, 用 To use, to expend, to employ; commonly, generally;

expenses; *iŭ ĕung*, 有用 useful; *ĕung sĭng*, 用心 careful; *bók-dĕung-ĕung*, 不中用 unfit; *tŭng hèng tŭng ĕung* 通行通用 current.

Ĕung, 潤 Moist, damp; to enrich; *ĕung-dĕk*, 潤澤 to fertilize.

Gă, 嘉 Good, excellent; to make happy.

Gă, 佳 Good of its kind, nice; COLL. *cáuk-gă*, 作佳 beautiful, fine.

Gă, 加 To add to, to increase; *gă gēng*, 加減 to add and subtract; *gă-tiĕng*, 加添 to increase; *gă-gá*, 加價 to add to the price; *gă-pĭ*, 加菲 coffee.

Gă, 家 A family, a home; domestic; COM., *gă-ngiĕk*, 家業 property; *gă-diòng*, 家長 the head of a family; *cé̤u-gă,* 自家 self, myself; *chĭng-gă,* 親家 father in law; COLL. *gă-sĭ,* 家私 tools, utensils; COM. *gă-gu̍óng,* 家眷 a family, household; *gă-huák,* 家法 a family; *gă-hó* 家父 or *gă-ngiè̤ng,* 家嚴 my father.

Gă, 膠 Read *gĕu:* viscid gums; to glue; *cūi-gă,* 水膠 glue; *ngṳ̀ gă,* 魚膠 isinglass.

Gă, 交 Read *gău:* *gău-hó,* 交付 to intrust to: *gău ké̤uk ĭ,* 交乞伊 deliver it to him; *gă-cé̤u-bău,* 交注包 a straw bag to cook rice in.

Gă: A coll. word: to cut; *gă-dọ̆,* shears; *gă-dọ̆-giăng,* scissors; *gă dọ̆i bèng,* to cut into two parts.

Gă: A coll. word: as *gă-lăng-kĭ,* slanting, oblique, tilted.

Gā, 假 Also read *gá*, q. v.: false, fictitious; feigned; supposing, if; COM. *gā-sṳ́*, 假使 if, supposing that; *gā hó̤*, 假好 hypocritical; *gā mō̤*, 假冒 to feign, to assume.

Gā 個 Read *gó*; also spoken *ā*, as *siŏh ā cièng*, 一個錢 one cash; *lâng gā nṳ̂ng*, 二個仈 two persons.

Gā, 絞 Read *giēu*: to twist, to bind a cord about.

Gā: A coll. word: *gā-cāu*, a flea.

Gā: A coll. word: *gā-gē*, to annoy, to disturb.

Gá, 價, 賈 The 2nd also read *gū* q. v: the price, as *gá-cièng*, 價錢; *sì gá*, 時價 the current price; *gŏng gá*, 講價 to ask a high price; *bók-nê-gá*, 不二價 "not two prices"; *kī-gá*, 起價 to raise the price; *lŏh gá*, or tŏk-gá, 落價 the price has fallen.

Gá, 假 Also read gā, q. v.: leave of absence; COM. gó-gá, 告假 to apply for a furlough; bóny gá, 放假 to give a vacation.

Gá, 駕 A title of respect; sir, your honor; in coll. used for divining blocks; as gá-buŏi, COM., gá-bĕng, 駕崩 demise of the emperor; séng-gá, 聖駕 his majesty.

Gá, 架 An open frame on which things are placed; a stand; a classifier of furniture except of tables and chairs; COM. sĕk-cĕ-gá, 十字架 a cross; cṳ̆-gá, 書架 a book case; huă-gá, 花架 a flowerstand; méng-gá, 面架 a washstand; dák-gá, 搭架 to erect a scaffold.

Gá, 嫁 To marry a husband;

Gă

COM. *gá-chéu*, 嫁娶 to marry; *gá-céng*, 嫁妝 dowry; *chók-gá*, 出嫁 to become a bride.

Gà, 敎 Read *gáu*: to instruct; to teach; *gá-hóng*, 敎訓 to instruct; *gá cǎ*, 敎齋 to teach school.

Gà, A coll. word: as in *gà-gŭng*, the common earthworm.

Gà, A coll. word; *gà-làu*, to roll about.

Gà, A coll. word: *gà-gà-giéu*, a clamor of voices.

Gà, A coll. word: *gà-lăk-chă*, crossed, intersecting as two lines.

Gà, 咬 Read *ngāu*: to gnaw, to bite, to chew; *gá-dáung*, or *gá dōng*, 咬斷 to bite off.

Gă, 街 A thoroughfare; *gă-chě*, 街市 a market place; *huàng-gă*, 橫街 a cross street: COLL.

gā-dŏng, 街中 a street.

Gā: A coll. word: gā-gā giéu, to cry as a child.

Gā: 解 Read gāi: to untie, unbind, loose, release; to comment, to explain; gā-siók, 解說 to explain; gā-mông, 解悶 to make sport of; gā-kák, 解渴 to quench thirst.

Gá, 解 Also read gāi, and hái, q. v.: to hand over to; to transfer an officer to another post.

Gá, 疥 Read gái: sāi gá, 沙疥 dry itch.

Gà: A coll. word: as gà-dēng, or gà-dēng-siè, above, aloft.

Gà: A coll. word: as gà-sùng, to tow a boat.

Gáe, 呼 Read hù: to call out, to shout; lā gáe, 禮呼 is calling out; gáe-gáe-giéu, 呼呼叫 or gáe huāng tiĕng, 呼反天 to vociferate.

Gáeh: A coll. word: a choking sound; to hiccough.

Gáek, 角 Read gáuk: a horn, a corner, a dime; sé gáek, 四角 four; cornered, gáek gŏ, a try-square; kēu gáek, 口角 to wrangle.

Gáek, 覺 Read gáuk: to perceive, to be aware of; giéng-gáek, 見覺 to realize.

Gáek, 雄 Read hùng, male of birds, animals and insects; ngù gáek, 牛雄 a bull.

Gáeng: A coll. word: same as gáe.

Gâeng, 共 Read géung; a preposition: with, by, to, for, in behalf of; an adverb: as, like to; gâeng ĭ dŏi chiū, 共伊對手 lend him a helping hand; gâeng diĕ, 共

弟 to tend little brother.

Gáh, 格 Read gáik: a pattern, a rule, a model; cṳ̆-gáh, 資格 qualification.

Gáh, 隔 Read gáik: to separate, or divide, as by a partition; gáh-biáh, 隔壁 adjoining; gáh màng, 隔暝 to pass the night at; kept over night, as food: gáh dék huông, 隔的遠 far removed, distant.

Găh: A coll. word: to test the weight.

Găh: A coll. word: a complete snarl.

Gáh: A coll. word: a bunch of paper; an apartment in a boat.

Gáh: A coll. word: găh kī, to pry up or open.

Găh: A coll. word: distress, grief.

Găh: A coll. word: ng tĕng diŏh

gäh, must not be offended,—
a polite phrase to a departing
guest.

Găh: A coll. word, as in sĕk cĕ-
găh, transverse, crosswise,
crossed, as two lines or sticks.

Găh, A coll. word;' to mutter,
to feel angry; bowels rum-
bling.

Găi, 皆 Uniform: sign of the
plural after nouns of multitude; găi iòng, 皆然 all the
same.

Găi, 偕 Associated; together;
găi lọ̄, 偕老 growing old together, as husband and wife.

Găi, 階, 堦 Steps; a degree, a
rank; guăng găi, 官階 an official grade.

Găi, 該 Fit, proper, necessary;
the aforesaid; găi-dŏng, 該當
or éng-găi, 應該 ought, proper,

just; *ng gái*, 唔該 ought not.

Gāi, A coll. word: as in *giĕ gāi*, a fowl's crop; *dēuk gāi*, to stuff a chicken's crop:—*scil.*, to make it weigh more.

Gāi, 改 COLL. *gūi*, q. v.: to change, to alter; *gāi guó*, 改過 to amend, to reform; *gāi-biéng* 改變 or *gāi-liòng*, 改良 to change for the better.

Gāi, 解 Also read *gá;* in coll. *gā,* q. v.: to open, to disperse, to comment: a commentary; *kuóng-gāi*, or *gāi-kuóng,* 解勸 to persuade; *gāi dŭk*, 解毒 to disperse bad humors.

Gái, 戒 To warn, to guard against; to refrain from; *gái dŭk*, 戒毒 to abstain from poison; *gái dŭk huôi*, 戒毒會 "anti-poison society"; *gĭng-gái,* 警戒 to caution.

Gái, 誡 Precepts, warnings; to exhort, to prohibit; COM., sĕk gái, 十誡 the Ten Commandments

Gái, 价 One who serves; COM., gói gái, 貴价 your servant boy; siēu gái, 小价 my valet.

Gái, 介 To assist; an attendant; numeral of persons; one alone; a frontier, border; ék gái, 一介 a single individual; gái é, 介意 to take umbrage at; gái-siēu, 介紹 to recommend, to be an agent.

Gái, 芥 The mustard plant; gái-chái, 芥菜 the mustard plant; gái-làng-chái, 芥藍菜 a course kind of mustard.

Gái, 疥 A scratch, a little sore; COM. gái-chŏng, 疥瘡 the itch; a refined term for gò-lô, 癆痨

Gái, 屆 A set time, a limit; gái-áing, 屆限 expiration of the time; gái-gĭ, 屆期 at the appointed time.

Gái, 界 A limit, a boundary; gái-bà, 界牌 land marks; gău-gái, 交界 adjoining; dê-gái, 地界 boundary of land; sié-gái, 世界 the world.

Gái, 丐 To ask alms; to bestow: COM., kéuk-gái, 乞丐 (COLL. kéuk-siăh, 乞儉) a beggar.

Gái, 蓋 A cover; to cover, relay: a conjunction: since, for, for that, now then; ciă-gái, 遮蓋 to cover; gái sié ù sęng, 蓋世無雙 in all the world has no equal; kī-gái, 起蓋 to build a house; huăng-gái, 翻蓋 to remove and relay, as tiles on a roof.

Gái, 再 Read cái; a second time; gái có, 再做 to do again.

Gáik 257

Gáik, 隔 In coll. read gáh, and găng, q. v.: a partition, a bulkhead; to separate, neighboring; gáik duâng, 隔斷 to cut off, to block, as a way.

Gáik, 翮 A feather including the quill; a large feather as distinguished from ṳ̄ 羽 a small feather.

Gáik, 膈 Coll. read káing, q. v.: the diaphragm; gáik mŏh, 膈膜 the midriff, between the thorax and stomach.

Gáik, 格 Coll. read gáh, q. v.: to examine, to understand thoroughly; excellent; a limit; gáik-dé, 格致 scientific; gáik ŭk, 格物 to enquire into (the nature of) things; gáik ŭk hŏk, 格物學 Physics; COM., gáik-nguôi, 格外 extraordinary.

Gáik, 革 To cure or break off a

habit; to degrade from office: to change; *gáik cék,* 革職 to deprive of office; *gáik á-piéng,* 革鴉片 to break off the opium habit.

Gáik, 結 Read *giék:* to tie, to fasten; tied, fixed: a numerative of skeins or knots as of thread and vermicelli; *gáik dáing,* 結有 to tie firmly; *chái-gáik,* 綵結 festoons; *gáik chái,* 結綵 to festoon.

Gáik, 鐭 Read *giék:* a sickle; a reaping hook, also called *lièng gáik,* and *lièng-dǒ,* 鐮刀

Gáik, 潔 Read *giék:* as in *táh-gáik,* clean, pure in physical or moral sense.

Gáing, 更 Read *gĕng:* often used in epistles; more, better, still, the more, the better; *gáing họ̆,* 更好 the better; *gáing-*

Gák 259

gáing, 更更 so much the more.

Gáing, 慣 Read *guáng*; q. v.: accustomed to, in the habit of; *có gáing*, 做慣 used to doing it.

Gáing, 縣 A district, the district city; COM. *dĭ-gáing*, 知縣 a district magistrate; also read *hièng*, and interchanged with *hièng* 懸 q. v.: to hang up, to suspend

Gáiu, 購 To buy, to barter; *gáiu mā*, 購買 to purchase, as goods for retail.

Gáiu, 覯 To meet with, to see suddenly.

Gáiu, 垢 COLL. *gāu*, q. v.: filth, impure, disgraceful.

Gáiu, 彀 COLL. *gáu*, q. v.: enough, full; COM. *nèng gáiu*, 能彀 and *bók nèng-gáiu*, 不能彀 able and not able.

Gák, 甲 The first of the "ten

stems"; met., the first, number one, the head, excellent; *gák-giāng,* 甲仔 a vest; *cī- (ciĕng) gák,* 指甲 finger nail; *kă-gák,* 胶甲 toe nail; *gák-tàu,* 甲頭 the headman of porters (at a landing); *lièng-gák,* 聯甲 unions, an organization of families by tens, constituting a committee of safety.

Gák, 夾 Coll. read *gĕk,* q. v.: assistants; to take under the arm; *gák-bēng,* 夾板 joined boards; *gák-bēng-sùng,* 夾板船 a house boat; *gák-mâng,* 夾慢 a money safe.

Gák, 合 Also read *hăk,* q. v.: a measure—ten make a *cĭng;* used in the COLL. to mix, to blend, to unite; *gák dĕk hō̤,* 合的好 living on good terms; *gák dĕk ngài,* 合的呆 disagreeing.

Găng 261

Gák, 鴿 A dove, a pigeon; COM. băh-gák, 白鴿 (spoken băh-dák), the domestic pigeon.

Gák, 蛤 A cockle, a muscle; gák-li póng, 蛤蜊縫 to halve the edges of boards, as in floors.

Gák, 割 To cut, as with a knife; to divide; COM., gák-dêu, 割稻 to reap rice; gák cāi dŏ, 割紙刀 a paper-cutting knife.

Găk, 聒 Read hák, and hăk; găk-găk-giéu, 聒聒叫 loquacious.

Găk, A coll. word; to adhere, adhesive; sŏi mặ găk, restless, cannot sit still; mò găk siăh, unimportant, trifling.

Găk, A coll. word: to be at or in; găk cī diē, is in here.

Găng, 干 Arms; to seek, to offend, to break laws; crime, guilt; găng-huáng, 干犯 to transgress; iŏk - găng, 若干

how much? *găng-céng,* 干証 to bear witness; *ô găng-quó,* 務干過 is concerned in.

Găng, A coll. word: to compel; *găng ĭ có,* compel him to do it.

Găng, 竿 A pole, a cane; *déuk-găng,* 竹竿 or *ngṳ̀ găng,* 魚竿 a fishing rod.

Găng, 肝 The liver, the feelings; *găng-ké,* 肝氣 the constitution, or state of the liver.

Găng, 奸 Inordinate desire; villainous, unprincipled; *găng-cá,* 奸詐 or *găng-gŭi,* 奸詭 false; *găng-sá,* 奸細 a spy.

Găng, 姦 Adultery; *găng-guāi,* 姦拐 to seduce and kidnap.

Găng, 柑 The cooly orange.

Găng, 杆 A wood used for spear handles; *gì-găng,* 旗杆 a flag staff; *ùi-găng,* 桅杆 a mast.

Găng, 桿 A lever, as *gáung-găng,*

Găng 263

槓桿; a post, a handle; numerative of spears.

Găng, 乾 Also read *gièng*, q. v.: dry, to dry; *met.*, clean, entirely; *găng-só,* 乾燥 parched.

Găng, 更 Read *gĕng:* the night watches of which there are five, from 7 p. m. to 5 a. m.; *sióh găng tiĕng,* 一更天 one watch; *páh găng,* 拍更 to beat the watches.

Găng, 粳 Read *gĕng;* a fine superior kind of rice.

Găng, 甘 Sweet to the taste; agreeable, willing; COM. *găng-ciá,* 甘樵 sugar cane; *găng-sĭng,* 甘心 or *găng-nguông,* 甘願 voluntary, willing.

Găng, 疳 As in *bâng-găng,* 病疳 atrophy.

Găng, 苷 As in *găng-chō,* 苷草 licorice root.

Găng, 艱 Hard, intractable soil; difficult, distressing; *găng-kŭ* 艱苦 miserable; *găng-nàng* 艱難 difficult; COLL. *găng-gái* 艱丐 destitute, poor.

Găng, 監 To inspect; an inspector, an overseer; usually read *gáng*, q. v.:—meaning, to look down upon, or into; to superintend; a jail, a prison; *gu̇óng-găng*, 關監 to imprison; *găng-diē*, 監裡 in the prison.

Găng, 間, 閒 Also read *gáng*, q. v.: a crevice; in the midst of; whilst, amongst; to make room for; a classifier of buildings and rooms; *sié-găng*, 世間 the world; *tiĕng-dê găng*, 天地間 in the world; *dŭng-găng*, 中間 in the midst of; *kĭng-káik-găng*, 頃刻間 in a moment.

Găng, 欄 Used in leases and

Găng

deeds; a room, a chamber; a classifier of houses and apartments: COLL. săng-găng-bà, 三橺排 three rooms in a row.

Găng, 隔 Read *gáik*: as in *găng biáh sié*, 隔壁勢 adjoining, neighboring; *găng-biáh chió*, 隔壁厝 the next house.

Găng: A coll. word: as in *găng-găng hō̤*, exactly right, just the thing.

Găng, 簡 A bamboo slip used for making notes on; an official document; *gāng cháh*, 簡册 the Bamboo Records; to abridge, to condense; terse in style; *gāng-sāng*, 簡省 to lessen, to reduce; *gāng-biêng*, 簡便 at hand.

Gāng, 柬 A visiting or business card, as *gāng-táik*, 柬帖

Gāng, 橄 The Chinese olive;

COM., *gāng-lāng*, (spoken *gā-lāng*), 橄欖 olives.

Gāng, 敢 To dare, to venture: rash, bold; to offend good manners; at the beginning of a sentence, it answers to how can; *ŭng-gāng*, 勇敢 intrepid; COM., *gāng-dŏng*, 敢當 to assume, as a trust; *bók-gāng*, 不敢 I dare not; *kī-gāng*, 豈敢 how can I presume to receive such a compliment.

Gāng, 感 To move the feelings: COM. *gāng-gék*, 感激 excited to gratitude; *gāng-ŏng*, 感恩 grateful for favor; *gāng-siá*, 感謝 (corrupt form, cumshaw), thankful; *gāng-dŏng*, 感動 to influence; *gāng-huá*, 感化 to improve, to convert.

Gāng, 趕 To pursue, to do quickly; busy, in a hurry:

COM., *gāng-gék* 趕急 hurried;
COLL., *gāng-gĭng* 趕緊 quickly.

Gāng, 哽 Read *gēng*: to choke, strangled.

Gāng: A coll. word: to cover, to spread over; *gāng nguā*, to lay tiles; *gāng puôi*, to spread the quilt over one.

Gāng, A coll. word: to wipe with a wet cloth; *gāng iē*, to wipe chairs; *gāng dă-dă*, wipe it dry.

Gáng, 諫 To remonstrate with; to testify against; to advise; *gáng cŭŏng*, 諫章 a memorial of censure or advice; *gáng sìng*, 諫臣 a censor to His Majesty; COM., *dĭk-gáng*, 直諫 to reprove directly.

Gáng, 鑑 A mirror, a speculum; a term for historical works; *dài gǎng*, 台鑑 for you, sir, to see—an epistolary phrase.

Gáng, 監 Also read *găng*, q. v.: to superintend; to search into; to control by inspection; *gáng-chák*, 監察 to investigate; *gáng-dók*, 監督 an overseer, a bishop; *gáng-iêng*, 監院 a college monitor; *tái-gáng*, 太監 a eunuch; *kĭng-tiĕng-gáng*, 欽天監 an astronomer royal; *gáng-sĕng*, 監生 a bought or purchased degree.

Gáng, 幹 Also read *guăng*, q. v.: capable, skillful; *gáng sẹ̆u*, 幹事 (*gáng-dái-giè* 幹代計) to attend to business; *nèng-gáng*, 能幹 ability.

Gáng, 閒, 間 Also read *găng*, q. v.: to interrupt, to alternate; to sunder, to part friends; *ĭng-găng*, 陰間 Hades.

Gău 269

Gáng, 癎 Read *háng*; spasms, convulsions.

Gáng, 澗 A stream in a valley, *gáng-ciòng,* 澗泉 a mountain spring.

Gàng, 街 Coll. read *hàng,* q. v.: rank, position, title; see *hàng-tàu,* 街頭; *gàng chói,* 街嘴 or 嘟嘴 to hold in the mouth.

Gàng, A coll. word: chilled; *gàng sī,* chilled to death.

Gáng, 汗 Sweat; *hộ gáng,* 浩汗 bright and splendid; *chók yáng,* 出汗 (COLL. *làu gáng*), to perspire.

Găn, 交 Coll. *gă,* q. v.: to unite, to join; together; a friend; COM. *găn-gă,* 交家 to form friendships; *găn-dái,* 交代 to hand over to, commit to; *găn-ĭk,* 交易 trade; *găn-cĕng,* 交針 to backstitch; *găn buó,* 交部

to hand over to a Board.

Gāu, 郊 Waste or forest land; *gău nguôi*, 郊外 remote wilds; COM. *găn tiếng*, 郊天 imperial sacrifices to heaven and earth.

Gāu, 溝 Read *gĕu*, a drain, a gutter, a ditch as *cūi gău*, 水溝.

Gāu, 勾 Read *gĕu*: to bracket, to reject; *gău kó*, 勾去 bracketed, rejected.

Gāu, 鈎 Read *gĕu*: a hook, a barb, a fluke; *ngù gău*, 魚鈎 a fish hook.

Gāu, 九 Read *giū*: nine; *met.*, many; *gāu-siàng-gāu*, 九成九 ninety-nine out of a hundred; *met.*, nearly done; *gău tàu lùng*, 九頭龍 the nine headed dragon—a sort of rocket.

Gāu, 垢 Read *gáiu*; scurf; *tàu gău*, 頭垢 dandruff.

Gāu, 詭 Read *gūi*; *gău-guái*, 詭

怪 cunning, tricky, crafty.

Gáu, 教 COLL. gá, q. v.: doctrines, tenets, to teach; to command; gáu-muòng, 教門 a sect, or school; gáu-uòng, 教員 a teacher; gáu-hóng, 教訓 to teach, instruction; gáu ŭk huôi, 教育會 an educational association; gáu huá, 教化 to instruct, to convert.

Gáu, 酵 Leaven, yeast; see bùi.

Gáu, 校 Also read háu, q. v.: stocks for the feet; to examine things, to revise books: hŏk háu, 學校 a school.

Gáu, 較 Also read gáuk, q. v.: to compare, as bī-gáu, 比較.

Gáu, 至 Read cé: to come, to extend to; at, to, unto; buŏh gáu, 剝至 about to arrive; gáu-dăng, 至伶 till now; gáu-muōi, 至尾 finally.

Gáu, 殼 Read gáiu: enough, sufficient.

Gáu, 磋 Read hăú: ciŭ gáu, 酒磋 a wine measure, containing half a pint; gáu-giăng, 磋仔 a little pot.

Gàu, 猴 Read hèu: a monkey; gàu ngê bèng, 猴耳丬 the monkey-ear radicals.

Gâu, 厚 Read hâiu: thick, not thin; dense; met., very superior; furred as the tongue; without shame.

Gáuk, 各 Every, each; COLL., strange, extraordinary; gáuk ói, 各位 every person or place; gáuk chéu, 各處 everywhere; gáuk-iông, 各樣 strange, odd, unusual.

Gáuk, 覺 COLL. read gáĕk, q. v. correct, upright intelligent; to manifest; dĭ-gáuk, 知覺 to perceive; *lìng-gáuk*, 靈覺 shrewd, intelligent.

Gáuk, 骨 The bones of the body; a framework; *gáuk bà* 骨牌 dominoes.

Gáuk, 較 Also read *gáu*; q. v.: to contend, to wrangle.

Gáuk, 斛 To adjust a measure; COLL., *gáuk bàng*, 斛平 to level the measure.

Gáuk, 刮 Read *huák*: to rub, to scrape with a knife.

Gáung, 降 Also read *hòng* q. v.: to descend; to send down, to confer, to degrade; *gáung siè*, 降世 to come into the world; *gáung hók*, 降福 to bless; *gáung giá*, 降下 degraded.

Gáung, 鋼 Read *gŏng*, in the dictionaries; iron assayed by fire, steel; *tiék gáung*, 鐵鋼 steel; in Foochow *gŏng*: hard, stiff; *gáung cáng,* a steel chisel.

Gáung, 槓 A load for two; a classifier of loads borne by two; *giêu gáung,* 轎槓 sedan poles.

Gé, 記 To remember, to register; a history, a signal; used on shop signs; *gé-cài,* 記才 the memory; *gé-cái,* 記載 to record; *gé-só,* 記數 to enter accounts; *â gé-dĕk,* 僱記的 can or do remember.

Gé, 冀 To desire, to expect; *gé-uông,* 冀望 to hope for; *gé-hâing,* 冀幸 to wish for good luck.

Gé, 既 Since, already; ended, finished; a sign of past time, and is placed before the verb; *gé-uōng,* 既往 past, gone; COM. *gé-iòng,* 既然 since, whereas; COLL. *gé-dĕk sé,* 既

Gék 275

的是 since it is, it being so.

Gé, 覬 COLL. read kāi, q. v.: to hope for good fortune, lucky; *gé-ù* or *gé éu*, 覬覦 or 覬覰 to covet and appropriate.

Gé, 忌 To fear, to dread; distasteful; COM., *gé-hâung*, 忌恨 to hate; *géng-gé*, 禁忌 to refrain superstitiously; *dó-gé*, 妒忌 to envy, jealous of.

Gé, 技 Skilful, inventive, apt at contriving; *gé-kiēu*, 技巧 ingenious; hence finely finished.

Gé, 伎 Interchanged with the last; *gé-liōng*, 伎倆 artful. Read *gì*: having six toes on a foot.

Gé, 妓 A prostitute.

Géh: A coll. word: to thrust, to pierce; *géh siŏh kĕng*, to pierce a hole through.

Gék, 吉 Lucky; advantageous;

happy, good; *dāi-gék,* 大吉 great luck—a felicitous phrase; *gék-hŭng,* 吉凶 lucky and unlucky.

Gék, 桔 Used for the next; an instrument for drawing water.

Gék, 橘 The mandarin orange; *gŭng-gék,* 金橘 a small yellow orange made into preserves; *gék páu,* 橘欒 large oranges.

Gék, 給 To give to, to provide the necessities; *gŭng-gék,* 供給 to furnish proper food.

Gék, 急 Hasty, impatient, urgent afflicted; poor, wretched; COM., *gék-siĕk,* 急舌 a stammering tongue; *gék sáng,* 急性 a hasty temper.

Gék, 亟 Haste, speed, prompt; *gék sók,* 亟速 urgently.

Gék, 戟 A lance, a halberd; *sěng ciĕ gék,* 雙枝戟 the double

crescent halberd carried in processions for good luck.

Gék, 擊 To strike, to tap; to rush upon, to charge.

Gék, 激 To excite to gratitude, to vex, to irritate; excitement, anger; COM. *gāng-gék*, 感激 grateful for kindness; COLL., *gék nèng séu ké*, 激仌受氣 to excite persons to anger.

Gĕk, 夾 Read *gák*, q. v.: to press, to hold tightly; *gĕk-góng*, 夾棍 an instrument of torture; *cṳ̆-gĕk*, 書夾 boards for pressing books.

Gĕk, 挟 Read *hiĕk*, q. v.: to clasp under the arms, as *gĕk góh-lóh-â*.

Gĕng, 庚 A way, a path; age; COM. *diòng-gĕng*, 長庚 the evening star; old, aged; *cŏng gĕng*, 尊庚 what is your age this year?—said to youth.

Gĕng, 更 Also read *gáing,* q. v.: to change; to alter: a watch of the night, read *găng,* in coll.; *gĕng-biéng,* 更變 to change, to fluctuate, as the markets.

Gĕng, 耕 To plow, to cultivate the fields; COM., *gĕng-cé̤ung,* 耕種 to till the ground.

Gĕng, 羹 A thick soup; a spoon or ladle; *gĕng tŏng,* 羹湯 soups; *dièu gĕng,* 調羹 to season soups; a soup-spoon.

Gĕng, 亙 A limit; *gĕng-yū é ùng,* 亙古未聞 an epistolary phrase—not heard of from most ancient times.

Gĕng, 減,减 To diminish, to subtract; COM. *gĕng kĭng,* 減輕 to lighten, as a load.

Gĕng, 梗 Thorny; sickness; a

Géng 279

resumé; in general; *gēng dĭk*, 梗直 upright, honest; *gēng-kái*, 梗槩 generally speaking.

Géng, 揀 To select; elected, chosen; COM. *gĕng-sōng*, 揀選 to select.

Géng, 敬 Respectfully; to esteem, to revere, to adore; *géng-òi*, 敬畏 to stand in awe of.

Géng, 禁 To prohibit, to forbid; *huáng géng*, 犯禁 to violate a prohibition; also read *gĭng*, to bear, to endure.

Géng, 噤 Used in COLL. for *géng*, q. v.: to refrain from speaking; silent, unable to speak.

Géng, 竟 To exhaust; the utmost limit; then, at last, finally; *géng iòng*, 竟然 finally; *géu-géng*, 究竟 certainly, entirely so.

Géng, 鏡 COLL. read *giáng*, q. v.:

a mirror; bright, clear, luminous; *gŏ dái ming géng*, 高臺明鏡 a bright mirror on a high terrace; *met.*, an astute officer.

Géng, 徑 A path, a by-way; straight through; *dĭk géng*, 直徑 a diameter.

Géng, 逕 Interchanged with the last; used in letters to mean "coming straight to the subject".

Géng, 勁 Read *gêng*: strong, brawny,

Gèng, 高 Read *gŏ*: high, tall; *gèng háng*, 高漢 a tall person; *gèng giá*, 高下 high and low, uneven, fluctuating, as prices.

Gèng, 鹹 Read *hàng*: salt, not fresh; *gèng puói*, 鹹配 salt condiments.

Gêng, 頸 The front part of the

Gĕug 281

neck, as *háung* for the nape of the neck.

Gĕng, 胎 A gizzard; *ák-gĕng,* 鴨胎 a duck's gizzard.

Gĕng, 競 To contend, to struggle for; great, abundant; *gêng cĕng,* 競爭 a race.

Gĕng, 姈 A sister-in-law on the wife's side. Read *ciĕng*: a pretty laugh.

Gĕng, 噤 Read *géng*: to shut the mouth; *géng chói,* 噤嘴 to diet.

Gĕng, 禁 Read *géng*: to warn, to exclude.

Gĕng, 工 Read *gŭng*: work, a day's work; workmanship; *gĕng-hŭ,* 工夫 skill in work; *gĕng-hŭ dà,* 工夫茶 Congou tea; *gĕng-ciĕng,* 工錢 wages.

Gĕng, 江 Read *gŏng*: a river; *gĕng-ò,* 江河 rivers and canals.

Gĕng, 港 An estuary, a cove; gĕng-kāu, 港口 the mouth of an estuary; Hiŏng-gĕng, 香港 Hong Kong.

Gĕng, 牷 A coll. word: the male of animals; gĕng-mō, 牷牝 male and female.

Gĕu, 勾, 句, COLL. gău, and gēu, q. v.: to reject; to entice.

Gĕu, 鉤 COLL. read gău: a hook, a sickle; crooked; to seduce, to tempt to do evil.

Gĕu, 溝 COLL. gău, q. v.: a ditch, a dam.

Gĕu, 膠 COLL. read yă, q. v.: glue; adhesive.

Gĕu: 勾 Read gĕu: gĕu-dáung, 勾當 underhand doings.

Gĕu, 苟 Grass, herbs; heedless, only, but, if so: COM., gĕu-chiă, 苟且 rudely, anyhow.

Gĕu, 狗 A dog; little, mean; gĕu-

háing 狗行 a dog's ways.

Géu, 救 To rescue, to save from evil; *Géu-Ciō*, 救主 the Savior.

Géu, 究 To examine into; *gōng-géu*, 講究 fitting, suitable; *géu-géng*, 究竟 finally.

Géu, 舅 Maternal uncles: COM., *niòng-géu*, 娘舅 a maternal uncle.

Géu, 舊 COM., read *gô* q. v.: old, before; venerable: COM., *gêu cĭk*, 舊疾 the old disease.

Géu, 倨 Proud, haughty as *géu ngô*, 倨傲.

Géu, 遽 Hurried, urgent, as *gĕk-géu*, 急遽.

Géu, 據 According to; *céng-géu*, 證據 testimony; *bìng-géu*, 憑據 proof, evidence.

Géu, 拒 Also read *gêu*, in the *Báik-'ing*: to ward off; *géu-ciŏk*, 拒絕 to renounce utterly.

Géu, 巨 Also read *gêu*: vast, mighty, large; how? *géu hāi*, 巨海 the vast sea.

Géu, 詎 Also *gêu*: how, in what manner? *géu-é*, 詎意 wholly unexpected.

Géu, 鉅 Also read *gêu*: hard, as steel, obdurate; *géu ngiĕk*, 鉅業 important matters; *géu kuāng*, 鉅欵 state monies.

Géu, 鋸 A saw; to saw, to divide; *géu kŏng*, 鋸糠 saw-dust.

Géu, 距 COLL. read *gêu*, q. v.; to oppose, to attack.

Géu, 踞 To squat, to sit on the feet; *buàng géu*, 盤踞 to sit improperly; *met.*, to seize as territory.

Géu, To fear, to dread.

Géu, 具 Implements, tools as *ké-géu*, 器具; *géu bīng*, 具禀 "prepared petition", an epistolary heading. COLL., lŏ-géu, 老具 an old man's staff.

Géu, 俱 Read gù: géu-dŏ, 俱多 for the most part, usually so; géu-ciòng, 俱全 all complete, perfect.

Géu, 颶 A tempest, a hurricane; géu hŭng, 颶風 a typhoon.

Géu, 距 Spurs; giŭ-géu 雞距 a cock's spur.

Géu, A coll. word, as géu huōi, to strike a light.

Géuk, 菊 The chrysanthemum; géuk huā, 菊花 the China aster; cūi dōng géuk, 水漲菊 a marigold.

Géuk, 掬, 匊 A handful; COLL., curdled, excited; géuk háik, 掬血 coagulated blood.

Géuk, 鞠 To nourish as géuk ŭk, 鞠育.

Géuk, 鞫 Read ŭk: to thrust into

water, to discover a leak.

Géuk: A coll. word: to run a seam.

Géung, 供 Also read gŭng, q. v. to offer or present to; géung hông, 供奉 to serve (the gods) with gifts.

Géung, 共 COLL. read gǎeng q. v. generally, all, altogether, to sum up; with, together with géung-cūng, 共總 the whole amount.

Géung, 僅 Exactly, nothing over, almost, a little short; géung nèng, 僅能 just able to; géung kō, 僅可 it will answer.

Géung, 饉 A famine of grains and vegetables, as gĭ géung, 饑饉.

Géung, 近 Near, to come near; according to; hô-géung, 附近 near to; ch'ing-géung, 親近 intimate; *gêung-biêng*, 近便 conveniently near; *gêung-lài*, 近來 recently; *gêung-sé* 近視 (coll. *gêung-né*) near-sighted.

Gêung, 覲 Introduced at court, as *diêu gêung*, 朝覲.

Gĭ, 箕 A winnowing fan as *buái gĭ*, 簸箕; *bóng-gĭ*, 糞箕 a hod-basket.

Gĭ, 基 A foundation, a basis, a commencement; *gĭ-cī*, 基址 a foundation; *gĭ-ngiĕk*, 基業 a patrimony; *dĕng-gĭ*, 登基 to ascend the throne.

Gĭ, 期 Times, seasons; to expect, to wait for; COM., *gĭ muāng*, 期滿 the time is up; *gĭ-áing*, 期限 the time agreed upon; *gĭ-piéu*, 期票 a promissory note; *sĭng gĭ*, 星期 Sunday (a term used since 1905).

Gĭ, 朞 An anniversary, a full

revolution of a year, 354 days.

Gĭ, 饑 Famine, as *gĭ-huŏng*, 饑荒; *gĭ gĕung*, 饑饉 See *gĕung*.

Gĭ, 飢 Hungry, famished; COM. *gĭ-ngô*, 飢餓 to starve; *gĭ-kák* 飢渴 hunger and thirst.

Gĭ, 幾 Also read *gī*; q. v.: moderately, a little, to examine.

Gĭ, 機 A machine, a loom, as *gĭ-ké*, 機器; *gĭ-huôi*, 機會 an opportunity, an occasion.

Gĭ, 嘰 To eat sparingly; *gĭ-gĭ-giĕu*, 嘰嘰叫 to peep as a chick.

Gĭ, 璣 Pearls not perfectly round.

Gĭ, 畿 An imperial park; a limit, a border; the threshold.

Gĭ, 譏 To slander, to ridicule; *gĭ-chiéu*, 譏笑 to jeer, to laugh at.

Gĭ, 乩 To divine; COM., *gĭ-bék*, 乩筆 the divining pen.

Gì 289

Gī, 肌 Muscle, as *gī-hŭ*, 肌膚 or *gī-nŭk*, 肌肉.

Gī, 己 I, myself; selfish, private; *cêṳ-gī*, 自己 (coll. *cê-gă*), one's self.

Gī, 圮 Also read *ī*, q. v.: to destroy, as a city.

Gī, 杞 The name of a state.

Gī, 紀 To record; history, annals; COM., *nièng-gī*, 年紀 a person's age; *gŏng-gī*, 綱紀 to govern.

Gī, 几 A stand; *dà-gī*, 茶几 a teapoy.

Gī, 幾 Also read *gĭ*, and in the coll. *gūi*, q. v.: an interrogative,—how, how many, or much?

Gì, 其 A relative or personal pronoun; he, she, it, etc.; also an indefinite pronoun, whoever, wherever; used in the

COLL. to mark the possessive; one, any one; a numerative; *gì-ù,* 其餘 the rest.

Gì, 棋, 棊 The game of chess.

Gì, 祈 To pray, to beseech, as *gì-dǭ,* 祈禱 or *gì-giù,* 祈求.

Gì, 祺 Fortunate, lucky; *sǐng gì,* 升祺 to be promoted—a complimentary phrase.

Gì, 祇 Used for *gǐ* (the Imperial domain); sometimes confounded with *ciĕ* (to respect; but, only); *dē-gì,* 地祇 *met.,* Earth, Terra.

Gì, 麒 As *gì-lìng,* 麒麟 male and female unicorns.

Gì, 旗 A flag, a standard; *gì-hǭ,* 旗號 signal flag; *gì hâ,* 旗下 Manchus; *gì-gǎng,* 旗杆 a flagstaff.

Gì, 耆 Aged; *gì-lǭ,* 耆老 the aged.

Gì, 奇 Also read *kiĕ* and in the COLL. *kiă*, q. v.: extraordinary, surprising; COM. *gì-děk,* 奇特 strange, unusual.

Gì, 岐 A hill with two peaks; *met.,* ambiguous, as words or conduct, as *uâ gōng liōng gì;* 話講兩岐 to speak with a double meaning.

Gì, 葵 As *gì huǎ,* 葵花 the holly hock; *hióng nĭk gì,* 向日葵 the sun flower.

Gì, 馗 The sides of the face; place where nine roads meet, a thoroughfare.

Giă, 迦 As *Sĕk-giă* 釋迦 a country in the west; also used for Sakya, a name of Budh.

Giă, 枷 A cangue; *dò giă,* 掏枷 to wear a cangue.

Giă: A coll. word: low, not elevated; cheap; *giă siŏh cèng*, 下一層 a step lower.

Giăk, A coll. word: angry, displeased; *giăk kó̤*, gone off displeased.

Giăk, 揭 Read *giĕng*: to carry on the shoulder; *met.*, displeased, petulant.

Giăng, 驚 Read *gĭng*: to fear, to be afraid; to apprehend; *giăng-huòng*, 驚惶 or *giăng-ói*, 驚畏 to fear; *ng giăng*, 伓驚 not afraid; *dĭng giăng nèng*, 頂驚伙 frightful! horrid!

Giăng 經 Read *gĭng*:

Giăng, 仔 Read *cṳ̄*: a son, a child; diminutive of animals, persons and things; young fruit.

Giáng, 鏡 Read *géng*: a mirror; *huōi giáng*, 火鏡 a reflector; *chiĕng-lĭ-giáng*, 千里鏡 a telescope; *hiēng-mì giàng,* 顯微鏡 microscope; *ngāng giàng,* 眼鏡 spectacles.

Giàng, 行, 跨 Read *hèng:* to walk, to proceed, to travel; met., to do evil.

Giàng, 健 Read *giông:* hale, hearty, lusty, vigorous in old age.

Giĕ, 圭, 珪 A baton; a measure equal to 64 grains.

Giĕ, 閨 Women, feminine, lady-like; *giĕ nṳ̄,* 閨女 a virgin, a young lady.

Giĕ, 雞, 鷄 The barnyard fowl; *giĕ gáek,* 鷄㹠 a cock; *giĕ mō,* 鷄牸 a hen; *giĕ cù,* 雞雛 a fledgling, a young chicken.

Giĕ, 階 Read *găi,* as in *giĕ-cô̤,* 階座 stone steps.

Giĕ, 規 A pair of compasses; regulation, custom; *giĕ-gṳ̄,* 規

矩 usage, custom; *giĕ-dèu*, 規條 rules, regulations; *că giĕ* 齋規 school rules; *nĭk-giĕ*, 日規 sun-dial.

Giĕ, 筓 As in *gĭk giĕ,* 及筓 to arrive at the age of puberty, as girls.

Giĕ: A coll. word: to tie, to fasten, to tether.

Giĕ: A coll. word: soon, quick; easily, rapidly; *giĕ duái,* to grow fast.

Gié, 計 To plan, to estimate; a plot; *gié-cháik,* 計策 or *gié-mèu,* 計謀 a plan, a scheme; *gié-sáung,* 計算 to reckon up; *gŭi-gié,* 詭計 a crafty scheme.

Gié, 桂 The Cassia tree; *met.,* literary reputation and honors; *gié-puòi,* 桂皮 cinnamon; *nguŏk gié,* 月桂 the monthly rose.

Gié, 繼 To adopt, to follow after; COM. *gié mū,* 繼母 a step-mother; *gié cióh,* 繼燭 to finish by candle-light.

Gié, 寄 To confide in, to deliver in charge; to send, as things; *gié táuk,* 寄托 to commit to; *gié sĕng,* 寄生 a parasite; COM. *gié séng,* 寄信 to send a letter or message; *gié kēu séng,* 寄口信 to send a verbal message.

Gié, 季 The last of a series; a season, a quarter of a year.

Giè, 岐 Read *gì:* used in names of places.

Giék, 結 COLL. read *gáik,* q. v.: a skein; to fasten, to bind parties; an agreement, compact; *giék huŏng,* 結婚 to betroth; *giék guŏh,* 給局 the final result.

Giék, 潔 COLL. *gáik*, q. v.: limpid, pure, untainted, above bribes; *giék ciàng*, 潔淨 pure, undefiled; *chĭng-giék*, 清潔 clean, chaste, pure.

Giék, 挈 To lift, to raise from the ground; *tì-giék*, 持挈 to lift and carry, *met.*, to recommend.

Giék, 揭 To lift up; to undertake; responsible for; COM., *giék gái*, 揭蓋 to lift the veil.

Giék, 鑷 Read *niék*: to take with tongs or pincers; *giék-niék*, 揭鑷 a pair of pincers, tweezers.

Giék, 擠 Read *gié*, to take with chopsticks;

Giék, 頰 The jaws, the cheeks; articulation; *huăng giék*, 緩頰 slow of speech.

Giék, 刧刦 To seize, to plunder,

to rob: COM. *chiōng giék*, 搶刼 (coll. *páh-giék*, 打刼) to rob.

Giék, 盤 Read *buàng:* to buy goods and retail.

Giék, 傑, 杰 A hero; proud, opinionated; COM. *ĭng-hṳ̀ng hò-giék*, 英雄豪傑 brave, heroïc.

Giék, 桀 Magnanimous. a hero; harsh, cruel;

Giĕk, 竭 To exhaust; to carry to the utmost; defeated; *giĕk lĭk*, 竭力 to exert one's strength to the utmost.

Giĕng, 鹼 Also read *ngiĕng:* salt, briny water; COM. *giĕng cūi*, 鹼水 lye.

Giĕng, 堅 Firm, solid, durable, as *giĕng-gó*, 堅固.

Giĕng, 肩 The shoulder; as *giĕng-tàu*, 肩頭.

Giĕng, 兼 A conjunction, moreover, and, also, with; additional; *bŏ giĕng,* 仅兼 or *gáing giĕng,* 更兼 still more.

Giĕng, 撿 To coerce; to gather and bind together, to collate; *giĕng-sók,* 撿束 to restrain; COM. *giĕng-diĕng,* 撿點 to arrange carefully.

Giĕng, 檢 An envelope, a book label, a pattern, to arrange, to collate, to compose a book.

Giĕng, 繭 A cocoon; *càng-giĕng,* 蠶繭 the silk-worm's cocoon; *giĕng-diù,* 繭綢 crape pongee. Read *gēng,* in coll., as in *chĕng-gēng,* 蠶繭 silk worms.

Giĕng, 襇 A plait, a fold; tucks, gathers; coll., *kák giĕng,* 拾襇 to make plaits.

Giéng, 見 Also read *hiéng:* q. v.: to see, to perceive; sign of the passive voice and past tense; COM. *gŏ-giéng,* 高見 your opinion;

kŏ giéng, 可見 from which it can be seen; giéng guó, 見過 seen; giéng chiéu, 見笑 laughed at; giéng-sék, 見識 knowledge; giéng chă, 見瘥 better in health; COLL., giéng-gáek, 見覺 to perceive.

Giéng, 劍 A sword, a rapier; COM. dŏ giéng, 刀劍 swords.

Gièng, 乾 Also read găng, q. v.: heaven; a sovereign; a father; strong, enduring; COM. Gièng-lŭng, 乾隆 the Emperor Kien-lung A. D. 1736—1796; giềng cṳ̆ 乾書 and kŏng cṳ̆, 坤書 a boy's and girl's betrothal cards.

Gièng, 墘 An edge, a border, a bank, or margin; eaves; cūi gièng, 水墘 the water's side; gièng ĕu kó, the edge worn off.

Gièng, 虔 Determined, sincere, correct, devout, to respect; *gièng gó,* 虔告 to inform respectfully; *gièng géng,* 虔敬 to revere; *gièng sìng,* 虔誠 sincere, devout.

Gièng, 儉 Economical as *giêng-sāng* 儉省; *ciék giêng,* 節儉 frugal, temperate; *kák giêng,* 太儉 stingy.

Giĕu, 嬌 Beautiful, graceful; to whine, or cry for; *giĕu-giĕu,* 嬌嬌 graceful, lovely; *giĕu-giāng,* 嬌仔 a dear, petted child; *có giĕu,* 做嬌 to whine and tease.

Giĕu, 驕 Proud, arrogant, as *giĕu-ngô,* 驕傲.

Giĕu, 皎 Clear, bright, effulgent, as the sun or the moon; *giĕu-giék,* 皎潔 white and spotless.

Giĕu, 狡 Artful, crafty and overbearing, as *giĕu ăuk,* 狡惡; de-

Giéu 301

ceitful and knavish, as *giēu-guái*, 狡怪.

Giēu, 姣 Beautiful, winsome; pretty, and captivating, as *giēu mê*, 姣媚.

Giēu, 疘 As *giēu dòng-sǎ*, 疘腸疹 colic or cholera morbus.

Giēu, 撟 COLL. also read *giéu*, q. v.: firm, unyielding; COLL.: to pry with a lever; *giēu kī lì*, 撟起梨 pry it up.

Giēu, 攪 As *giēu sǒi*, 攪衰 frets himself lean.

Giēu, 餃 Read *gáu*: a dumpling.

Giēu, 絞 To bind, to strangle; COM., *giēu sī*, 絞死 to execute by strangling.

Giēu, 繳 To deliver up; to pay back; COM., *giēu só*, 繳數 to render an account; *giēu dèng*, 繳還 to return, to hand back.

Giéu, 叫 To call, to call upon;

to cry out; to name; to command; to persuade; termed: *giéu éng,* 叫應 call and answer; *nệng lā giéu nū,* 仅禮叫汝 some one is calling you; *diê-nệng giéu nū có,* 俤仅叫汝做 who told you to do so? *giéu lō̤ sié-nó̤h miàng,* 叫囉世毛名 by what name is it called.

Giêu, 僑 An inn; *giêu gụ* 僑居 to visit, to sojourn.

Giêu, 喬 High, stately; aspiring; crooked; proud; a surname; *met.,* father; *giêu mŭk,* 喬木 stately trees; *giêu cṳ̄,* 喬梓 father and son.

Giêu, 橋 A bridge, a viaduct: a stately tree; *met.,* father; *giêu cṳ̄,* 橋梓 father and son.

Giêu, 轎 A sedan; *giêu guăng,* 轎舘 coolie stand; *giêu cièng,*

轎錢 sedan fare; *giêu băng*, 轎班 sedan bearers; *giêu liềng*, 轎簾 curtains of a sedan; *báik cộ giêu*, 八座簥 a sedan with eight bearers; COLL., *sội giêu*, 坐簥 to ride in a sedan; *giêu gáung*, 簥槓 sedan thills; *iā giêu*, 野簥 a wild sedan, i. e., one not of the regular establishment.

Giêu, 撟 Read *giêu*, q. v.: to pry heavy things; *giêu siĕk*, 撟折 to break in prying.

Gĭh: A coll. word: to thrust, to pierce; *gĭh diŏh*, pierced, perforated.

Gĭh: A coll. euphonic prefix, as in *gĭh găh*, to pry up; crosswise.

Gĭk, 極 A superlative; extremely, very, the limit; *báek gĭk*, 北極 the north-pole, the north-star; COLL., *kŭ dék gĭk*, 苦的極 the very extreme of misery; *diōng gĭk*, 轉極 crisis; *gĭk diĕng*, 極點 to the extreme.

Gĭk, 及 A verb and conjunction; to effect, to reach to, to go to; to communicate; and, with, also, at, to; *gĭk dĭng,* 及丁 the age of puberty for boys; *gĭk giĕ,* 及筓 ditto for girls,—for both it is 16 years.

Gĭng, 京 Great, lofty, extensive; the capital of a kingdom; *gĭng dŭ,* 京都 a metropolis.

Gĭng, 勍 Strong, powerful; *gĭng dĭk,* 勍敵 a powerful enemy.

Gĭng, 黥 To mark the face with black spots; *gĭng miĕng,* 黥面 to tattoo the faces of criminals.

Gĭng, 鯨 As *gĭng ngù,* 鯨魚 a whale.

Gĭng, 擎 To raise with the hands, to elevate.

Gĭng, 驚 Coll. read *giăng*, q. v.: to frighten, to alarm; terrified, astonished; *gĭng dông*, 驚動 have disturbed you—a polite phrase.

Gĭng, 兢 To forbear, to refrain; *gĭng-gĭng*, 兢兢 cautious, respectful, guarded.

Gĭng, 經 Laws, canons; standard works, classics: COM. *séng-gĭng*, 聖經 the Sacred Scriptures; *ī gĭng*, 已經 has, already have; *gĭng guó*, 經過 to pass by.

Gĭng, 今 Now, at this time, presently; COM. *gĭng-nièng*, (coll. *gĭng-nièng-màng*,) 今年 this year; COLL. *gĭng-dáng*, 今旦 or *gĭng-dáng-nĭk*, 今旦日 to day; *gĭng-buŏ*, 今晡 to night;

gĭng - dáng - cā, 今旦早 this morning.

Gĭng, 金 Gold, metal, gilt; a piece of money; precious, true, imperial; a surname.

Gĭng, 鈞 As gĭng ăng.

Gĭng, 均 To equalize; even, level, flat.

Gĭng: A coll. word: to last long, enduring; gĭng-sāi, good for use, will last long.

Gĭng, 景 Circumstances, as guŏng-gĭng, 光景; gīng-dĕ́, 景致 scenery, landscape; uāng-gĭng, 晚景 the evening prospect; met., old age.

Gĭng, 境 A limit, a boundary; condition in life; gĭng-gái, 境界 boundary; sŏng gĭng, 順境 in good circumstances; COM., gĭng siá, 境社 a village temple.

Gìng, 謹 Diligent, careful; solemn; to venerate; *gìng-séng,* 謹慎 careful, cautious, circumspect.

Gìng, 警 To caution, to enjoin, as *gìng-gái,* 警戒; *gìng-gái â chéu,* 警戒下次 to warn against a repetition of.

Gìng, 錦 Embroidered, worked in colors, as *gìng-séu,* 錦繡.

Gìng, 緊 To bind fast; pressing; *gìng-gék,* 緊急 very pressing; *iéu-gìng,* 要緊 important.

Gìng, 荊 Spinous, prickly; *gìng chā,* 荊妻 my wife; *ciók-gìng,* 拙荊 a stupid thorn—i. e., my wife.

Gìng, 瓊 Precious coral; small pretty gems; COM. *Gìng ciū hū,* 瓊州府 the Island of Hainan.

Gìng, 煢 Alone, solitary as *gìng dŭk,* 煢獨.

Giò, 橋 In the dictionaries read *gièu*, q. v.; a bridge; *uăng sêu giò*, 萬壽橋 bridge of myriad ages;—the great bridge at Foochow.

Giò, 蕎 Read *gièu*: *giò măh*, 蕎麥 buckwheat—used medicinally.

Giò, 茄 Read *gă*: a name for *ciē-chái*, 紫菜 the egg plant.

Gióh, 脚 Read *giók*; as in *gióh-sáik*, 脚色 ability, skill; *met.*, laborers, workmen, coolies.

Giók, 決 To cut off; to pass sentence; *giók ciŏk*, 決絕 to renounce utterly; *giók lié*, 決裂 determination to separate, as countries going war; *giók-é*, 決意 to decide mentally; *giók-duáng*, 決斷 to decide;

Giók, 抉 Used for the coll., *dŏng*

Giŏng 309

q. v.; to castrate as *giók dụ*, 抉豬

Giók, 鴂 The shrike, the butcher-bird, called *báik lọ*, 伯勞.

Giók, 鴃 The tailor bird, called *kiĕu hó*, 巧婦 (the cunning woman, etc.)

Giók, 訣 A farewell; an art, a rule; a trick; COLL., *giók-dáiu*, 訣竇 rule, methods in doing.

Giók, 譎 Also read *kiók*: feigned, counterfeited; *giĕu giók*, 矯譎 crafty,

Giók, 脚 The foot, the leg; *met.*, firm, stable; skill, talent, in which sense the coll., is *gióh*, p. v.: *họ chiū gióh*, 好手脚 clever, handy; *ló gióh*, 露脚 to show the (cloven) foot.

Giŏng, 姜 A surname. *Giŏng Tái-Gŭng*, 姜太公 a famous general, B. C. 1122.

Giŏng, 娟 Beautiful, handsome; slender; distant.

Giŏng, 蠲 Pure, bright; *giŏng-miĕng,* 蠲免 to remit as taxes.

Giŏng, 殭 Lying as if dead; stiff; *giŏng càng,* 殭蠶 the larvae of of silk worms.

Giŏng, 薑 Ginger as *giŏng-mō̤,* 薑姆.

Giŏng, 疆 Limits, borders, to bound; *giŏng - gái,* 疆界 a boundary.

Giŏng, 捐 To reject, to renounce, to contribute, to buy office or title; *giŏng-dà̤,* 捐題 to subscribe.

Giŏng, 鵑 The cuckoo, as *dô̤-giŏng,* 杜鵑.

Giŏng, 強 Also read *giòng,* q. v.: to urge, to force; *giŏng-miĕng,* 強勉 to constrain.

Giŏng, 薔 Read *giòng;* small

roots, a lily; *giōng-sŭk,* 薑術 the tuberose.

Giōng, 窖 To beg, to supplicate; hard, difficult; good honest advice as *giōng-giōng,* 窖窖.

Gióng, 絹 Read *giōng: gióng-să,* 絹紗 a sort of gauze, lustring?

Gióng, 建 To establish, to constitute; to build; *gióng lik,* 建立 to establish, to found.

Gióng, 毽 The shuttlecock; *tĕk-gióng,* 踢毽 to kick the football.

Giòng, 強 Also read *giōng,* q. v.: violent, headstrong, obstinate; strong, brawny; 40 years old; *giòng-cáung,* 強壯 vigorous; hale; *giòng-páik,* 強迫 to forcibly compel.

Giōng, 健 COLL. read *giâng,* q. v.: strong, robust, unwearied, enduring; COM. *kŏng-giông*, 康健 hale, vigorous.

Giông, 件 COLL. read *iông*, q. v.: a classifier used to denote a particular article, subject, or affair; a, an, one.

Giŭ, 瘦 Read *giĕu*: bent with pain; *giŭ-dòng-sáu*, 瘦腸嫩 the whooping cough.

Giŭ: A coll. word: to shorten, to shrink, puckered; *giŭ kó̤*, shrunk; *met.*, silent from bashfulness;

Giŭ, 久 A long time, enduring, lasting; *diòng-giŭ*, or *dòng-giŭ*, 長久 forever.

Giŭ, 灸 COLL., *gó̤*, q. v.: to cauterize with the moxa.

Giŭ, 羑 Read *iū*, in the dictionaries; right principles, reason; just, proper;

Giŭ, 九 COLL. read *gău*, q. v.:

nine; *met.*, many, the highest; *Giū-gŏng*, 九江 nine rivers, *Kiū-kiāng*.

Giū, 糾 Also read *giēu*: to combine, to examine, to inform, to elevate, to head a sedition; perverse.

Giū: 韭 Scallions or chives, a salad onion, as *giū chái*, 韭菜.

Giù, 求 To seek; to beg, to ask, to supplicate; ardently desirous of; *gì-giù*, 祈求 to pray; *kōng-giù*, 懇求 to beg earnestly.

Giù, 毬 A ball, a globe, a sphere; *siók-giù*, 雪毬 the snow-ball (flower.)

Giù, 球 A round gem; a ball, a globe, a sphere; *tiĕng-giù*, 天球 a celestial globe; *dê-giù*, 地球 the earth; *Liù-giù*, 琉球 Loochoo.

Giù, 虯 A horned dragon; to wriggle as a snake; a quick, agitated movement.

Gó, 固 Determined, firm; assuredly, certainly, firmly; *gó-é*, 固意 wilful; *giěng-gó*, 堅固 stable, firm.

Gó, 痼 A chronic, incurable disease, as *gó-cĭk*, 痼疾

Gó, 錮 To fuse copper, or iron; to mend cracks; *met.*, to bind, to prevent.

Gó, 故 Also read *gū* in the coll., q. v.: a cause, a reason for; therefore, on that account; old, long in possession; *gó-iū*, an old friend; *ù gó*, 無故 causeless; *iòng-gó*, 緣故 a reason, a cause; *gó-chū*, 故此 therefore.

Gó, A coll. word: a comparative; more, still more; an

adverb; yet, still again; *gó họ*, better; *gó ó*, yet have, have more; *gó muôi*, not yet; *gó dék họ*, luckily.

Gó, 顧 To look after, to care for; an initial word: but, on the contrary; a surname; *ciéu-gó,* 照顧 to look after; *ng gó,* 怀顧 to disregard.

Gó, 僱 To rent, to hire workmen; as *gó gḙng,* 僱工.

Gô, 灸 Read *giū:* to cauterize.

Gô 舊 Read *gêu:* old, worn out; formerly; anciently; *gó-dā,* 舊底 formerly.

Gọ, 蒿 Used with names of different plants; *dòng-gọ,* 塘蒿 celery; *chǐng gọ,* 青蒿 wormwood.

Gọ, 高 Coll. read *gèng,* q. v.: high, eminent; excellent, sublime, noble; a periphrasis for *your* in direct address; *gŏ-séu*, 高壽 (your) exalted age? *gŏ-sĭng*, 高陞 to be promoted; *gŏ-ngô*, 高傲 proud, arrogant: *Gŏ-là guók*, 高麗國 Corea.

Gŏ, 篙 A pole; *déuk gŏ*, 竹篙 a bamboo pole; *gáek gŏ*, 角篙 a try-square.

Gŏ, 膏 Fat, ointment; rich food; *gŏ-dĕk*, 膏澤 grace, favor; *gŏ-iŏh*, 膏梁 a medicinal plaster; *gŏ-liòng ĕng*, 膏梁紅 a dull red.

Gŏ, 羔 A lamb, as *gŏ-iòng*, 羔羊.

Gŏ, 糕 Unleavened cakes, pastry; *giĕ-láung gŏ*, 雞蛋糕 sponge cake.

Gŏ, 歌 A song, a ballad: *chióng gŏ*, 唱歌 to sing songs.

Gŏ, 哥 Coll. a term of respect for boys and girls; an elder brother; a polite term for an elder or stranger: *duâi gŏ*, 大

哥 my elder brother; *niè-giāng - gŏ* 伲仔哥 children; *muói gŏ,* 妹哥 his or your daughter; sister! Miss!

Gŏ, 皋 To inform, to announce; *gŏ gŏ,* 皋皋 rude, uninformed.

Gŏ, 藁 Straw for huts; a draft or copy.

Gŏ, 稿 Straw; an original, the first draft of a writing; a proof.

Gó, 箇, 个 A classifier for human beings and round, compact, inanimate things; an individual; the pronoun this; used in the coll., mandarin and for the coll. ciáh, q. v.: *gó-gó,* 个个 severally, all; *gó-ing, gó-ing,* 个人, 个人 each one.

Gó, 告 To accuse, to impeach; to tell, to ask, to request; *gó-*

só, 告訴 to inform; gó-sē (coll. gộ-cế,) 告示 a proclamation, an edict; ngwòng-gó, 原告 the plaintiff; bê-gó, 被告 the defendant; gó áng, 告案 a lawsuit; gọ́ băh, 告白 a placard.

Gọ́, 誥 To order, to enjoin; hóng gọ́, 訓誥 to instruct; gọ́-hŭng, 誥封 to confer rank, as on the parents or wife of an officer.

Gò, 㿀 Read gō: gò-lộ, 㿀瘵 the itch; săng gò-lộ, 生㿀瘵 to have the itch.

Gò: A coll. word: as gò-giăng, a fish resembling a shark.

Gọ́h, 閣 The posts of a door, a council chamber; met., the court; COM., nội-gọ́h, 內閣 the Inner Council; gọ́h á, 閣下 Your Excellency! chók gọ́h 出閣 to become a bride.

Gói 319

Góh, 擱 To obstruct, to impede; to delay; *kéuk ū dăng góh*, 乞雨擔擱 delayed by the rain; *góh chiēng*, 擱淺 to ground on shallows.

Góh, 袼 Read *lŏk* and *gáuk*, the under seam of a sleeve; *góh-lŏh* (or *láuk*) *â*, 袼落下 under the arm, the armpit.

Góh: A coll. word: *góh biāng*, to stuff cakes, to make sandwiches.

Gói, 貴 Honorable, noble, dignified, good; your, thine, in direct address; high-priced; COM,, *hó-gói*, 富貴 riches and honor; *gói-ìng*, 貴人 the gentry, the officials; *gói séng*, 貴姓 your surname.

Gói, 瑰 A perfect pearl; *met.*, rare, precious, admirable; COM. *muòi-gói*, 玫瑰 the jasper; a species of red rose.

Gói, 癸 The last of the ten stems; to consider, to calculate; COM., *tiĕng-gói*, 天癸 the menses. puberty.

Gòi: A coll. word: *gòi sĭng-diĕ*, to carry (a child) under one's garment; *gòi-gòi lạ*, to place in the bosom.

Gói, 櫃 A chest, a locker; COM., *cièng gói*, 錢櫃 a money safe.

Gói, 餽 A term for sacrificing; to offer.

Gói, 饋 Food, victuals; to prepare food; *gói-ìng*, 饋人 a king's baker.

Gói, 跪 To kneel, to bend the knee to the ground; COM., *gói-bái*, 跪拜 to kneel and worship; *săng gói giŭ káiu*, 三跪九叩 three kneelings and nine knockings (of the head) as in profound obeisance.

Gók, 谷 A valley, a ravine; to nourish; embarrassment; the east wind; COM., *săng gók*, 山谷 a ravine.

Gók, 穀 Grain; excellent; *bók gók*, 不穀 "the unworthy"— I, your humble servant; COM., *ngū gók*, 五穀 rice, cereals in general.

Gók, 轂 A wheel, as *gŭ-gók*, 車轂.

Gók, 梏 Manacles and fetters, as *cék-gók*, 桎梏.

Gók, 鵠 A little bird.

Gók, 酷 Severe, inhuman; extremely; *gók lê*, 酷吏 a cruel, extortionate officer; *ngièng gók*, 嚴酷 severe.

Gók, 趜 Read *kuók*: *gók-gók-diōng*, 趜趜轉 squirming about; restless, as a child.

Gók: A coll. word: *gók kī*, to

322   Gŏng

rise up (from a seat or bed)).

Gŏk, 滑 Read *huăk:* slippery; *gŏk-siŏh-dō̤,* 滑一倒 to slip down; *gŏk ciáh gŏk,* 滑隻滑 very slippery.

Gŏng, 缸 An earthen jar; *mī gŏng,* 米缸 rice jars; *cūi gŏng,* 水缸 water jars; *gŏng-buòng,* 缸盆 a large bowl.

Gŏng, 罡 A star; *tiĕng gŏng,* 天罡 The Dipper, in Astronomy; much used in charms.

Gŏng, 扛 To bear burdens on a pole between two; COM. *gŏng giĕu,* 扛轎 to carry a sedan; COLL., *gŏng mā̤ kī,* 扛賣起 can't carry it.

Gŏng, 根 Coll., *gŭng,* q. v.: roots, of plants; the origin, root, foundation; a classifier of trees; *gŏng-buōng,* 根本 the the source; *gŏng-nguòng* 根原

the origin; *gŏng-gĭ,* 根基 the foundation.

Gŏng, 江 Coll. read *gĕng*, q. v.: a river; *gŏng-săng,* 江山 rivers and mountains,—the empire; COLL., *ngiê gŏng,* 外江 other provinces.

Gŏng, 肛 The colon; the anus; COM., *gŏng muòng,* 肛門 the rectum; COLL., *tŏk gŏng,* the piles.

Gŏng, 剛 A sharp in music; hard, solid; enduring; an adverb of time; now, just now, recently; *gŏng-gióng,* 剛健 strong, resolute; *gĭng-gŏng siŏh,* 金剛石 a diamond.

Gŏng, 綱 A bond of society, a great principle; *gŏng-gĭ,* 綱紀 a narrative, a series; *săng gŏng,* 三綱 the three bonds— i. e., the relative duties of king, father, and husband; cūng-gŏng, 總綱 the essence of; gŏng-gáng, 綱鑑 a history.

Gŏng: A coll. word: as in gŏng cŭ, to make offerings in school in the 4th moon.

Gōng, 講 To narrate, to discourse, to explain; COM., gōng uâ, 講話 to speak, to talk; gōng-lī, 講理 to state the reason; gōng-cŭ, 講書 to explain books, to preach; gōng puái, 講破 expose thoroughly; páng gōng, 有講 to chat; iā-gōng, 野講 to lie.

Góng, 貢 Tribute, taxes; COM., céng-góng, 進貢 to offer tribute; góng-sĕng, 貢生*, băk-góng, 拔貢 or iŭ-góng, 優貢*; góng-iêng, 貢院 the provincial examination hall; góng-dáung, 貢緞 a superior kind of satin.

---

*See Baldwin Manual p. 189.

Gú   325

Góng, 棍 A round stick, a club, as *chà-góng*, 柴棍; *liēng-giāng góng*, 輦仔棍 a flail; *dū góng*, 賭棍 gamblers.

Gòng, 閂 Coll. also read *cháung*, q. v.; a bar for fastening a door; *mùong-gòng*, 門閂 a door bar; *gòng mùong*, 閂門 to bar a door.

Gòng: A coll. word: hot; to cook thoroughly, to boil soft.

Góng, 郡 An inhabited place, a small district.

Gŭ, 孤 Fatherless; desolate, alone; unprotected; *gŭ-cṳ̄*, 孤子 a fatherless child; *gŭ-ăi-cṳ̄*, 孤哀子 an orphan.

Gŭ, 菰 The Caladium; COM., *hiŏng-gŭ*, 香菰 a small edible mushroom..

Gŭ, 枯 Rotten wood; decayed, withered; *gŭ-gō*, 枯稿 emaciated, cadaverous; COLL. *gŭ-dă*, 枯乾 withered.

Gŭ, 姑 A polite term for ladies; lenient, lax, indulgent; just, merely; *sṳ-gŭ*, 師姑 a young lady, Miss; also a married daughter; COLL., *duâi sạ gŭ*, 大細姑 husband's sisters.

Gŭ, 沽 Name of a river in the Chinchew prefecture, Fukien; to contract bargains, to trade; *gŭ mìng*, 沽名 to purchase office.

Gŭ, 辜 A fault, a crime; sin, guilt; necessary; to monopolize; *cô̤i gŭ*, 罪辜 sins.

Gŭ, 鴣 Partridge, as *ciá-gŭ*, 鷓鴣

Gū, 罟 A bird net; *met.*, the net of the law; *cô̤i-gū*, 罪罟 the meshes of sin, involved in guilt.

Gū, 股 The rump; firm, stable;

a chapter or head of an essay; a share, a classifier of shares; *săng gū*, three shares.

Gū, 籃 A vessel, a utensil: COM., *dà gū*, 茶籃 a teapot.

Gū, 古 Ancient, from of old; antiquity; *gū-lọ̃*, 古老 old, antique; *gū-cā sì-hâiu*, 古早時候 ancient times; *gū gĭng*, 古今 ancient and modern; *gū-céĕk*, 古蹟 relics, sacred spots; *gū-guái*, 古怪 odd; tricky; *cáuk gū*, to die; *mạ gū-dūng*, to sell curiosities.

Gū, 嘏 Great; distant; strong; blessed; propitious; *céuk-gū*, 祝嘏 to bless.

Gū, 估 To estimate, to value; price; COM., *gū gá cièng*, 估價錢 to set a price.

Gū, 牯 The female of kine.

Gū, 蠱 A slow poison; to seduce;

gū-hĕk, 蠱惑 to delude; gū-dŭk, 蠱毒 poison; COM., gū-dióng, 蠱脹 the dropsy.

Gū, 買 Also read *gá*, q. v.: a resident tradesman; gū-ché, 買市 a market.

Gū, 鼓 A drum; to drum; to arouse; to soothe; a watch of the night; gū-ciŏng, 鼓掌 to clap the hands; COM., gū-làu, 鼓樓 a drum tower; uăng-gū, 晚鼓 the evening drum; COLL., páh găng gū, 拍更鼓 to beat the watches.

Gū: A coll. word: to stir up, to stir; gū hùng, to roil by stirring.

Gū, 瞽 Blind; leader of an orchestra.

Gū, 故 Read *gó*: gū-séu, 故事 antiquated matters; gū-é 故意 or gū sĭng-é, 故心意 purposely and hypocritically.

Gù, 糊 Read *hù*: paste, gluten; *gù-ciŏng*, 糊漿 paste.

Gù: A coll. word: as *gù-cŭi*, the turtle-dove; *gù-cŭi-mĕk*, a staple of brass or iron.

Gù: A coll. word: as in *gù-lŭng-chiòng*, to squat; *gì-lĭ-gù-dŭ*, (or *lù*), muttering, grumbling; *gù-dók*, to wriggle.

Gù, 拘 To detain; to restrain; COM., *gŭ-sók*, 拘束 to bind, as by fixed rules; *bók-gŭ*, 不拘 not insist; no matter how or what; COLL., *mŏh gŭ*, 莫拘 don't stand on ceremony.

Gù, 居 To reside, to inhabit; to fill an office; COLL., *sŏng-gŭ*, 孀居 a widow; *gŭ-cĕu*, 居住 to reside, to live at.

Gù, 車 Used for *chiă*, q. v.: a cart, a carriage.

Gŭ, 矩 A carpenter's square; a rule, a law; *giék gŭ,* 絜矩 rules which influence others; COM., *giĕ-gŭ,* 矩規 a rule, a usage.

Gŭ, 舉 To raise; to recommend; to extol, to praise; COM., *gŭ-ciéng,* 舉薦 to recommend one; *gŭ-dóng,* 舉動 movements, actions; *gŭ-chiū,* 舉手 to raise the hands.

Gù, 俱 Coll. read *gêu,* q. v.: altogether, jointly; *gù-ciòng,* 俱全 complete, perfect, entire.

Gù 渠 A drain; a pool; a personal pronoun; he, she, it; *gù dĕng,* 渠等 they.

Gù, 衢 A street, a highway; *tŭng gù,* 通衢 a thoroughfare; *tiĕng gù,* 天衢 the equator.

Guă, 瓜 General name for the gourd family; COM., *guă-cī,* 瓜

Guá　　　331

子 melon seeds; gǐng guǎ, 金瓜 a pumpkin; sa̤-guǎ, 西瓜 a water-melon; chái guǎ, 菜瓜 cucumbers; guā hŭng, 瓜分 divide the melon, *met.*, dismemberment of a country.

Guá: A coll. word: to catch; caught, as a sleeve on things in passing.

Guā, 剮 A form of punishment; chói guā, 碎剮 cut (him) in bits—sometimes used facetiously.

Guá, 寡 Few, little; rarely; a widow; gŭ-guǎ, 孤寡 orphaned and widowed; COM., guā-hó, 寡婦 a widow; dọ̆-guā, 多寡 much or little, some.

Guá, 卦 To divine; guá cụ̆, 卦資 a divination fee; báuk guá, 卜卦 to divine.

Guá, 挂 To suspend, to hang up;

to distinguish; anxious; *guá-lêu*, 挂慮 in suspense, anxious about; *guá-niêng*, 掛念 to bear in mind.

Guá, 袿 A jacket worn over the robe; *bò-guá*, 袍袿 robe and jacket.

Guăi, 乖 Perverse, obstinate; to contradict; cunning, crafty; in the coll., good, amiable, tractable; *guăi-diŏng*, 乖張 stubborn; *guăi-pék*, 乖癖 a perverse temper; COLL., *cêng guăi*, 盡乖 very good, as a child.

Guăi: A coll. word: old, hard, stringy, as vegetables.

Guăi: A coll. word: to turn aside, to stop at; *guăi diē lì*, call in; *guăi nguāi siá á*, call at my lowly dwelling.

Guāi 拐 To swindle, to deceive;

to entrap persons; *guāi piéng*, 拐骗 to gull; *guāi-dái*, 拐带 a kidnapper.

Guāi. 枴 An old man's staff as *guāi-tiông*, 枴杖.

Guāi, 踝 Also read *guài*, and *kuá*: q. v.: to shuffle, to limp.

Guái, 怪 Strange, marvelous, extraodinary; wonderful; to be offended at; *gŭi-guái*, 詭怪 trickish; *cáuk-guái*, 作怪 intelligent, as a child; *guái nguāi*, 怪我 offended at me; *mộh giéng-guái*, 莫見怪 don't be offended; *guái dék sẽ*, 怪的是 why, it is just so! (about as *huà dék sẽ*, q. v.)

Guái: A coll. word; a trick, a malicious art; *sāi guái*, to use black art.

Guák, 括 To include or embrace

as the ideas in a sentence, as in *bău-guák,* 包括.

Guák, 活 Also read *uăk,* q. v.: *guák-guák-giéu,* 活活叫 the croaking of frogs.

Guák, 刮 Coll. read *gáuk,* q. v.: to scrape off.

Guák, 豁 An open valley; to understand; liberal; *guák-dăk,* 豁達 perspicacious; COM. *guák-miĕng,* 豁免 to remit, as taxes.

Guăng, 官 An officer of government; the authorities; a title of respect; official business; *ngū - guăng,* 五官 the five senses,—eyes, ears, nose, mouth and eyebrows; *guăng-hū,* 官府 mandarins; *ùng ū báik guăng,* 文武百官 all civil and military officials; *guăng uá,* 官話 the court dialect, mandarin; *guǎng gái,* 官界 the official class; *láu-guǎng* 佬官 a husband's father.

Guǎng, 棺 To encoffin; a coffin, as *guǎng-mŭk,* 棺木 or *guǎng-cài,* 棺材.

Guǎng, 冠 Also read *guáng,* q. v.: a cap or bonnet as *guǎng-miēng,* 冠冕; *miēng guǎng,* 免冠 take off your caps! *huà-guǎng,* 華冠 a crown.

Guǎng, 觀 Also read *guáng,* q. v.: to observe, to travel and see; a sight, a spectacle; *gì-guǎng,* 奇觀 a rare sight; *guǎng-ing hŭk,* 觀音佛 the goddess of mercy, Kuanyin.

Guǎng, 鰥 An old bachelor; alone, single; *guǎng hŭ,* 鰥夫 a widower.

Guǎng, 關 Coll. *guŏng;* q. v.: to bar a door; to fasten, to fix;

a custom house; a limit, a boundary; results; a surname; *guăng-hiĕ,* 關係 consequences; *hāi-guăng,* 海關 maritime customs; *guăng-ngái,* (coll. *guăng-buáng,* 關礙) an obstacle, a difficulty in the way of; *guăng siĕk,* 關涉 concerned with.

Guāng, 管 A reed, a tube; a classifier of tubular things; to govern, to control; *guāng-li,* 管理 to rule, to manage; *guāng-gă,* 管家 a steward, butler; *guāng-sók,* 管束 to restrain, control; *guāng-â,* 管下 subject to (his) rule; *guāng só,* 管數 an accountant; COLL. *guāng mặ hŭk,* 管賣服 unmanageable.

Guāng, 館 An inn; a hall; a saloon; a school-room; *gŭng-*

guāng, 公館 a temporary official residence; suói-guāng, 稅館 a custom house; ī-guāng, 醫館 a hospital; guāng-dáing, 館店 a restaurant; huôi-guāng, 會館 an exchange, a guild; giêu guāng, 轎館 a sedan-men's lodge.

Guāng, 逭 To run away, to escape from; to revolve.

Guāng, 幹 Also read gáng, q. v.: the trunk of a tree, the stems or stalks of plants.

Guáng, 冠 Also read guăng, q. v.: to cap a young man at twenty or at marriage; able, superior.

Guáng, 貫 A string of cash, as ék guáng cièng; guáng chióng, 貫串 to thread, to string upon, met., connected, as ideas in a discourse.

Guáng, 慣 Coll. gáing, q. v.: accustomed to, habitual; COM., *guáng-liéng,* 慣練 drilled, practiced in; COLL., *cọ́ guáng,* 作慣 accustomed to doing it.

Guáng, 觀 Also read *guǎng,* q. v.: a hermitage, a retreat; to make known.

Guáng, 罐 An earthen pot, a water pot; *dà-guáng,* 茶罐 a teapot or kettle; *ngù-nèng-guáng,* 牛朧罐 a quart measure.

Guǎng, 灌 To water, to moisten; to collect; many, numerous; to water (meat), as *guáng cūi.* 灌水

Guàng: A coll. prefix, as in *guàng-guáng,* earthen pots; *guàng-guáng,* a bail, a handle.

Guáng, 扣 Read *kuáng,* and *siù;* to carry by a bail, or by a string; a bail, as of a pail, bucket, or basket; *guáng gèng,* 扛高 to lift high.

Gŭi, 龜 The tortoise; also to advance; adorned, ornate; *cūi gŭi,* 水龜 a water turtle; *gĭng gŭi,* 金龜 a species of beetle.

Gŭi, 歸 To revert to; to go home; a house, a native place, a refuge; *gŭi tiēng,* 歸天 deceased; *gŭi lŏi,* 歸彙 classified, arranged.

Gŭi, 飢 Read *gĭ*: as *bŏk lŏ gŭi,* 腹老飢 hungry.

Gŭi, 鬼 A ghost, apparition, spectre, devil; a miserable person, a wretch; COM., *gŭi-sìng,* 鬼神 spirits, gods; *gŭi-guái,* 鬼怪 hobgoblins; *huáng gŭi,* 犯鬼 possessed by demons; *gŭi huōi,* 鬼火 an ignis fatuus; *sŏ gŭi,* 鎖鬼 a foreign lock;

gūi niăh gūi, 鬼拿鬼 "devil catch devil",— two rogues cheating each other.

Gūi, 宄 Banditti, villains; *găng gūi,* 奸宄 domestic and foreign plots.

Gūi, 軌 An orbit; a law, a rule; *gūi dô,* 軌道 a constant path, a planet's orbit.

Gūi, 詭 To deceive, to cheat; to censure; odd; *gūi ê,* 詭異 strange, incredible; COM., *gūi guái,* 詭怪 wily, dishonest.

Gūi, 幾 Read *gī*: an interrogative of quantity,—how many, much, or many of? a few; *gūi ciáh,* 幾隻 how many, as persons or things; *gūi dēng,* 幾點 what o'clock is it? *gūi dēng cǔng,* 幾點鐘 how many hours is it? *gūi huòi,* 幾歲 several times.

Gŭk 掘 To excavate, to open, to hollow out; *gŭk chīng*, 掘深 to dig deep; *gŭk huāng-sṳ̆*, 掘番茹 to dig potatoes; *gŭk kī lì*, 掘起犁 to dig up.

Gŭk: A coll. word: thick, thickened; *chīng gŭk*, thin and thick; *gŭk ciáh gŭk*, very thick.

Gŭng, 公 The opposite of selfish or mean; public, universal; just, fair; a duke; a lord, a master; a term of respect and dignity (*for the deceased*); *gŭng-bàng*, 公平, *gŭng-lī* 公理, just, fair; *gŭng-nêng*, 公認 all agreeing; *gŭng-ô*, 公務 official business; *gŭng-sṳ̄*, 公所 a public place; *gŭng-céung*, 公衆 the public; *ngiê-gŭng*, 外公 maternal grandfather; *gŭng-sṳ̆*, 公私 public and private.

Gŭng, 工 Coll. read gĕng, q. v.: a laborer, artizan, mechanic; art, craft; an officer; *báik gŭng,* 百工 all kinds of work; *cĭng gŭng,* 精工 fine work.

Gŭng, 攻 To fight; to apply diligently; to stimulate the vital powers; *gŭng cṳ̆,* 攻書 to study hard; *gău gŭng,* 交攻 to join battle.

Gŭng, 功 Meritorious, worthy; honor; *gŭng-háu,* 功效 efficacious; *gŭng-lò,* 功勞 merit; *gŭng-mìng,* 功名 fame, high rank.

Gŭng, 蚣 An insect; *ngù gŭng,* 蜈蚣 the centipede: called in the coll. *ĕng ĕng,* q. v.

Gŭng, 君 A ruler, to rule; a prince; honorable, exalted; a term of respect (*for the living see gŭng p.* 341.) given to others and used by all persons, *hŭ-gŭng*, 夫君 my husband; *sạ-gŭng*, 細君 my wife; *gŭng-uòng*, 君王 the emperor; COM., *cŏng gŭng*, 尊君 your father; *gŭng-lòng*, 君郎 your son.

Gŭng, 軍 An army of 12,500 men; military, warlike; *gŭng ìng*, (coll. *gŭng iàng*,) 軍營 a camp; *dàu-gŭng*, 投軍 to enlist.

Gūng, 滾 Boiling, welling up; to boil; *gūng-cūi*, (or *tŏng*,) 滾水 boiling water; *gūng-ciéng*, 滾箭 hasty, urgent; *páh gūng-dāu*, 拍滾斗 to turn a somersault.

Gùng, 羣 A flock a herd; a concourse, a company; a plural number; *gùng-sĕng*, 羣生 all living; *gùng-gŭ*, 羣居 to dwell together; *gùng-dêng*, 羣陣 a group, a flock.

Gùng, 裙 A skirt; dŭng-gùng, 中裙 petticoats; ùi-sĭng gùng, 圍身裙 an apron.

Gùng, 拳 Read guòng: the fist as gùng-tàu, 拳頭.

Gŭng, 弓 A bow; archery; to measure; gŭng-ciéng, 弓箭 bow and arrows; gŭng-hièng, 弓弦 a bow string.

Gŭng, 芎 A medicinal plant, used to purify the blood.

Gŭng, 躬 One's person, personally.

Gŭng, 恭 To respect, respectful, courteous; gŭng-géng, 恭敬 to respect, to venerate.

Gŭng, 供, Read géung, q. v.: to supply with; to provide, to succour; to give in evidence; COM.. kēu-gŭng, 口供 verbal evidence; gŭng-gĕk, 供給 to furnish, to succour;

Gŭng, 龔 Read gŭng: a surname; respectful, reverential; to give.

Gŭng, 宮 A mansion; the palace. gŭng-dáing, 宮殿 a palace; gŭng-uōng-diĕ, 宮宛裏 the imperial harem; gŭng-dĭng, 宮燈 a hexagonal lantern.

Gŭng, 斤 A pound, varying from 12 to 21 oz., the standard being 16 oz., and about equal to the English pound; céuk gŭng, 足斤 a full pound; hṳ̆ gŭng, 虛斤 a pound of 12 oz.

Gŭng, 筋 A sinew, a muscle; muscular, strong; háik gŭng, 血筋 veins.

Gŭng, 根 Read gŏng, q. v.: the roots of plants, the origin; a foundation; gŭng-dā, 根底 a support, as one's wealth; origin, source of.

Gŭng, 跟 Read gŏng: the heel;

to follow up; to pursue an inquiry; *gŭng-sùi*, 跟隨 to follow; attendants; *gŭng giêu*, 跟橋 a sedan attendant; COLL., *gŭng á-dāu*, 跟後斗 to follow on behind.

Gŭng, 斤 Formerly used for *gŭng* (a catty), now usually an adz, or a plane.

Gŭng, 巾 A neck cloth; a napkin, a handkerchief; COM., *chiù-gŭng*, 手巾 a towel, *dóh-gŭng*, 棹巾 a napkin; *gáng-gŭng* 汗巾 a handkerchief.

Gŭng, 拱 To join the hands before the breast when bowing; to encircle; *gŭng-hī*, 拱喜 joy to you! congratulate you!

Gùng, 窮 Poor, destitute; to search thoroughly; to exhaust; COM., *gùng-kŭ*, 窮苦 poor and miserable; *ù gùng* céng, 無窮盡 exhaustless; gùng-géu, 窮究 to investigate thoroughly.

Guŏ, 鍋 A saucepan; a skillet, a deep frying pan; hài-guŏ, 孩鍋 earthen pots or basins, same as buák; ngùng-guŏ, 銀鍋 a crucible.

Guŏ, 過 Usually read guó, q. v.: to pass by; in the coll., too much, excessive; cū kák guŏ, 煮恰過 boiled too much; guŏ só, 過燥 to dry.

Guō, 果 Coll. read guōi, q. v.: fruits with seeds or kernels; to over come, to surpass; to conclude; courageous; really, truly; báik guō, 百果 all kinds of fruit; guō-iòng, 果然 or ù̀ - guō, 如果 certainly, truly; COLL., guō cóng, 果俊 truly, excellent.

Guó 過 Also read guŏ, q. v.: to exceed, to pass along; to spend, as time; to transgress; an error; denotes past time; the pluperfect; a sign of comparison—the more, rather, much, great; COM., guó sié, 過世 to die, deceased; nàng guó, 難過 hard to pass by or over; gĭng guó, 經過 to pass by; guó ngū, 過午 past noon; guó-sék, 過失 a transgression; tŏ guó muòng, 討過門 to take a wife; gó guó, 故過 a comparative, the more, rather; kák guó, 恰過 too much, excessive; guó diô, 過路 to pass by; guó buŏ, 過哺 to pass a night; mò dék guó, 毛的過 impassable.

Guó, 句 Read géṳ: a stop in reading, a comma; a sentence;

a classifier of phrases; COLL., *ng siàng guó*, 怀成句 poorly composed.

Guóh, 擴 To expand; *met.*, to enlarge the mind.

Guóh, 郭 A surname; the suburbs of a city.

Guóh, 廓 to enlarge as *kăi guóh*, 開郭.

Guóh, 椁 Another coffin; *sĭk guóh*, 石椁 a sarcophagus.

Guŏh, 局 A square on a chessboard; an important establishment; to delude, to bait; COLL., complete; *gŭng-cŏng guŏh*, 軍裝局 an arsenal; *cièng guŏh*, 錢局 or *bō-hók guŏh*, 寶福局 a mint; *éng cṳ̆ guŏh*, 印書局 a printing establishment; *cṳ̆ ngiê guŏh*, 諮議局 the deliberative assembly; *guŏh piéng*, 局騙 to gull one;

gáh guŏh, 格局 one's appearance; *giék guŏh,* 結局 result; *sák guŏh,* 煞局 finale.

Guōi 果 Read *guō*: *guōi-cī,* 果子 fruits; *guōi-cī-tăng,* 果子攤 fruit stalls.

Guōi, 粿 To cleanse rice; steamed rice cakes; *tòng guōi,* 糖粿 steamed cake of rice and red sugar; *huăng-sù guōi,* 番茹粿 steamed cakes of potato flour.

Guōi, 改 Read *gāi*: to change, to alter the form of; to correct, as essays; *guōi gō,* 改稿 to correct proof; *guōi ciáng,* 改正 to alter to correct form.

Guói, 劊 To cut off, to decapitate; *guói-cŭ-chiŭ,* 劊子手 an executioner.

Guói, 澮 A rill in a field; *gĕu-guói,* 溝澮 ditches and pools.

Guói 獪 Crafty, fraudulent, as

giēu-guói, (gāu-guái) 狡獪.

Guói, 髻 Read gié; the coiffure of Chinese women.

Guói: A coll. word; to lean, to rest, as the hand or foot on something.

Guók, 國 A state, country, kingdom; a nation, a people; guók-gŭng, 國君 a sovereign; guók-gă, 國家 the state; Dáichĭng guók, 大清國 China; buŏng guók, 本國 native country; guók mìng, 國民 the nation; guóh - céng, 國政 the government.

Guók, 蟈 A small green frog; COLL., guók-dáẹng, also called hà-mà, 蝦蟆.

Guók, 蕨 Read kuók: an edible fern.

Guók, 笏 Read huók: a piece of ink; a classifier for ink.

Guŏk: A section, a bit: a classifier of long things; as wood; the whole length is a *huók*, while the half length is a *guŏk*.

Guŏng, 光 Light, splendour, brilliant, illustrious; honor, éclat; *guŏng áng*, 光暗 light and dark; *guŏng-gīng*, 光景 the prospect, circumstances; COLL., *guŏng-gŏk*, 光滑 slippery; *guŏng-biăng*, 光餅 wheaten biscuits; *tiĕng guŏng-cā*, 天光早 early dawn.

Guŏng, 胱 The bladder, called *bòng-guŏng*, 膀光.

Guŏng, 關 Read *guăng*; to inclose, to confine; to shut, as a door; *guŏng găng*, 關監 to imprison; *guŏng muòng*, 關門 to shut a door.

Guŏng, 卷, 捲 Spiral, curled,

rolled up; a classifier of things rolled up; the second also read *guóng*, q. v.

Guōng, 廣 COLL. *kuōng*, q. v.: diffuse; COM., *Guōng-děng*, 廣東 Canton; *guōng-kuák*, 廣闊 wide, spacious; *guōng-gău*, 廣交 a wide circle of friends.

Guōng, 鑛 The ore of iron and other metals; *tiék guōng*, 鐵鑛 iron ore; *gĭng guōng*, 金鑛 gold ore.

Guōng, 管 Read *guāng*; as in *cŭi guōng*, 水管 a water dipper; *mĭ-guōng*, 米管 a rice measure; *huōi-guōng*, 火管 a blower.

Guóng, 卷 A roll, a manuscript, a scroll; a section or division of a book; a classifier of books; *cŭ guóng*, 書卷 books; *guōng nê*, 卷二 Vol. II; *ĭ cŭ-guóng* hō, 伊書卷好 he is well-read.

Guóng, 眷 To love, to care for; relative, kindred; *guóng-gó*, 眷顧 to care for tenderly; *gă-guóng*, 家眷 one's family or household.

Guóng, 劵 A bond, a deed; a book, a section; *kié-guóng*, 契劵 deeds, agreements.

Guòng, 權 The weight of the steelyard; to balance, to equalize; power, influence; as *guòng-sié* 權勢; *chọ-guòng*, 操權 to wield power; *guòng-lê*, 權利 rights; privilege.

Guòng, 顴 The cheek bones.

Guòng, 惓 Careful, earnest, diligent.

Guòng 拳 COLL.; read *gùng*, q. v.: the fist; attentive.

Guòng, 狂 Mad, raving; rash, imprudent; *diĕng-guòng*, 顛狂

mad, crazy; *guòng-hŭng*, 狂風 a violent wind; *huák guòng*, 發狂 delirious.

Guòng: A coll. word; large, of a large denomination; *guòng piéu*, large bank-bills.

Guóng, 倦 Tired, fatigued; *pī-guóng*, 疲倦 fagged out.

Guóng, 誑 Read *guóng*: wild talk, to deceive, as *kĭ guóng* 欺誑; *guóng-ngiòng*, 誑言 lying words.

Hă, 哈 Read *hák* and *hăk*: *hă-hă-chiéu*, 哈哈笑 noise of laughing.

Há 孝 Read *háu*: mourning, funereal; *dái há*, 帶孝 to wear mourning.

Hà, 霞 Clouds tinged with red; vapor, smokiness; *èng hà*, 紅霞 crimson clouds.

Hà, 瘕 A female complaint;

hùng hà, 痕瘕 a cicatrix. Read *gā*: chronic pain in the stomach.

Hà, 遐 Remote, distant; why, what.

Hà, 蝦 Small crustaceans; shrimps, etc.; *hà-mà*, 蝦蟆 a toad; *hà-mī*, 蝦米 dried shrimps.

Hà: A coll. word; as in *hà-diāng*, soon, shortly; *hà-diāng kó*, will go shortly.

Hā, 下 Coll. read *á*, q. v.: below, down, bottom, inferior, vulgar; to descend; to fall, as rain; as a verb, in the Classics read *ū*; *siòng hā*, 上下 above and below; *káik-hā*, 刻下 at this instant; *hā ū*, 下雨 to rain; *hā cūng*, 下種 to plant seeds; *met.*, to inocculate; *góh hā*, 閣下 or *dài hā*, 臺下

your excellency! *há liù*, 下流 inferior person or business.

Há, 夏 Summer; a mansion; name of a dynasty; *dṳng há*, 中夏 China; *há tiĕng*, 夏天 the summer season; *lĭk há*, 立夏 the beginning of summer.

Há, 厦 A mansion; a side room; *siá há*, 舍厦 or *á 下* my humble dwelling.

Há, 暇 Leisure, relaxation; self-indulgence.

Há: A coll. word; to transport in a boat or carriage; *há mī*, to transport rice.

Hạ̄, 睍 Read *ngạ̄:* to look askance at; *hạ̄ mọ̄*, 睍娼 to cast hateful glances at.

Hạ̄, 蟹 Also read *hāi* and *hái*: a crab; *mò há* 毛蟹 crab with hairy claws,

Hạ̤: A coll. word: to sob, to

Há̤: A coll. word: as in *hạ lŏh lì*, to sag down.

Hae̤: A coll. word: to call out, to vociferate; *háe̤ huāng-tiĕng*, to cry loud enough to turn the heavens.

Háe̤: A coll. word: to shame, to disgrace; *háe̤ nè̤ng mò̤ méng-puòi*, to reproach one for being shameless.

Háe̤k: 蓄 Read *héuk*: to collect, to get or buy for use; *háe̤k ngiĕk*, 蓄業 to purchase property.

Háe̤ng, 譽 Read *héng*: to swell up as *háe̤ng kī-lì*, 譽起梨

Háe̤ng, 巷 A lane; a street of dwellings; *gă-háe̤ng* 街巷 streets and alleys.

Háe̤ng, 烚 Read *hṳ̆ng*: to throw out heat.

Hài 359

Hạh: A coll. word: as in *hạ-hạh*, to sneer at, to jeer.

Hăi, 哈 To laugh and joke; in the coll., an exclamation.

Hāi, 海 The sea, ocean; maritime; marine: COM., *hāi-iòng,* 海洋 the ocean; *hāi-huòng,* 海防 the superintendent of maritime customs; *hāi-guăng,* 海國 a custom house.

Hāi, 醢 Seasoned, minced meat; to simmer.

Hài, 孩 A child, youth; generally applied to boys; *siĕu-hài,* 小孩 little children.

Hài, 骸 Bones of the human frame; *hài-gáuk,* 骸骨 human bones, a skeleton.

Hài, 諧 To harmonize, as *huò-hài,* 和諧.

Hài, 硋 A coll. character; crockery, as *hài-ké,* 硋器.

Hâi, 亥 A horary character, the 12th of the Branches; *hâi nièng,* 亥年 years of the cycle containing this character; *hâi nguŏk,* 亥月 the 10th month; *hâi sì,* 亥時 from 9 to 11 P. M.

Hâi, 閡 Also read *ngâi:* to shut, to prevent entrance; stopped, obstructed.

Hâi, 械 Military weapons as *ké-hâi,* 器械.

Hâi, 懈, 解 Remiss, slow, inattentive; the 2nd read *gāi* and *gá,* q. v.: *hâi-dâi,* 懈怠 lazily, slowly.

Hâi, 廨 Read *gāi* and *gái:* a hall, a suite of rooms.

Hâi 獬 A fabulous animal, as *hâi-câi,* 獬豸 the lion-unicorn, embroidered on the robes of censors and judges; *met.,* haughty, stern.

Hâi, 喊 Also read *hái*; to cry out, to bawl; in the coll., stop that! you must not!

Hâi, 害 To injure, to prejudice; calamitous; a sense or fear of, a feeling; COM., *càng-hâi,* 殘害 to injure; *lê-hâi,* 利害 formidable; *cāi-hâi,* 災害 calamity. Read *hăk:* why not? how not?

Háik, 血 Read *hiĕk:* blood; *háik-măh,* 血脈 blood and pulse; *met.,* race, stock; *háik-kĕ,* 血氣 blood and breath,— vigor, bodily stamina; *háik-gâng,* 血汗 bloody sweat; *met.,* excessive toil.

Háik, 黑 Black, sooty, obscure; dull; *met.,* wicked, malicious. COM. *háik-áng,* 黑暗 pitchy dark.

Háik, 赫 Bright, luminous, like

a fire or sun; angry; *háik-nô,* 赫怒 very angry; *háik-háik,* 赫赫 fiery, as the sky in a drought; glorious, effulgent.

Háik, 嚇 Coll. read *hiáh*, q. v.: *háik cá,* 嚇詐 to terrify by threats.

Háing, 橫 Also read *huàng*, q. v.: perverse, mulish; COLL. *iā háing,* 野橫 insufferably mulish.

Háing, 荇 As *háing chái,* 荇菜 a kind of spinach.

Háing, 幸 Fortunate, lucky; to hope, to long for; to rejoice: *hǒ-háing,* 何幸 how so lucky? COLL. *háing-dék,* 幸的 fortunately.

Háing, 倖 Lucky, fortunate; *hiĕu - háing,* 徼倖 a lucky hit.

Háing, 行 Also read *hèng* and

hòng, and in coll. *òng* and *giàng*, q. v.: actions, conduct; COM., *dáik-hâing*, 德行 virtious deeds; *pīng-hâing* 品行 conduct, character.

Hâing, 杏 A kind of plum; *hâing ìng*, 杏仁 almonds.

Hâiu, 候 To wait; to inquire for; to congratulate; a time, as *sì-hâiu*, 時候; *sêu-hâiu*, 伺候 to serve; *hâiu-buō*, 候補 to wait for appointment.

Hâiu, 後 Coll. read *háu* and *áu*, q. v.: after in time; then, next, posterity; *cièng-hâiu*, 前後 before and after.

Hâiu, 堠 A bank or tumulus, used to make fire signals on.

Hâiu, 厚 Liberal, kind; well, very; substantial; rich, as soil; to esteem; COM., *chīng hâiu*, 親厚 intimate; *hâiu-*

dái, 厚待 to treat well; háiu é, 厚味 a rich flavor; háiu é, 厚意 a generous mind.

Háiu, 后 A queen, a ruler, a tributary; sovereign; behind; huòng-háiu, 皇后 the Empress; huòng-tái-háiu, 皇太后 the Empress Dowager.

Háiu, 逅 Pleased to meet, as hái háiu, 邂逅.

Hăk, 瞎 Blind; met., ignorant, uneducated: COM., hăk-cṳ̆, 瞎子 a blind person.

Hăk, 喝 To call out loudly; to shout at; to reprove, to reprimand, etc.

Hăk, A coll. word: hăk-ché, to sneeze.

Hăk, 合 To unite, to close, to collect, suitable, a pair; united together, with; a measure, 1/10 of a cĭng; COLL., suitable, cheap; as hăk-ngì, 合宜 and hăk-sék; huò-hăk. 利合 harmonious; hăk-gùng, 合羣 a united people; hăk-sièng, 合蟾 hinges; siŏh hăk 一合 a pair.

Hăk, 洽 To harmonize; united, blending.

Hăk, 闔 A leaf of a door, a two-leaved door; a family: COM., hăk-gă, 闔家 a whole family.

Hăk, 轄 A linch pin; to regulate, to control; guāng-hăk, 管轄 to govern.

Hăng, 邯 As dăng-hăng, 諽邯 a city in Hupeh. Read hàny, as hàng dăng 邯鄲 a district in Chili. Read hâng as in hâng-dâng 邯淡 full, abundant.

Hăng, 蚶 A salt water cockle; a small clam; hăng-káek, 蚶亮 clam shells.

Hăng, 憨 Silly, stupid as *ngù hăng,* 愚憨 also *giĕu-géu.*

Hăng, A coll. word as *hăng-diù,* a closet, a food-safe.

Hăng, 罕 Rare, scarce, seldom; a bird or rabbit net; COM., *hāng-giéng,* 罕見 rarely seen; *hāng-iŭ,* 罕有 scarce, rare; *hāng-giāng,* 罕仔 an only child.

Hāng, 悍 An energetic disposition; fearless; hasty, cruel, as *hāng áuk* 悍惡.

Hāng, 旰 Sunset, evening; *sièu hāng,* 宵旰 night and day.

Hāng, 喊 Angry cries; to call for; to vociferate; *hāng géu,* 喊救 to call for help; *hāng giéu,* 喊叫 to cry out, to bawl.

Háng, 漢 Chinese, as *ŏh háng ùng,* 學漢文 to study Chinese; *tiĕng háng,* 天漢 the

Milky Way,—in poetry called *ngùng háng*, 銀漢 silvery river: COM., *muāng háng*, 滿漢 Manchus and Chinese; COLL., *háng nèng*, 漢仆 the Chinese; *háng mā*, 漢馬 the stature; *ngàung háng*, 歇漢 stupid.

Háng: A coll. word: to suppose, as *háng-dĕk*; to ask, to request; to give notice, to inform; *háng dáik cŏi*, to confess a fault; *háng siá*, to express thanks; *háng kī-dâeng*, to thank one for his trouble.

Hàng, 閑 A barrier, a bar, an inclosure; to obstruct; to regulate by law; to forbid; *huòng hàng*, 防閑 to guard against.

Hàng, 咸 All, jointly, altogether; completely; always; all around. Used in letter writing interchangeably with 緘 q. v.

Hàng, 閒 Also read *găng,* q. v.: leisure, rest; unoccupied: COM., *ăng-hàng,* 安閒 repose, quiet.

Hàng, 嫺 Skilled, accustomed to; elegant; refined; *hàng ngā,* 嫺雅 polished, elegant; COM., *hàng-sŭk* 嫺熟 versed in.

Hàng, 緘 To close or bind up to seal; *nôi séng ék hàng,* 內信一緘 the enclosed letter; *ngŭk hàng,* 玉緘 your esteemed favor; an epistolary phrase

Hàng, 函 To contain, to enfold, to envelope; a letter; COM., *băn-hàng,* 包函 to infold, to contain; magnanimous.

Hàng, 鹹 Coll. read *gèng,* q. v.: saltish, as salt water; salted, preserved in brine.

Hàng, 含 To hold something in

Hàng   369

the mouth; to contain; in the coll., incomplete, confused; COM., *baŭ hàng*, 包含 to hold, to contain; *hàng-chiéu*, 含笑 to smile; *hàng tiè*, 含啼 to be in tears; *hàng-hàng*, 含含 incomplete; *hàng-mìng*, 含眠 or *hàng-káung*, 含困 half asleep; *hàng áng-buŏ*, 含暗哺 dusk, evening.

Hàng, 銜 Usually read *gàng*: official rank, station, as *hàng-tàu*, 銜頭; *ĭ sié-ngḣ hàng-tàu*, 伊世毛銜頭 what is his official rank?

Hàng, 韓 A feudal state of the Chow dynasty; a surname.

Hàng, 涵 Submerged; to leak; marshy; to contain. as *hàng-ùng*, 涵容; *hàng iōng*, 涵養 kind, meek.

Hàng, 寒 Cold, wintry; shivering; poor; my, mine; *hàng tiēng*, 寒天 winter; *hàng só*, 寒素 unpretending; COM. *hàng-sṳ̄*, 寒暑 cold and heat; *hàng-lēng*, 寒冷 shivering; *hŭng-hàng*, 風寒 a cold; *hàng-gă*, 寒家 my family; *hàng-sĭng*, 寒心 discouraged.

Hàng: A coll. word: to consume, to burn up; *hàng huŏi dŏi*, to burn a heap of refuse.

Hàng: A coll. word: a bride's furniture, as *hàng gá*; *hàng-gá dáing*, a furnishing shop.

Hàng, 翰 Usually read *hàng*: the Imperial College as *hàng-lìng-iêng*, 翰林院 or *guăng*.

Hâng, 翰 Writings; a plume or quill to write with; *cṳ̌ hâng*, 書翰 written with a pen; *hâng mĕk* 翰墨 literary.

Hâng, 陷 To fall down or into;

Hău   371

overwhelmed, ruined; to involve another; *háng gói*, 陷櫃 criminal's cage; *háng hái*, 陷害 to inveigle one.

Háng, 餡 Coll. read *áng:* pastry, stuffed cakes.

Háng, 銲 Coll. read *áng*, q. v.: to solder; *háng iŏh*, 銲藥 soldering.

Háng, 頷 The jaws, the chops; *hâ háng*, 下頷 the chin.

Háng, 含 Read *hàng;* to close partially; *muòng ná háng lā*, 門佛含禮 shut the doors partly—the leaves overlapping.

Hău, 哮 To howl, bellow, roar, grunt; as beasts when angry; to pant; *hău chuāng*, 哮喘 asthma.

Hău, 薅 Read *gŏ;* to weed; *hău chāu*, 薅草 to pull grass.

Hāu, 吼 The cries of animals, as cattle and feline animals; *sāi hāu,* 獅吼 a lion roaring.

Hāu: A coll. word; to call one, to direct to do, to inform one; *hāu ĭ lì,* tell him to come; *kó̤ hāu,* go and call him; *hāu siŏh hiŏk,* to call a while.

Háu, 孝 Used for the coll. *há,* q. v.: filial duty, respect to parents; mourning for parents; COM., *háu-sóng,* 孝順 dutiful to parents; *háu-géng* 孝敬 to obey and revere; *bók hiu,* 不孝 unfilial.

Háu 鱟 The king crab; COLL., *háu-giĕ* 鱟主 a crab-shell dipper.

Háu, 效 To imitate, to copy, to verify; effects, results, COM., *háu ngiéng,* 效驗 fulfilled; *giĕng háu,* 見效 efficacious.

Háu, 効 To toil, to labor, to imitate, effects, results; COM., *găng-háu,* 功効 meritorious effort.

Háu, 校 Also read *gáu,* q. v.: a school, a college, as *hŏk háu,* 學校

Háu, 後 Read *háiu; háu-săng,* 後生 young, youth, between 16 and 30 years of age; *háu-săng-giăng,* 後生仔 young persons.

Háuk, 㨃 Read *káuk;* to pound, to beat with a stick.

Háung, 桁 Read *hèng;* floor beams, as *dé bàng háung,* 地棚桁

Háung, 恨 Indignation, resentment; dislike, hatred; vexed, sorry; *kō̤ háung* 可恨 detestable; *hièng-háung,* 嫌恨 to hate.

Háung, 項 A surname; great

the nape of the neck; used for a species, class, etc.. In the coll., a sum of money; funds; *ciòh háung,* 借項 borrowed money; *gŭng-háung,* 公項 public funds; *kiéng háung,* 欠項 debts.

Háung, 行 Usually read *hèng* and *hâing,* q. v.; strong, powerful.

Hé, 懿 Mild, virtuous, excellent; *hé-mī,* 懿美 mild and excellent.

Hé, 亟 Usually read *gék,* q. v.: frequently; repeatedly; hasty.

Hĕ, 齁 Read *kuŏ:* to emit breath.

Hĕ, A coll. word: eaten; *hĕ chĭng-chū,* all eaten up clean.

Hè, 喉 Read *hèu;* also read *hò* in the coll. q. v.: *hò-lèng,* 喉嚨 the windpipe, the throat.

Hè: A coll. word: to steam; *hè*

Hék 375

sŭk, to steam it done; *hè ièk*, to warm food.

Hék: A coll. word: to sniff, to snuff up.

Hék, 翕 To unite, to collect; to revile, to slander as *huò hék*, 和翕,

Hék, 燙 Hot, burning; coll. to steam, to smother, to take a sweat; *hék buông*, 燙飯 to cover and steam rice—after cooking it; *hék ák-giăng* 燙鴨仔 to hatch ducklings by heat, (incubating.)

Hék, 洫 A moat, a sluice for water; overflowing.

Hék, 淢 Read *mĭk*: to flow rapidly; a current.

Hék, 侐 Quiet, silent, taciturn; *hék cêng*, 侐靜 peaceful, undisturbed.

Hék: A coll. euphonic prefix, as

in *hék hiék*, to dry by the fire; *hék hók*, to brush off.

Hĕk, 獲 Also spoken *lĕk*, q. v.: to take in hunting; to catch thieves as *hĕk dô̤*, 獲盜; to get, to obtain, as knowledge. In the coll. denotes cause, means, manner or instrument; with, by, in use of; to use, to employ; *hĕk cṳ̆ gá nè̤ng*, 獲書敎仈 to teach people by books.

Hĕk, 畫 Also read, in coll., *uâ*, q. v.: to draw, to paint, to draw a plan: COM., *cê hĕk*, 字畫 the strokes forming a a character.

Hĕk, 劃 To carve, to engrave; to cut glass; an engraver.

Hĕk, 或 Uncertain, doubtful; perhaps, if, perchance; a certain person as *hĕk ìng* or *hĕk-ciă*, 或者. When repeated means either—or, this—that, *hĕk cuòi,* 或聚 *hĕk huòi,* 或回; *hĕk-chiā,* 或且 probably, perhaps.

Hĕk, 惑 To deceive, to lead astray; to excite doubt or suspicion; COM., *ièu-hĕk,* 誘惑 or *mì-hĕk,* 迷惑 to delude.

Hĕk, 趞 Read *háik:* to pant, to puff, to gasp for breath; *kĕ-hĕk,* 氣趞 panting; *hĕk sïŏh hĕk,* 趞一趞 to take a breathing spell.

Hĕk: A coll. word: to fuse metals, to smelt; *hĕk gĭng,* to smelt gold.

Hĕng, 亨 To pervade, to penetrate; prosperous, successful as *hĕng-tŭng,* 亨通.

Hĕng, 很 Read *hōng:* also *tēng,* a corruption of *hĕng:* a sign of the superlative, very much, great, exceeding as *hēng sà*, 很價; *hēng hó* 很好 very good, all the better; *dăng hēng (tēng) lò*, 佇很囉 now we are at a sad pass! (slang); *hēng-hēng á* 很很下 severely, harshly; *heng-hēng sīng*, 很很心 harsh, unfeeling; *bāng iā hēng*, 病予很 very sick.

Héng, 興 Read *hīng*, q. v.: to desire; a desire, a passion delighted with; COM., *sī héng*, 詩興 poetical inspiration; *dū héng*, 賭興 a passion for gambling.

Hèng, 行 Also read *háing*, *hâung*, *hòng*, and *òng*; in the coll. *giàng*, q. v.: to go, to proceed; to do; to appeal a case; the elements; COM., *hèng-úi*, 行為 to do, to act; *hèng-ĭ*, 行醫 to practice medicine; *hèng sêu*,

行事, or *hèng báing*, 行辦 to transact business; *hèng lā*, 行禮 to salute; *hèng siēng*, 行善 to act virtuously; *hèng-lī*, 行李 luggage; *piéng hèng*, 遍行 to go all around; *hèng hŏ sèu*, 行好事 to be benevolent.

Hèng, 衡 A balance; to weigh; transverse.

Hèng, 恆, 恒 Constant, according to rule, or law; persevering; *hèng-sīng*, 恆心 the mind constant, as in virtue.

Hèng, 宏 Wide, extensive; grand, as a prospect; *hèng guōng*, 宏廣 spacious.

Hèng, 還 Read *huàng*; same as *dèng*, q. v.: to restore, to return, to pay back; to offer a lower price, as *hèng gá*, 還價; *dò dèng i̇́*, 掏還伊 take and return it; *hèng lāu*, 還了 returned; *hèng chìng-chú*, 還清楚 fully paid up.

Hèng: A coll. word: suspended, hanging down, as cord; *hèng lòh lì*, hanging down.

Héng: A coll. word: reserved, taciturn, as *hêng-hêng*.

Hěng, 烘 Read *hùng*; to toast; to warm at the fire, as *hěng-huōi*, 烘火; *hěng chiŭ*, 烘手 to warm the hands; *hěng bău*, 烘包 to toast bread.

Hěng, 魟 Read *gŭng*, or *hùng*: a saltwater, scaleless fish.

Hèu 痔 Read *hău*: the asthma; *hèu cŭ*, 痔子 an asthmatic.

Hèu, 侯 A marquis; a surname; *cŭ-hèu*, 諸侯 a petty prince.

Hèu, 喉 Coll. read *hĕ* and *hò*, q. v.: the throat; *hèu ngò*, 喉蛾 the quinsy; *băh hèu*, 白喉 diphtheria.

Héung 381

Héu, 猴 Coll. read *gàu*, q. v.: a monkey, an ape.

Héu, 煦 The genial warmth of the sun; kind, gracious, as *héu-héu*, 煦煦.

Héu, 呴 Usually read *hṳ́*, to blow with the mouth.

Heu, 酗 Mad with drink; *héu ciū*, 酗酒 delirium tremens.

Héuk, 畜 To rear, to feed; to domesticate cattle; domestic animals as *sĕng-héuk*, 牲畜.

Héuk, 蓄 To accumulate, to hoard; *còng-héuk*, 藏蓄 to nourish; good vegetables, as *cī héuk*, 旨蓄; COM., *cék-héuk*, 積蓄 to amass.

Héung, 釁 To offer blood in sacrifice; an offense, a wrong; a pretext for a quarrel as *héung-kek*, 釁隙; *hiĕk-héung*, 挟釁 to avenge.

Hĭ, 非 Not, negative; not so, opposite; not right; false, bad; COM., *sĕ hĭ*, 是非 yes and no; right and wrong.

Hĭ, 希 Few, rare; to hope, to desire, as *hĭ-uóng* 希望; *hĭ-hāng*, 希罕 scarce, few.

Hĭ, 熙 Flourishing, prospering, as *hĭ huò*, 熙和; *hĭ chŭng dà*, 熙春茶 Hyson tea; *hĭ diêu*, 熙朝 a flourishing dynasty; *Kŏng-hĭ*, 康熙 the Emperor Kang-hi, A. D. 1662—1723.

Hĭ, 稀 Open, wide apart; loose; careless, remiss; *hĭ-hĭ*, 稀稀 coarse, as cloth.

Hĭ, 嬉 Pretty, handsome; sports or games of children, as *hĭ-hié*, 嬉戲; COM., *hĭ-chiéu*, 嬉笑 playing and laughing.

Hĭ, 妃 A partner, a consort; *gŭng-hĭ*, 宮妃 imperial concubines; *hĭ-bĭng,* 妃嬪 a maid of honor.

Hĭ, 嘻 The sound of mirth; in harmony, delighted; *hĭ-hĭ-chiéu,* 嘻嘻笑 to laugh pleasantly.

Hĭ, 飛 Coll. *buŏi,* q. v.: to fly, to flit; *hĭ-neu,* 飛鳥 birds.

Hĭ, 喜 Pleased, as *huăng-hĭ,* 歡喜; to give joy to, to congratulate as *gŭng-hĭ,* 恭喜; *hĭ-séu,* 喜事 a joyful event.

Hiă, 罅 Read *há,* and *chá;* to open, to crack open, as wood in drying; yawning, gaping as *hiă-hiă kŭi,* 罅罅開; *ngū hiă,* 五罅 scattered, in utter confusion.

Hiā: A coll. word: that, that one; the other, the opposite of *ciā* (this); very, exceedingly; *hiā nęng,* that person; *hiā kuāng*, that way, shape or fashion; *hiā huòi*, or *hiā ngh̀*, that time or thing! *hiā má ciáh sẽ má*, such scolding is scolding indeed!

Hiáh, 嚇 Read *hiák*; an angry tone, to threaten, to frighten, as *hiáh chǎ* 嚇叱.

Hiák: A coll. word: to deceive, to cozen, to cheat.

Hiák: A coll. word: to fall forward or backward; to flap a door as *hiák guó*.

Hiăng 兄 Read *hĭng*, q. v.: an elder brother; *hiăng-sō*, 兄嫂 elder brother's wife.

Hiè, 廢 A house in ruins; to abandon when half done, as *buáng dù ì hiè*, 半途而廢; *huōng-hiè*, 荒廢 desolate; *hiè-chiē*, 廢地 obsolete.

Hiè, 費 To spend, to use; expense, cost; waste; *dóng-hiè*, 動費 to spend money; *huă-hiè*, 花費 to squander; *căk hiè*, 雜費 miscellaneous expenses; *lô-hiè*, 路費 traveling expenses.

Hiè, 戲 To sport; a play, a comedy; *có hiè*, 做戲 to play, as actors.

Hiè, 肺 The lungs; *hiè-lò*, 肺癆 consumption of the lungs.

Hiè, 奚 Why? how? a page to an officer as *duâi hiè*, 大奚 (spoken *iè*); a waiting maid.

Hiè, 攜 To lead by the hand, as *hiè tì*, 攜提.

Hiè, 惠 Gracious; benevolent; charity; *ŏng-hiè*, 恩惠 grace, mercy; *sêng*, or *hâiu-hiè*, 厚惠 your great favor; an epistolary phrase.

Hiè, 繫 To tie, to bind; to continue; *guăng-hié,* 關繫 important results, consequences involved.

Hié, 慧 Intelligent, wise; *dé-hié,* 智慧 wise, discerning; wisdom.

Hiĕk, 熁 Read *hiĕk;* heat rising up, as *hiĕk siöng* 熁上; *hiĕk diŏh,* 熁着 burnt; *hiĕk-siŏh* 熁石 loadstone, magnet.

Hiĕk, 血 Coll. read *háik,* q. v.: blood.

Hiĕk, 俠 Generous, noble-minded, as *hiĕk-ké,* 俠氣; *hò-hiĕk,* 豪俠 a hero.

Hiĕk, 挾 Used in coll. for *gĕk,* q. v.: to carry under the arm; to conceal; arrogant; *hiĕk-hièng,* 挾嫌 to cherish hatred.

Hiĕk, 脅 The sides of the body; the ribs; to intimidate, as *páik hiĕk,* 迫脅.

Hiĕk, 穴 A cave, formerly used for dwellings; a den, a hole, as *kūng-hiĕk*, 孔穴; *muó-hiĕk*, 墓穴 graves, vaults.

Hiĕk, 協 Agreement, harmony; united; *hiĕk-dài*, 協臺 a brigadier.

Hiĕk, 頁 The head; in the coll. the numeral for leaves of books or flowers, etc.

Hiĕng, 掀 Read *hŭng:* to remove, as a cover; for which *huăng* is more commonly used.

Hiĕng 顯 Light, manifest; *hiĕng-mìng*, 顯明 or *hiĕng-hiĕng*, 顯現 to make manifest.

Hiĕng, 險 A precipice; dangerous, insecure, in danger; *met.*, corrupt, wicked; *ngùi-hiĕng*, 危險 dangerous.

Hiĕng, 炫 Brilliant, dazzling.

Hièng: A coll. word: to throw, to pitch, to fling away; *hièng guó,* toss it over (here or there).

Hièng, 賢 Virtuous, wise; excellent; to surpass: to praise; *hièng cài,* 賢才 superior abilities; *séng-hièng,* 聖賢 sages and philosophers; *hièng-ing,* 賢人 a virtuous man; *hièng chā* 賢妻 a faithful wife.

Hièng, 嫌 To dislike, to hold in contempt, to despise; prejudiced; *hièng-hâung,* 嫌恨 to hate.

Hièng, 懸 To suspend, to hang down, undecided; unlike, as *hièng-ciŏk,* 懸絕 very unlike; *ciā dâi gó hièng lā,* 者代故懸禮 the matter still undecided.

Hièng, 玄 Dark, somber, like the deep sky; *hièng dá,* 玄帝

the Shangti of the somber heavens.

Hièng, 弦 The string of a bow; the moon in quarter on the 8th and 23rd days of the month, also called *sióng hièng*, 上弦 and *hȧ hièng*, 下弦.

Hièng, 絃 Silken strings of musical instruments; COM. *sŭk hièng*, 續絃 "join the guitar string"—a widower marrying his second wife.

Hièng, 眩 Also read *hiĕng*: confused vision, dizzy; defective sight; not discerning, mistaken.

Hièng, 衒 Also read *hiĕng*: bragging, boasting; *cêu hièng*, 自衒 self praise.

Hièng, 現 A vulgar character. To divulge; *hièng chók*, 現出 to become manifest; *hièng-cái*,

現在 now; *hiêng-káik,* 現刻 this instant; *hiêng-cièng,* 現錢 ready money.

Hiêng, 見 Also read *giěng,* q. v.: to appear, to be manifest; revealed; *huák-hiêng,* 發見 to be manifest; the new meaning,—recently made manifest or revealed: just discovered.

Hiěu, 僥 False, hypocritical; *hiěu-háing,* 僥倖 to be wholly intent on gain; in the coll., a lucky hit.

Hiěu, 磽 Stony ground; *pì-hiěu,* 肥磽 rich and poor soils.

Hiěu, 澆 To irrigate; false, hard-hearted as *hiěu-bŏk,* 澆薄. Read *lièu,* an eddy, a whirlpool.

Hiěu, 梟 A kind of owl that eats its mother; met., strong, wicked; *hiěu-tò,* 梟桃 a winter peach.

com., *hiĕu-sĭng* 梟心 ungrateful.

Hiĕu, 曉 Light, clear, in the morning; plainly stated, intelligible; to understand, as *hiĕu-dék*, 曉的.

Hĭng, 興 Also read *héng*, q. v.: to rise, to flourish; as *kīng kī*, prosperous; raised, elevated; *hĭng-uóng*, 興旺 flourishing; *hĭng săng bái láng*, 興三敗二 the buyer (pays) three, and the seller two, *per cent*, (to the go-between).

Hĭng. 兄 In the coll., read *hiăng*, q. v.: an elder brother; a senior, a superior; a term of respect; *bàu hĭng-dá̤*, 胞兄弟 own brothers; *hĭng-dài*, 兄台 exalted Sir!—an epistolary phrase.

Hĭng, 扃 A door bar; *hĭng*

muòng, 局門 to bolt the door.

Hìng, 形 Form, shape, appearance, as hìng-sék, 形式 or hìng-cáung, 形狀; hìng-chiŏng, 形像 a likeness, or image; COLL., mò̤ hìng-cék, 毛形質 no clue.

Hìng, 型 An example, to be an example; diēng hìng, 典型 a law, a precedent; ngì hìng, 儀型 good example.

Hìng, 刑 Legal punishments; torture; hìng-huák, 刑法 criminal laws; hìng-huák, 刑罰 punishments; hìng-buô, 刑部 Board of Punishments.

Hìng, 眩 Read hièng and hiĕng; dizzy, confused; lightheaded, as tàu hìng, 頭眩; hìng-sùng 眩船 seasick.

Hìng: A coll. euphonic prefix, as in hìng-hàng, to burn; hìng-

hèng, to restore, to pay back.

Hiŏk, 歇 To rest, to desist; to discontinue, as *hiŏk-sék*, 歇息; *mò dìng mò hiŏk*, 毛停毛歇 incessantly.

Hiŏk, 蠍 A scorpion.

Hiŏk, 謁 To visit a superior as *hiŏk-giéng*, 謁見; to intimate; a card; *hiŏk siá*, 謁舍 a guest chamber.

Hiŏng, 香 Fragrant, aromatic; incense; aroma; met., reputable, fragrant, as a name; COM., *hiŏng-gŭ*, 香菰 a fragrant mushroom; *hiŏng-iòng*, 香櫞 a finger-lemon, the "Budh's hand"; *Hiŏng-gĕng*, 香港 Hong-kong.

Hiŏng, 鄉 A village, a hamlet; the country; rude, rustic; COM., *hiŏng-lĭ*, 鄉里 neighbors; *hiŏng-chŏng*, 鄉村 a village;

hiŏng-dōng, 鄉黨 a society; *hiŏng-sĭng,* 鄉紳 village gentry; *hiŏng-lō,* 鄉老 village elders; COLL., *hiŏng-â,* 鄉下 the country; *hiŏng-â-nĕng,* 鄉下仈 rustics.

Hiŏng, 喧 Noise of talking; to vociferate; COM., *gĭng-cī hiŏng-huà* 禁止喧嘩 noise is forbidden!

Hiŏng, 暄 A genial warmth; a pleasant heat; *hàng hiŏng,* 寒暄 cold and heat.

Hiŏng, 晅 A bright hot sun; to dry, to parch.

Hiŏng, 萱 The fleur-de-lis; *met.,* a mother; *chŭng-hiŏng* 椿萱 father and mother; *hiŏng-dòng,* 萱堂 a mother.

Hiŏng, 軒 The hood of a car; a balcony; pleased, satisfied as *hiŏng-hiŏng,* 軒軒

Hióng 395

Hiōng, 晌 Read *siōng* in the dictionaries; noon; midday as *hiōng-ngū,* 晌午.

Hiōng, 響 Noise, a sound, echo: COM., *īng-hiōng,* 影響 a shadow and echo; *met.,* a trace, an inkling of; COLL., *hiŏng siŏh siăng,* 響一聲 it sounds.

Hiōng, 享 To offer up; to enjoy; a feast; *hiōng sêu,* 享壽 to enjoy long life; *hiōng-hók,* 享福 to be happy, blessed.

Hióng, 向 Towards, facing, opposite to; inclined to; an intention; former, heretofore; points of the compass; *é-hióng,* 意向 intention; COM., *huŏng-hióng,* 方向 the direction of; *sèu - huŏng - hióng,* 四方向 everywhere; *hióng-lài,* 向來 heretofore; *hióng-háiu,* 向後 hereafter; *hióng-siéng,* 向善

inclined to good; *hiòng-sèng,* 向前 to advance.

Hióng, 餉 Provisions for workmen and troops; rations; taxes; duties in general; *hióng dăng* 餉單 a duty chop; *ciĕ hióng,* 支餉 to receive or pay rations; *cŏ hióng* 助餉 contributions to aid government.

Hióng, 憲 A rule, a precept; an office of any rank from prefect to viceroy; *hióng hióng,* 憲憲 pleased, gratified; *lĭk hióng gì huák* 立憲其法 method of establishing constitutional government; *hióng céng piĕng că guăng,* 憲政編查館 Constitutional Bureau in Peking.

Hióng, 獻 To offer up, as *hióng siòng,* 獻上.

Hióng, 獻 Read *ngiĕk,* in the

dictionaries; to judge or decide a case; *hióng géuk*, 讞鞫 to examine a criminal; *hióng ngŭk*, 讞獄 to sentence; *chiŭ hióng*, 秋讞 the autumnal assize.

Hiŭ, 休 To cease, to desist; a negative; good, excellent; as *hiŭ gă*, 休嘉; *hiŭ é*, 休矣 could not accomplish.

Hiŭ, 幽 In a ravine or shady dell; secret, retired; obscure, mysterious; to rusticate; *hiŭ áng*, 幽暗 very dark; *hiŭ pék*, 幽僻 solitary; COM., *hiŭ ngă*, 幽雅 retired and tasteful, as a room.

Hiŭ 朽 Also read *hiĕu*: decayed wood; rotten; *mìng bók hiŭ*, 名不朽 an imperishable name; COM., *hiŭ-huái*, 朽壞 ruined, destroyed.

Hó, 富 Coll., read *bó,* q. v.: rich, affluent, wealth, riches; to enrich; COM., *hó gói bìng ciêng,* 富貴貧賤 rich and poor, high and low; *hó-céuk,* 富足 abundance, wealth.

Hó, 副 To assist, to aid; to investigate; an assistant, a lieutenant; a deputy; in the coll. a classifier for sets of certain things; COM., *hó cūng còi,* 副總裁 a subexaminer of Kujin at Peking; *ciáng hó,* 正副 principal and assistant; *hó-lī,* 副理 an assistant.

Hó, 付 To give, to deliver, to hand over; COM., *hó-táuk,* 付託 to charge with; *gău-hó,* 交付 to deliver to; COLL., *uāng siŏh hó,* 碗一付 a set of 10 bowls; *dęu siŏh hó,* 箸一付 ten pairs of chopsticks; *sŏh* siŏh hó, 鈿一付 a pair of bracelets.

Hó, 赴 To go to, to repair to; to arrive at; hó gó, 赴告 to go and inform, to present a petition.

Hó, 訃 To announce the death of a parent or relative by the nearest mourner.

Hó, 傅 To annex; to lay on as colors; to superintend; a workman; a surname; să-hó, 師傅 (coll. să-hó, q. v.) a tutor: COM., hó-huói, 傅會 to imitate a bad example; in the coll., to do carelessly, any how.

Hó, 賦 To exact, to levy; to require; tribute from fiefs; taxes, imposts as hó-suói, 賦稅 or hó-kuāng; hó-lièng, 賦斂 to levy taxes.

Hó, 呬 To blow, to breathe; in

coll., to charge one with, as *hŭng-hó,* 吩咐 (*hŭng-nó,*) to instruct, to direct one how to do.

Hó: A coll. word: time enough for; *hó ng hó* or *â hó mṳ̄* is there time enough? *â hó,* there is time enough.

Hó: A coll. word: to dampen, to bedew; *hó cūi,* to sprinkle with water; *hó 'lâng,* to wet by sprinkling.

Hô, 父 A father; in a met., sense, kind, loving; COM., *hô-mū* 父母 parents; *hô cṳ̄,* father and son; *tiĕng hô* 天父 Heavenly Father; *gă hô,* 家父 my father; *hô chĭng,* 父親 father—an epistolary phrase; *siĕng hô,* 先父 my late father: COLL., *sṳ̆-hô,* 司父 a master, skilled workman.

Hô, 扶 Read *hù;* to support with

the hands; to raise, to lift up as *hô-tì*, 扶提; also to second.

Hô, 輔 To succor, to help, as *hô-có*, 輔助; also to second.

Hô, 婦 A wife, a married woman; a lady; female; COM., *hô-nṳ̄* 婦女 (*hô-nṳ̄ nẹng*) women; *sék-hô*, 媳婦 (spoken, *sĭng-mô*) a daughter-in-law; *liĕk hô*, 烈婦 A Chinese suttee.

Hô, 負 To owe as *hô kiéng*, 負欠; to be ungrateful as *gŭ hô*, 辜負.

Hô, 戶 To protect, to screen; an inner door; a family; a household; COM., *mùong-hô*, 門戶 a door; *hô-buô*, 戶部 Board of Population and Revenue.

Hô, 護 To guard, to preserve; *hô-có*, 護助 to aid, to succor;

hó hŭng, 護封 "safely sealed"—used on envelopes.

Hô, 附 Near, tributary; adjacent as *hô-gêung,* 附近.

Hô, 腐 Corrupted: *hô-lâng,* 腐爛 spoiled, as food.

Hô, 互 Interlocking, like cog-wheels fitting into each other; with, together with; *gău hô,* 交互 united.

Hō, 好 Also read *hó*, q. v.: good, right, excellent, well, very; in the coll., an intensive adverb; COM., *hō é,* 好意 good intention; *hō sệu,* 好事 (coll. *hō dái*) meritorious actions; *siông hō,* 上好 very good; *hō káng,* 好看 pretty, beautiful: COLL., *iā ô hō,* 野務好 passably good; *hō chiéu,* 好笑 amusing; *hō miáng,* 好命 a lucky state; *hō dā,* 好底 "good bottom"—

i. e, wealthy; hō ká-uăk, **好快活** in good circumstances; báng hō lāu, **病好了** recovered from sickness.

Hó, **好** Also read hō, q. v.: to love, to take pleasure in; to desire, to wish for; COM., céi hó, **最好** greatly to wish for; hó hŏk, **好學** fond of study; hó hăk, **好合** domestic harmony; hó séu, **好事** fond of meddling.

Hó, **耗** To diminish; to squander; hŭ-hó, **虛耗** wasted, squandered; COM., hó-hiê, **耗費** to expend larg,ely; căk-hó, **雜耗** trifling expenses,

Hò, **何** Also read hó, q. v.: which, who, what; how, as hò iá, **何也** COM., ù-hò, **如何** how? in what, why? hò-ù, **何如** how is it? hò-bìng hò-géu,

何憑何據 what evidence?— i. e., no proof whatever; coll. *mò nài-hò,* 毛奈何 no resource, impossible.

Hò, 荷 Also read *hŏ,* q. v.: the lotus, as *hò huā,* 荷花; *bŏk-hò,* 薄荷 mint; peppermint.

Hò, 豪 A porcupine, as *hò-dŭ,* 豪猪; brave; a leader; *hò-giĕk,* 豪傑 a hero.

Hò, 毫 Long, fine hair; atoms, motes, anything very minute: COM., *hò-liè,* 毫釐 or *sĭ-hò,* 絲毫 a very little, a mote.

Hò, 號 Also read *hŏ,* q. v.: to roar, as a tiger; a cock's crow.

Hò, 喉 Read *hèu:* as in *hò-lèng,* 喉嚨 the throat.

Hŏ, 號 Mark, designation; a "chop", a label, a countersign; COM., *cŏng hŏ,* 尊號 or *dài-hŏ,* 台號 what is your honourable surname; *biĕk hộ,* **別號** your literary name; *ná hộ,* **畫號** to affix the signature.

Hộ, **賀** To congratulate, as *hộ-hī,* **賀喜**; *gŭng-hộ,* **恭賀** "respectful salutations"; as written on presents,

Hộ, **皓** The light of heaven, luminous; *tái hộ,* **太皓** the firmament; *hộ siū,* **皓首** a hoary head.

Hộ, **浩** Great, swelling waters; superabundant; *hộ dáung,* **浩蕩** or *hộ-dái,* **浩大** vast as the firmament.

Hộh : A coll. word : to cook or heat up, as cold food; *hộh buông,* to warm up rice.

Hội : A coll. word : same as *ŏi,* q. v. : an exclamation of regret or surprise; *hội ộ,* Oh! Ah!

Hói, 諱 To shun, to respect; to muffle; *hói cê,* 諱字 sacred names; COM., *ngêu hói,* 御諱 sacred names of the emperor; *huâng hói,* 犯諱 to trespass on forbidden subjects; *cŏng hói,* 尊諱 the sacred name—*scil.,* of your deceased relative.

Hói, 緯 The woof of cloth; transverse lines; *gīng hói,* 經緯 warp and woof; *ngū hói,* 五緯 the five planets; *hói siáng,* 緯線 parallels of latitude.

Hók, 福 Happiness, good fortune; lucky; to bless; a blessing; COM., *hók-ké,* 福氣 happiness; *hiōng hók,* 享福 to be happy; *tò hók,* 叨福 happy or blessed by your favor.

Hók, 撫 To wipe, to dust; to

oppose; *hŏk ìng cī séng*, 拂人之性 to thwart one's wishes; COM., *hŏk iē dŏh*. 拂椅棹 to dust chairs and tables; *hŏk chiū*, 拂手 a small dusting-broom.

Hŏk, 福 Happiness, luck; *hŏk-lŭk*, 福祿 happiness and official income.

Hŏk, 綍 By *met.*, fine, elegant; *lùng hŏk*, 綸綍 eloquent, persuasive, as imperial sayings.

Hŏk, 幅 A wide strip of cloth; a classifier of maps, pictures, rolls, flags, strips of cloth, etc.; *sé hŏk*, 四幅 a set of four scrolls.

Hŏk, 彿 Like, as if: *huōng hŏk*, 彷彿 resembling.

Hŏk, 弗 A negative; not, it should not be; contrary; *hŏk dĭ*, 弗知 not to know, ignorant of; *hók gĭk,* 弗及 to fail of.

Hók, 蝠 A bat; in the coll., *biĕng-hók,* 蝙蝠 used for the embroidered figures of the bat.

Hók, 覆 Also read *páiu,* q. v.: to repeat, as *huāng-hók* 反覆; *hók kŏ,* 覆考 to repeat an examination.

Hók, 腹 Coll. read *bók,* q. v. that which embraces; the abdomen; the seat of the mind; the affections; *hók sĭng* 腹心 very dear; intimate.

Hŏk, 鶴 A crane; an emblem of age.

Hŏk, 學 Coll. read *ŏh,* q. v.: to learn; learning, science, doctrines, tenets; a college; COM. *hŏk-sĭk,* 學習 to study and learn; *hŏk-séu,* 學士 academicians; *hŏk-sĕng,* 學生 a scholar; *hŏk-nṳ̄,* 學女 a female

Hōng 409

pupil; *hŏk hâu*, **學校** a college; *hŏk-gái*, **學界** the student and literary class.

Hŏk, **劾** To judge, to examine into; *hŏk-sĭk*, **劾實** to ascertain the facts; *hŏk bâing*, **劾辦** to revise a case.

Hŏk, **核** To investigate, to ascertain the facts as *hŏk sĭk*, **核實**; the kernels or seeds of fruits, as *guō hŏk*, **果核**; COM., *hŏk-tò*, **核桃** walnuts.

Hŏng, **煙** Read *iĕng*: tobacco, opium; *gáik hŏng*, **革煙** to cure the habit of smoking; *hŏng-bău*, **煙包** tobacco pouch; *hŏng-dęng*, **煙筒** tobacco or opium pipe.

Hōng, **很** Disobedient, perverse, quarrelsome; a superlative:— very, much, in which sense read *hēng* in the coll., q. v.

Hóng, 俸 Salary of officers, stipend : COM., *hóng-lŭk,* 俸祿 official income ; *hóng háiu,* 俸厚 a fat salary.

Hóng, 訓 To instruct, to explain; a doctrine, a precept ; *gáu-hóng,* 教訓 to instruct.

Hóng, 糞 Coll. read *bóng* q. v. : ordure, dung ; to manure.

Hóng, 奮 To endeavor after, to rouse one's energies, as *hóng cé,* 奮志.

Hòng, 行 Also read *hèng, háing,* and *òng* q. v. : a row, a line or column of characters. Read *òng,* a warehouse. Read *hèng* to do. Read *háing,* deeds. In the coll. read *giàng,* to walk.

Hòng, 桁 Read *hèng*: used for the coll. prefix *hòng,* as *hòng háung,* 桁桁 floor beams.

Hòng, 杭 The Capital of Chehkiang as *Hòng-ciŭ*, 杭州 Hangchow.

Hòng, 航 A scar, a cicatrix; COM., *cūi hòng*, 水航 a trace in water, *met.*, flaws in glass and gems.

Hòng, 降 Also read *gáung*, q. v.: to submit, to return to one's allegiance; to descend; *hòng-hŭk* 降服 to submit to; *dàu-hòng*, 投降 to submit, as rebels.

Hòng, 防 Read *huòng*; to prepare, to be on one's guard against, as *hòng-bê* 防備; *hòng chĕk*, 防賊 to guard against thieves.

Hōng, 鳳 A fabulous bird; the Chinese phoenix; COM., *hōng-guăng*, 鳳冠 a cap ornamented with the phoenix—worn by brides.

Hông, 奉 To receive or offer respectfully in both hands; to revere, to obey; *hông-sẹ̆u,* 奉事 to serve; *hông gáu,* 奉教 to embrace the doctrines (of a sect).

Hông, 混 Confused; mixed: COM., *hông-diĕng,* 混癲 crazy.

Hông, 分 Also read *hŭng,* q. v.: duty, the duties of an office or situation; a part, a share; *tiĕng hông,* 天分 natural endowments: COM., *cĕk-hông,* 職分 duties of a position; *buŏng-hông,* 本分 one's own duty; *uŏk-hông,* 越分 to go beyond one's proper sphere: COLL., *ô hông,* 務分 to have a share in.

Hŭ, 夫 Also read *hù,* q. v.: to help, one who can assist; a scholar, a man, a workman, a husband as *tióng-hŭ*, 丈夫; an exalted lady, your wife, as *hŭ-ìng*, 夫人; *hŭ-hó*, 夫婦 husband and wife; *mā-hŭ*, 馬夫 hostler.

Hŭ, 膚 The skin, as *puòi-hŭ*, 皮膚.

Hŭ, 孵 To hatch, as eggs.

Hŭ, 鄅 The outermost wall beyond the citadel; the suburbs.

Hŭ, 桴 A raft of wood or bamboo: also read *pèu* when meaning a ridgepole, a drumstick, a barrow to carry earth.

Hŭ, 敷 To spread out, to diffuse; to issue an order; *hŭ siĕ*, 敷施 to promulgate, as laws: COM., *hŭ ĕung*, 敷用 sufficient for use; *bók hŭ*, 不敷 insufficient.

Hŭ, 灰 Ashes, cinders, as *huōi-hŭ*, 火灰.

Hū, 虎 A tiger, the king of beasts (China); *met.*, brave, awful, violent: COM., *hū cāu*, 虎爪 tiger's claws: *met.*, tailor's shears: COLL., *láu-hū*, 佬虎 a tiger; *láu-hū guá sŭ-ciö*, 老虎掛素珠 a tiger wearing Soochow pearls; *met.*, feigned gentleness; *hū tàu siè-muòi*, 虎頭蛇尾 a tiger's head and a snake's tail; *met.*, a fierce beginning and cowardly ending.

Hū, 府 A store house, a house; a record office, a library, a prefecture; a prefect; *buōng-hū*, 本府 I, the prefect; *hū-siông*, 府上 your house; *céng 'hū*, 政府 the government.

Hū, 俯 To stoop, to bow; to consider: *hū-hŭk*, 俯伏 to fall prostrate.

Hū, 腑 The inferior viscera:

COM., *câung hū*, 臟腑 the superior and inferior viscera.

Hū, 父 Usually read *hô*, q. v.: a suffix of names; a title of respect and honor as, *Nà hū*, 尼父 the honorable *Nà* (Confucius); to address respectfully.

Hū, 斧 A hatchet, an ax; to cut, to chop; *hū-siók*, 斧削 to criticise, to correct.

Hū, 脯 Preserved or dried meat; *siŭ-hū*, 修脯 or *sók-hū*, 束脯 slices of dried meat sent to a teacher; teacher's salary.

Hū, 甫 Large, beautiful; eminent; I, myself; *hū-hū*, 甫甫 much, numerous.

Hù, 胡 A surname; why, wherefore; the Tartars, Mongols or Huns; lasting, eternal; in the coll., remiss, careless, as *hù-*

dù, 胡塗: COM., *hù-chṳ*, 胡鼠 squirrel: COLL., *hù-siók*, 胡說 to lie, to talk ridiculously.

Hù, 鬍 The beard; *hù-sṳ*, 鬍鬚 beard and whiskers.

Hù, 糊 Pepper, as *hù-ciêu*, 糊椒.

Hù, 蝴 A butterfly, as *hù-diĕk*, 蝴蝶.

Hù, 湖 Coll. *ù*, q. v.: a lake; *ngū hù*, 五湖 the five lakes —the Poyang, in Kiangsi; Lungting and Tsingtsau in Hunan, and the Tai and Tanyang in Kiangsu.

Hù, 餬 Congee; to seek a living.

Hù, 糊 Also read *gù* in the coll., q. v.: paste, gluten; to paste: COLL., careless, slovenly, as *hù-dù*.

Hù, 瑚 Coral as *sāng hù*, 珊瑚 (coll. *dăng-hù*).

Hù, 夫 Also read *hŭ*, q. v.: an

initial particle, now, therefore; *hù ìng ciā*, **夫仁者** now as to the benevolent man; *chiā hù*, **且夫** moreover.

Hù, 扶 Coll. *hô*, q. v.: to aid, to uphold as *hù-tì* **扶持**; *hù-có*, **扶助** to assist.

Hù, 狐 Suspicious, mistrusting; a fox, as *hù-lì*, **狐狸**; *hù-ngì*, **狐疑** to doubt; COLL., *hù-lì-mà*, **狐狸貓** a fox elf.

Hù, 弧 An arc in mathematics; curved, arched.

Hù, 符 A tally made of two slips; to correspond to; to testify; to evidence; a warrant; COM., *hù hăk*, **符合** to fit, to match.

Hù, 乎 An interogative adverb; interjection of doubt, admiration, or inquiry placed at the end of the sentence; **after** nouns, a sign of the vocative; after verbs, a preposition; sign of the accusative; an expletive.

Hù, 呼 To breathe; an expiration: COM., *chĭng-hù*, 稱呼 to address one by his title; *hù-ngék*, 呼吸 expiration and inspiration.

Hù: A coll. word, as in *hù-chiŭ*, (spoken: *hù-diŭ*) a mud eel.

Hù, 和 Read *huò*, as in *hù-siông*, 和尚 a Buddhist priest.

Hṳ̆, 虛 Empty; unsatisfactory; void, vain; humble; space; *hṳ̆-kŭng*, 虛空 the firmament; COM., *hṳ̆-sĭng*, 虛心 humility; *hṳ̆ cê*, 虛字 particles, as adverbs, etc.,

Hṳ̄, 許 To grant; to accede to; to promise; a surname; used in the coll. for the demonstrative

Huǎ

pronoun, *that*, also for the adverb, *so, thus*: COM., *hṳ̄ nguóng*, 許願 to vow; *éng-hṳ̄*, 應許 to promise; COLL., *hṳ̄ ciáh* 許隻 that one; *hṳ̄-uái*, 許塊 there; *hṳ̄-běng*, 許邊 in that direction; *hṳ̄-diĕ*, 許裡 in there.

Huǎ, 花, 華 Second also read *huà*, q. v.: a flower; *met.*, pleasure, vice, ornamental; to exaggerate; COM., *huă buòng*, 花盆 a flower-pot; *huă lūi*, 花蕊 a flower bud; *huă-sěng*, 花生 peanuts; *chéng-huă*, 秤花 the notation on steelyards; *siŏh huă*, 石花 less than a picul; *huă-huói*, 花會 a lottery.

Huǎ, 畫 Read *uă*; as in *huă-mì*, 畫眉 a large hopping bird.

Huǎ: A coll. word: as *huă kó̤*, to have been blown out by the wind.

Huá, 化 To change; to transform; to digest; COM., *biéng huá*, 變化 to change, to reform; *siéu-huá*, 消化 to digest (food); *gāng-huá*, 感化 to transform; *gáu huá*, 敎化 to improve by instruction; *huá sĕng*, 化生 produced by metamorphosis; COLL., *cô huá*, 造化 fortunately.

Huà, 華 Used for *huà* (a flower), q. v.: the elegance of flowers; charming; splendid; hoar headed; a designation of China; COM., *huà-lâ*, 華麗 splendid; *ìng-huà*, 榮華 glorious; *chià-huà*, 奢華 extravagant.

Huà, 嘩 Clamor, noise; *huà iòng*, 嘩然 hurrah: COLL., *huà-huà-giéu*, 嘩嘩叫 the rustling (of leaves), noise (of rain or running water).

Huăi   421

Huà, 划 A boat, a pinnace, as *huà cṳ̄*, 划子.

Huà: A coll. word: to estimate, to calculate; *huà káng*, to calculate and see; *huà-dék sé*—I reckon so, it is just so.

Huà: A coll. word: a spade.

Huáh: A coll. word: to joke, to jest, to riot; dissipated; *mŏh huáh*, don't jest; *páh-huáh*, to live riotously.

Huăi: A coll. word: to pass out of the mind, as *huăi sĭng*; *sĭng-séṳ mă huăi*, can't get rid of the tho't or feeling.

Huài, 懷 To cherish in the heart; to embrace, to favor; to cherish, as ill-will; private, selfish; the heart, the affections; *huài dáik*, 懷德 to meditate on virtue: COM., *huài-niĕng*, 懷念 to think of; *huài*

422 Huák

ēng, 懷孕 or huài-tăi, 懷胎 pregnancy.

Huài, 槐 A species of Cassia of which the yellow flowers are used for a dye.

Huái, 壞 To spoil, destroy; injured, ruined; useless; bái-huái, 敗壞 to destroy; hūi-huái, 毀壞 ruined.

Huák, 法 A rule, a law; regulations; legal infliction; an art; an industry; a sect: COM., lī-huák, 理法 reason and law; huák-dô, 法度 rules; chiū huák, 手法 handicraft; guók-huák, 國法 the laws of a country; constitution; huŏng-huák, 方法 a way of doing; huák-dèu, 法條 a watch spring; COLL., mò̤ huák niăh ĭ ài, cannot come up to; mò̤ huák dék, 毛法的 unavoidable.

Huák, 發 To issue; to send forth, to germinate; to dispatch; to manifest; met., spring and summer; COM., *huák-lêng*, 發令, to issue commands; *huák kī*, 發起 to prosper; to rise, as dough; to instigate, to originate; *huák mặ*, 發賣 to offer for sale; *huák-dăk*, 發達 to prosper, to succeed.

Huák, 髮 Coll., read *huók*, q. v.: hair of the head; met., trees, herbs, moss; *háik huák*, 黑髮 black haired, youth; *bĕk huák*, 白髮 white haired, aged: COM., *sṳ̆-huák*, 鬚髮 beard and hair.

Huák, 伐 To destroy, to fight; to punish; to brag; a meritorious deed; *cáuk huák*, 作伐 a go-between; *huák côi*, 伐罪 to punish crime.

Huák, 罰 A crime; to punish;

to fine; a forfeit; COM., *cáik-huăk*, 責罰 to punish; *hìng-huăk*, 刑罰 punishment; *huăk cièng*, 罰錢 to fine.

Huăk, 乏 Want, destitution, failure; deficient; to fail; to injure; empty, poor: COM., *kuók-huăk*, 缺乏 destitute, in want.

Huăk, 滑 Smooth, slippery; polished; sharp, knavish; *guŏng huăk*, 光滑 shining and smooth; *huăk siŏh*, 滑石 soapstone.

Huăng, 歡 Joyous, merry; pleased; to like, as in *huăng-hī*, 歡喜; *hī-huăng*, 喜歡 (coll. *huăng-huăng hī-hī*) jubilant; *huăng-ngìng*, 歡迎 to wellcome.

Huăng, 番 A beast's footprint; a time, a repetition of; to

Huăng 425

reckon; to change; a term applied to all foreigners; *ék huăng*, 一番 once: COM., *chū huăng*, 此番 this time, now; *huăng guók*, 番國 foreign countries; *huăng-sù*, 番茹 the potato; COLL., *huăng nệng*, 番仈 foreigners; *guŏng-huăng*, 光番 an unchopped dollar; *huăng-cièng-giăng*, 番錢仔 fractions of a dollar.

Huăng, 藩 A fence, a boundary; to inclose; to protect: COM., *huăng-dài*, 藩臺 a title of the provincial treasurer.

Huăng, 翻 To fly to and fro; to change, to vacillate; to revise a case; to translate books; *huăng-áng*, 翻案 to rejudge a case; *huăng-ĭk*, 翻譯 to translate (books); *huăng-uá*, 翻話 to retract one's word; COLL., *huăng có,* 翻做 to do differently; *huăng-siăng,* 翻聲 to take back a promise.

Huāng, 反 To turn, as the leaves of a book, as in *huāng guó,* 反過; to rebel, as in *có huāng,* 做反; *huāng-kí,* 反起 to remove, as tiles from a roof; but, contrary; again; COM., *siŏng-huāng,* 相反 opposed to; *huāng-dói,* 反對 to oppose, to contradict.

Huáng, 喚 To call to, out and for; to bid, to name: COLL., *huáng i că kó,* 喚伊齊去 call him to go with.

Huáng, 奐 Great, beautiful, variegated; at ease; *mī căi huáng iòng,* 美哉奐焉 how excellent and beautiful!

Huáng, 販 To traffic, to deal in; COM., *huáng huó,* 販貨 to deal in goods; *huáng má,* 販賣 to sell off (goods).

Huáng, A coll. word: to act as nurse, to tend children; *nèng huáng,* and *găng-huáng,* wet and dry nurses.

Huàng, 還 Used in the coll. for *hèng* and *dèng,* q. v.: to return, to revert; to give back, to repay; to give attention to; still, furthermore; now, immediately: COM, *huàng chiū,* 還手 to strike back; *huàng-hùng,* 還魂 to revive, as the sick; *gău huàng chĭng chū,* 交還清楚 to pay up in full.

Huàng, 繁 Much, numerous, many: COM., *huàng-căk,* 繁雜 heterogeneous, as a crowd; *huàng-huà,* 繁華 pomp and show.

Huàng, 凡 All, everybody; common, useful; generally; the world: COM., *cụ̈ huàng,* 諸凡 all, every; *huàng sū iū,* 凡所有 all that there is; *dái-huàng,* 大凡 whatever, whoever; COLL., *huàng sẹu diỏh sǎng sụ̈,* 凡事着三思 in all matters think thrice.

Huàng, 煩 Troubled, perplexed; impertinent; grieved, sorry: COM., *huàng lọ̀,* 煩勞 to trouble one; annoyed; *huàng-nọ̈,* 煩惱 troubled and anxious.

Huàng, 橫 A cross-bar; transverse, athwart, as *dā-lāng-huàng,* 打攪橫; perverse, unreasonable; *huàng-áuk,* 惡橫 refractory.

Huàng, 礬 Mineral salts; alum; to dye with alum; to tan or cure (leather) in lime and copperas; *băh huàng*, 白礬 alum.

Huáng, 範 A rule, a guide; a custom; a mould; to imitate; *mùò-huáng*, 模範 a pattern.

Huáng, 幻 A trick, sorcery; apparitions; dreams, visions, as *huáng móng*, 幻夢; *huáng chiöng*, 幻象 to imagine; imagination.

Huáng, 患 Evil, distress, affliction: COM., *huáng nâng*, 患難 misfortune, troubles.

Huâng, 犯 To rush against; to transgress; a culprit; to be possessed by: COM., *huáng huák*, 犯法 to violate law; *huáng gŭi*, 犯鬼 possessed by a devil; *huáng cội*, 犯罪 to transgress: COLL., *huáng báng*, 犯病 taken sick.

Huâng, 緩 Leisurely; careless; easily; gradually; to delay;

in the coll., to tie loosely, as *muōng kặ ĭ huáng sïŏh â.*

Huáng, 豢 To rear domestic animals; to bait, to bribe.

Hŭi, 輝 Brilliant, glistering, as *yuŏng-hŭi,* 光輝.

Hŭi, 暉 Effulgent, glorious; *siâ hŭi,* 斜暉 slanting sunbeams; *sŭk hŭi,* 夕暉 the evening sun.

Hŭi, 揮 To rend open; humble, unassuming; *cī-hŭi,* 指揮 to point out.

Hūi, 毀 To break down, to level, as a house; ruined; destroyed; to vilify, to slander: COM., *hūi-huâi,* 毀壞 ruined; *hūi-báung,* 毀謗 to backbite.

Hūi, 燬 Fire; blazing; bright; *siĕu hūi,* 燒燬 burned up.

Hŭk, 佛 To see indistinctly; contrary, unreasonable: COM., *hŭk gáu,* 佛教 Budhism: COLL.

chái hŭk, 菜佛 a vegetarian.

Hŭk, 伏 To lie or fall prostrate; to humble, to subject; to conceal; to confess: COM., *hŭk uông*, 伏望 to hope for—an epistolary phrase; *hŭk cô̤i*, 伏罪 to confess faults; COLL., *hŭk diô*, 伏路 to lie in ambush by the roadside.

Hŭk, 復 Again, reiterated; to return; to restore: COM., *hŭk mêng*, 復命 to report on a commission: COLL., *hŭk diōng li̍*, 復轉來 to revert.

Hŭk, 茯 China root, as *hŭk-lìng*, 茯苓.

Hŭk, 服 To use; to wait on, to serve: COM., *ĭ-hŭk*, 衣服 garments; *hŭk-séu*, 服事 to serve: COLL., *hŭk ĭ guāng á*, 服伊管下 to submit to his rule.

Hŭh: A coll. word: as in *hŭk-*

dŭk, gruff, peevish; cêng kó hŭk-dŭk, exceedingly gruff.

Hŭng, 風 Breath, spirit; air gusts, a gale; manners, etiquette; institutes; policy; influence: COM., liòng hŭng, 涼風 to take the air; hŭng ê, 風味 taste, flavor; hŭng-sŭk, 風俗 customs; sì-hŭng, 時風 the winds of the season; hŭng-hàng, 風寒 a cold; hŭng-cūi, 風水 geomancy; ŭi-hŭng, 威風 dignity: COLL., hŭng-tăi, 風颱 a typhoon, a hurricane; hŭng-ké, 風氣 spirit; hŭng-dièu, 風潮 sudden trouble, trouble without cause.

Hŭng, 楓 The maple; hŭng-sìng, 楓宸 the maple palace: met., the emperor.

Hŭng, 瘋 The leprosy, scrofula; insane; palsy; hŭng-dièng, 瘋

Hŭng   433

癲 crazy; *hŭng-niōng,* 瘋軟 paralysis.

Hŭng, 丰 Good looking melodious; *hŭng-chāi,* 丰釆 a graceful gait; *hŭng ông,* 丰韻 a fine harmony.

Hŭng, 鋒 A sharp point; the vanguard, as *cièng hŭng,* 前鋒: COM., *bék hŭng,* 筆鋒 the point of a pencil.

Hŭng, 吩 Read *hŭng,* and *hóng:* to give orders to, to bid, to direct as *hŭng-hó,* 吩咐 or *hŭng-nó.*

Hŭng, 分 Also read *hông;* in the coll. read *buŏng,* q. v.: to separate, to divide; to distribute; a candareen, tenth of a mace; tenth of an inch: COM., *hŭng-biĕk,* 分別 to separate as friends; *hŭng-biĕk,* 分別 to discriminate; *hŭng-sáng,* 分散

to scatter; *hŭng-mìng,* 分明 clear, plain; *sĕk hŭng,* 十分 a superlative, very, perfectly.

Hŭng, 枌 Also read *hùng*: as in *hŭng-ù,* 枌榆 the elm: met., the ancestral home.

Hŭng, 紛 Perplexed, confused, as *hŭng căk,* 紛雜; *hŭng-hŭng-luâng,* 紛紛亂 confused, as a crowd; distracted; *hŭng-hŭng bók-ék,* 紛紛不一 contradictory reports.

Hŭng, 氛 Fume, vapor; *àuk hŭng,* 惡氛 noxious vapors; *hāi-hŭng,* 海氛 marine vapors; met., pirates.

Hŭng, 封 A prince's domain; to appoint to office; to seal up, to close; an envelope, a classifier of letters: COM., *hŭng giŏng dái-sìng,* 封疆大臣 the high provincial officers; *nôi* séng ék hŭng, **內信一封** one letter; hŭng éng, **封印** to close the seals; hŭng séng, **封信** to seal a letter; hŭng sùng, **封船** to impress boats.

Hŭng, **豐** A full goblet; full, abundant; fertile; talented: COM., hŭng-nièng, **豐年** a year of plenty; hŭng-muāng, **豐滿** abundant.

Hŭng, **蚊** Read ùng: hŭng-muòng, **蚊蚋** a mosquito.

Hŭng: A coll. word: as in hŭng-hŭng-áng, evening twilight, dusk.

Hūng, **粉** Broken rice; flour of any kind of grain: COM., mī-hūng, **米粉** rice flour; miéng-hūng, **麵粉** wheaten flour; hūng-gāng, **粉乾** dry vermicelli; cūi-hūng, **水粉** moist vermicelli; hūng-bēng, **粉板**

a writing tablet; *ṳ-hṳ̄ng*, 雨粉 a drizzling, a falling mist.

Hṳ̄ng, 憤 Impatient desire, zeal, ardor; anger: *huáng hṳ̄ng*, 發憤 ardent, as for study.

Hṳ̄ng, 忿 Anger, indignation: COM., *hṳ̄ng-nô*, 忿怒 or *hṳ̄ng-ké*, 忿氣 anger, vexation.

Hṳ̄ng, 恐 Read *kṳ̄ng*: coll., *hṳ̄ng-pá*, 恐怕 to fear lest.

Hùng, 雲 Clouds, mist on the hills; numerous like the clouds; *hùng-ṳ̄*, 雲雨 clouds and rain; *hùng-mū*, 雲母 mother of pearl: COM., *hùng ciă* 雲遮 or *hùng bé*, 錫蔽 or *hùng dáu*, 雲罩 covered by the clouds; *hùng ô*, 零霧 a fog: COLL., *hùng siŏh*, 雲石 figure stone, (used for seals) wrongly called soap-stone.

Hùng, 紅 Used for *gŭng*, (work);

Hùng 437

in the coll., read *èng*, q. v.: red color, reddish, fiery, ruddy as the complexion; *hùng dăng*, 紅丹 red lead; *nṳ̄ hùng*, 女紅 ladies' work.

Hùng, 馮 A surname.

Hùng, 鴻 A postman, large, profound; learned: COM., *hùng ŏng*, 鴻恩 great grace.

Hùng, 洪 An inundation, a deluge; a surname; *hùng-cūi*, 洪水 a flood: COM., *Hùng-săng giò*, 洪山橋 the Upper Bridge, 4 miles west of Foochow.

Hùng, 渾 A roaring, dashing torent; turbid, roily; confused; the whole of; *hùng sĭng* 渾身 the whole body; COM., *hùng-hùng*, 渾渾 roiled; *hùng-huá*, 渾化 careless; COLL., *hùng siàng*, 渾成 suitable, fitting.

Hùng, 虹 Used for *kêung,* in the coll., q. v.: a halo near the sun; *hùng giò,* 虹橋 the arched rainbow—a poetic phrase.

Hùng 墳 A grave, a tomb; an embankment; vast; *săng hùng,* 三墳 heaven, earth and man: COM., *hùng muó,* 墳墓 a grave; *hùng săng,* 墳山 hills covered with graves.

Hùng, 逢 To meet undesignedly, to fall in with; great, wide: COM., *hùng nièng,* 逢年 a propitious year.

Hùng, 魂 The soul: COM., *sìng hùng,* 神魂 the spirit or mind; *huàng hùng,* 還魂 to revive, as one very sick; *lìng-hùng,* 靈魂 the soul, the spiritual part of man.

Hŭng, 勳 Meritorious; *gióng hŭng,* 建勳 to establish merit.

Hŭng 439

Hŭng, 昕 The morn, the dawn; *dái hŭng*, 大昕 early dawn.

Hŭng, 烘 Also read *hùng*, in the coll. read *hĕng*, q. v.: the heat of fire rising up.

Hŭng, 熏 Smoke rising; to fumigate; harmonious, agreeable; evening: *hŭng-hŭng*, 熏熏 agreeable; *hŭng sĭk*, 熏夕 twilight.

Hŭng, 凶 Unfortunate, unhappy, unpropitious; calamity; *hŭng diéu*, 凶兆 a bad omen; *hŭng-séng*, 凶信 bad news.

Hŭng, 兇 Malevolent, cruel, vicious; a cry of fear: COM., *hŭng-chiú*. 兇手 a murderer; *hŭng áuk*, 兇惡 wicked.

Hŭng, 洶 The bubbling of a spring: *hŭng éung*, 湧胸 gurgling of a fountain.

Hŭng, 洶 The bosom, the chest;

the mind, the heart, the feelings: COLL., *hŭng-sèng,* 胸前 the bosom.

Hŭng, 忻 Joy, happiness; delighted, pleased as *hŭnghuăng,* 忻歡.

Hùng, 雄 A cock bird; courageous, heroic, energetic: COM., *sĭng hùng* 心雄 or *dāng hùng,* 膽雄 brave, heroic; *hùng cáung,* 雄壯 burly and strong; martial: COM., *hùng giĕ,* 雄雞 a cock; *hùng-hùng chiū,* 雄雄手 to do quickly.

Hùng, 熊 A bear.

Hùng, A coll. word: as *gīng*: tight, taut; the opposite of *nèung* (slack).

Huō, 火 In the coll. read *huōi,* q. v.: fire, flame; to consume; heat, feverish:

Huō, 伙 Read in the coll. *huōi,*

q. v.: a messmate, a comrade.

Huō, 夥 In the coll. read *huōi*, q. v.: a colleague, an associate; a company, a party; *huō-giĕ*, 夥計 (coll. *huō-gé* or *huō-é*) partners, fellows.

Huó, 貨 Goods, merchandize; to trade: COM., *huó ŭk*, 貨物 goods; *mā huó*, 買貨 to buy goods; *tū huó*, 土貨 native goods: COLL., *huó dă*, 貨底 inferior goods; *huó siâng*, 貨賤 the goods are cheap.

Huò, 禾 Growing grain, as paddy and wheat.

Huò, 和 Also read *huŏ*, q. v.: harmony, agreement; to unite, to join company: COM., *huò hŏ*, 和好 or *huò-bìng*, 和平 or *huó-mŭk*, 和睦 on peaceable terms; *huò-iók*, 和約 a treaty of peace; COLL., *huò-huò-iĕk*,

和和熱 tepid, lukewarm.

Huô, 稐 To accord, to respond, as in singing refrains.

Huô 禍 Evil; adversity, sorrow, woe; unhappy; *căi-huô,* 災禍 calamity, judgment: used in the coll., for rain, as in summer; a shower, as *dâung huô,* 遏禍.

Huŏh, 局 Read *guŏh:* q. v.: to cheat, to deceive.

Huŏi, 灰 Coll. read *hŭ,* q. v.: ashes, lime; to plaster; discouraged as *sĭng huŏi* 心灰 com., *huŏi lù,* 灰爐 a lime kiln; *siĕu huŏi,* 燒灰 to burn lime; *huŏi-cūi,* 灰水 whitewash.

Huōi, 火 Read *huō:* fire, flame; *met.,* quick, rapid, fiery, as the disposition: *huōi-ĭng,* 火烟 smoke; *huōi-hŭ,* 火灰 ashes;

huōi siŏh, 火石 flint; *cê̤ṳ-lài-huōi*, 自來火 (self-come-fire) matches; *huōi-iŏh*, 火藥 gunpowder; *huōi-piéu*, 火票 a hasty warrant; *huōi-bā*, 火把 a torch; crullers; *huōi-guŏng*, 火管 Chinese bellows; *huōi siĕu chió*, 火燒厝 a conflagration; *huōi-iêu*, 火鵁 fire hawks—plunderers at a conflagration.

Huōi, 伙 Read *huō*: as in *gă-huōi*, 家伙 household furniture; *huōi-sĭk*, 伙食 food, provisions.

Huōi, 夥 Read *huō*: as *huōi-gé* 夥計 (pronounced *huō-é*) a fellow-workman.

Huói, 晦 Obscure, as *huói-mìng*, 晦明: COM., *huói ké*, 晦氣 unlucky.

Huói, 誨 To teach; to admonish;

444   Huòi

gáu-huói, 敎誨 to teach diligently.

Huói, 悔 To repent, to change as *tọi-huói,* 退悔: COM., *huói-gāi,* 悔改 or *huói-cọi gāi-guó,* 悔罪改過 to repent and amend: COLL., *tọi huói,* 退悔 to regret having done.

Huói, 歲 Read *suói:* a year; a year of one's age; *huói-só,* 歲數 years of age; *gūi-huói,* 幾歲 how old?

Huòi, 回 To revolve; to return back; returning: COM: *huòi séng,* 回信 (coll. *huòi piĕ*), to answer by letter; *huòi-ĭng,* 回音 "the reply"—an epistolary phrase; *huòi-gă,* 回家 to return home; *huòi-huòi-gáu,* 回回敎 Mohammedanism; *huòi chiū,* 回手 or *huòi giêu,* 回轎 to set down (the sedan); *lài-*

Huôi 445

huòi, 來回 to come and go— i. e., to make a round trip: COLL., *gūi - huòi*, 幾回 how many times; several times.

Huòi: A coll. word: the correlative of *cuòi* (this); *huòi họ, cuòi ngài*, that good and this bad; *hiā huòi*, that! that there!

Huòi, 廻 To curve, to bend; to turn round; *huòi kuàny*, 廻環 circling, as hills: COM., *huòi lòng*, 廻廊 porches about a court.

Huòi, 茴 Fennel or caraway seed as *huòi-hiŏng* 茴香, or *siēu-huòi*, 小茴.

Huôi, 會 To collect, to assemble, as *huôi-cĭk*, 會集; a club, a meeting; a church, a congregation; to meet; to understand, to perceive, as *huôi-*

nguó, 會悟; gáu-huói, 教會 the Christian church; huói-iŭ, 會友 a fellow-member; huói-guāng, 會館 a guild hall; gĭ-huói, 期會 an opportunity; bái-huói, 拜會 to visit one.

Huói, 繪 To embroider; to paint: huói dù, 繪圖 to draw plans or maps.

Huói, 潰 To run in drops, to separate: huói-bái, 潰敗 dispersed, broken, as troops.

Huói, 䃜 As in huói miêng, 䃜面 to wash the face.

Huók, 忽 A single floss of silk; the smallest fraction; a millionth; neglectful: COM., huók-iòng-gāng, 忽然間 suddenly, abruptly.

Huók, 髮 Read huák: tàu-huók, 頭髮 the hair of the head.

Huŏng, 方 Square, angular; a

place, a region; manner, means; then, in that case; like; to compare; a prescription; *huŏng-chiā,* 方且 then, consequently: COM., *séu-huŏng,* 四方 everywhere; *huŏng-hióng,* 方向 the direction; *dê-huŏng,* 地方 a situation, employment; *huŏng-huák,* 方法 the mode of doing; *huŏng-cĕng,* 方針 bent, inclination, purpose.

Huŏng, 坊 A neighborhood; a street, an alley; a country house, a shop; an honorary portal: COM., *siŏh huŏng,* 石坊 a stone arch or gateway; *cṳ̌-huŏng,* 書坊 a book-store: COLL., *kié huŏng,* 竪坊 to erect an honorary portal.

Huŏng, 芳 Fragrant, odorous: *met.,* agreeable; virtuous, excellent.

Huŏng, 婚 Marriage; to take a wife: COM., *huŏng-ĭng,* 婚姻 nuptials; *huŏng-lă,* 婚禮 marriage etiquette; *huŏng-cṳ̆,* 婚書 (coll. *duâi táik,*) betrothal contract.

Huŏng, 荒 Deserted, wild, barren; a famine: *huŏng-hié,* 荒廢 waste, uncultivated; *huŏng-iā,* 荒野 a desert, a waste; *gĭ-huŏng,* 饑荒 famine: COLL., *huŏng-dòng,* 荒唐 random talk.

Huŏng, 慌 Confused, nervous, agitated, as *huŏng-mòng,* 慌忙.

Huŏng, 謊 To talk in sleep, incoherent; *huŏng-ngiòng,* 謊言 lies.

Huŏng, 訪 To inquire, to search out; to consult, to deliberate: COM., *huŏng că,* 訪查 to investigate.

Huòng, 仿 To copy, to imitate; a model: COM., *huōng iông*, 仿樣 to copy the form or pattern: COLL., *huōng ǐ iông*, 仿伊樣 imitate him.

Huòng, 貺 Sometimes read *huóng*: to give, to bestow; *hâiu-huōng*, 厚貺 to bestow abundantly.

Huóng, 放 In the coll. also read *bóng*, q. v.: to reject; extend, to liberate; to indulge; COM., *huóng-séu*, 放肆 dissolute, impudent; COLL., *huóng à*, 放鞋 to stretch shoes; *huóng báuk*, 放駁 burst in stretching.

Huóng, 況 More, moreover, further: COM., *huóng-chiā*, 況且 still more; *hò-huóng*, 何況 how much more!

Huóng, A coll. word: a boil; *sāng huóng*, to have boils.

Huòng, 皇 High, exalted; imperial; Heaven; an emperor, as in *huòng-dá,* 皇帝; *huòng-háiu,* 皇后 the empress; *huòng-siòng,* 皇上 His Imperial Majesty.

Huòng 隍 An empty ditch, a dry moat around a city; *met.,* the municipal guardian, as in *siàng-huòng,* 城隍.

Huòng, 煌 A great blaze, luminous, glorious, effulgent, as in *hŭi-huòng,* 輝煌.

Huòng, 惶 Apprehensive, frightened, as in *giăng-huòng,* 驚惶.

Huòng, 園 A garden, an orchard as *huă huòng,* 花園; imperial sepulchers: COM., *chái-huòng,* 菜園 a vegetable garden; *huòng-dĭng,* 園丁 a gardener; *huòng dìng,* 園亭 a summer house.

Huòng, 防 Coll. read *hòng,* q. v.:

a levee, a dike; to guard against; *huòng-bê*, 防備 to be ready for, on one's guard; *huòng mạ déu*, 防賣薅 unable to prevent.

Huòng, 磺 Firm, strong; native sulphur: COM., *liù-huòng*, 硫磺 Loochoo sulphur.

Huòng: A coll. word: oppressed with cares.

Huóng 遠 Read *uōng*: distant, far off; a superlative, very much, extremely; *huóng gę̆ng*, 遠近 far and near; *huóng dió*, 遠路 a long road; *huóng dọ̆i*, 遠塊 a remote place; *chă dék huóng*, 差的遠 very different from.

Ĭ, 衣 Also read *é*, q. v.: clothes; a case or wrapper; *băh ĭ*, 自衣 (coll. *băh săng*,) students: COM., *ĭ-siòng*, 衣裳 or *ĭ-hŭk*, 衣

服 clothes; *ŭ-ĭ,* 雨衣 rain garments; *sêu ĭ,* 壽衣 a shroud: COLL., *ĭ-sìong-kŭ,* 衣裳襪 the skirts.

I, 依 To rely on; to conform to; as, according to: COM., *ĭ nṳ̄,* 依汝 as you like.

I, 伊 He, she, it; an initial particle, only, because, that; a surname: *ĭ-dēng,* 伊等 they, them: COLL., *ĭ-gáuk-nẹng,* 伊各人 they all; *ĭ ciā nẹng,* 伊茖人 that person; *ĭ cọ̆ ĭ sé,* 伊做伊是 he acts in his own peculiar way.

I, 醫 In coll., used for *muŏk,* q. v.: to heal, to cure; medical, medicine: COM., *ĭ-sēng,* 醫生 a physician; *ĭ-guāng,* 醫館 a dispensary, a hospital; *ĭ-dé,* 醫治 to cure; *hèng ĭ,* 行醫 to practice medicine.

I   453

Ĭ, 阿 Read *ŏ*: common appellative prefix; *ĭ-diă*, 阿爹 father! *ĭ-mā*, 阿媽 grandma! *ĭ-ciă*, 阿姐 elder sister!

Ī, 以 By, with; for, that; in order to; according to; and, next: preceded by *sū* 所, therefore, wherein, as *sū-ĭ-iòng*, 所以然: preceded by *họ̆*, 何 how? how could? COM., *họ̆-ī*, 何以 suitable, will answer; *ī-ciéng*, 以前 (coll., *ĭ-sèng*), formerly; *ī siông*, 以上 the preceding; *ī-dé*, 以致 so that.

Ī, 苡 As in *é-ī*, (coll. *ī-mī*) pearl barley.

Ī, 爾 Thou, you, your; a final particle, also forms adverbs: *séuk ī*, 倏爾 suddenly; *ī-dēng*, 爾等 you all; *nāi ī*, 乃爾 it is thus, just so.

Ī, 邇 Near, next to; to approach: *ī-lài*, 邇來 until now, near (in time).

Ī, 倚 Coll. read *āi*, q. v.: to rely on, to depend on; *piěng ī*, 偏倚 partial.

Ī, 已 Sign of the perfect: COM., *ī gǐng*, 已經 has, already has: as a final,— excessive, no more.

Ì, 圯 Also read *gī*, q. v.: a bridge; an embankment.

Ì, 夷 Even; to equalize; great, ample; remote, foreign; applied to all foreigners; *ì-ing*, 夷人 or *ì-dǐk*, 夷狄 a foreigner.

Ì, 姨 A wife's sister: COM., *mū ì*, 母姨 a maternal aunt; *ì-mā*, 姨媽 and *ì-gǔng*, 姨公 grandmother's sisters and sister's husband.

Ì, 而 The whiskers; a copulative conjunction, and also, to-

Ì 455

gether; and yet, even: a disjunctive, but, yet, contrariwise; still, as: used for the person spoken to, thou: an initial particle; *ì-gǐng ì hâiu*, 而今而後 now and henceforth; *ì-ǐ*, 而已 that and nothing else: COM., *ì chiā*, 而且 moreover; *ì huóng*, 而况 still further, much more.

Ì, 輀 A funeral car, a hearse.

Ì, 兒 A boy, an infant; a suffix to nouns in the Court dialect: *hài-ì*, 孩兒 a boy: COM., *sièu-ì*, 小兒 my son.

Ì, 飴 Sweet cakes; sweet, pleasant; to feed.

Ì, 頤 The chin; to nourish, to feed; one of the diagrams.

Ì, 匜 A pitcher or goblet with a handle and spout; a waterpot or basin.

Iā, 冶 To fuse metals; to alloy; a smelter.

Iā, 墅 A separate residence; a cottage; *biĕk iā,* 別墅 a country house.

Iā, 野 A wilderness; a desert; wild, savage; uncultivated; rude, ill-mannered: COM., *iā é,* 野味 wild game; *kuōng-iā,* 曠野 a desert; *iā-séu,* 野獸 wild beasts: coll., *iā-giāng,* 野仔 a vagabond.

Iā: A coll. word: confused, disorderly; false, lying; also a superlative, very extremely: *iā siăh,* careless in one's diet: *iā-gōng,* to lie; *iā siăng,* very cheap; *iā hēng,* very bad or wicked.

Iā: A coll. word: followed by *ô* (to have, to be): slightly, partially: *iā-ô-hō,* somewhat good, pretty well; *iā-ô-ạ*: pretty well-able to; *iā-ô-sṳ̍k*; tolerably well-cooked.

Iá, 也 Used for the coll. *iá,* q. v.: a final euphonic particle, after a noun, makes the vocative: as a connective: and, also, even further, likewise: before a negative, it makes a question and implies an alternative; before *sê* (to be, is) it intensifics the meaning: repeated with *iū* (to have) it means also, too, likewise: used after verbs, to arrest the attention: *sê hȯ iá,* 是何也 what is it? what is meant? *ék iá,* 一也 the same, just alike; *kọ̄ dĭ iá,* 可知也 (from which) it is perceived; *ê cĭ iū iá,* 未之有也 there's no such thing!

Ià, 椰 The cocoanut, as in *ià-cī,*

椰子; *ià uāng*, 椰碗 cocoanut dippers.

Ià, 耶 An appellation of a father; an interrgative particle at the end of a sentence; *kī iū sḗ ià*, 豈有是耶 how is it so? COM., *Ià-Sŭ*, 耶穌 Jesus; *Ià-Sŭ-gáu*, 耶穌教 Protestant Christianity.

Iâ, 夜 After the sun's setting, night; late at might; *cŏk iâ*, 昨夜 last night; *iâ dài*, 夜台 the night terrace—the grave: COM., *diéu iâ*, 晝夜 or *nĭk iâ*, 日夜 day and night.

Iâ, 也 Read *iá*: and, also, too, when repeated it is a correlative, both, and: *iâ hǭ*, 也好 also good or well; *iâ ciŏng có*, 也將做 also do thus; *iâ ô gùng iâ ô bó*, 也務窮也務富 there are both rich and poor.

Iáh, 益 Read *ék*: to benefit, to profit: *ŏ iáh*, 有益 profitable; *lé iáh*, 利益 benefit, advantage.

Iăh, 役 Read *ĭk*: a policeman, a runner, as *chă iăh*, 差役.

Iăh, 驛 Read *ĭk*: a stage, a post, a posthouse, as *iăh cáng*, 驛站; *iăh hŭ*, 驛夫 a courier.

Iák: A coll. word, analagous to *hiák*: inverted, turned over: *iák gwó*, turned over, as a leaf by a sudden puff of wind; blown or puffed out.

Iăk: A coll. word: to beckon with the hand, as *iăk chiū*; *iăk nęng lì*, to beckon one to come.

Iăk: A coll. word: to use the fan, as *iăk siĕng*; *iăk huôi*, fan the fire.

Iăng: A coll. word: same as *hiăng*: *cháu iăng-iăng*, an

offensive order, a stench.

Iāng: A coll. word: to receive, to contract by exposure; *met.*, conveyed, as news; *mò hŭng-iāng*, no intelligence (to verify it).

Iāng: A coll. word: efficacious, as medicine: *ó iāng, mò iāng*, is it efficacious or not?

Iàng, 映 Read *ióng*: to expose to the sun or one's gaze; *dò nĭk-tàu iáng*, 掏日頭映 take and expose it to the sun a while.

Iàng, 營 Read *ìng*: a camp, an intrenchment; an army; *gŭng-iàng*, 軍營 the army; *iàng-buàng*, 營盤 a camp; *diē iàng*, 入營 to enlist; *cák iàng*, 札營 to encamp; *iàng-hióng*, 營餉 rations, wages.

Iàng, 贏 Read *ìng*, q. v.: to win,

as in a game or lawsuit; to conquer; *siŏ-iàng*, 輸贏 to lose and win.

Iàng: A coll. word: to spread, as grass growing or as any cutaneous eruption: *iàng muāng dói*, to spread everywhere; *iàng siŏh sŭng*, to spread over the whole person,

Iăng: A coll. word: bright, shining, glittering.

Iē, 椅 Also read *ĭ* and *ī*, in the dictionaries: a chair, a couch: COM., *gŭng cô iē*, 公座椅 an arm chair; *dĭk buói iē*, 直背椅 strait back chair: coll., *iē-tàu* 椅頭 and *iē-dèu*, 椅條 short and long benches; *iē-giāng*, 椅仔 a small chair; *iē-giāng dĕu*, 椅仔篼 a small mountain sedan.

Ié, 縊 The warp of cloth; to hang,

to strangle one's self; *ié sṳ̌*, 縊死 strangled to death.

Iè, 移 To transplant rice; to transpose, to shift; to transmit, as an infection; to migrate: COM., *iè kŭi*, 移開 to move aside: coll., *iè cêu hṳ̌ gáek*, 移就許角 move it to that spot; *iè siŏh hióng*, 移一向 to change the position of.

Iè, 爺 A father, a sire; a title of respect given to officers and gentlemen: COM., *iè mùong*, 爺門 an officer's household; *sṳ̌-iè*, 師爺 a private secretary: coll., *duái lō̤-iè*, 大老爺 your honor! term of address for district magistrates, etc..

Iè, 穧 Read *côi:* to sprinkle about: *iê cṳ̄ng*, 穧種 to sow seed; *iê muāng dê*, 穧滿地 to scatter all over the ground.

Iĕk, 夜 Read iâ: as in iê ṳ, 夜於 to work in the night; iê siŏh gĕng, 夜一工 to do a job of work by night.

Iĕk, 饇 Provisions for a journey; to carry food, as to workmen in the fields.

Iĕk, 熱 Warm; ardent, warm-hearted; feverish; to warm food: COM., iĕk ké, 熱氣 hot air, caloric; iĕk chéng, 熱冷 hot and cold; huák iĕk, 發熱 feverish; huò-huò iĕk, 和和熱 tepid; iĕk sĭng, 熱心 zealous; nâu iĕk, 鬧熱 a bustle a great stir; chĭng iĕk, 親熱 very intimate; iĕk bâng, 熱病 a fever.

Iĕk, 葉 Used for the coll. niŏh, q. v.: the leaves of plants; a leaf of a book; the thin plates of metal, foil; an age, posterity.

Iĕk: A coll. word: to shake, to loosen: *iĕk tiék-dĭng,* to pull out a nail.

Iĕng, 咽 The throat, the esophagus, in distinction from *hèu,* the windpipe. Read *iēng:* to swallow. Read *iĕk:* a stoppage of heath. Read *ĭng;* the roll of drums.

Iĕng, 烟 In the coll. read *ĭng,* and *hŏng,* q. v.: smoke, vapor; tobacco or opium, because they are smoked: COM., *huōi-iĕng,* 火烟 (or *ĭng*) smoke; *iĕng-dĕng,* 烟筒 a chimney, a flue.

Iĕng, 掩 Read *iēng:* To cover, to conceal, as with the hands; *iĕng mêng,* 掩面 to cover one's face; *iĕng ngê,* 掩耳 to stop the ears.

Iĕng 淹 To soak, to saturate.

Iēng 465

Iĕng, 醃 Used for the coll. siéng, q. v.: to lay in salt, to pickle.

Iĕng, 蚦 A large snake, said to be edible.

Iĕng, 髯 Also read iĕng: the whiskers; the beard.

Iĕng, 冉 To advance; slowly; gradually; Iēng-iŭ, 冉有 a disciple of Confucins.

Iēng, 苒 Luxuriant, tender herbage; by turns, successively.

Iēng, 偃 To lie down, to repose; to desist; prostrated; *iĕng nguô*, 偃卧 to lie down to sleep.

Iēng, 掩 In the coll. read *iĕng*, q. v.: to shade, to conceal from view: *iĕng muòng*, 掩門 to shut a door; COM., *iĕng-sék*, 掩飾 to hide or cover up (a matter); *ciă-iĕng*, 遮掩 to keep secret.

Iēng, 演 To spread out, to amplify, to practice, to drill: COM., *chàu-iēng*, 操演 (or *chàu-liēng*,) to drill troops; *iēng-siók*, 演說 to lecture.

Iēng. 衍 To inundate: to spread out; much, wide, far; elegant, handsome; *Iēng séng gŭng*. 衍聖公 title given Confucius and his descendants.

Iéng, 宴 Rest, ease; an entertainment; a feast, as *iéng-sĭk*. 宴席; *iéng lŏk*, 宴樂 joyful: COM., *sièk iéng*, 設宴 or *là iéng*, 排宴 to spread a feast.

Iéng, 燕 A feast; to rest; peaceful; a swallow, a martin: COM., *iéng-uŏ*, 燕窩 edible bird's nest.

Iéng, 厭 To dislike, to loathe; filled, satisfied, sated: COM., *iéng-ké*, 厭棄 to loathe and reject: COLL., *káh-di'u iéng*, 客調厭 tired of play. Read *ièng*, peaceful, tranquil. Read *iěng*, to conceal. Read *iěk*, wet, damp. Read *ák*, to subdue.

Iéng, 饔 To eat to repletion, as *siăh iéng*, 食饔.

Iéng: A coll. word: to take all, to engross, to retain for one's own use: *iéng lā cŏ̤*, to monoplize work; *iéng lā gōng*, to keep the floor, not allow others to speak.

Iéng, 炎 Fire blazing up; a fire spreading; luminous, bright: COM., *ièng iěk*, 炎熱 the severe heat of summer.

Iéng, 圓 Read *uòng*: round, circular; to collect, to assemble: *ièng kuàng*, 圓環 a ring; *ièng séu*, 圓壽 the character for longevity in a round form, as on scrolls, etc.; *ièng-ièng*, 圓圓 very round, circular; *ièng cièng*, 圓錢 to collect money; *ièng siŏh-dŏi*, 圓一堆 to collect together, as persons or things.

Iêng, 焰 The same as *ièng*, 炎 fire blazing up; a flame, a blaze; bright, brilliant: COM., *huŏi-ièng*, 火燄 the flame of fire.

Iêng, 豔 Beautiful; captivating; brilliant, as flowers: COM., *ièng lâ*, 豔麗 pretty, elegant.

Iêng, 院 A walled enclosure; a public establishment; a court, a hall; a college, a hospital: COM., *góng-ièng*, 貢院 a provincial examination hall; *hŏk-ièng*, 學院 a literary chancellor; *cṳ̆-ièng*, 書院 a college;

ĭ-iêng, 醫院 a hospital.

Iĕu. 幺 Small, tender, as a newborn child: things, diminutive; *iĕu dòng,* 幺豚 the runt.

Iĕu, 要 Also read *iéu,* q. v.; to search out the facts.

Iĕu, 腰 The loins, the waist, *met.,* the middle of a thing: COM., *iĕu-gáuk,* 腰骨 the haunch bone; *iĕu-cī,* 腰子 the kidneys; COLL., *iĕu-biĕng-páu,* 腰邊薹 Indian corn; *hāi-iĕu,* 海腰 a channel.

Iĕu, 邀 To cover, to conceal; to obstruct; to salute: COM., *hŭ-iĕu,* 虛邀 my poor invitation or feast.

Iĕu: A coll. word: to lead, to conduct, to show the way; *iĕu chiū,* to lead by the hand; *iĕu ĭ cà kó,* to take him along.

Iĕu, 妖 Beautiful, enchanting:

strange, unusual; to flatter, to enchant: *iĕu ngiòng,* 妖言 enticing words.

Iĕu, 夭 Also read *iĕu,* q. v.: pleasing, attractive; delicate, calamitous.

Iĕu, 殀 Short lived; a premature death, a calamity: COM., *iĕu sióng,* 殀相 a physiognomy indicating an early death, said of one having a short chin.

Iĕu, 擾 To give trouble, to annoy; to confuse; to infest, as banditti do: COM., *iĕu-luảng,* 擾亂 to produce anarchy; *chāu-iĕu,* 吵擾 to trouble, to annoy.

Iĕu, 窈 Also read *miĕu;* used for coll. *liĕu,* q. v.: deep, obscure, profound; *iĕu-tiĕu,* 窈窕 at leisure; gentle, quiet; handsome, as a lady.

Ièu, 舀 To lade, to dip out: COM., *ièu cūi*, 舀水 to lade water; *ièu kó siăh*, 舀去食 to dip it up and eat it.

Ièu, 要 Also read *ièu*, q. v.: to want, to wish; important, essential; a compend, an epitome: *ièu dộ*, 要道 the essential principles: COM., *cháuk ièu*, 撮要 a compend, an abridgment.

Ièu, 姚 A surname; beautiful, elegant. Read; *tiéu*: light, airy.

Ièu, 搖 Also read *ièu*: to shake, to move; to disturb, as *ièu-dóng*, 搖動.

Ièu, 謠 A song, rustic ditties; to villify: COM., *ièu-hĕk*, 謠惑 to lure, to tempt.

Ièu, 遙 Far, distant, remote in place.

Ièu, 飄 Fluttering, floating on the breeze, as a flag.

Ièu, 曜 The light of the sun: *chék ièu,* 七曜 the seven lights—i. e, sun, moon and five planets.

Ièu, 耀 To shine upon, to illumine; glorious, splendid: COM., *ing-ièu,* 榮耀 glory, distinction.

Ièu, 鷂 A hawk, a kite: variegated plumage: COM., *cāi-ièu,* 紙鷂 a paper kite.

Ĭh: A coll. euphonic prefix, as in *ĭh uăh,* by *met.,* to write quickly.

Ĭk, 易 Also read *ê,* q: v.: to change, to exchange, to barter: COM., *mâiu-ĭk,* 貿易 or *gău-ĭk,* 交易 commerce, barter: *găng-bàng gău-ĭk,* 公平交易 to trade fairly.

Ik, 疫 A pestilence, an epidemic, as *sì-ĭk,* 時疫: COM., *ŭng-ĭk,* 瘟疫 a plague; *chŭng ŭng, há ĭk,* 春瘟夏疫 spring and summer contagions.

Ik, 翼 A counsellor; to assist, to support; *ū ĭk,* 羽翼 wings; *met.,* adherents.

Ik, 液 Fluid secretions: COM., *cĭng-ĭk,* 精液 secretions of the body.

Ik, 伶 A musician, as *ĭk-sĕng,* 伶生.

Ik, 亦 A conjunction: and, also, too: *ĭk sê,* 亦是 also is; *ĭk iū,* 亦有 moreover; *ĭk kō,,* 亦可 also can or ought.

Ik, 奕 Large, great; beautiful; enduring, as generations: *ĭk iĕk,* 奕葉 an old family.

Ik, 役 Coll., read *iăh,* q. v.: border; official underlings, a police man; a servant; *chă-ĭk*, or *chă-iăh*, 差役 police.

Ĭk, 譯 To explain, to translate; an interpreter: *diòng-ĭk*, 傳譯 to interpret: COM., *huăng-ĭk*, 繙譯 to translate.

Ĭk, 繹 To unravel, get the clue to, as in *iù ĭk*, 紬繹.

Ĭk, 懌 Happy, pleased, contented.

Ĭk, 掖 Side apartments of the imperial palace, as *ĭk dìng*, 掖庭.

Ĭk, 腋 The armpit. *ĭk hâ*, 腋下 under the arms.

Ĭk, 驛 Coll., read *iăh*, q. v.: a post for the government; a stage; a courier; *ĭk câng*, 驛站 a post, a stage; *ĭk-guăng*, 驛官 a postmaster.

Ĭk, 弋 To shoot, as at birds flying.

Ĭk, 入 Used in the coll. for *diĕ*, q. v.: to enter, as a house; to become a member of; receipts, income; *ĭk hŏk,* 入學 to enter on one's studies: COM., *chók-ĭk,* 出入 to go out and in.

Ĭk: A coll., euphonic prefix, as in *ĭk-ŭk,* to wave, as a flag.

Ĭng, 仍 As, according to; again; just so, thus: COM.., *ĭng-nguòng,* 仍原 still, yet, as before.

Ĭng, 因 A cause, a reason; because, on account of, as *ĭng-ói,* 因爲 COM., *ĭng-chṳ́,* 因此 on account of this, hence: COLL., *ĭng ciŏng-uâng,* 因將換 hence, thus.

Ĭng, 暗 As in *ĭng ā,* 暗啞 dumb from sobbing or grief.

Ĭng, 音 A noise; a musical note; the voice: *siăng-ĭng,* 聲音 a sound, voice; *báik-ĭng*, 八音 the eight tones; *guăng-ĭng*, 官音 and *tū-ĭng*, 土音 the mandarin and local pronunciation.

Ing, 姻 Affinity; a bride: COM., *huŏng-ĭng*, 婚姻 betrothal, marriage; *giék-ĭng*, 結姻 to settle a marriage contract; *ĭng-gă*, 姻家 families related by marriage.

Ing, 凐 To dam up, to dike; *ĭng mŭk*, 凐沒 sunk in the water, drowned.

Ing, 烟 Read *iĕng:* smoke; *huŏi-ĭng*, 火烟 the smoke of a fire.

Ing, 應 Also read *éng*, q. v.: that which is proper and right; suitable, ought, should: COM., *ĭng-găi*, 應該 or *ĭng-dŏng*, 應當 ought.

Ing, 膺 The breast; to receive,

to assume, responsibility.

Ing, 瘖 Dumb from disease; *ĭng-lùng*, 瘖聾 dumb and deaf.

Ing, 癭 The goiter.

Ing, 罌 A canister, an earthen pitcher as *hài-ĭng*, 硋罌.

Ing, 甄 To mold; a potter; to distinguish; *ĭng biék ìng cài*, 甄別人才 discern men's abilities.

Ing, 氤 The elements.

Ing, 纓 A fringed ceremonial cap worn in summer, as *ĭng lĭk*, 纓笠.

Ing, 英 Luxuriant; excellent; brave, virtuous: *ĭng-huà*, 英華 beautiful; Anglo-Chinese: COM., *ĭng-hùng hò-giĕk*, 英雄豪傑 brave, manly, heroic.

Ing, 茵 As in *ĭng-dìng*, 茵蔯 wormwood.

Ing 闉 The inner gates in the

city wall, as *dṳng ĭng*, 重闉.

Ĭng, 陰 Obscure, dark; hades; secret; matter quiescent: COM., *ĭng-iòng*, 陰陽 the male and female principles in nature; *ĭng-hū* 陰府 or *ĭng-găng*, 陰間 hades; *ĭng-mèu*, 陰謀 to scheme secretly; *guŏng-ĭng*, 光陰 time.

Ĭng, 鷹 The falcon, the hawk: *ĭng-cēu*, 鷹烏 the eagle.

Ĭng, 永 Perpetual; final, complete; forever: COM., *ĭng-uōng*, 永遠 or *ĭng-siè*, 永世 forever: COLL., *ĭng-gū*, 永古 never.

Ĭng, 引 To precede; to induce; to recommend; a prefatory notice: COM., *siĕu ĭng*, 小引 a short preface; *ĭng-dô̤*, 引道 to show the way.

Ĭng, 飲 See also coll. *siăh* and *chiŏk*: to drink, to imbibe.

Read *éng*, to give to drink.

Īng, 飪 To season and dress food as *pĕng īng*, 烹飪.

Īng, 頴 A full head of grain, as *sĭk īng*, 實頴.

Īng, 袵 As in *liēng īng*, 斂袵 to put the hands together and bow, as ladies do.

Īng, 荏 Gentle, kindhearted: *īng-iēng*, 荏苒 to come and go, as of night and day.

Ing: A coll. euphonic prefix, as in *ing-iong*, to nourish, to rear.

Ìng, 人 Sometimes used for *nèng*, in the coll.: a man, a person: placed after nouns, a person having a calling: COM., *dŭng-ìng*, 中人 a broker; *tū-ing*, 土人 aborigines; *nŏi-ìng*, 內人 my wife; *cŏng hŭ-ìng*, 尊夫人 your wife; *ìng-cṳ̄*, 人子

sons; the Son of man; *gă-ìng,* 家人 domestics; *ìng-gă,* 人家 families; *ìng-sĕng,* 人參 ginseng: *ìng-gă chió,* 人家厝 family residences.

Ìng, 仁 In coll. read *nìng,* q. v.: humanity, benevolent, merciful; insensible; paralyzed: COM., *ìng-ái,* 仁愛 love, charity; *ìng-dáik,* 仁德 benevolence; *ìng-háiu,* 仁厚 trusty; *háing-ìng,* 杏仁 almonds.

Ìng, 盈 Full, overflowing; increasing, as the moon; *nguŏk-ìng,* 月盈 full moon; *ìng-kuók,* 盈缺 waxing and waning; *ìng-muāng,* 盈滿 full; conceited.

Ìng, 楹 A column, a prop, a support.

Ìng, 寅 To reverence; a colleague; one of the twelve

branches: COM., *ìng sì chĕ,* 寅時初 3 A. M.; *dùng ìng guăng,* 同寅官 fellow officers.

Ìng, 夤 To respect; to gain promotion; *ìng-iòng,* 夤緣 to intrigue.

Ìng, 壬 One of the ten stems great, to flatter.

Ìng, 任 Also read *êng,* q. v.: sincere, worthy of trust; friendship; a surname,

Ìng, 淫 The rising of water; immoral; great, as faults: COM., *găng-ìng,* 姦淫 fornication.

Ìng, 榮 Glory, fame, honor: COM., *ìng-guŏng,* 榮光 brilliant, as stars; *ìng-ièu,* 榮耀 glory, distinction; *ìng-huà hó gói,* 榮華富貴 splendor, wealth and honors.

Ìng, 熒 The sparkling light, as of an illumination; doubtful, intermitting light: *ìng dài*, 熒臺 a volcano.

Ìng, 瑩 The color of gems; bright, lustrous; *téng ìng*, 聽瑩 to hear indistinctly.

Ìng, 絍 Also read *êng*: threads used in weaving: *cék ìng*, 織絍 to weave.

Ìng, 縈 To wind, to twine about as *ìng nàu*, 縈繞.

Ìng, 塋 A tomb, a cemetery.

Ìng, 蠃 To bud, to expand; a family surname.

Ìng, 贏 In the coll. read *iàng*, q. v.: profits; overplus; to win, to conquer.

Ìng, 瀛 The broad ocean.

Ìng, 營 Coll. read *iàng*, q. v.: to dwell in a market; to plan, to scheme; a camp; military; the army.

Iō: A coll. word: weak, ex-

Iŏh 483

hausted, as *iô-iô*, or *iô chióh*.

Iô, 曳 To saunter, to walk leisurely, as *iô-iô*, 曳曳.

Iô, 睿 Wise, astute: *iô séng*, 睿聖 wise, sapient; *iô dé*, 睿智 intuitive perception.

Iô, 蜹 A gnat, a musquito.

Iô, 裔 The skirt of a robe; descendants: COM., *háiu-iô*, 後裔 one's posterity.

Iô, 銳 Sharp-pointed; ardent, zealous; courageous; quick-witted: *iô mĭng*, 銳敏 keen, quick, ready: COM., *iô-ké*, 銳氣 a zealous spirit; studious, as a learner.

Iŏh: A coll. word: to calculate, to make a rough estimate of, as *iŏh lā mô*.

Iŏh, 藥 Medicinal herbs; drugs, physic; to heal: COM., *iŏh cài*, 藥材 medicines; *iŏh hŭng*, 藥

粉 or *iŏh sāng*, 藥散 powders; *iŏh-uòng*, 藥丸 pills: COLL., *iŏh ké giàng*, 藥氣行 the operation of a dose; *iŏh siŏh táik*, 藥一貼 or *hŭk*, 服 a dose of physic; *iŏh că*, 藥渣 refuse of medicinal herbs.

Iŏh, 籲 Also read *ĕu:* to invoke, to implore; *kōng-iŏh*, 懇籲 to invoke earnestly.

Iŏh, 鑰 A lock, a bolt: COLL., *muòng iŏh siŏh â*, 門鑰一下 just give the bolt a push and fasten the door.

Iŏh: A coll. word, as in *láu-iŏh*, a large hawk or kite.

Iók, 約 To bind with a cord; to contract, to bind by rules; an agreement, a contract: COM., *iók cê*, 約字 a written contract; *mìng-iók*, 明約 a plain agreement; *iók dăng*, 約單 a bill of sale; *iŏk-liŏk*, 約畧 or *dái-iŏk*, 大約 in general, for the most part; *iŏk-sók*, 約束 to bind by contract.

Iŏk, 閱 To examine, to inspect; *iŏk chău*, 閱操 to review troops.

Iŏk, 弱 Read *iŏk*: weak, fatigued: *iŏk mŏ lĭk*, 弱毛力 the strength wasted by fatigue.

Iŏk, 悅 說 The second also read *siŏk* and *suói*, q. v.: to feel happy, contented; gratified; to submit gladly; COM., *iŏk é*, 悅意 pleased, delighted.

Iŏk, 弱 Used for the coll. *iók*, q. v.: weak, feeble, delicate; COM., *sŏi-iŏk*, 衰弱 emaciated and weak.

Iŏk, 若 A conjunction, if, supposing that: COM., *iŏk-sṳ̄*, 若使 if, supposing that.

Iŏk, 躍 To leap, to jump, as *tiéu iŏk*, 跳躍.

Iŏng, 央 In the center; to request as a favor: COM., *dŭng-iŏng*, 中央 the center, middle of: COLL., *mò đói iŏng*, 毛塊央 no one whom I can beg to do it.

Iŏng, 殃 Punishment, calamities, judgment, as *cāi-iŏng*, 災殃.

Iŏng, 鳶 A kite or sparrow hawk: *cāi-iŏng*, 紙鳶 a paper kite.

Iŏng, 蔫 Not fresh, putrid: *iŏng-iŏng-é*, 蔫蔫味 a stench, as of spoiled meat.

Iōng, 壤 Loamy soil; *gái iōng*, 蓋壤 cover and ground—heaven and earth; *gék iōng*, 擊壤 an ancient game.

Iōng, 養 Also read *iông*, q. v.: to feed, to nourish; to maintain, as the indigent: COM., *iōng-*

uăk, 養活 to support life; iōng-ŭk-dòng, 養育堂 a foundling asylum; tiĕng-iōng, 添養 to bear children.

Iōng, 癢 Used for the coll. *sióng*, q. v.: to itch; a desire to scratch.

Ióng, 怏 Discontented: *ióng-iòng*, 怏然 conceited.

Ióng, 恙 Grief, melancholy; *biĕk lài ù ióng*, 別來無恙 have you been well since we parted?— an epistolary phrase.

Ióng, 映 Used for the coll. *iáng*, q. v.: the sun past the meridian: COM., *ièng ióng*, 掩映 to shimmer.

Iòng, 羊 A sheep, a goat; a gazelle: COM., *mièng-iòng*, 緜羊 a sheep; *săng iòng*, 山羊 a goat; *gŏ-iòng*, 羔羊 a lamb.

Iòng, 佯 To pretend: *iòng bók*

dĭ, 佯不知 to pretend not to know—an epistolary phrase.

Iòng, 洋 The sea, the ocean, as *hái-iòng*, 海洋.

Iòng, 沿 To follow a stream; to conform, as to others' wishes *hŭng-sŭk siòng iòng*, 風俗相沿 the custom has been perpetuated.

Iòng, 鉛 Lead, COM., *iòng-cī*, 鉛子 a bullet; *iòng cê*, 鉛字 foreign type.

Iòng, 鎔 Read *ùng*. to smelt, to fuse metals; *iòng ngùng*, 鎔銀 to fuse silver.

Iòng, 揚 To publish, as *bó̤-iòng*, 播揚; COM., *iòng-diòng*, 揚傳 to spread abroad.

Iòng, 颺 Blown about by the wind; *bó̤ iòng*, 播颺 to winnow grain; *iòng-ngiòng*, 颺言 loud, hasty words.

Iòng, 楊 As in *iòng-liŭ*, 楊柳 the willow.

Iòng, 陽 Lofty and clear; the superior of the dual powers in nature: as heaven, the sun, day; male; virility: COM., *tái-iòng*, 太陽 the sun; used together, *iòng hóng ĭng ŭi*, 陽奉陰違 manifestly obeying, secretly disobeying; *iòng găng*, 陽間 or *iòng-sié*, 陽世 the world.

Iòng, 然 Used as a final particle, yes, truly, verily, certainly; as a disjunctive, but, then, if, so then; used as the sign of adverbs: *côi iòng*, 卒然 suddenly; *iòng iá*, 然也 just-so: COM., *guō-iòng*, 果然 truly, surely; *cĕu-iòng*, 自然 of course; *iòng-hăiu*, 然後 afterwards, then.

Iòng, 燃 To burn; to catch fire; a conflagration: coll., *iòng-ęu*, to smoulder.

Iòng, 延 Slow, dilatory: COM. *ă-iòng*, 挨延 to procrastinate.

Iòng, 筵 A spread table: *met.*, a feast, as *iòng sĭk*, 筵席 or *iòng iéng*, 筵宴.

Iòng, 緣 Used for the coll. *iông*, q. v.: a cause, a reason, as *iòng-gó*, 緣故.

Iông, 件 Read *siông*: a classifier for an article, an affair, a subject, etc., a, an, one: COM. *cī siŏh iông*, 只一件 this one: COLL., *iông-iông dŭ ẹ̆*, 件件都儜 can do everything.

Ióng, 養 Also read *iōng*, q. v.: to provide for, to support one's parents.

Iōng, 樣 A rule, a pattern: *met.*, a guide, an example; *muò-*

iông, 模樣 a pattern: coll., ciŏng-iông, 將樣 how, in what manner? ciŏng-iông-gì, 將樣其 why? how? ŏh ĭ iông, 學伊樣 imitate him.

Ióng, 讓 Used for the coll., niông, q. v.: to give up, to yield; yielding, retiring; humble.

Iông, 禳 As in iông-tái-suói, 禳太歲 to sacrifice to the great Cycle.

Iŭ, 憂 Sorrowful and anxious, as iŭ-lêṳ, 憂慮.

Iṳ̆, 優 Abundant, excessive; iŭ iŭ iŭ ṳ̀, 優優有餘 enough and more.

Iŭ, 友 A friend, a companion; to act as a friend: COM., bèng-iŭ, 朋友 a friend; huôi-iŭ, 會友 a fellow member.

Iŭ, 牖 A square window; to instruct, to bring up: iŭ mìng,

牖民 to instruct the people.

Iŭ, 誘 To lead on to evil, as *ĭng-iū*, 引誘; *iū-hĕk*, 誘惑 to tempt, to seduce.

Iŭ, 有 Sometimes used for *ó* in the coll.: to have, to be; forms the past tense; and, also, more: *iū sì*, 有時 sometime; *iū-áing*, 有限 limited in amount; *iū é*, 有意 purposely; *iū ṳ̆*, 有餘 overplus.

Iù, 柔 Easy, flexible; complaisant; gentle, mild; COM., *iù-niŏng*, 柔軟 gentle, yielding.

Iù, 遊 To ramble, to roam, to saunter: *iù gă*, 遊街 to saunter in the streets; *siông há iù*, 上下遊 northern and southern Prefectures in Fukien Province.

Iù, 游 To float, to drift; to go abroad: *iù mìng*, 游民, *iù chiū*

游手, *iù ụng*, 游勇 idle people.

Iù, 油 Oil, fluid grease, paint: COM., *iù huŏi*, 油灰 putty; *siŏh iù*, 石油 petroleum.

Iù, 由 A preposition: through, by, from: *iù chụ̄*, 由此 hence, therefore: COM., *iù lài*, 由來 heretofore: COLL., *iù cái nụ̄*, 由在汝 as you please, it rests with you; *mò lài iù*, 毛來由 no reason for it.

Iù, 郵 A post house; *iù ĭk*, 郵驛 a post-station; *iù céng guŏh*, 郵政局 the Post Office.

Iù, 猶 As in *Iù-tái nệng*, 猶太仆 the Jews; *iù-ẹu bók giŏk*, 猶豫不決 doubting and undecided.

Iù, 尤 Extraordinary, remarkable; adverb of comparison very, excessively; a surname; *kiĕng-iù*, 愆尤 a fault.

Iù, 疣 As in *săng iù,* 生疣 to have a tumor, or swelling.

Kă, 胶 Read *ngàu:* the foot; also a numerative of one of a pair; same as *kiă,* q. v.: *kă-tōi,* 胶腿 the thigh; *kă-kók-tàu,* 胶屈頭 the knee; *kă-ngù-mĕk,* 胶牛目 the ankles; *kă-cāi,* 胶指 the toes; *piāng-kă,* 跛胶 lame; *kă-buó,* 胶步 a step, a pace; *kă-kó,* 胶靠 fetters.

Kă: A coll. word, as in *kă-chióh,* the magpie.

Kā: A coll. word; as *kā-dák,* (*lák*), to mend.

Ká, 敲 Read *kiĕu:* to beat, to pound to crack, as nuts; *ká muòng,* 敲門 to knock at a door.

Kă, 溪 A mountain stream: COM., *kă ò,* 溪河 streams and

Káeng 495

rivers; *kă-sùng,* 溪船 up-river boats: COLL., *kă-năk,* 溪筒 or *năk-giăng,* 筒仔 a bamboo tracking rope.

Kă, 襟 Read *kĭng:* the skirts of a garment, called *ĭ-sìong-kă,* 衣裳襟

Kă, 齟 Read *cū:* to bite, to gnaw; *met.,* to appropriate.

Ká, 快 Read *kuái:* to hurry, to make haste; *ká-chuói,* 快脆 very expeditiously; *ká-uăk,* 快活 in easy circumstances.

Káek, 壳 Read *káuk:* the skin, shell, or covering of fruits or of eggs; *huă-méng-káek,* 花面壳 a mask; *táung káek,* 脱壳 to shed the skin.

Káeng, 空 Read *kŭng:* a void, an interstice; *káeng-láeng,* an interval.

Káeng, 欬 Read *kái:* to cough, to

hack, as kâeng-sáu, 欮嗽

Káh, 客 Read káik: a guest, a friend; a dealer, a trader; nèng-káh, 仆客 a guest; káh-siŏng, 客商 a foreign trader; káh-tiăng, 客廳 a parlor.

Káh: A coll. word, as káh-dièu, (or ka-dièu) to recreate, to play.

Kăi, 開 In the coll., kŭi, q. v.: to open, to unfold; to institute, to explain; kăi huôi 開會 to open a meeting; kăi tŭng muòng hô, 開通門戶 the "open door"—commercial relations.

Kăi, 揩 To rub, to wipe, as kăi chék, 揩拭.

Kāi, 劏 A sickle; kāi chiék hiêu-êu, 劏切曉諭 fully make it known to you—a phrase used in edicts.

Kāi, 凱 Victrious, trimphant;

Káik 497

kāi gŏ, 凱歌 peans of victory.

Kāi, 覬 Read *gé*: to covet and appropriate, as *kāi-ęu*, 覬覦.

Kāi, 楷 A straight, graceful tree; *muò-kāi*, 模楷 a model, an examplar; *kāi cê*, 楷字 a full, square form of character.

Kái, 慨 The disappointment of a brave man; loyal; noble, generous as *kōng kái*, 忼慨.

Kái, 概 As in *ké-kái*, 氣概 determined, resolute; COM., *dâi-kái*, 大概 generally speaking, on the whole; *ék-kái*, 一概 altogether.

Káik, 克 To be able, superior to; overbearing; *káik gī*, 克己 to subdue self: COM., *káik kùng káik giêng*, 克勤克儉 to be diligent and economical.

Káik, 尅 To subdue, to overcome: in the coll., to deny

self; *káik gĭ*, 尅期 a set time; *cêng káik*, 盡尅 very crowded.

Káik, 刻 To cut, to engrave; one quarter hour, as *siŏh káik cŭng:* 一刻鐘: COM., *káik cê*, 刻字 to cut characters; *káik bēng*, 刻板 to cut (on) blocks; *sì-káik*, 時刻 coustantly; *kīng-káik*, 頃刻 a short time; *káik hâ guŏng-gīng*, 刻下光景 present prospects; *káik bŏk* 刻薄 to cheat; insulting: COLL., *siŏh káik gŭ*, 刻古 a little while.

Káik, 客 Coll. *káh*, q. v.: a guest, a friend, a stranger, as *sĕng káik*, 生客: COM., *uōng káik*, 遠客 strangers from afar; *bĭng-káik*, 賓客 (or *lài-bĭng*, 來賓) guests.

Káik, 唫 Read *iék:* to close, as

Káiu 499

the eyes; *měk-ciŭ káik,* 目睛瞌 to shut the eyes;

Káing, 挭 To oppress, to obstruct: COM., *káing sŭk,* 挭熟 to obstruct the redemption of property.

Káing, 膈 Read *gáik,* the diaphragm: *káing tiáng,* 膈痛 pain in the chest.

Káing: A coll. word: to put on a cover; to cover.

Káiu, 叩 To strike, to tap; to knock the head when in worship, or saluting a superior; *káiu siŭ,* 叩首 the kotow: COM., *săng gôi giŭ-káiu,* 三跪九叩 three kneelings and nine knockings, of the head, as in Confucian worship.

Káiu, 扣 To beat, to knock; to deduct, a reduction: COM., *gāu ngū káiu*, **九五扣** a reduction of 5 *per cent*, i. e., 95 paid on 100; *káiu buó*, **扣布** a kind of narrow cotton cloth; *káiu gĕng ciĕng*, **扣工錢** to cut wages.

Káiu, **釦** A gold or silver rim on vessels; to carve buttons; to button: COM., *káiu muòng*, **釦門** button holes.

Káiu, **寇** To rob, to plunder; thieves, outlaws, as *káiu-chĕk*, **寇賊**.

Káiu, **蔲** Nutmegs as *dáiu-káiu*, **荳蔲**.

Kák, **渴** Dry, thirsty; eager, longing for: COM., *chói káh*, **嘴渴** thirsty; *cī kák*, **止渴** to quench thirst.

Kák, **恰** Opportunely; exactly, just right as *kák hō̤*, **恰好**; *kák cóng*, **恰俊** very nice—often said in irony.

Kák, 拾 Read *sĭk*: to collect, to pick up, as *kák kī*; 拾起.

Kák: A coll. word: to collect, as money; to take (a census): *kák hóng ciềng*: to collect the quotas (for a village temple); *kák dĭng-kēu*, to take a census of males and females.

Kák, 太 Read *tái*: used for the coll. *kák*, a superlative, too, very; *kák guó*, 太過 excessive; *kák dòng*, 太長 too long; *kák ciĕng*, 太賤 very mean or low; *kák ciŭ-mĭk*, 太周密 excessively polite.

Kăng, 刊 To cut, to carve, to engrave, as *kăng-káik* 刊刻; *bók kăng*, 不刊 unmutilated; *met.*, imperishable, as the doctrines of a sage.

Kăng, 龕 To contain, to hold; a niche for tablets and images:

COM., *bù-sák-kăng,* 菩薩龕 an idol shrine.

Kăng, 坑 A ditch, a hollow; a hole, a den, as for wild beasts: COM., *săng-kăng,* 山坑 a mountain precipice.

Kăng, 堪 To sustain; capable of, fit, worthy of; *kăng éng,* 堪任 able to bear a responsibility: COM., *bók kăng,* 不堪 unfit, unworthy.

Kăng, 嵌 Rocky, precipitous ledges as *kăng-ngàng,* 嵌巖

Kăng, 戡 To stab, to kill.

Kāng, 坎 A pit, a dangerous place: COLL., *kāng séng,* 坎囟 the brainpan, the soft spot on the head of an infant.

Kāng, 砍 To fell, to cut down; *kāng dọ̤,* 砍倒 to fell trees.

Kāng, 檻 A baluster; a cage or den for wild beasts: a win-

Kău 503

dow, as *kāng-mùong*, 檻門.

Kāng, 艦 A man-of-war; *ciéng kāng*, 戰艦 a gunboat; *Mī kāng*, 美艦 the American fleet.

Kāng: A coll. word, as in *kāng-bèng*: bits of broken tiles.

Káng, 看 Sometimes read *kăng*: to see; to inspect: COM., *káng-giéng*, 看見 to see; *káng-kĭng*, 看輕 to disesteem; *káng-pó*, 看破 to penetrate; to discover (the folly of): COLL., *káng mạ chók*, 看賣出 can't understand it.

Káng, 瞷 To view, to watch one furtively.

Káng, 勘 To examine; to ascertain facts: COM., *káng-ngiêng*, 勘驗 to hold an inquest.

Kău, 鬮 Read *kiŭ* in the dictionaries: a lot, a ballot; to draw lots, as *niĕng kău*, 拈鬮.

504   Káuk

Kău: A coll. word: to mix, to mingle, as *kău siŏh-dŏi.*

Kău: A coll. word: difficult, troublesome, as *kău-ké.*

Kāu, 口 Read *kēu:* a mouth; *gă-kāu,* 街口 entrance to the street; *hāi-kāu,* 海口 passage to the sea.

Káu: A coll. word: a tone of displeasure, chiding; *káu ĭ tĕk cṳ̆,* to urge to study; *káu ĭ cọ́ dái,* to urge to diligence.

Káuk, 壑 A ditch, a pit; a gully: COM., *cūi-káuk.* 水壑 a plash, a puddle.

Káuk, 榷 A plank or timber over a stream; a drawbridge where toll is paid: *káuk suói,* 榷税 to receive toll.

Káuk, 恪 To revere, to respect.

Káuk, 愨 Careful, diligent, as *sìng káuk.*

Káung   505

Káuk, 確 Hard, solid; truthful, sincere; certainly: *bók káuk*, 不確 doubtful: COM., *káuk iòng*, 確然 surely; *dék káuk*, 的確 faithful; *káuk-sĭk*, 確實 or *káuk cĭng*, 確眞 true, verily.

Káuk, 磕 Read *kái*: to "knock the head" before superiors; *káuk tàu*, 磕頭 the *kotow* ceremony; *káuk tàu páh chiěng*, 磕頭拍禩 to knock the head, kneeling on one knee.

Káung, 伉 To mate, to match; *káung lá*, 伉儷 a pair, husband and wife.

Káung, 抗 To raise with the hand: COM., to oppose, to resist, as *káung-géu*, 抗拒, *káung ùi*, 抗違 to rebel against.

Káung, 匡 As *káung-chòng*, 匡床 a couch, or *kang* as used in the north.

Káung, 炕 To roast; to toast; *káung chòng*, 炕床 a bed of brick, heated underneath.

Káung, 困 A house in ruins; needy, in want; distressed, as in *káung-kū*, 困苦.

Káung, 睏 To sleep: *kó káung*, 去睏 to go to bed; *káung diōh*, 睏着 asleep; *káung lŏh mìng*, 睏落眠 fast asleep.

Káung: A coll. word: to lay by, to store away.

Ké, 氣 Vapor; air; the breath the temper of men and things; aspect, bearing: COM., *tiĕng-ké*, 天氣 weather: *sék-ké*, 濕氣 dampness; *ké-sáik*, 氣色 complexion; *nó-ké*, 怒氣 anger; *cé-ké*, 志氣 energy, nerve; *siĕu-ké*, 小氣 miserly, avaricious: COLL., *ké dĕuk*, labored breathing; *sĕu ké* 受氣 get angry.

Kék 507

Ké, 器 A vessel, a dish; utensils as *ké-gêu;* 器具; *siêu-ké,* 小器 mean, littleminded.

Ké, 棄 To reject, to cast off: COLL., *ké-hièng,* 棄嫌 to dislike; *ké sié,* 棄世 dead; *iéng ké,* 厭棄 to loathe; *ké-siá gŭi ciáng,* 棄邪歸正 to reform.

Ké, 柿 Read *sĕu:* the persimmon: COLL., *kê biăng,* 柿餅 persimmons—dried and pressed.

Kẹ, A coll. word: doltish.

K'ẹ: A coll. word: the same as *kù;* dull and stupid.

Kék, 泣 As in *kók-kék,* 哭泣 to cry and sob; *kék hiék,* 泣血 to weep blood—written on funeral cards.

Kék, 隙 A hole in a wall; a crevice; a pretext; COM., *sìng kék,* 尋隙 to seek pretexts for a quarrel.

508   Kĕng

Kék, 喫 Read *ngék:* to suffer, to endure; *kék-kŭi,* 喫屈 suffering, in pain; *mậ kék dék,* 賣喫的 indisposed.

Kĕk, 獲 Read *hĕk*, q. v.: denoting cause, manner or instrument; with, by, through; to use.

Kĕng, 牽 Used for the coll. *kèng,* to grasp and pull: to lead, as by a cord; to guide; to influence: COM., *kĕng chiū,* 牽手 to take hold of hands; *kĕng sĭ,* 牽絲 to spin webs, or coccoons.

Kĕng, 莖 Read *hèng:* a stem, a twig.

Kĕng, 鏗 Used for *kiăng, kiăng* and *kiàng* in the coll.: a ringing metallic sound; *cièng kĕng* 籛鏗 a man who reached the fabulous age of 767 years.

Kēng, 犬 A dog; the 94th radical.

Kěng, 肯 Coll. read kǐng, q. v.: to be willing; bók kěng, 不肯 unwilling, to refuse.

Kéng, 慶 To congratulate; kéng-hô, 慶賀 good, excellent; hǐ kéng, 喜慶 happy congratulations; dòng kéng, 堂慶 mother's birthday congratulations.

Kěng, 空 Read kŭng: empty, hollow; in vain, to no purpose; kěng-kěng, 空空 a hole; kěng-páng, 空冇 hollow; kěng-páng-káęk, 空冇壳 an empty shell; met., a weak constitution.

Kěu, 摳 Also read chěu: to lift up the skirts, in ascending a flight of steps, as kěu ǐ, 摳衣.

Kěu, 口 In the coll., read kāu and kěu; the mouth, a door, a narrow passage into; a classifier: COM., hô kěu, population;

kēu-cái, 口才 eloquence; *kēu-é*, 口意 the meaning of what one says; *kēu é*, 口呷 taste, flavor; *kēu-gŭng*, 口供 testimony; *kēu-ĭng*, 口音 dialect; *gēng-kēu*, 減口 voluntary lessening of food; *kēu séng*, 口信 a verbel reply.

Kéu: A coll. word: stiff, starched: *mạ kéu*, limber.

Kéu, 臼 Coll. read *kó*, a mortar; *kéu tū*, 臼杵 a mortar and pestle.

Kéu, 去 Coll. read *kó̤*, q. v.; to go away; to go out, from or through; to advance; past, former; *kéu sié*, 去世 dead.

Kéuk, 乞 To ask alms; to implore: in the coll., to give, to bestow; also a sign of the passive, to let, to allow: COM. *giù kéuk*, 求乞 to beg: COLL., *kéuk ĭ páh,* 乞伊拍 beaten by him; *kéuk ĭ piéng,* 乞伊骗 deceived by him.

Kéuk 曲 Coll. read *kuŏh,* q. v.: crooked, distorted; as *kók kéuk,* 屈曲.

Kêung, 梠 Read *kêu:* the tallow tree, as *kêung chéu,* 梠模.

Kêung, 虹 Read *hùng:* the rainbow; *uák siŏh kêung,* 挖一虹 to give a scratch with one's nails.

Kĭ, 欺 To impose upon, as *kĭ hô* 欺負; to cheat, as *kĭ-piéng,* 欺骗

Kĭ, 崎 Used for coll. *kié,* q. v.: Steep, rugged, as *kĭ-kŭ,* 崎歁 precipices, dangerous defiles.

Kĭ, 欹 Inclined; *kĭ ké,* 欹器 vessels easily upset: coll., *gă-lăng-kĭ,* oblique, toppling.

Kĭ, 豈 How! what! a particle

implying a strong affirmation, as kĭ-bók-sê, 豈不是 how is it not! kĭ-bók-dĭ, 豈不知 how do I not know it! kĭ-gāng, 豈敢 how dare!—a polite reply to a compliment.

Kĭ, 起 To rise; to build; to undertake: COM., kĭ-chiū, 起手 or kĭ-diĕng, 起點 to begin; kĭ gá, 起價 to raise the price: COLL., kĭ buáng-làng-chiàng, 起半欄成 half-built, as a house.

Kĭ, 齒 Read chĭ: the teeth.

Kĭ, 蜞 Read gĭ: a leech as mā-kĭ, 螞蜞

Kĭ, 鉗 Read kièng: to fasten china with clamps as kĭ uāng, 鉗碗.

Kiă, 奇 Read kiĕ: also gĭ q. v.: one, a single one; odd numbers as kiă kiă; kiă nĭk, 奇日 the odd days in a month.

Kiâng 513

Kiă, 跨 Read *kuă* and *kuá*: to treat persons harshly, as *kiă nęng*, 跨仸.

Kiă, 跨 Read *kuă* and *kuá*: to bestride.

Kiák, 谷 Read *gók*: a depression between hills, as in *săng-kiák*, or *săng gók*, 山谷

Kiák, 㨃 Read *hăk*: to press; pinched; *lŏ-chṳ̄-kiák*, 老鼠㨃 a rat-trap; *kiák sióng*, 㨃相 to photograph.

Kiák: A coll. word: to add; *kiák ngài cièng*, to mix in bad cash.

Kiăng, 鏗 Read *kĕng*: also coll. read *kiāng* and *kiàng*: a ringing, metallic sound.

Kiáng: A coll. word: to nod, to bow the head, as *kiáng tàu*.

Kiâng: A coll. word: to shut, to close the door, as *mùong kiâng siŏh â*.

Kiĕ, 奇 also read *gì;* in coll. read *kiă,* q. v.: odd; surplus; odd numbers, as *kiĕ só;* 奇數.

Kiĕ, 暌 To oppose; separated from; *kiĕ ùi nĭk giū,* 暌違日久 a long time sundered—used in letters.

Kiĕ, 稽 To examine into, to investigate; *kiĕ chák,* 稽察 to search a record. Read *kiē* to bow down.

Kiĕ, 稽 The name of a place as *kiĕ săng* 稽山; a surname.

Kiĕ, 窺 To peep at, as through a crevice; *kiĕ táng,* 窺探 to spy out; *kiĕ-sęu,* 窺伺 to wait for.

Kiĕ, 啓 To open out, to explain; to teach: COM., *kiĕ ciă,* 啓者 to the writer—opening phrase in a letter; *êu kiĕ ciă,* 又啓者 a postscript; *ăng kiĕ,* 安啓

"open it calmly"—a superscription on letters; *kiĕ-mìng sĭng,* 啓明星 the morning star.

Kiē, 綺 A figured summer silk called *kiē lò* 綺羅 or *lò-kiē.*

Kié 跂 To raise the foot. Read *kié:* to stand on tiptoe.

Kié, 騎 A horse; *chiěng-kiē* 千騎 a thousand horse; *gŭ kiē,* 車騎 horse and carriage.

Kié, 企 To stand erect; to eagerly expect as *kié uông,* 企望.

Kié, 契 Also read *siék,* q. v: a deed, a contract; adopted: COM., *kié iŏk,* 契約 deeds; *kié nā,* 契奶 adopted mother.

Kié, 崎 Read *kĭ:* inclined, steep: *cêng kié,* 盡崎 very steep.

Kié, 竪 Read *sêu:* to set upright: *kié huŏng,* 竪坊 to erect an honorary portal; *kié hàng-tàu*, 豎銜頭 to display one's official titles.

Kiè, 騎 Also read *kie*: to ride a horse, as *kiè mā*, 騎馬.

Kiê, 跬 Read *kiē*: to stand: *kiê dáing*, 跬店 employed in a shop; *kiê siŏh gū*, 跬一股 to stand for (have) one share.

Kiék, 怯 Also read *kiŏk*: of little courage, as *kiék dāng*, 怯膽.

Kiék, 愜 Pleased, gratified, as *kiék é*, 愜意

Kiék, 慊 Contented; read *kiĕng*, dissatisfied.

Kiék, 缺 Read *kuŏk*: a flaw, a nick, as in a knife or pottery; *kiék chói*, 缺嘴 a harelip.

Kiĕng, 嗛 A bird's crop. Read *gàng*: to hold in the mouth.

Kiĕng, 謙 As *kiĕng-hṳ̆* 謙虛 humble, unassuming, lowly.

Kiĕng 517

Kiĕng, 愆 A fault, error; excess, crime, as kiĕng-iù, 愆尤 COM., cŏi-kiĕng, 罪愆 or kiĕng-guó, 愆過 a transgression.

Kiĕng, 繾 As in kiĕng guóng, 繾綣 intimate, as friends.

Kiĕng, 譴 As in kiĕng-cáik, 譴責 to blame, to criminate.

Kiĕng, 遣 To send, to commission, as chă-kiĕng, 差遣.

Kiéng, 欠 To owe; COM., kiéng cái, 欠債 to owe debts; kiéng kuó, 欠課 to owe taxes; kiéng-kuók, 欠缺 deficient in.

Kiềng, 岑 A high, tapering peak; a surname.

Kièng, 擒 To seize, to grasp: COM., kièng chiū, 擒手 to grasp with the hand.

Kièng, 鉗 In the coll. used for kìng and kì: q. v. to grasp

with pincers; pincers, nippers, forceps.

Kièng, 鈐 As in kièng éng, 鈐印 to stamp edges of letters in P. O. as of official documents or to match bank bills.

Kiĕu, 撬 To raise with a lever.

Kiĕu, 敲 Used in coll. for ká, q. v.: to rap, to beat on one side with a club; kiĕu muòng, 敲門 to knock at a door.

Kiĕu, 蹺 To lift up the foot: used in the coll. in the sense of tricky: COLL, kiĕu-da, 蹺打 to take advantage of, so as to injure.

Kiéu, 巧 Coll. kiéu q. v.; skillful, ingenious; wily, crafty.

Kiĕu, 豈 Read kī: COLL. kiĕu, a corruption of kī iū; kiĕu chụ lī, 豈此理 it is unreasonable.

Kiéu, 竅 A hole, an interstice.

Kĭng 519

met., the mind, as intelligent or dull: COM., *lìng-kiéu*, 靈竅 intelligence.

Kiéu, 巧 Read *kiéu*: skill, ingenuity: *kiéu-miéu bók dùng*, 巧妙不同 their talents are different.

Kĭk, 檄 An official summons or reprimand, as *kĭk ùng*, 檄文.

Kĭk, 頸 Read *giék* in the dictionaries: a stiff or strait neck.

Kĭk: A coll. euphonic prefix, as in *kĭk-kŏk*, to strike against: *kĭk-kiăk*, to mix in, as cash, goods, etc.; *kĭk dŭk kiăk*, tilting, as a stone or board.

Kĭng, 傾 Coll. read *kìng*: inclined; to subvert; to waste, to squander; *kìng cháik*, 傾側 inclined.

Kĭng, 頃 Read *kìng*: *kìng-káik* 頃刻 a little while.

Kĭng, 卿 To revert towards: a noble, a high officer, *kĭng sióng,* 卿相 a prime minister; *kĭng gă,* 卿家 our ministers *ái kĭng,* 愛卿 my wife.

Kĭng, 欽 To respect, to reverence; imperial: COM., *kĭng-chă,* 欽差 an imperial envoy; *kĭng-gói,* 欽貴 valuable, precious; *kĭng-gă,* 欽加 to confer an additional title.

Kĭng, 矜 To compassionate; to esteem; to maintain one's self respect; *kĭng i bók cĕng* 矜而不爭 to maintain one's dignity without wrangling; *kō̤ kĭng,* 可矜 pitiable: COM., *kĭng kuā,* 矜誇 to brag.

Kĭng, 輕 A light carriage: frivolous: COM., *kĭng sĕng,* 輕生 bold, audacious; *kĭng sĕng,* 輕信 credulous: COLL., *kĭng-*

King 521

ùng-ê, 輕容易 carelessly or easily.

Kĭng, 頃 Coll. read *kìng*: a hundred meu; an instant, a moment: COM., *kĭng-káik,* 頃刻 or *kĭng-káik cĭ gáng,* 頃刻之間 a very short time.

Kĭng, 肯 Read *kĕng*: *kĭng có,* 肯做 willing to do; *kĭng tĕk,* 肯讀 willing to study.

Kìng, 禽 The feathered tribe; COM., *kìng nëu,* 禽鳥, birds; *kìng séu,* 禽獸 birds and beasts.

Kìng, 琴 A Chinese lute of five or seven strings, also applied to foreign musical instruments: *dàng-kìng,* 彈琴 to play musical instruments.

Kìng, 傾 Read *kĭng*; to pour, to pour tea, as in *kĭng dà,* 傾茶

Kìng, 鉗 Read *kièng*; a pair of

tongs, as in *huŏi kìng,* 火鉗

Kiók, 孑 Solitary, alone: COM. *kiók iòng ék sĭng,* 孑然一身 one without relatives.

Kiók, 攫 As in *kiók chū,* 攫取 to seize, to take forcibly.

Kiók 訐 Read *giók* in the dictionaries: to reprove one; to reveal: *miêng kiók,* 面訐 to reprimand personally; *kiók ìng duāng chéu,* 訐人短處 to talk about people's faults.

Kiŏk, 劇 Very; distressing; a comedy: *bêng kiŏk,* 病劇 a distressing illness.

Kiŏk, 謔 Also read *ngiŏk:* to jest, to sport; to ridicule; *chiéu kiŏk,* 笑謔 to laugh at.

Kiŏng, 腔 A hollow bone; a dialect: COM., *tū kiŏng,* 土腔 the native dialect; *ừng kiŏng* 榕腔 the "banyan" (i, e., Foochow) dialect.

Kiŭ, 邱 A low hill, a mound; a surname: *săng kiŭ* 山邱 the three hills of the immortals; *kiŭ lūng* 邱壟 a mound, graves; *kiŭ ling* 邱陵 tumuli; high mound or hill.

Kiŭ 鳩 A pigeon; to assemble; to dwell; coll: to collect, as money for public use; *kiŭ cĭk* 鳩集 a band of people.

Kiŭ: A coll. word: warped, bent, as *kiù-kiù*. *Cê siā dék kiù* the words badly written.

Kó 庫 An armory, a treasury; a magazine: COM: *chŏng kó* 倉庫 granary and treasury: *tū kó* 土庫 a store-room; *hūi iŏk kó* 火藥庫 a powder magazine

Kó 袴 Trowsers, COM. *tó kó* 套袴 overalls.

Kó 臼 Read *kêu*; coll *kó*: a mortar; *cĕng kó* 舂臼 a stone mortar; *kó tùi* 臼錘 a pestle; *muòng*

kó 門臼 a door socket; *siŏh dái kŏ* 石碓臼 large stone mortar.

Kŏ 柯 An ax handle; a surname.

Kŏ 苛 small plants, troublesome: COM. *kŏ giù* 苛求 to importune; *kŏ káik* 苛刻 to harrass; *kŏ ngiŏk* 苛虐 to oppress: COLL *kŏ káik*, parsimonious.

Kŏ, 可 To be willing, to consent, to permit; can, may; fit, proper; *bók kŏ* 不可 ought not; *kŏ pēu,* 可否 will it do, or not; *kŏ bī* 可比, to illustrate; *kŏ chiéu,* 可笑 laughable; *kŏ ó,* 可惡 odious; *kŏ sék,* 可惜 alas! *kŏ ngì,* 可疑 to doubt; *siēu kŏ,* 小可 unimportant; COLL., *kŏ lèng,* 可憐 compassionate.

Kŏ, 考 Old; complete; to examine as *că kŏ* 查考; *kŏ géu* 考據 to examine evidence, as in books. *kŏ óng* examination.

Kó, 靠 To rely on; contrary: in the coll, fetters: COM. *kó săng*, 靠山 to rely on a firm friend. COLL., *ăi kó*, 倚靠 to rely on; *kó dék cêu*, he can be relied on; *kă chiu kó* fetters and manacles.

Kó, 魛 Small dried fish used as condiment as, *ngù kó* 魚魛

Kó, 去 Read *kéu*, coll. *kó*: to go away, to depart; *chók kó*, 出去 gone out; *diē kó*, 入去 to go into; *kó că*, 去齋 to go to school; *kó dò* 去掏 go and fetch it; *mò dék kó* 無的去 can't go; will not contain it; *kó nièng* 去年 last year.

Kò, 峇 Read *kó*; coll. *kò*, to run aground as a boat, as *sùng kò chiĕng*. 船峇淺

Kò, a coll. word, to knock against; *kò láu*, a boat made

Kói, 愧 Abashed; contrite: *siŭ kói* 羞愧 ashamed; COM., *cĕu kói* 自愧 mortified.

Kŏk, 哭 To cry aloud; to wail, *tóng kŏk* 痛哭 to weep bitterly; *tiè kŏk* 啼哭 to mourn.

Kŏk, 屈 Bent; to stoop; to submit; wrong; affliction; *kŏk sĭng* 屈身, to submit to suffering; *uŏng kŏk* 枉屈 ill-treated.

Kŏk, A coll word: to hide, to conceal one's self; to be in, or at, a place; *kŏk dĕng nĕ*, hid where? *kŏk siŏh dŏi*, to be together; *ă kŏk dék lŏh*, can stay at, as a place.

Kŏk, 搉 to take; to strike; to knock: *kŏk náh* 搉凹 indented; *kŏk siŏh á*, gave it a knock: *ciā nèng mă kŏk dék*, can't touch that person! *scil.,* for he has a quick temper.

Kŏk, A coll. word as in *kŏk-kŏk-cŭng*, to shake, to shiver.

Kŏk, A coll. prefix as in *kŏk-káuk*, a depression in the ground.

Kŏng, 坤 The 2nd diagram; COM., *gièng kŏng*, 乾坤 heaven and earth; *kŏng-cṳ* 坤書 a girl's betrothal contract.

Kŏng, 昆 an elder brother; *kŏng dḕung* 昆仲 brothers.

Kŏng, 崑 as *kŏng-lùng-săng* 崑崙山 the Kwanlun range, between the Desert of Gobi and Tibet.

Kŏng, 康 Rest; peaceful; blessed; excellent: *kŏng cáung* 康壯 hale, as an old man; *kŏng giòng*, 康強 strong, robust, *Kŏng-hĭ* 康熙 the Emperor Kang-hĭ, A. D. 1662—1723; *kŏng-hĭ cê-diēng* 康熙字典 Kanghi's dictionary.

Kŏng, 糠 Husk of grain: chaffy; troublesome; *chŭ-kŏng* 粗糠 husks; *géu-kŏng* 鋸糠 sawdust; *kŏng buŏng* 糠飯 bran (mixed in) boiled rice, (for fowls.)

Kŏng, 亢 Read *káung*: overbearing: to resist, as in *káung ngę̆u*.

Kōng, 墾 To open new land: *kōng dê* 墾地 new land; *kūi kōng* 開墾 to clear land.

Kōng, 慷 Noble, magnanimous; *kōng kái* 慷慨 liberal; unmoved by slander; grieved, as at the faults of others,

Kōng, 懇 To request, to importune, as in *kōng giù* 懇求

Kóng 空 Coll. *kę̆ng;* to empty, to exhaust; a deficiency: also read *kŭng* q. v.: *kóng huăk,* 空乏 defalcation: COM. *kŭi kóng* 虧空 a deficit, as of revenue.

Kóng, 控 To draw, to rein in;

to accuse, to impeach as *siòng kóng* 上控; *kóng gó* 控告 to petition against.

Kòng, A coll. word as in *kòng giĕng-tàu*, to bear on the shoulder.

Kŭ 坵 Read *kiŭ*, pomace; *dà kŭ* 茶坵 pomace of tea-nut oil, used as soap; *dâu kŭ* 豆坵 bean pomace.

Kŭ 箍 A hoop; to bind with hoops: COM: *kŭ buák* 箍砵 and *kŭ tĕng*, 箍桶 to hoop earthen basins and buckets; *kŭ bā* 箍把 bound bundles of wood; coll. *kŭ-tĕng dáng* a cooper's block.

Kŭ 古 Read *gū*; coll. *kŭ*, as in *Kŭ chèng*, a district city in north Fukien, 70 miles from Foochow.

Kŭ, A coll. word: to call animals; to recite, to repeat: *kŭ giĕ* to call fowls; *kŭ dŭ* to call pigs; *kŭ báik-ĭng* or *kŭ bàng cáh*, to hum or repeat the tones.

Kū 苦 A marshy plant; bitter; painful; urgent; painstaking: as a verb to feel grieved for, to dislike: COM. *kū chŭ* 苦楚 extreme grief; *kū miâng* 苦命 a hard lot in life; *kū nâng* 苦難 affliction; *sĭng-kū* 辛苦 wearied:

Kù, A coll. word, to crouch.

Kŭ, 區 Read *kŭ*: to classify; a boundary; a police precinct; a surname: *buŏng kŭ,* 分區 to divide into precincts.

Kŭ, 嶇 A steep ascent: COM., *kĭ kŭ* 崎嶇 rough, as roads.

Kŭ, 樞 A sort of spinous tree, the socket of a door; the axle; fundamental: *kŭ gĭ*, the hinge, *met.,* a controlling power.

Kŭ 軀 The body, the person: *kŭ káek* 軀殼 very thin, emaciated.

Kŭ, 驅, 敺, A fleet horse; to urge; *siĕng kŭ* 先驅 vanguard; *háiu kŭ* 後驅, the rear-guard: COM., *kŭ dŭk* 驅逐, to drive away; *kŭ dŭk hàng ìng* 驅逐閒人 "exclude idlers",— a notice.

Kŭ, 劬 Read *gŭ*, labor, care; the anxiety of parents, as in *kŭ-lò* 劬勞.

Kŭ, 佉 as in *kŭ lù*, 佉盧 Greek or Phoenician.

Kŭ, 去 Also read *kéu*, q. v., to expel, as in *kŭ áuk*, 去惡 "expel badness", to reform; *kŭ* or *kéu dŭk siá*, 去毒社 "expel poison", anti-poison society.

Kŭ, A coll. word: slow, dull, stupid, as *kŭ dęk hēng*, very dull,

Kuă, 誇 To boast, to brag; *kuă kēu,* 誇口 boastful; *cêu kuă* 自誇 self laudation: COLL. *ói yŏng kuă vâ,* fond of bragging; *kuă ciáh kuă,* very boastful.

Kuá, 跨 Also read *kuă,* to bestride: to encroach on; COLL. *sêu nèng kuá-á,* domineered over by others.

Kuá, 掛 Read *guá;* used for the coll. *kuá* as in *kuá i só,* or *kuá siŏh bék,* to take account; *kéuk i kuá kiéng,* he is indebted as per account.

Kuá, A coll. word, as in *kuá-chiēng,* to run aground on shallows, same as *kò-chiēng,* q. v.

Kuāi, 夬 Different; absolute; the 54th of the 64 diagrams.

Kuāi, 蒯 A surname: a kind of grass, used for making sandals, ropes and mats.

Kuāng 533

Kuái, 快 Happy, prompt: in the coll. read *há* q. v.: *kuái chạ* 快差 a swift messenger; *kuái séng*, 快信 a special delivery letter; *kuái cṳ̄* 快子 "nimble lads,"—chopsticks: COLL., *sōng kuái*, 爽快 well and happy; *ng sōng kuái*, indisposed.

Kuák, 濶, 闊, Wide, liberal; diligent: COM. *guōng kuák*, 廣闊 extensive: COLL. *kuák dúai*, 闊大 ample, capacious.

Kuăng, 寬 Large, ample: indulgent; forgiving. COM. *kuăng-ōng*, 寬恩 gracious; *kuăng ṳ̀ng*, 寬容 lenient; *kuăng-sẹ̤u*, 寬恕 to forgive; *kuăng-áing*, 寬限 to allow a larger time.

Kuăng, 款, Something desired; sincere: to revere; to seek for; to reach; a record; a numerative of articles, classes, affairs, etc: *gŭi kuāng*, 歸欸 to repay a loan; *kuāng dái*, 欸待 to treat politely. COLL. *ciā kuāng*, this form or mode.

Kuāng, A coll. word, as in *kuāng-kuāng-giéu*, a clattering as of tiles rattling.

Kuàng 圜, Complete, round, a circle; to revolve, to environ, coll. *kuàng-kuàng-ùi*, encircling, as walls; *kuàng-kuàng gièng*; the border on all sides; *kuàng-sióh-làu*, to go about once; *kuàng-bái* a tonal mark at the corner of a character.

Kuàng 環, A circlet, to encircle. COM. *giū-lièng-kuàng*, a chain puzzle; *kuàng giù* 環球 to encircle the globe, a traveler: *kuàng-kuàng-diōng*, around; the circumference of a ball.

Kuàng 鐄, A metal ring; COM. *cī*

kuàng 指鐶 a finger ring; *chiū kuàng* 手鐶, bracelets.

Kuáng, A coll. word, as *kuáng kuáng*, sound of a gong, clang! clang!

Kŭi 虧, Short breath, to pant; deficiency: COM. *kŭi kóng* 虧空 defalcation; *kŭi buŏng* 虧本 loss of capital: coll. *kék kŭi* distress, suffering.

Kŭi, 開 Read *kăi*, COLL. *kŭi*; to open; to institute; to enact; to explain; to remove; to write, as shop bills; to show (favor): *kŭi kĭ* 開起 to unfold; *kŭi-huă* 開花, to blossom; *kŭi huŏng*, 開方, to write a prescription; *kŭi ŏng* 開恩, to show favor to; *kŭi géng*, 開禁 to remove a prohibition; *kŭi siăng* 開聲, to speak out; *kŭi gā* 開解, to explain; *kŭi tàu or kŭi sùng* 開頭 or 開船, to set sail; *kŭi kwóh* 開缺, to resign, to ask to resign.

Kŭi, 揆 To measure; to examine *báik kŭi* 百揆, a general superintendent.

Kŭk, 禿, Read *tŭk*; blunt, short *kŭk muōi* 禿尾, a blunt end: *kák kŭk* 恰禿 too short, as a cord.

Kŭng, 空 Empty, vacant; wide; the sky, the firmament; also read *kŏng*: COLL. *kĕng* and *láeng*, q. v.: *kŭng-dŭng* 空中, heaven; *kŭng ké* 空氣, the atmosphere.

Kŭng, 孔, An opening; a cave; through; deep; excellent; a surname; *kŭng dŏ* 孔道, a thoroughfare: COM. *Kŭng-cū* 孔子 or *Kŭng-hŭ-cū* 孔夫子 Confucius; *kŭng chiŏk*, 孔雀 a peacock.

Kùng 537

Kŭng, 綑, To bind; to hem; a border on a garment: in coll. a numerative of packages, rolls or bundles: COM. *kŭng dèu* 綑條, strips for binding hems; *kŭng siŏh kŭng* 綑一綑, to bind in a bundle; *kŭng buŏh* 綑縛 to bind; met., distressed; *kŭng gièng* 綑墘, to bind edges.

Kùng, A coll. word: to coil as rope, as in *kùng ièng ièng;* *kùng siŏh uòng,* coiled in a bunch; *kùng siŏh dŏi,* cuddled together, as animals.

Kṳ̆ng, 穹 Lofty, vast and high, as the firmament; *kṳ̆ng chŏng* 穹蒼, the azure sky.

Kṳ̆ng, 恐 Apprehensive: *kṳ̆ng gêṳ,* 恐懼 to dread; *kṳ̆ng pá* 恐怕, fearful of, apprehensive lest.

Kṳ̀ng, 勤 Diligent, industrious:

538　　　　Kuŏ

COM. kùng gĭng 勤緊, diligent: kùng-qiêng kĭ-gă 勤儉起家, to exalt one's family by diligence and economy.

Kùng, 懃 Diligent, earnest: COM., ùng kùng 慇懃, anxious about duties.

Kùng, 芹 Celery, as kùng chái 芹菜.

Kùng, 困 Read kŭng: kùng and kŭng: a stack, a pile: kùng siŏh dŏi 困一堆 to gather into a heap.

Kuŏ, 戈 A kind of halberd; a spear: gāng kuŏ 干戈 shields and spears.

Kuŏ, 科 A root, the hollow culm of grain; a vacuum; medical practice; a class, series, rank, as kuŏ mŭk 科目: COM. kuŏ hŏk 科學, subjects studied in school; nôi kuŏ 內科, physic;

Kuóh 539

nguôi kuŏ 外科 surgery: COLL. *kuŏ buōng* 科本, estimate the capital: *mạ kuŏ dék gáu*, 賈科的至 inestimable.

Kuŏ, 靴 Boots: COM., *dáung kuŏ*, 緞靴, satin boots; *iòng kuŏ* 洋靴 foreign boots.

Kuŏ, 刳 Read *kŭ*; to cut, to pare off as in *kuŏ siŏh gièng* 刳一墘 pare off an edge.

Kuó, 課 To try; to deliberate; a series; a task, a lesson; COM., *gŭng kuó* 功課, literary work; *nĭk kuó* 日課, a daily task; *siŏng kuó* 上課 opening of a school term.

Kuò, 踒 Read *uŏ*; sprained, as in *kă bĕuk kuò* 胶跌踒 the foot sprained by a fall.

Kuóh 曲, Read *kĕuk*, COLL., *kuóh*: bent, crooked; a ditty; *kuóh chióh* 曲尺 a carpenter's square; *uăng kuóh* 彎曲 or *kĭ kuóh* 欹曲 crooked, winding: *chióng kuók*, to sing songs.

Kuŏi, 盔 A basin; a helmet; COM. *kuŏi gák* 盔甲, armor.

Kuók, 亅 A hooked stroke; the barb of a weapon; to mark off.

Kuók, 缺, 鈌 Defective; deficiency; a vacancy in office: COM. *kiéng kuók* 欠缺 deficient; *kuók huăk* 缺乏 destitute; *kŭi kuók* 開缺 to ask to resign; to resign.

Kuók, 橛 Read *huŏk*, COLL. *kuŏk*: a block, a stick; *géu siŏh kuŏk* 鋸一橛, saw off a block.

Kuŏng, 匡 A vessel for containing rice; a square box, case or frame; to reform: used in coll. for *kuóng*, q. v. *kuŏng géu* 匡救 to reform one; COM. *muòng kuŏng* 門匡 door-frames.

Kuòng 541

Kuŏng 誑 Lying talk; to swindle: COM. *kuŏng tó* 誑套, a scheme to entrap one.

Kuŏng 圈 A coop; a prison; a snare; a circle, a period; to punctuate: COM: *kuŏng tó* 圈套 a gin, a snare; a plot to entrap one.

Kuŏng 壙, A vault of a tomb.

Kuōng 曠 Read *kuóng*; COLL, *kuōng*; as in *kuōng iā* 曠野 a wilderness.

Kuóng 勸 To advise; to encourage; COM. *kuóng huò* 勸和 to urge to peace; *kuóng siĕng* 勸善, to exhort to virtue; *kuóng ngiĕk dọ̆* 勸業道 a Commissioner of Industry.

Kuóng 曠, In coll. read *kuōng*, q. v.: clear, vacant, waste: COM. *kuóng iā* 曠野 a wild, a desert;

Kuòng 横, Read *hèng*; used for

COLL. kuòng, a tub, large at the top; a barrel; tierce; kuòng tęng 禈桶 large tubs; kuòng diāng 楎鼎 a cooking pan surrounded by a wooden cylinder.

Kuòng A coll. prefix as in kuòng kuŏng, frames, as for doors.

Kuòng, A coll. word to govern, to rule, as kuòng gă to manage the household.

Kuŏng 匡 Read kuŏng; used for the COLL. kuóng; squares, rectangular spaces; the eye-socket, called mĕk ciŭ kuŏng.

Lă, 拉 Read lăk; used for the coll. lă; to pull, to drag along; met, to embezzle, as lă chiĕ.

Lă, A coll. word, as in lă că, foul, filthy.

Lā, 喇 Used for the coll. lā; a particle like ciā: a, an, a certain one: ó lă nęng, there was a

Lā̤ 543

man; *mò̤ lā̤ mā̤ có̤*, nothing that he can't do.

Là, A coll. word as in *là-lī* a name for the *chiŏng săng gák*, the manis.

Lā̤, 禮, 礼, Rites, ceremonies; etiquette; *lā̤ máu* 禮貌 good manners; *lā̤ bái* 禮拜 worship; offerings: COM. *lā̤ só* 禮數, or *lā̤ ciék* 禮節 rules of decorum; *lā̤ ŭk* 禮物 a gift; *lā̤ ngì* 禮儀, forms of propriety: *met.*, gifts, offerings; *lā̤ buó* 禮部 the Board of Rites; *sáeng lā̤* 送禮 to send presents to a bride before marriage; *ù lā̤* 無禮 impolite; *sék-lā̤* 失禮 have failed in manners.

Lā̤, A coll. word, using the character 禮, before verbs, makes the active participle; after certain verbs, is euphonic or implies completion of the action; after nouns means in, at, from, out of; *kiě lạ* 跬禮 standing; *lạ sīŏng* 禮想 is thinking; *diŏh chió lạ* 着唇禮, at home.

Là, 犁 A plow; to plow the fields; as *là chèng*; day break; 犁頭 or *là tàu tiék* 犁頭鐵 a plowshare.

Lạ: A coll. word: to strike, to rub against; to strand as in *sùng lạ chiēng*, boat stranded on shallows; *lạ-bă* persevering; *lạ miáng*, to have a hard lot: *lạ guó* to press by.

Là, 璃 A precious stone, a gem; *pờ-là* 玻璃 (coll. *bŏ-là*), glass.

Là, 黎 Dark brown, black, as *là-mìng* 黎民, the black-haired people—the Chinese.

Lậ, 厲, Strict and stern, as in *ngièng-lậ* 嚴厲.

Lá, 勵, To animate: COM. *lá cé* 勵志 to do resolutely; *miēng-lá* 勉勵 to rouse to effort.

Lá, 麗 A stag; an adjective of praise; elegant: COM. *huà lá* 華麗 splendid, magnifical.

Lá, 隸 As in *Dĭk-lá sĕng* 直隸省 the Chihli province; *lá cṳ̄* or *lá cê*, the plain square character.

Láe, 鑢, A file; to file, to scour: *láe géu* 鑢鋸 to file a saw; *láe dĕng* to scour brass; *láe guóng* to polish bright; *láe méng*, to rub the face.

Láe, A coll. word: to claw, to scratch; *láe siŏh dŏi* to scrape together; *bà láe*, to scratch, as a hen.

Láek, A coll. word: to become loose; separated; *láek dé*, stem separated, as of ripe fruit; *pì láek kó*, the scab has come off;

kéuk láek, to tire of and give up; *mò dék láek*, can't get rid of.

Lâeng: A coll. word: an interval of time or space; *láeng siŏh nĭk*, interval of one day; *láeng huông*, a wide interval; *láeng póng*, an interstice; *diāng láeng*, to watch for leisure time; *láeng lā diô*, to leave a passage-way.

Lâeng, 術, 衕, The first read *dùng*, and *dông*, the second read *háeng*; used for the coll. *háeng*: a narrow street, an alley; *lèng lâeng*, a lane; *diô lâeng*, a passage to; *huōi chiòng lâeng*, a way between walls.

Lâeng, 弄 Read *liông*; COLL. *lâeng*: to tease; *hié lâeng* 戲弄 to annoy; *cáuk lâeng* 作弄

to trifle with; *mŏh lāẹng ĭ*, 莫弄伊 don't tease him; *lâẹng bê* 弄弊 to embezzle.

Lāi: A coll. word: untidy appearance.

Lāi: 籟, Read *lūi*: for the coll. *lāi*: a small bamboo basket, called *dáek-lāi*; *lāi-giūng* 籟子, small fish baskets.

Lài 瀨 Water flowing over sand; rapids: coll., *lái iā chiēng*, the rapid is very shallow.

Lài 來 To come; to reach; to induce; denotes the future; after verbs, implies action; with a negative, expresses impracticability; joined with *kéu*, denotes here and there; again and again; after the verbs *kī* and *chók*, it means to begin; in the coll. read *lì*, q. v.:

COM., *lài uōng* 來往, coming

and going; *lài huòi* 來回, to and fro, both ways; *cùng lài* 從來 hitherto; *hâiu lài* 後來 hereafter; *gêung lài* 近來 just now, recently; *lài sié* 來世 the future life; *lài iù* 來由 the origin, cause; *lài lĭk* 來歷 the history of; prestige as of rank; *lài é* 來意 the object of one's *coming*: *nguòng lài* 原來 originally, yes, so of course; *lài hŭk*, a term for a week; *lài ék*, Monday, etc.: COLL., *lài diŏ*, an opening, as for one without employment; *lài ké* 夾器 a vice, also called *lâu hū kìng* and *lòi sṳ̆ gṳ̆*.

Lài 箂 A species of bamboo: used for the coll. *lài*, a bamboo basket; *lài dáng* 箂担 a cooly's two baskets.

Lài, 雷 Read *lòi*; COLL. *lài-gŭng*, 雷公, the god of thunder; thunder.

Láiu 549

Lâi, 癩 A virulent eruption; specifically leprosy: *lâi chŏng* 癩瘡 ulcers: COM., *siông-lâi* 上癩 (coll. *báng lâi*) leprosy; *găng lâi* 乾癩 dry leprosy.

Lâi, 賴, To depend on; to rely on; to trump up; to accuse falsely: *āi lâi*, 倚賴 dependent upon; *uŏng lâi* 寃賴, to defame; *dù lâi* 圖賴 to criminate the guiltless: COLL., *lâi guó*, lean further along; *lâi dĕ-dău*, to lie sulkily on the ground: *sī-lâi*, involve one by suicide.

Láing, A coll. word as in *bà-láing* to invert: *ĭ chói ậ bà-láing*, his talk is contradictory; *bà-láing lì bà-láing kó*, to turn up and down; full of inconsistent (assertions).

Láiu, A coll. word, as in *láiu á*, or *láiu lŏh kó*, to slip as a child from a chair; to slide down a steep place.

Láiu, 廖 A man's name; a surname; the name of a state.

Láiu, 料 Read *liêu*; commonly read *láiu* as stuffs, glass, immitation jade; talent, cleverness as of an employé; grain, manure; to consider: also read *lièu* and *liêu*, q. v.: *nguòng láiu* 元料 raw material; *láiu ké* 料器 glass ware, like imitation jade; *láiu ciö* 珠料 glass beads; *iŏk láiu* 藥料 materia medica; *mā láiu* 馬料 horse's provender; *ciěu láiu* 椒料 spices; *chà láiu*, 柴料 lumber; *gěng láiu* 工料 work and materials; *láiu siōng* 料想 to suppose: COLL., *guōi-cī-láiu*, 果子料 dried fruits; *chók láiu* 出料 to give out strength, as things steeped.

Lăk 551

Láiu 漏 To leak; to let slip; to escape from, *met.*, to divulge; a leak: in the coll., read *láu* and *láu*, q. v.

Láiu, 陋 A narrow place; a vile residence as in *bě láiu gì chió*.

Lák, A coll. word: bald; worn off: *lák tàu*, a bald head; *lák ták cêng guŏng*, completely stripped, all gone.

Lák, A coll. word, as in *kà-lák*, to repair; to put in order.

Lák, A coll. word: to entrap, to overreach, to injure by cunning: *céng kéuk nẹng lák kó*, insnared by others; *lák ĭ tàu lā*, noosed his head— i. e., entrapped him.

Lăk, 剌 To turn over; to spread out; in the coll. to take off; to slip up or down: *chiŭ-uōng lăk gèng* 手袖剌高, to shove up the sleeve; *lăk kó̤* 捋去 scrape it away; *lăk guŏng guŏng diŏh,* rub it smooth.

Lăk, 粒 A kernel of rice or other grain; *met.,* food, a pellet; a numerative of small things: COLL., *buóng lăk* 飯粒 grains of cooked rice.

Lăk, 爁 Fiery, blazing; used in the coll. in a sense similar to *bŭk* q. v.: COLL., *bóng huōi-ĭng lā̤ lăk,* to cure in the smoke.

Lăk, 獵 To hunt wild animals; the chase; COM., *lăk hô̤* 獵戶, huntsmen; *dă lăk* 打獵 to hunt; *lăk kēng* 獵犬 a hunting dog.

Lăk, 臘 Dried meats; *lăk nguŏk* 臘月 the 12th month.

Lăk, 蠟 Wax, bees-wax: as *uòng lăk* 黃蠟; *băh lăk* 白蠟 white wax; *lăk mùi* 蠟梅 a flower: *lăk ciŏh,* 蠟燭 wax candles.

Lāng 553

Lăk 辣, 辞 Hot, as pepper; biting, pungent: used in the coll. in a *met.* sense; severe, formidable; *lăk giòng* 辣薑 ginger-root; *gái lăk* 芥辣 mustard: coll., *lăk cŭah lăk*, very pungent; *chiŭ iă lăk*, has a very hot hand—is formidable in his plots.

Lăk 涉, Read *sièk*; used for the coll. *lăk*: to wade in water or across a stream, as *lăk cūi* 涉水 and *lăk quó kă* 涉過溪.

Lăk: A coll. word, as in *bà lăk*, to turn, as a key in a lock; *bà lăk tàu*, to shake the head—unwilling, dissenting.

Lāng, 懶 Lazy as *lāng dŏ:* COLL. *lāng sĭ* 懶尸, you lazy lout! *lāng cō̤* 懶做 to idle.

Lāng, 覽 To behold; to look at carefully; *ĕk lāng* 一覽 at one view; *báuk lāng* 博覽 learned.

Lāng, 欖 The Chinese olive, called *gāng lāng* 橄欖; COLL. *gā-lāng,* olives; varieties of olives called *dòng ièng* and *sièu uòng.*

Lāng, A coll. word: saliva; *chói lāng,* spittle; *pói lāng,* to spit; *lāng ciǎ,* a child's bib; *lāng tàng* phlegm; *làu lāng,* to drool.

Làng, 婪 Covetous; to covet; COM., *tăng làng* 貪婪 avaricious.

Làng, 窟 As in *làng tàng,* thin and widely spread: in the coll. means large rocks, bowlders.

Làng, 籃 Baskets: COM., *chái làng* 菜籃 a vegetable basket; COLL., *huōi sĭk làng* 火食籃 a provision basket.

Làng, 藍 A surname; indigo: COM. *làng sáik* 藍色 a blue or indigo color; *làng dáing* 藍靛 native indigo; *iòng làng* 洋藍 Prussian blue; *chiēng làng*, light blue; *nê làng* 二藍 navy blue.

Làng, 襤 A coverlet; a single garment; mean, ragged clothes; COM., *làng lŭ* 襤褸 or *làng lêu* shabby, as raiment.

Làng, 閬 A door screen, as *muòng làng* 門閬.

Làng, 攔 To hinder; to impede; as in *làng cū* 攔阻.

Làng, 欄 A balustrade; a pen, a den; to cage; COM., *làng găng* 欄杆 a railing: in the coll. also means dress trimmings; COLL. *làng dò*, a balustrade.

Làng, 蘭 A general name for gynandrous flowers; *met.*, fragrant, excellent; a surname: *diêu làng* 吊蘭 an air-plant; COM., *làng huă* 蘭花 a very fragrant flower much prized by the Chinese; other varieties of the *làng* are *ciờ làng* 球

蘭, *mŭk làng* 木蘭, *só sĭng* and *bó suói*: *Hò làng* 荷蘭, Holland: *Hŭk làng* 佛蘭 or *Huák làng* France.

Láng, 濫 A freshet; overflowing; to soak; excessive; intruding; careless, lawless: in the coll. wet, soaked with water: COM., *láng gău* 濫交 to associate with the lowbred: COLL. *páh láng*, to become wet.

Lâng, 爛 To cook thoroughly; corrupted; tattered; spoiled; splendid; splendor: *cṳ́ lâng* 煮爛 to boil soft; *dông lâng* 炖爛 cook soft; *cháng lâng* 燦爛 refulgent; COLL., *hô lâng* 腐爛, decayed.

Lâng, 二 Read *nê*; used for the coll. *lâng*: two: *lâng ciáh* 二隻, or *lâng gì* 二其 two persons or things; *lâng gā nẹng*, two persons; *lâng bā* 二把, two bundles of wood; *láng tàu muōi*, the two ends.

Lăŭ, A coll. word: to lift, as the skirts in walking; to embezzle; to cook slightly, as *lăŭ siŏh ă* or *lăŭ siŏh gŭng*.

Lāu, 了 Read *liĕu*; COLL. *lāu*: done, finished; always, of course; after verbs a sign of the past tense; have, has: *cŏ lāu* 做了 finished; *uòng lāu*, 完了 completed; all exhausted.

Láu, 溜 Read *léu*; COLL. *láu*: to flow, to run out; to drop, as grains from a hole; to pour, as melted lead in adulterating money; to go about; *láu iòng* 溜鉛 to adulterate with lead; *láu tŏng* 溜湯, to drink broth; *láu láu sŭk*, thoroughly acquainted.

Láu 漏, Read *láiu*; coll. *láu*, to drip; to ooze out; to overlook; to miss: *láu só* 漏數 to miss entering into the account; *láu suói* 漏稅 to smuggle; *láu siŏh cê* 漏一字, to leave out a word.

Làu 劉; Read *liù*; coll. *làu*: a surname.

Làu 樓 Read *lèu*; coll. *làu*; a loft; the upper story: *làu bàng* 樓棚 a wooden platform on a roof; *làu dīng* 樓頂 *lău â* 樓下 the upper and lower stories: *làu tăi* 樓梯 a ladder; *làu cāng* 樓井 a skylight; *gū làu* 鼓樓 the Drum Tower, as over South Street: coll., *cāu-mā làu* a veranda; *iòng làu* the north tower of Focchow; *cųng làu* a belfry.

Làu 流, Read *liù*; coll *làu*: to flow, as water; to float; a time, once over: *làu gék* 流急 to flow swiftly; *cūi làu* 水流

Lâu 559

water flowing; *làu měk cāi* 流目滓 to shed tears;

Làu 留 Read *liù*; coll *làu*; to detain; to keep back; *làu nẹng káh*, to stay a guest; *làu sṳ* 留鬚 to leave the whiskers unshorn; *làu lā muōi*, to leave a balance, as of debts, work etc.

Làu: A coll. word, as in *gà-làu*: to roll about; *gà làu hìng* dizziness.

Lâu 老, 佬 The first read *lọ* and the second *liẹu*: coll. *lâu*; aged; venerable; to die, dead, deceased—said of the aged and adults: *lâu nẹng* 佬伏 an aged person; *lâu mā* 佬媽 a wife; *lâu siè*, a snake; *lâu iǒh*, a species of hawk: *lâu kọ́*, deceased.

Lâu 漏 Read *lâiu*; coll. *lâu*, to leak, to run out: *lâu dā̤*, a leaky bottom as of a tub.

560 Lâung

Láuk, A coll word; to saunter about, as in *láuk láuk*; *láuk láuk kuăng*, fitting loosely, as shoes.

Láung 崙, 崘, A mountain; a classifier of hills and mountains.

Lâung 浪 Waves, billows, as in *pŏ lâung* 波浪; *lâung cū* 浪子 a spendthrift; *lâung ęung* 浪用 wasteful.

Lâung 蛋 Read *dáng* in the dictionaries: a tribe of the Miautsz; an egg: COM. *giĕ lâung* 鷄蛋 hens eggs: *lâung cĭng* 蛋精 or *lâung băh* 蛋白 the white of an egg; *lâung uòng* 蛋黃 the yelk; *lâung gŏ* 蛋糕, sponge cakes; *bó lâung* 抱蛋 to hatch eggs.

Lâung 論, To discourse about; to reason, to consult; according to, by the, as in *lâung nĭk* 論

Lé — 561

日 by the day: COM., tŏ láung 討論 to search into; gōng láung 講論, to discourse upon; lī láung 理論 to remonstrate with one; COLL., mọ̀ láung, without regard to, no matter (how, what, how many, etc.,)

Láung 亂, 乱. Read luáng; COLL. láung; to confuse; disordered; anarchy; láung gōng láung tiăng, to lie, lying, mendacious.

Lé 利, Profitable, useful; happy; interest on investments; also read lè, q: v.: COM., bó lé 不利 unlucky; lé sék 利息 interest on money; buŏng lé 本利 (COLL mọ̄ lé) principal and interest; COLL., lé-iăh, profit, advantage.

Lé A coll. euphonic prefix, as in lé-láe, to file; lé léu, to saw off with a knife; lé lié, to slit open; lé lọ̆i, to bore.

Lê 利, A sharp point or edge, keen edged; acute, clever; covetous; to benefit: COM., *lê hái* 利害 formidable, hurtful; stingy: *giù lê* 求利 to seek wealth.

Lê 俐, Clever, as in *lìng lê* 伶俐; *mà lê*, expert, active.

Lê 痢, Dysentery as in *lê-céng* 痢症; *háik lê* 血痢, a bloody flux.

Lê 吏 An officer; rulers; to rule; *cṳ̌ lê* 書吏 government writers.

Lè, A coll. euphonic prefix, as in *lè lô̤* to go on a round of inspection; *lè lái*, to lean against; *lè-liê*, to withdraw.

Lè̤, A coll. word, as in *lè̤ dō̤*, to recline at full length; *lè̤ siŏh dō̤*, to fall down sprawling.

Lē, 魯 Read *lū*; COLL. *lē*, as in *lē-*

Lĕk 563

lḙ, dull, obtuse; *lḙ cŭ,* a dull person.

Lè, 驢 Read *lù;* COLL. *lè:* an ass: *lè gēng* 驢牡. a jackass.

Lè, A coll. word: to project, to extend: *lè tàu,* to thrust the head forward.

Lè, A coll. word: to curse, to rail at: *lè nèng,* to blackguard people.

Lék, A coll. euphonic prefix, as in *lék-laék,* loose, falling apart.

Lĕk, 勒 A bridle-bit, a curb; to restrain; to force to do: COM. *mā lĕk* 馬勒 a horse's bit; *lĕk mā,* 勒馬, to curb a horse; *lĕk sáuk* 勒索, to extort from: COLL. *ák lĕk* 押勒 to force by oppression; *lĕk sī* 勒死 to strangle to death—to oppress severely.

Lĕk, 瘝 Read *lĭk;* COLL. *lĕk:* the

scrofula, as in *săng lĕk*, 生癧 to have scrofula.

Lĕk, 六 陸 The second read *lŭk* in other senses; used as a complex form of the first: the cardinal number six: COM., *sĕk lĕk* 十六, sixteen; *lĕk sĕk gák-cŭ* 六十甲子 the cycle of 60 years.

Lĕk, 鹿 Read *lŭk*, COLL. *lĕk*; a deer; *lĕk hū* 鹿脯 dried venison.

Lĕk, A coll. word, as in *lĕk cūi*, to wade, or walk about in the wet.

Lĕk, A coll. word: to dip up; to filter; *lĕk pièu*, to dip duckweed; *lĕk buŏng*, to lade rice.

Lĕng, A coll. word as in *lĕng-tĕng*, sated and indifferent to, as food, small gains etc.

Lēng, 冷 Cold and chilly, as

in *hàng lēng* 寒冷: COM, *tiĕng lēng*, 天冷 chilly weather; *lēng chiéu*, 冷笑 to smile coldly at; *lēng dáng*, 冷淡 cool towards, distant.

Léng, A coll. word: a carpel; a triangular section of round things, as in *găng siŏh léng*, a section of a cooly-orange.

Léng, A coll euphonic prefix, as in *léng liéng*, rolling or tossing about, as on one's bed.

Lèng 蓮, The lotus: COM.. *lèng huā* 蓮花, the water lily; *lèng cī* 蓮子, lotus nuts.

Lèng, 菱, Read *lìng*: COLL. *lèng*, as in *lèng gáęk* 菱角, water caltrops.

Lèng 龍, Read *lùng*; COLL. *lèng*, as in *lèng-gēng*, 龍眼 the lungan or dragon's eye; *lèng-gēng-gŏ̤*, lungan jelly.

Lèng 憐, Read *lìng*; COLL. *lèng*, as in *kŏ lèng*, to pity; to show sympathy toward.

Lêng 令, 令, Law, rule; to command; a period of time, a season; COM. *mêng lêng* 命令, a command; *huák lêng* 發令, to issue orders.

Lêng 另, to be or dwell apart, separate, alone; *lêng nguôi* 另外 besides, in addition, *lêng cè*, by itself; *lêng gŭ*, to dwell apart; *lêng nĭk*, another day.

Lêng 吝, 悋, 悋, Avaricious, stingy; *lêng sáik* 吝嗇, close, niggardly; *pī lêng* 鄙吝, avaricious, sordid.

Lĕng, A coll. word, as in *lĕng liè muòng*, a screen with doors.

Lĕng, A coll. word: *săng lĕng*, a mountain cave; *kè-lĕng*, a hole, an orifice.

Lèng 567

Lẹng 攏, Read lủng: COLL. lẹng: to cause to approach, to draw close to; giàng lẹng, 行攏, to walk close to, lẹng siŏh dŏi 攏一堆, to gather (things) together; lẹng kó̤ 攏褲 overalls-worn by boatmen.

Lẹng 籠, Read lùng: COLL. lẹng, as in déuk lẹng or lẹng siŏng 籠箱 a bamboo box or chest.

Lèng 籠, Read lùng: COLL. lèng, a cage; giĕ lèng dáu 鷄籠罩, a movable hen coop; cēu lèng 鳥籠, a bird cage; huōi lèng 火籠 a hand stove.

Lẹng 礱 Read lùng, COLL. lẹng; a handmill for hulling rice; to hull: lẹng chiŏh to hull paddy.

Lẹng 曨 Read lùng; COLL. lẹng, as in hò̤ lẹng, the trachea.

Lèng 瓏, Read lùng; COLL. lèng:

clear, translucent, as in *tĕng lĕng* 通瓏.

Lèng 聾 Read *lṳ̀ng*; COLL. *lèng*; deaf, as in *ngê lèng* 耳聾.

Lèng, A coll. word: to stir up, as in *sĕ ĭ lèng guó lì*, it is he that stirred up (the quarrel.)

Lĕu, A coll. word, as in *lĕu chók lì*, to reject food, as a babe does.

Lēu 簍 Also read *lèu*: a bamboo basket, as *dĕuk lēu* 竹簍; *táng lēu* 炭簍 a coal basket.

Lēu 鏤 Read *ĕu*: COLL. *lēu* to dig through a wall as in *lēu tĕng táu* 鏤通透; *lēu siŏh kĕng* 鏤一空, dig a hole through.

Lèu 樓 An upper story; a tower; a peak; used in the coll. for cheap, low in price: *uòng lèu* 望樓, a lookout tower; *gō lèu* 高樓, a high story or loft;

pùng lèu 篷樓, a mat covered lodge.

Léu 屢, Often, many times, as in *léu ehéu* 屢次.

Léu 褸 Also read *lū*: torn, ragged garments: in the coll. read *lèu: làng léu* 襤褸 a ragged garment.

Léu 鑢 A file, a rasp: in the coll. to cut off with a knife, as in *léu dói dòng.*

Léu 慮 To feel concern; anxiety: *sṳ́ léu* 思慮 to think seriously of; *guá léu* 掛慮, anxious about.

Léu 濾, To filter, to strain: in the coll. to wade about: COM. *léu eiöng* 濾漿 to strain starch; *lèu că* 濾渣 to separate by filtration: COLL. *léu cūi*, to tramp about in water.

Lī 李 A plum, prune, apricot: a

surname: *hèng lī* 行李 luggage.

Lī 里 A residence; a village; a street; Chinese mile: *lìng lī* 鄰里 the neighbors; *hiŏng lī* 鄉里 a village; townsmen; *sĕk lī* 十里, ten Chinese miles, one *puó*.

Lī 理 To govern; to manage or put to rights; reason in man; *tiĕng lī* 天理 heavenly reason—analogous to over-ruling Providence; *dĕ lī* 地理 geography; *cìng lī* 情理 natural feeling; *lièu lī* 料理 to manage; *lī-huôi* 理會 to comprehend.

Lī 裏, 裡, A lining: *lī méng*, inner and outer surface; *bĕng-diŏng-lī*, to turn inside out.

Lì 梨 黎, A pear: *tòng lì* 糖梨, sugar pear; 黃梨, a pineapple.

Lì 蜊, A small yellowish clam: COLL. *gák lì póng*, to halve the edges of boards in laying floors.

Lì 來, Read *lài*, q. v.: COLL. *lì*; to come, to arrive; *diē lì* 入來 come in; *lì lāu* 來了 has come; *có má lì*, can't do it; *ā có dék lì*, can do it; *ciēu dék lì*, he rarely comes; *lì káng*, come and see.

Liáh 剌, Read *lĭk*; COLL. *liáh*; to rend apart; to split open, as with a knife: *liáh dói bèng*, split in two.

Liáh 靂, Read *lĭk*; COLL. *liáh*; the crashing sound of thunder, as in *liáh siŏh siàng*.

Liáh 舔, Read *ták*; used for the COLL. *liáh*; to lap, as a dog.

Liák 鞹, Read *ngék* and *sák*: used for the COLL. *liák* as in *liák kă*, slipshod; *liák ą̊ liák*, 鞹鞋鞹 to wear shoes slipshod.

Liāng 嶺, Read *līng;* a pass in a mountain; a ridge of mountains; *báek liāng,* 北嶺 the mountains north of Foochow; *liāng dīng,* 嶺頂 summit of a ridge.

Liāng 襟 領 Read *līng;* COLL. *liāng*: a collar; also used as the numerative of mats, carpets, etc.; *kiê liāng,* 豎嶺 a standing collar.

Liāng, 領 Read *līng;* COLL. *liāng;* to take; to govern; to command; *liāng cièng* 領錢 to receive money; *guāng liāng,* 管領 to govern; *liāng séu* 領事 a consul.

Liāng, A coll. word: to expose to the air, as in *liāng dáeng,* cool it in the air.

Liĕ, A coll. word: to lay, as bricks in building, as in *liĕ* ciŏng; liē gĭ, to lay a foundation; liē cáu, to build a kitchen range.

Liè, 離, Scattered, separated from; to cut in two; also read lié, q. v. liè hiĕk 離別, to part from, as friends; liè cŭ, a bill of divorcement.

Liè 籬, A bamboo fence, as in liè bă 籬笆.

Liè 嫠, A woman whose husband is dead; liè hó 嫠婦 a widow.

Liè 釐, 厘. Used for lī (to govern): the 1000th part of a tael: the hundredth, as of an inch; a grain: liè dīng 釐戥, a small money-steelyard; liè hó 釐毫, a small fraction, a trifle; liè gĭng, 釐金, an extra local duty levied on goods; likin.

Liè 荔, Read lié; COLL liè: a fruit tree; the lichi, called liè-ciĕ-chéu 荔枝棵.

Lié, 例, To compare, to classify; laws, regulations, as in *lŭk lié* 律例 laws; *sŭk lié* 俗例 common practice; *mọ̀ ciā lié* 毛者例, there is no such custom; *gŭng lié* 公例 recognized custom.

Lié 離, Also read *liè*, q. v.: to retire, to separate from; distant: *lié gă* 離家 to leave home; *lié kŭi* 離開 to separate from;

Liék 烈 Read *liék*, used for the coll. *liék*, fiery: *ẹng liék liék* 紅烈烈 fiery-red.

Liĕk 列, To separate; to arrange in order, as in *bà liĕk* 排列; *liĕk ói* 列位, you, gentlemen!

Liĕk, 冽 A cold air, as in *hăng liĕk* 風冽 a chilly wind.

Liĕk 烈, A raging fire; impetuous; zealous; fierce; faithful to principles; used for *liĕk*, in the coll. q. v.: *liĕk sṳ̆u* 烈士, a patriot; *liĕk cū* 烈祖, eminent ancestors; *liĕk hó* 烈婦 a chaste woman.

Liĕk 裂, To rend in two; as in *liĕk kŭi*, rent asunder.

Liĕng 臉 The cheek; the face; met., one's reputation; *liĕng miêng* 臉面, the face; modesty; *ù liĕng* 無臉, brazen-faced

Liŏng, A coll. word: to turn about, to revolve, as in *liéng sìŏh diŏng*, turn the thing round.

Lièng 連 To connect; contiguous; a connective particle at the beginning of a sentence, and also, even; in the coll. unexpectedly; *lièng káik* 連刻 instantly; *bô lièng* 伐連 in addition to, besides.

Lièng 廉 Pure, incorrupt: *lièng tī* 廉耻 modest; *ù lièng tī* 無廉耻 shameless; *chǐng lièng* 清廉 incorruptible.

Lièng, 簾 A curtain, as in *muòng lièng* 門簾 a door screen.

Lièng, 簾 A curtain of bamboo splints, as in *déuk lièng* 竹簾.

Lièng, 鐮 A sickle, as in *lièng dǒ* 鐮刀.

Lièng, 奩 A lady's dressing case: *cǒng lièng* 粧奩 a bride's trousseau.

Lièng, 聯 Connected; to combine: *lièng gák* 聯甲 union, an organization of famlies by ten:— a home-guard.

Lièng, 煉, 鍊, To fuse metals; to forge; *met.,* discipline: *báik lièng* 百鍊 thoroughly refined; *tiék lièng* 鐵鍊 an iron chain.

Lièng, 練 To learn by experience

as *liêng sŭk* 練熟; *chău liêng* 操練 parade-drill.

Liêng, 殮 To dress a corpse; *siŭ liêng* 收殮 to shroud and en-coffin.

Lièu 了, A sign of the past tense; finished, done: settled, fixed; before a verb, in the coll. read *lāu*, q. v.: it means very, wholly: *lièu iòng mìng běk* 了然明白 to understand very clearly; *bŏk lièu* 不了 interminable.

Lièu, 廖 Empty, void; solitary; *lièu lŏk* 廖落 deserted.

Lièu, 遼 Remote, far off; *Lièu-děng* 遼東 and *Lièu-să* 遼西, East and West Liau, now Shingking in Manchuria.

Lièu, 蜆 Read *hiěng*; used for the coll. *lièu*: a bivalve, a clam, as *lièu giăng* 蜆子 small clams; *lièu diăng* 蜆埕 a clam bed.

Lièu, 料, To oversee, to manage as in *lièu lī.*

Lièu, 料 To judge, to measure, to calculate; also read *láiu*, stuffs, materials; ability; talent; grain, provender; *lièu sióṳng* 料想 to judge, to estimate; *mặ lièu dék chók,* incalculable, inscrutable.

Lĭk, 力. Strength, brawn, nerve, force, mental energy; *lụ̄ lĭk* 㩳力 strong; *lĭk lióng* 力量 capacity; *chók lĭk* 出力 to exert one's self.

Lĭk, 立 To stand erect; to establish, to perfect; *dŭk lĭk* 獨立 independent; *lĭk chŭng* 立春, beginning of spring; *lĭk cé* 立志 to resolve: *lĭk káik* 立刻 instantly.

Lĭk, 笠 A rain hat: *cháu lĭk* 草笠 a straw hat; COLL. *dāu lĭk*

Lìng

斗笠 an umbrella hat.

Lĭk, 栗 As in *lĭk cī* 栗子 chestnuts.

Lĭk, 歷 A series, as in *lĭk nièng* 歷年 a series of years; *lĭk lài* 歷來 from the first till now.

Lĭng, 鈴 Read *lìng,* used for the coll. *lĭng* as in *lĭng lĭng,* the tinkling of a bell.

Līng, 禀 To nourish: *līng mêng* 禀命 to receive orders; *līng hŏ* 禀賦 natural endowments.

Lĭng, 領 To lead, to direct; in the coll. read *liăng,* q. v. *lĭng sêu* 領袖 a leader.

Lìng, 伶, Smart, clever as in *lìng lê* 伶俐.

Lìng, 鈴 A small bell: COM. *mā lìng* 馬鈴 sleigh-bells; *báng lìng* 柄鈴 bells with handles.

Lìng, 苓 A tonic medicine, COM., *hŭk lìng,* 茯苓 China root.

Lìng, 林 A clump of trees; a surname; *Hàng lìng iêng* 翰林院 the Hanlin College.

Lìng, 綾 Thin silk: *huă lìng* 花綾 damask.

Lìng, 凌 To disgrace, as in *lìng ŭk* 凌辱.

Lìng, 零 A remainder: in numeration means "and."

Lìng, 靈 A spirit, a soul as in *lìng hùng* 靈魂 the human soul; *sĕng lìng* 生靈 living beings; *lìng-kiéu* 靈竅 intelligent, astute; *Séng-lìng* 聖靈 the Holy Spirit.

Lìng, 憐 To compassionate as in *lìng mīng* 憐憫 (coll. *kŏ lèng*)

Lìng, 鄰 Near, neighboring: *lìng lĭ* 鄰里 the neighbors; *lìng guŏk* 鄰國 adjacent countries: *lìng gŭ* 鄰居 or *lìng siá* 鄰舍 the next house.

Lìng, 臨 To condescend; to descend; to visit; when: *lìng sì* 臨時 at the time.

Liō, 虜, 擄 To seize, to capture for ransom: used for *lū* in the coll. ᖰ. ᴅ.: *liō ǐng* 擄人 to kidnap people.

Liō, 裸 Nude, bare backed; to strip, to make bare the upper part of the body as *liō sǐng* 裸身.

Liŏh, 綠 Read *lŭk*; COLL *liŏh*: green color; *liŏh cì cì* or *liŏh pàng pàng,* very green; *liŏh dǎng* 綠丹 verdigris.

Liŏh, 錄 Read *lŭk* in the dictionaries; a metallic luster; veins on a shell; to copy; to register; an index as in *mŭk liŏh* 目錄.

Liŏh, 斜 Read *liŏk*; in the *Báik ǐng, liŏh*: to level; to smooth with the hand; *liŏh bàng* 斜平 to level; *liŏh kŭi* 斜開 to brush aside; *liŏh tàu-huŏk* 斜頭髮 to comb the hair.

Liŏk, 劣 Infirm, weak; poor, humble; a little, scarcely; rustic, rude; *iŭ liŏk* 優劣 capable and incapable.

Liŏk, 署, 略. In general, as in *iók liŏk* 約署; *gĭng liŏk* 經署 to manage; *mèu liŏk* 謀署 to contrive; *huŏk liŏk* 忽署 cursorily.

Liōng, 兩, 両, Two, a pair; double; a tael, equal to 1⅓ oz, or 583⅓ grains; a Chinese ounce, worth about $1.39, or 6s. 8d.: COM. *ngṳ̀ng liōng* 銀兩 silver ingots, sycee; *liōng hù* 兩湖 Hupeh and Hunan; *liōng ciòng* 兩全 both complete;

Liòng, 凉, 涼, Cool; refreshing;

poor, in need; COM. *liòng hŭng* 涼風 a cool breeze; *chă liòng* 凄涼, pitiable; *liòng hŭng huói,* 涼風會 a summer pleasure party.

Liòng, 梁, A ridge pole; as in *dóng liòng,* a beam; by *met.,* the chief; trustworthy: *gŏng liòng* 杠梁 a beam, a girder; *pé liòng* 鼻梁 the bridge of the nose.

Liòng, 梁 Large grained millet: COM. *gŏ liòng siĕu* 膏梁燒 spirits distilled from tall millet.

Liòng, 糧, 粮, Food; victuals; soldiers' pay; land taxes; COM. *mī liòng* 米糧 rice; *liòng chó,* 糧草 food, victuals; *siáh cièng liòng* 食錢糧 to eat rations, as soldiers.

Liòng, 良, Gentle; kindhearted;

a term of praise; loyal; capable; *liòng ìng* 良人 my goodman; my good-wife; *liòng dĭ* 良知 human instinct; *liòng sĭng* 良心 a good conscience; *liòng mìng* 良民 a loyal people; *liòng siēng* 良善 virtuous; *sùng liòng* 循良 gentle, mild.

Liòng, 量, To consider, to deliberate upon, as in *sŏng liòng* 商量.

Liông, 量 To measure, to estimate; good feeling, generosity; also read *liòng*, q. v.: COM., *âing liòng* 限量 limited quantity; *dô liòng* 度量 ability to forgive.

Liòng, 亮 Clear, transparent; bright as in *guŏng liòng* 光亮; COLL. *siăng ĭng iā liòng* 聲音也亮 very clear voice; *liòng liòng méng* 亮亮面 an open, honest face.

Liông, 諒 To trust in; faithful to suppose; COM., *liông bék* 諒必 to regard as quite probable; *tā liông* 體諒 to make allowance for.

Liŭ, 丟 Read *diū*; used for the coll. *liŭ:* to throw away; to run away from, as in *liŭ cău* 丟走 has absconded.

Liŭ, 柳 The willow; *met.*, dissipation; the 24th zodiacal constellation: *chák liŭ* 插柳 to stick up willow-twigs, as at the *Chĭng-mìng* festival.

Liŭ, 綹 In the coll. a classifier of beards, lappets and periwigs: COLL. *cĕng siŏh liŭ* 綹一鬚 one false cue.

Liŭ, 劉 In the coll. read *làu*, q. v.: a surname.

Liŭ, 流 To flow, as water; to be transported; as *liŭ mìng* 流民

vagrants; *liù lôi* 流淚 to shed tears; COM., *liù huâng* 流犯 banished for crime; *liù tăng* 流通 current, as good bills: COLL, *muóng liù* 倜流 banishment.

Liù, 硫 Sulphur; COM., *liù huòng* 硫磺 flowers of sulphur.

Liù, 留, 酉, 畱, To detain, as guests; to procrastinate; a surname; in the COLL. read *làu*, q. v.: COM., *liù êng* 留任 to keep in office.

Liù, 榴 The pomegranite tree: COM., *siŏh liù* 石榴 the pomegranite; *huăng siŏh liù* 番石榴, the guava.

Liù, 瘤 A tumor; a wen: COM., *háik liù* 血瘤 bloody tumors.

Lô, 露 Dew; to bedew; to bless; to make manifest: COM, *lô dài* 露臺 the terrace (of a house), a staging; *ló tā* 露體 naked; *ló gáuk* 露骨 "exposed bone" —i. e., an evil deed exposed.

Lô, 滷 Read *lū*: COLL. *lô*: brine, pickle, as *lô cáik* 滷汁; *lô hó* brine besprinkled; *met.*, scandalous.

Lô, 路 A road, a path, a passage: *met.*, a way of action; in the coll. read *diô*, q. v.: COM., *lô géng* 路徑 or *lô tiàng* 路程 ways, roads.

Lô, 鷺 A heron; COLL., *lô lì* (or *sì*) 鷺鷀 the fishing cormorant.

Lô, 賂 Bribe: in the coll. to deceive, annoy: *uōi-lô* 賄賂 bribes.

Lŏ, 囉 Read *lò*; COLL. *lŏ*, as in *cêng kŏ lŏ sŏ*, exceedingly vexatious.

Lŏ, A coll. word: *lŏ-lŏ bēng* or *lŏ-lŏ diŏh*, negligent, slack.

Lŏ, A coll, word, also spoken *lŏ*; a euphonic particle, as *iē lŏ*, *dóh lŏ*, *cṳ̄ lŏ*, chairs, tables, books.

Lŏ, 老 Old, seventy years of age; out of date; skilful; a term of respect; Mr.; in the coll. read *láu* q. v.: COM., *lŏ éu* 老幼 old and young; *lŏ chiū* 老手, skilled at; *lŏ iè*, 老爺, Sir, your Honor; *lŏ sĭk* 老實 honest; COLL., *lŏ sièu* 老小 a wife; *lŏ bēng* 老板 the boss; *gŭ lŏ* 孤老 a leper: *lŏ uă* 佬鴉 a raven.

Lò, 勞 To toil, to labor, as in *lò kū* 勞苦 toilsome labor; *kùng lò* 勤勞 to be diligent; *gŭng lò* 功勞 merit; *lò dông* 勞動 or *dŏ lò* 多勞 to trouble one.

Lò, 癆 Consumption, as in *lò céng* 癆症, phthisis; *tiè lò*, settled consumption.

Lò, 羅 A surname; *met.*, a snare; COM., *lò gĭng* 羅經 a compass.

Lò, 囉 In the coll. noise, clamor, as in *lò cò* 囉嘈; *hō̤ lò* good; *sê lò*, yes.

Lò, 蘿 Parasitic plants; COM. *lò bŭk* 蘿蔔 a carrot; termed in the coll. *chái tàu* 菜頭.

Lò, 鑼 A gong: COM. *lò gū bĕng* 鑼鼓板 gongs, drums, and rattling sticks.

Lò, 燶 Read *iŏh*; used in the *Báik ĭng* for the coll. *lò*: to scald: *lò miéng* 燶麪 to scald vermicelli.

Lò, 勞 To reward labor; to console as in *ói lò* 慰勞.

Lò, 邏 To make a circuit, to inspect; a patrol; COM: *sùng lò* 巡邏 to patrol; *lò gă* 邏街 to go about the streets.

Lò, 癆 Read *lŏ*; COLL. *lò* as in *gò lò* 癆瘃 itch.

Lŏh, 絡 Read *lŏh*; used for the coll. *lŏh*: a case or cover: *sáng lŏh* 傘絡 an umbrella case; *chiū lŏh* 手絡 gloves, mittens; *lŏh diē* put it into.

Lŏh, 落 Read *lŏk*; coll *lŏh*; to fall, to descend; *met.*, to degenerate; to set, as the sun; *dáung lŏh* 邊落 to fall down as things: *nĭk lŏh sáng* 日落山 sunset: *lŏh sùng* 落船 to take a boat; *lŏh dặ* 落底 formerly, originally.

Lŏi, 橤 Read *cŭi*; a knot in wood, as in *chà lŏi* 柴橤; knots in wood; *lŏi tàu*, a knot.

Lŏi, 纇 Read *lói*: knots in silk, thread or cord: *lŏi páh siŏh ciáh*, tie a knot; *páh giék lŏi*, knotted, tangled, as thread.

Lòi, 雷 Thunder; a surname: in the coll. read *lài*, q. v.: *lài* gŭng, 雷公 Jupiter tonans; *lòi hiōng* 雷嚮 the sound of thunder.

Lòi, 螺 A name of spiral univalves; a screw: COM. *diè lòi* 池螺 pond snails: *lòi sī*, 螺絲 a screw.

Lôi, 累 To invlove, to implicate, as in *dâi lôi* 帶累; COLL., *lôi diŏh bĕk nèng*, to involve others.

Lôi, 彙 A class, a series: *cê lôi* 字彙 a dictionary: COM., *lôi cṳ̄* 彙書 to arrange books.

Lôi, 類 Good, excellent; a class, sort: *dùng lôi* 同類 of the same sort.

Lọ́i, 鑢 To perforate: *lọ́i lā kĕng kĕng*, 鑢喇空空 to bore a hole.

Lộï, 擂 Read *lòi*: to drum: *lộï gū* 擂鼓 to beat a drum.

Lŏk, 絡 Hemp; joined: *liêng lŏk*

連絡 to have friendly relations with.

Lŏk, 樂 Pleasure, delight; to rejoice: COM, *ăng lŏk* 安樂 peaceful and happy; *cáuk lŏk* 作樂 to make merry.

Lŏk, 駱 As in *lŏk dọ̀* 駱駝 a camel.

Lōng, 朗 Clear, bright: *mìng lōng* 明朗 clear, light.

Lōng, 襴 A garment worn next the person; *dōi lōng* 短襴 a shirt.

Lòng, 廊 Rooms, porches, corridors.

Lòng, 狼 A wolf; *met.*, cruel, oppressive; *cài lòng* 豺狼 a wolf: COLL., *lòng buôi kék-kŭi*, in very great distress.

Lòng, 郎 A gentleman; COM. *sìng lòng* 新郎 a bridegroom; *lêng lòng* 令郎 your son; COLL. *lòng bá* 朗罷 (spoken *nòng má*), a father.

Lu*â*ng   593

Lù, 盧 A vessel for holding rice; a surname.

Lù, 蘆 High rushes, as in *lù chāu* 蘆草

Lù, 爐 A furnace, a brazier; a stove; a censer; COM., *huōi lù* 火爐 a fire place; *chiŭ lù* 手爐 a hand stove.

Lṳ̄, 呂 The spine: a surname.

Lṳ̄, 侶 A colleague; to associate with: *puáng lṳ̄* 伴侶 a partner; *bŏng lṳ̄* 帮侶 comrades, helpers.

Lṳ̄, 旅 A battalion of 500 men; a guest, a lodger: *lṳ̄ dáing* 旅店 a lodging house.

Lṳ̄, 膂 The back bone, the spine: COM., *lṳ̄ lĭk* 膂力 strong, strength.

Luâng, 亂 To confuse, to disorder; insurrection: *cáuk luâng* 作亂 to rebel, to make riot; *ieu luâng* 擾亂 to make confusion.

Lūi, 壘 Ramparts, fortifications.

Lūi, 蕊 The stamens: COM., *huá lūi* 花蕊 a flower bud.

Lŭk, 律 A fixed law, a statute; *lŭk huák* 律法 laws; *lŭk gái* 律誡 commandants.

Lŭk, 縲 A large bamboo rope; in the coll. to raise or lower by cords: COLL. *lŭk sŏh* a pulley rope; *lŭk biāng*, a pulley.

Lŭk, 陸 High, dry land, terra firma: *lŭk diô tì-dók* 陸路提督 a major general.

Lūng, 隴 A dike: used in the coll. for all, the whole: *lūng cūng* all, the whole.

Lùng, 倫 Constant, regular; a series, a class; national law; to choose: COM., *ngŭ lùng* 五倫 the five social relations.

Lùng, 輪 A wheel with spokes;

a revolution; by turns; COM. *chiă lùng* 車輪 a wheel.

Lùng, 龍 A dragon; dragon like; imperial; a fruit, the lungan or dragon's eye.

Lùng, 隆 Grand; exalted; COM., *Gièng-lùng* 乾隆 the Emperor Kienlung.

Mā, 嬤 A common name for mother; COLL., *mă-mă* or *ĭ mă,* 依嬤 mamma! mother!

Mă: A coll. word, to take with the hand; to grasp as in *mă gĭng,* to grasp tightly; *mă siŏh ba,* to grasp a bunch.

Mā, 馬 A horse; cavalry as in *mā bĭng* 馬兵; *kiè mā* 騎馬 to mount a horse: *mā hŭ* 馬夫, a hostler; *mā diŏ* 馬路 a horse road.

Mă, 媽 A mare; a dame, a grand-mother: COLL., *láu-mā* 佬媽 a wife.

Mā, 瑪 The agate: COM., *mā-nọ* 瑪瑙 the carnelian.

Mā, 碼 Weights, as in *huák mā* 砝碼; also used for the English yard: COLL., *mā cī*, abreviated numerals: *siŏh mā* 一碼 one yard.

Mā: A coll. word, as in *mā-dái-*(or *lái*) *iè*, a large spider.

Má, 罵 To scold; to vilify as in *ŭk má* 辱罵: COM., *có má* 詛罵, to curse; *sŏng má* 相罵 to altercate.

Mà, 痲 Numb, benumbed: in the coll. read *muài*, q. v.: COM. *mà-hŭng* 痲瘋 leprosy.

Mà, 麻 Hemp, the female plant; in the coll. read *muài*, q. v.: the linen of the Chinese: sackcloth; in the coll., mean, troublesome, as in *mà cà*.

Mà, 猫 Read *mièu*: a cat: COM.

iā-mà 野貓 a wild cat: COLL., *mù-giāng* 貓仔 a kitten; *mà-huòng cēu*, an owl.

Mà, 蟆. A striped frog: COLL., *hà mà* 蝦蟆, the edible frog.

Mà, A coll. word, as in *mà hù*, the dragon fly.

Mà, A coll. word, as in *tiè-mà*, to cry, to weep.

Mạ̄, 買 To buy; to obtain: *mạ̄ mạ̄* 買賣 trade; *mạ̄ bâing* 買辦 a comprador; *mạ̄ mìng sĭng* 買民心, to win the people's hearts (by cunning): *mạ̄ diô* 買路 to "buy (right of) way," as of highwaymen.

Mạ̣, 賣: To sell, to dispose of for money; to betray: COM. *chŏi mạ̣* 碎賣 to sell in small quantities; *mạ̣ sĭng* 賣身 to sell into slavery.

Mạ̣; A coll. word: cannot, will

not, is not: with *iông*. means not much, not very, somewhat: *mạ dōi*, not too short; *có mạ lì*, or *siăh mạ dă*, can't be done; *ạ ā mạ*, can or can't? *mā sāi dék*, will not do, must not; *mạ iông iĕk*, not very hot.

Máek, 抹: Read *muák*; COLL. *máek*: to daub, to besmear, to stain.

Máeng, 夢 Read *móng*; COLL. *máeng*: a dream, a vision; *met.*, vain hopes, visionary; *siòng máeng* 詳夢, to interpret dreams.

Máeng, 緟 A fishing net: COLL. *ngù máeng* 魚緟 a fish net.

Măh, 脈 Read *mĕk*; COLL. *măh*: the pulse; the circulation; a descent, as in *háik măh*, 血脈 race or stock; *káng măh* 看脈, to feel the pulse.

Mài 599

Măh, 麥 Wheat: *siēu măh*, winter wheat; *măh puō* 麥麩 wheat bran; *săng gáek măh* 三角麥, buck-wheat; *duái măh* 大麥 barley.

Mạh, 哶 Read *miéh*; COLL. *máh*, the bleating of sheep and goats.

Mặh, A coll. word, as in *cháu gău mặh*, a puddle, a plash.

Māi, 魅 Read *muói*; used for the coll. *māi*; a hobgoblin; *kéuk māi dáh* 乞魅壓 to have the nightmare; *met.*, unlucky.

Māi: A coll. word: to fade, to decay; worthless; *miàng siăng māi*, his reputation decayed, as said of a physician.

Mài, 埋: To bury, to inter; to secrete: in the coll. read *muài*, q. v.: COM., *mài cáung*, 埋葬 to bury a corpse; *mài còng*, 埋

藏 to secrete; *mài hŭk*, 理伏, to lie in ambush.

Mái, 邁 To go away; senile, aged; to go beyond, to surpass: *nièng mái* 年邁 or *lŏ mái* 老邁 old.

Mái, A coll. word: to carry on the back; *met.*, to owe; in debt.

Mâing, 孟 The eldest, senior; the first of the series, the first months of a quarter; a surname: COM., *Mâing cṳ̄* 孟子 or 孟夫子, Mencius,

Mâing, 慢 Read *mâng*; COLL. *mâing*: slow, dilatory: *dì mâing* 遲慢 tardy; *cŏ dék mâing* 做的慢, to do leisurely; *kák mâing* 恰慢, too slow.

Mâiu, 茂, Exuberant foliage; thrifty; a high rank; fine, elegent; strong: *mâiu sêng* 茂盛 flourishing; *séu mâiu* 秀茂 rich foliage.

Mǎiu, 貿 To barter, to trade: *mǎiu-ĭk* 貿易 commerce.

Mǎng, 胖 Read *màng*; coll. *mǎng*, met., dull, stupid as in *mǎng-mǔng* 胖儚; *tì-tǔ-mǎng* 蜘蛛胖 a spider's web.

Mǎng, 猛 Read *měng*; coll. *mǎng*; strong and active; vigorous; hot, glowing, as fire: *mǎng-mǎng-huōi* 猛猛火 a very hot fire.

Mǎng, 蠓 Read *měng*; coll. *mǎng*, as in *chāu-mǎng* 草蠓 a grasshopper.

Mǎng, 滿 Read *muǎng*; coll. *mǎng*; a corruption of *muǎng* (full, fully), following *cī* or *hṳ̄*, so very, so much: *cī-mǎng-hō* 只滿好 so very good; *hṳ̄-mǎng-gèng* 許滿高, so very high.

Mǎng: A coll. word; a corruption of *mô̤-gāng*, as in *mǎng có*, dare not do it.

Màng, 蒙 Read *mùng;* coll. *màng,* as in *màng-muôi* (or *buôi*) 蒙昧, simple, ignorant.

Màng, 盲 Blind, the eye sightless; blind in mind, deceived: COLL., *chăng-màng* 瞽盲.

Màng, 蠻 A very weak worm; the aboriginal tribes of the south; as in *màng-ì* 蠻夷 barbarians; in the coll. to jest, to joke: COLL., *áu-màng* 拗蠻 fierce; *màng-chiéu* 蠻笑 to laugh at, to jest.

Màng, 明 Read *mìng;* coll. *màng,* as in *màng-nièng* 明年 or *màng-nièng-màng,* 明年明 next year; *kó-nièng-màng* 去年明, last year; *siŏh-màng,* yesterday.

Màng, 暝 Read *mìng;* coll. *màng;* dark, obscure; night, as in *màng-buŏ* 暝晡; *nĭk-màng* 日

Màu 603

暝 day and night, constantly.

Màng, 暝 Evening, the evening meal: *siăh-màng* 食暝, to eat supper.

Máng, 幔 A curtain, or screen, as in *dióng-mâng* 帳幔; COM., *buó-mâng* 布幔 an awning.

Mâng, 慢 To treat with disrespect as in *dâi-mâng* 怠慢; *ū-mâng* 侮慢 to insult.

Mâng, 謾 To deceive superiors, as in *kĭ-mâng* 欺謾; *dâi-mâng* 大謾 great disrespect.

Mău: A coll. word: to close the lips or mouth, as in *chói măn*; also spoken *māu*.

Māu; A coll. word: to turn or fold over; to clinch as nails: *māu-diĕ,* fold it in.

Màu, 茅 High rank grass: COM., *màu-châu,* 茅草 rush-thatch; *màu-săik* 茅塞, ignorance, mental darkness.

Máu, 貌 The outward mien; the appearance, countenance; COM., ùng-máu 容貌 the form, the figure; nguôi-máu 外貌 the outward appearance; lạ-máu 禮貌 etiquette.

Máuk, A coll. word, soft, tender; decayed, as fruit, paper; máuk kọ́, soft, as by cooking.

Máung, 言 Read mòng: used for the coll. máung: to eat as the aged; to eat with the gums.

Mé: A coll. euphonic prefix, as in mé-má, to scold; mé-mọ́, to pound, to beat.

Mê, 媚 Smiling, smirking; ogling; to flatter, as in tiẽng-mê 諂媚: COM., hẹ̀-mê, to cajole.

Mê, 謎 An enigma, a riddle: coll., cūng-mê 準謎 to guess riddles.

Mê; A coll. word: to search for

stolen things; to study, as a lesson, *mê-diŏh*, or *mê-dék-diŏh*, searched out.

Mê: A coll. euphonic prefix, as in *mê-mô*, to grind in a mill; *mê-má*, to sell off.

Mĕk, 默, 嘿 Dark, cloudy; night; memory: *mĕk-sê* 默示 a revelation; *mĕk-cṳ̆* 默書 to write from memory.

Mĕk, 目 Read *mĕk*; coll. *mĕk*, as in *mĕk-ciŭ* 目睭, the eye.

Mĕk, 密 Read *mŭk*; coll. *mĕk*: close together, as in *mĕk-mĕk* 密密.

Mĕk, 墨 Read *mĕk*; ink; black, as ink: *met*, writings, letters; *ùng-mĕk* 文墨 literature.

Mĕk, 茉 Read *muăk*; coll. *mĕk*, as in *mĕk-lê-huă* 茉莉花, the jasmine.

Mĕk, 目 Read *mŭk*; coll. *mĕk*,

also read *měk*, q. v.: a theme, the eye; as in *měk-ciŭ* 目睭; *měk-cāi* 目滓 tears; *dà-měk* 題目 a theme; *gù-cŭi-měk* 鵠鵴目, a staple.

Měk; A coll. word, as in *měk-sáik*, a bed-bug.

Měng, 猛 A strong, fierce dog; stern; cruel; hot, as fire: in coll. read *māng* q. v.: *měng-liěk* 猛烈 ferocious.

Méng, 面 Read *miéng*: coll. *méng*: the face; the surface; in front honor, character; *méng-máu* 面貌, the expression; *méng-sèng* 面前 in one's presence.

Mèng, 盟 An oath, a contract: COM, *mèng-iók* 盟約 a sworn contract, *dùng-mèng* 同盟 an alliance.

Mêng, 命 To order; a decree; a polite request; heaven; luck,

Mēu 607

fortune: in the coll. read *miáng*, q. v.: COM., *tiĕng-mêng* 天命 the decree of heaven; *mêng-lêng* 命令 a command; *séng-mêng* 性命 life, existence.

Mĕng; A coll. word: light and spongy, as in *mĕng-mĕng*.

Mĕng, 疹 Read *cīng*; used in the *Báik-ĭng* for the coll. *mĕng*; the measles; *chók mĕng* 出疹, to have measles.

Mĕng, 蠓 Read *mūng* and *mùng*; coll. *mĕng*, gnats; sand flies.

Mĕng, 芒 Read *mòng*; coll. *mĕng* as in *mĕng-sáu* 芒掃 a whisk-broom.

Mēu, 牡 The male of quadrupeds; a male screw: in the coll. read *mū*, q. v.: *mēu-dăng* (coll. *mū-dăng*), 牡丹 the Mowtan peony.

Mēu, 畝, 畒, A Chinese acre;

met., fields, arable land; in the coll. read *mū*, q. v.: *dièng-mēu* 田畝 fields and farms.

Mèu, 謀 To make plans; to scheme: to plot: a scheme: *dùng-mèu* 同謀 to conspire; *mèu-sēng* 謀生 to plan a livlihood: *mèu-hái* 謀害, to plot against.

Mĭ: A coll. word: the mewing of cats: *mĭ-mĭ* and *mĭ-giāng*, terms used in calling cats.

Mĭ: A coll. euphonic prefix, as in *mĭ-mă*, to grasp; *mĭ-muŏ* to touch, to feel of.

Mī, 米 Husked or hulled rice, as in *mī-gók* 米穀 rice; *mī-hŭng* 米粉 rice flour.

Mī, 美 Sweet, delicious; good; beautiful; to commend: *mī-lâ* 美麗 fine: COM., *cáng-mī* 讚美, to praise.

Mì, 眉 The eyebrows; old, aged: COM., *mì-mò-nguŏk* 眉毛月 the moon, crescent or waning: *huā-mì,* a song-bird.

Mì, 惟 To think on: to have, to be, is; but, only; COM. *mì-dŭk* 惟獨, but, only; *mì-iū* 惟有, only have or is.

Mì, 維 To tie, to bind; to think on, to consider: *mì-tì* 維持 to support, to promote.

Mì, 糜 Rice gruel, thin congee, as in *mì-cĕuk* 糜粥.

Mì, 微, 徴 Small, insignificant; obscure: *mì-sá* 微細 small, fine; *cĭng-mì,* 精微 subtle; *mì-ciĕng* 微賤 base, servile; COM., *mì-mì-huōi,* a little fire; *mì-mì-ŭ,* fine rain.

Mì, 迷 To deceive, as in *mì-hĕk* 迷惑; *huŏng-mì* 惛迷 in a stupor, insensible.

610 Miàng

Mì, 遺 To leave, as at death; to bequeath; a will, testament; COM., *mì-mêng* 遺命 a will; *mì-diòng* 遺傳 handed down, as property or a profession; tradition.

Miák: A coll. word: to smear, to plaster; *miák ngài*, spoiled, as by a muddy splash: *miák nguāi sĭng-sióng*, has come on me (for liquidation).

Miák: A coll. word: old and shabby; prostrated by sickness: *miák miák*, strength all gone; *ĭ-siòng iā miák siŏh làu*, is wearing very shabby clothes indeed!

Miăk: A coll. word: to beat, as the heart: *miăk-miăk-dâęng* (or *giéu*) palpitating.

Miàng, 名 Read *mìng;* coll. *miàng;* a name; the given

name; *met.*, a person; reputation as in *miàng-siăng* 名聲; distinction, as in *miàng* (*mìng*) *ę̆u* 名譽; *chók-miàng* 出名, to act for (others); noted, famed.

Miăng, 命 Read *mêng;* coll. *miâng:* the natural life or being; fate; fortune: *uăk-miâng* 活命, one's natural life; *káng-miâng* 看命 to tell fortunes; *miâng-ngài* 命呆 a wretched lot.

Miĕ, 剔 Read *piĕ;* used for the coll. *miĕ:* to trim; to pare, to whittle off, as in *miĕ-siŏh-tùng,* to pare off one thickness.

Miéh, 乜 Read *miā* in the dictionaries meaning oblique; in the coll. read *miéh*, what; the same as in the coll. *sié,* q. v.: *miéh-ngṅh,* what? *miéh-ngḣ-ngḣ* what things? *miéh-sì-háiu,* what time?

Miĕk, 威, 滅, To extinguish; to destroy utterly: *càu-miĕk* 剿威, to extirpate: COM. *dù-miĕk* 除滅 to abolish; *miĕk-uòng* 滅亡 exterminated.

Miĕk, 蔑 Interchanged with the last; to scrape thin; small, minute; worthless.

Miĕk, 篾 The skin of the bamboo: COM., *miĕk-nòng*, 篾瓤 inner splints; *miĕk-kŭ* 篾箍 bamboo hoops: COLL. *miĕk-năk* 篾繳, (or *kă-năk* 溪繳) a bamboo tow-line.

Miĕ·g; A coll, word, as in *miĕng-mŏng*, adjusted, well arranged, as things.

Miēng, 免 To put away, to free from; to forgive, as in *siá-miēng* 赦免; escape from; *nàng-miēng* 難免 can't escape, as a penalty: coll., *miēng-dék* 免的

to avoid, so that it may not; *mạ-mièng-dék-kọ́* 賣免的去 inexcusable, unavoidable.

Mièng, 娩 㜽 To bear children: the first also read *uăng* q. v.: *hŭng-mièng* 分娩 parturition.

Mièng, 勉 To urge, to animate, as in *mièng-lặ* 勉勵 com., *mièng-lĭk* 勉力, to be diligent in; *giōng-mièng*, 強勉 to constrain.

Mièng, 棉 The cotton plant: com., *mièng-huă* 棉花, raw cotton; *mièng-cāi* 棉紙 cotton paper; *mièng-sặ-siáng* 棉紗線 cotton yarn or thread; coll., *mièng-puói* 棉被 cotton wadded bed-clothes.

Mièng, 綿, 緜 Interchanged with the last; soft cottony silk, as raw silk or floss: *sĭ-mièng* 絲綿, silk sheets—like cotton batting.

Mièng: A coll. word: to shave off; to pare, as fruit: *mièng lī* to pare plums; *mièng kă-něng* to shave off the hard skin of the feet.

Miêng, 面 The countenance, the top or surface of: a classifier of drums, gongs, and mirrors; the 176th radical; in the coll., read *méng*, q. v.: COM., *tā-miéng* 體面 honor, respectability.

Mièng, 麪, 麵, Wheaten flour; vermicelli made of flour: COM., *mièng-băŭ* 麪包 lit., vermicelli and small loaves, as presents; wheat bread; *mièng-hūng* 麪粉 (coll., *mièng-muŏk* or *miéng-mŏk*) wheat flour; *chiék-mièng,* 切麪 and *sŏh-mièng* 索麪, the sliced and the thread like kinds of vermicelli: COLL. *mièng siŏh gáik,* a knot of thread-vermicelli; *miêng siŏh piāng*, a fold of sliced vermicelli.

Miĕu, 渺 The boundless appearance of the ocean.

Miĕu, 藐 Small, petty; to regard contemptuously: COM., *miĕu-sĭ* 藐視, to slight, to regard with disdain.

Miĕu, 描 To trace, to design and sketch as in *miĕu-uâ* 描畫.

Mièu, 貓 Also read *màu* in the dictionaries; a cat, a puss: in the coll. read *mà*, q. v.

Miĕu, 妙 Admirable of its kind, excellent, perfect; as in *mī-miĕu* 美妙 wonderful; subtle, supernatural: COM., *miĕu-chiŭ* 妙手, skillful, as an artist, or a physician; *kiĕu-miĕu* 巧妙 capable, has genius.

Miĕu, 廟, 庿 An idol temple, an ancestral hall: COM. *miĕu-cĕuk*

廟祝 (coll. *káng-miéu*) a temple curator.

Miéu, 謬 Read *méu* in the dictionaries: an error: to err; to defraud, to mislead; silly, extravagant gabble as in *miéu-ngiòng* 謬言; *miéu-nguó* 謬誤, an error: COM. *buói-miéu* 背謬 refractory; wrong, as the idea in an essay.

Mĭk, 密, 蜜, Thick, close together; fine, minute; secret; friendly: in the coll. read *mĕk*, q. v.: *bé-mĭk* 秘蜜 hidden, secret; *chĭng-mĭk* 深蜜 very intimate: COM. *ciŭ-mĭk* 周蜜 complete, well done, as work; faultless.

Mĭk, 濫 Full, overflowing as waters; in the coll. submerged: COLL. *kéuk cūi mĭk* 乞水濫 covered with water; *mĭk-guó-tàu* 濫過頭 overflowing higher than one's head.

Mĭng 617

Mĭk, 蜜, 蜜, Honey; luscious; *met.*, honeyed, flattering: COM., *mĭk-pŭng* 蜜蜂, the honeybee; *mĭk-cọ̄* 蜜棗 sweet dates; *mĭk ciéng pĭč-sŏng*, 蜜浸砒霜 "arsenic steeped in honey"—the flattering words of a scoundrel.

Mĭk, 域 A frontier; a region; lands: *Sặ-mĭk*, 西域, states beyond the western frontier.

Mĭng, 皿 Dishes; the 108th radical: *ké-mīng* 器皿 utensils used in eating.

Mĭng, 敏 Active, clever, as in *chŭng-mĭng* 聰敏: COM., *mĭng-ciĕk* 敏捷 ready, prompt, of quick perception.

Mĭng, 憫, 愍, To feel concern for: COM., *lìng-mĭng* 憐憫, (coll. *kọ̄-lèng*, 可憫) to pity.

Mĭng, A coll. euphonic prefix, as in *mĭng-miĕng*, to forgive; to avoid.

Mìng, 名 In the coll. read *miàng*, q. v.: a name; the given name; *met.*, a person; a title; fame, honor, renown; to name; to designate; *sìng-mìng*, 成名, to obtain a reputation; *gŭng-mìng* 功名 merit, official honors; *mìng-gă* 名家 an illustrious family; *mìng-sẹ̆u* 名士 a distinguished scholar.

Mìng, 明 Bright, clear; open, manifest; brightness, splendor; to illustrate, as by explanations: in the coll. used for *màng*, q. v.: COM., *mìng-bĕk*, 明白 to understand clearly; *Mìng-dièu* 明朝, the Ming dynasty, A. D. 1368—1628; *kiĕ-mìng-sĭng* 啓明星, the morning star; *mìng-tiĕng* 明天 (coll., *mìng-dáng*) tomorrow.

Mìng, 民 The people, as in *mìng-*

gă 民家: COM., mìng-ké 民氣, the spirit of the people; mìng-gŭ 民居 the dwellings of the people; nguàng-mìng 頑民 the canaille; lìong-mìng 良民 loyal people; mìng-biéng 民變 the people changing—i. e., becoming rebellious.

Mìng, 眠 Read mièng; coll. mìng; to sleep; drowsy as in mìng-nệu; mìng-chòng 眠床 a bedstead; chŭng-mìng 瞓眠 sleepy.

Mìng, 閩 A species of serpent; the ancient name of Fukien; the river Min in the province; COM., Mìng Uŏk 閩粵 the Fukien and Canton provinces.

Mìng, 鳴 The cry of a bird: giĕ mìng 鷄鳴 cock crowing; mìng cŭng, 鳴鐘 to sound a bell: cệu mìng-cŭng 自鳴鐘 a clock.

Mŏ: A coll. word: to swell, as

from the bite of an insect: *siŏh sĭng dŭ sĕ mŏ̤-mŏ̤*, covered with bunches (from bites).

Mŏ̤: A coll. word, borrowed from Shantung and equivalent to *bău*, bread, as *mŏ̤-mŏ̤*, loaves of bread.

Mō̤, 母 Read *mū:* coll. *mō̤*: the female of animals; *met.*, principal, substance; *ngù-mō̤* 牛母, a cow; *giĕ-mō̤* 鷄母 a hen; *chó-mō̤* 醋母 the mother in vinegar; *dăi-mō̤* 大母 or *cūng-mō̤* 準母, the substance; an epitome.

Mō̤, 拇 Read *mū;* coll. *mō̤*, as in *duái-mō̤-cāi*, 大拇指 the thumb; *kă duái-mō̤-cāi* 胶大拇指 the great toe.

Mò, 麼 A final interrogative in questions answered by "yes" or "no:" coll., *káng-mò* 看麼 lo! behold!

Mò, 摩 To rub; to polish, to destroy, as *siêu-mò* 消摩: COM., *chōi-mò* 揣摩 to search out the sense of.

Mò, 磨 To grind; to polish; *met.*, to study; afflicted; also read *mô* and in the coll. *muài*, q. v.: COM., *mò-nâng* 磨難, to be afflicted; *mò-liéng* 磨鍊 to become skilled in.

Mò, 魔 A demon; COM., *mò-gūi* 魔鬼 a devil.

Mò, 毛 Hair, fur; feathers; the 82nd radical; used in coll. books for no, not, none; COLL., *mò-báng* 毛病 a failing; a defect (in a thing); *mò mò-báng* 毛毛病 faultless; blameless.

Mò, 無 Read *ù*; used for the coll. *mò*; not, no, none; wanting; equivalent to *un* in English: *mò iéu-gīng* 無要緊 un-important; *mò-huák-dék* 無法的, no help for it; *ô ā mò* 有吓無 yes or no; *mò-nóh gōng* 無毛講, nothing to say; *mò ciā sęu* 無者事 no such thing; *mò-dăng-dŏng* 無擔當 cannot; *mò-méng* 無面 ashamed.

Mộ, 冐, 冒, A head covering; to assume; to counterfeit as in *gā-mộ* 假冒; *mộ-hiēng* 冒險 to brave danger, to risk.

Mộ, 帽 A hat, a cap: *hŭng-mộ* 風帽 a hood or winter bonnet.

Mộ, 磨 A hand-mill; to grind grain; also read *mò*, q. v.: *cūi-mộ* 水磨, a water mill; *ngừ-mộ* 牛磨 a buffalo mill; *mộ miĕng-hūng* 磨麫粉 to grind wheat.

Mǒh, A coll. word: to guess at; *muōng mǒh* just say or guess.

Mǒh, 莫 Read *mŏk*; coll. *mǒh*; do

not, must not, no need of: *mŏh-gŭ* 莫拘, don't be ceremonious; *gó mŏh niăh nguāi iông*, 故莫拿我樣 still not equal to my style.

Mŏh, 膜 Read *mŏk*, coll. *mŏh*, a thin film; *gaik-mŏh* 隔膜 a separating partition.

Mŏk: A coll. word, as in *mók-ĭ*. fine sewing silk.

Mŏk, 莫 A negative of prohibition: in the coll. read *mŏh*, q. v.: COM., *mŏk bók sè* 莫不是, it must have been.

Mŏk, 漠 Also read *máuk:* a sandy plain, as in *să-mŏk* 沙漠.

Mŏk, 膜 The thin film inside of eggs, grasses and certain fruits; any membrane as the cornea, mesentery, etc.: in the coll. read *mŏh* q. v.

Mŏk, 幕 A curtain, a screen, as in *mì-mŏk* 帷幕.

Mŏng, A coll. word: a kind of grass, called *mŏng-chāu*, gathered for fuel.

Mŏng, A coll. word, as in *miĕng-mŏng*, all properly arranged, as things.

Mŏng, A coll. word, as in *mŏng-mŏng-hìng*, fluttered, harassed.

Mōng, 莽, 莽, Confused, tangled; rude, boorish: COM., *lū-mōng* 鹵莽 rough, impertinent.

Mŏng, 夢 To dream; a dream; in the coll. read *máeng*, q. v.

Mòng, 忙 The mind distressed with cares: COM., *huŏng-mòng* 慌忙 hurried; COLL., *mòng-mòng-cāu* 忙忙走 to hurry to and fro, driven with work and cares.

Mòng, 茫 Vast, and indistinct, as in *miĕu-mòng* 渺茫 incapable of proof.

Môngˊ, 悶 Sad, sorrowing; afflicted: COM., *iĕu-môngˊ* 憂悶 unhappy: COLL., *tói-môngˊ* 碓悶 captious; troublesome.

Mū, 母 A mother; a female; *met.*, earth; in the coll. read *mọ̄*, q. v.: COM., *mū-chˊing* 母親 a mother; *chˊing-mū*, 親母 a mother-in-law; *dùngˋ hô ê mū* 同父異母 step brothers and sisters.

Mū, 姆, 姥, A childless widow of fifty years; a school mistress; COM., *mū-sīng* 姆嬸 sister-in-law.

Mū, 某 A certain time, place, person, or thing; also for the pronoun I; *mū nı̆k* 某日 a certain day: COLL., *mū nẹngˋ* 某仸 a certain person.

Mū, 畝 Read *mēu*, coll. *mū*: a Chinese acre: 6.61 *mū* equal to an English acre.

Muài, 埋 Read *mài;* coll. *muài:* to bury, as in *muài-cáung* 埋葬, to inter; *muài-hŭk* 埋伏 buried, as one's ability.

Muài, 痲 Read *mà;* coll. *muài;* a skin disease, like *mĕng* (measles); *chók muài* 出痲, to have the *muài* eruption.

Muài, 麻, 蔴, Read *mà;* coll. *muài:* hemp; sack-cloth; *muài-buó* 麻布 hempen cloth; *muài-iù* 麻油, oil of sesame.

Muài, 磨 Read *mò;* coll. *muài;* to whet, to grind; to polish: *muài dŏ* 磨刀 to whet a knife.

Muăk, 抹 To daub, to smear; to sweep away; to erase; in the coll. read *máek* q. v.: COM., *dù-muăk,* 塗抹, to blot out.

Muăk, 末 The end; the last of, the least important; used for I, myself; *buōng-muăk* 本末

origin and end; *mì-muăk* 微末 insignificant.

Muāng, 滿, Full, abundant, as in *chṳng-muāng* 充滿, or *muāng-céuk* 滿足 abundant; *muāng-sĭng* 滿心 the whole mind or heart; *Muāng-ciŭ* 滿洲 Manchuria: COLL, *muāng-sié* 滿世 or *muāng-dói,* 滿塊 everywhere; *cī muāng hō̤,* 只滿好 so very good.

Muàng, 瞞 A flat eye; to deceive, to cheat: COM., *muàng-piéng* 瞞騙 to deceive; *ciŭ-muàng* 遮瞞 to hide from: COLL., *céṳ muàng céṳ* 自瞞自 self-deception.

Muàng, 鰻 An eel: *dâng-cūi-muàng* 淡水鰻 fresh water eels.

Muk, 木 Wood, wooden: a tree; honest, unbending; the 75th

radical: COM., *chŏ-mŭk* 草木 plants; *mŭk-lâiu* 木料 timber: COLL., *chéu-mŭk* 楳木 trees.

Mŭk, 目 The eye; *met.*, the mind, mental perception: an index, as in *mŭk-liŏh* 目錄: in the coll. read *mĕk* and *mĕk* q. v.

Mŭk, 睦 A kind eye; kind, peaceful; harmony among relatives; COM., *huò-mŭk* 和睦 concord.

Mŭk, 牧 To tend cattle; a shepherd; to superintend; a religious teacher, a pastor, as in *mŭk-sŭ* 牧師.

Mŭng, 濛 Read *mùng*; coll. *mŭng*, as in *mŭng-mŭng-tiĕng* 濛濛天, dark, gloomy weather.

Mùng, 蒙 A kind of moss; dull, simple; thankful, grateful for favors: COM., *mùng-muôi* 蒙昧 ignorant: *mùng-ŏng* 蒙恩 to receive favors; *kiĕ-mùng* 啓蒙

Muò 629

to teach the ignorant; *Mùng-gū* 蒙古 Mongolia.

Muŏ, 摸, 捫, The first read *muŏ*, the second *muòng;* coll. *muŏ:* to lay the hand on, to feel as in *muŏ măh* 摸脈 to feel the pulse; to soothe as in *muŏ sŏk*, 摸抄.

Muō, 奺 A coll. character, used in the *Baik-ĭng:* a wife; *muō-giāng* 奺仔 wife and children.

Muó, 墓 A tomb, a grave: COM., *muó-dê* 墓地, a cemetery; *muó-bà* 墓牌 a grave stone.

Muò, 模, 摹, A model; a guide for imitation; a rule, a law; COM., *muò-iông* 模樣 a pattern.

Muò, 謨 Counsel, a matured plan; to imitate; *mèu-muò* 謀謨 to devise plans.

Muò: A coll. word, as in *muò-ó*, fog, mist.

Muò: A coll. word: dim, obscure, as in *muò-muò*, obscure as the weather, glass, etc.

Muô, 慕 To long for, as in *sṳ̆-muô* 思慕 or *siōng-muô* 想慕; *ngiōng-muô* 仰慕 to revere.

Muô, 暮 The evening, the sunset: COLL., *mĕk-ciŭ muô* 目睭暮, dim-sighted.

Muōi, 每 Each, every, all, any one; usually, constantly, as in *muōi-muōi* 每每; *muōi-huòi* 每回 or *muōi-chék* 每次 every time.

Muōi, 莓 Read *muòi;* coll. *muōi,* as in *muōi-sì* (or *lì*) 莓蒔 water-chestnuts.

Muōi, 尾 The tail of an animal; the end, extremity; the bottom, a stern; a classifier of fishes: COM., *muōi-duái* 尾舵 a rudder; *muōi-chiū* 尾手 afterwards, at last: COLL., *ò tàu mò muōi* 務頭毛尾 a beginning without end, incomplete; *lēng-muōi* 瀧尾 and *kŭi-muōi* 開尾 to swing the boat's stern towards and from the shore.

Muói, 妹 A younger sister, one's daughter; a miss: *ciā-muói* 姐妹 sisters; *muói-hŭ* 妹夫 younger sister's husband: COLL., *muói-gŏ* 妹哥 Miss.

Mùoi, 媒 A matchmaker, as in *mùoi-nẹng* 媒仈.

Mùoi, 煤 Coal; charcoal; embers: COM., *mùoi--táng* 煤炭 hard coal; *cāi-mùoi* 紙煤 a paper-match.

Mùoi, 梅 An apricot; the flowering almond as in *mùoi-huā* 梅花; *iòng-mùoi* 楊梅 (coll. *chiŏ-ùng*), the Chinese tree-strawberry.

Muòi, 玫 A bright red stone, red coral: COLL., *muòi-gói* 玫瑰 red jasper: *muòi-gói-huä* 瑰玫花 a kind of red rose.

Muòi, 霉 Summer rains, damp molding weather, as in *muòi-tiĕng* 霉天: COLL., *muòi-máuk* spoiled by mildew.

Muôi, 未 Read *é;* used in the coll. *muôi:* not yet, not now; *siăh buông ā muôi* 食飯吓未, have you eaten rice yet? *muôi gáu gĭ* 未至期 the appointed time not yet come.

Muôi, 昧 No sun, twilight, somber; blind, ignorant; false, perfidious: used in the coll. books for *muôi* 未 not yet; *mộ-muôi* 冒昧 rash, inconsiderate: COM., *mùng-muôi* 蒙昧 ignorant.

Muŏk, 醫 Read *ĭ;* used for the

Muóng 633

coll. *muŏk*, to heal, to cure : *muŏk-bâng* 醫病 to heal disease.

Muōng, 晚 Read *uāng*; used in the *Báik-ĭng* for the coll. *muōng*, as in *muōng-děng* 晚冬 the second crop of rice—reaped in the 10th moon.

Muŏng, 莽 Read *buŏng*; used for the coll. initial particle *muŏng*: merely, only, only just; the more, still more; in any way, no matter how; *muōng ciĕu* 莽少 fewer and fewer; *muōng bó* 莽富 increasingly rich; *muōng gōng,* 莽講 just say on; to lie.

Muóng, 倜 A coll. character: to ask, to inquire of or about; to demand of, to investigate; to banish: *diŏh muóng* 着倜 you must ask; *muōng muóng* 莽倜 just ask; *muóng-dù* 倜徒 to exile for three years; *muóng cội* 徇罪 to exile for crime.

Muòng, 門 A door, a gateway; *met.*, the family; a sect, a class, a profession; a classifier of cannon, etc; the 169th radical; *ĭ-muòng* 醫門 the medical profession; COM., *chók-muòng* 出門, to go out; *muòng-sĕng* 門生 or *muòng-dù* 門徒 a disciple; COLL., *muòng-kāu*, 門口, the entrance.

Muòng, 們 The sign of the plural of persons: *ngō̤-muòng* 我們 we, us; *tă-muòng* 他們 they.

Muòng, 文 Read *ùng*; used for the coll. *muòng* as in *muòng-cṳ̆* 文書 an official dispatch.

Nā, 拿, 拏. To lay hold of; to apprehend; *met.*, to ascertain; in the coll. read *niăh*, q. v.

Nā, 那 A demonstrative and interrogative pronoun; an adverb of place: that, that one; then, which, what, where, how: in the coll. read nò, q. v.: nā gộ 那个 that one, nā lī 那裡 where? how?

Nà: A coll. word: to evacuate, to void: *nà-niêu*, to urinate; *nà-lê* dysentery, flux.

Nà: A coll. word: to measure with the thumb and middle-finger extended: *nà káng niõh-uâi*, measure and see how much.

Ná, 郍 Read nò; used for the coll. *ná:* but, only, simply, merely; if, but if: *ná cuòi* 郍嘴 only this; *ná ng-kīng* 郍怀肯 but if unwilling; *ná mọ̀,* if none.

Ná; A coll. initial particle, as in *ná lā-cộ,* to do frequently.

Nạ, 奶 Read nĭ and nāi in the

dictionaries: a common term for mother; a nurse: *niòng-nā* 娘奶 mother; *nā-mă* 奶嬤 a nurse; COLL., *bâ-nā* 罷奶 parents; *siéu-nā-nā* 少奶奶 an officer's daughter-in-law.

Nà̤, 尼 To agree; agreeing; a nun as in *nà̤-gŭ* 尼姑 a Buddhist nun.

Nà̤, 泥, 坭, 埿, Mud, mire; earth, soil; in the coll. to plaster; soiled; *met.*, to defame; also read *nă̤*, q. v.: COLL. *nà̤ huŏi,* 泥灰 to plaster with lime.

Nà̤, 泥 To decide rigidly; inflexible; in the coll. similar to *nà̤,* to daub, to plaster.

Ná̤: A coll. word: fat, corpulent as *buòi-ná̤-ná̤.*

Náe̤ng: A coll. word: soft as *iā náe̤ng* very soft; *kĕ-náe̤ng,* the soft persimmon.

Náing 637

Náh: A coll. word; to abate, as rain, as in *ṳ̄ náh,* the rain slackens.

Náh, 凹 Read *ău;* coll. *náh:* the opposite of *tŭ* 凸 (to protrude); indented: same as *náh,* q. v.

Náh, 凹 Read *ău;* coll. *náh:* concave, indented: *tŭ gì tŭ, náh gì náh* 凸其凸, 凹其凹, rough and uneven.

Nāi, 乃, 廼, But, doubtless.

Nài, 柰, 奈. A wild plum; to occur; a remedy; how, in what way? COM., *nài-hò* 奈何 what resource?

Nāi, 耐 Patient; to forbear; COM., *ṳ̄ng-nāi* 忍耐 to bear patiently, *nāi gĕng* 耐工, patient in work.

Náing, 跉 Read *niĕk;* in the *Báik-ĭng* for the coll. *náing:* to stand on the toes, as in *kă náing kī* 胶跉起.

Nāing, 念 Read *niéng;* coll. *nāing;* to repeat memoriter: *nāing-gĭng siăh-chái,* 念綹食菜 to say prayers and live on a vegetable diet.

Năk, 納 To collect; to pay; to give to, as presents: COM., *năk-suói* 納稅, to pay duties; *siŭ-năk* 收納 to receive; *sêu-năk* 受納 to embrace as doctrines.

Năk, 衲 In the coll. to stitch together, to quilt; to patch; patched: *chék - buō báik - năk* 七 補 八 衲 all covered with patches.

Năk, 筲 A bamboo-splint rope, as in *kă-năk* 溪筲: COLL., *bĕk năk* 扷筲 to pull the tow-line.

Nāng, 搣 To grasp with the hand; to push away or out, as with the hand or foot; used for *nàng* in the coll.: *nāng kŭi* 搞開 to push open.

Nàng: A coll. word: to force one's self, as when weak or fagged; *náng mạ kī*, unable to rise, as from weakness.

Nàng, 南 The south, to face the south; southern: COM., *Nàng-gĭng*, 南京 Nanking.

Nàng, 楠, 枬, A kind of plum: COM., *nàng-mŭk*, 楠木 a hard wood used for furniture.

Nàng, 男 The male of the human species; a man: COM., *nàng nṳ̄* 男女 boys and girls.

Nàng, 難 Hard, difficult as in *găng-nàng* 艱難; also read *náng*, q. v.: often means cannot; to trouble, as in *nàng-ùi* 難爲.

Nàng: A coll. word, as in *nàng-mŭŏi-sĭng*, a glow-worm.

Nâng, 難 Trouble, adversity; misfortune; to reprimand: also read *nàng,* q. v.: COM., *huáng náng,* afflictions: *biĕ-nâng* 避難 to avoid evil; *mò-nâng* 磨難 distressed.

Nău, 撓 Read *nāu;* used for the coll. *nău;* to grasp, to crumple by clutching; puckered as in *nău-nău* 撓撓.

Nāu, 撓 Also read *nàu:* to disturb; to trouble, to pervert: *nāu-luâng sê hĭ,* 撓亂是非 to confound right and wrong.

Nāu, 繞 To wind, to cord about, as in *diêng-nāu* 纏繞.

Nâu, 鬧, 閙, A great stir, bustle, as in *iĕk-nâu* 鬧熱; *nâu-chê* 鬧市, a lively market.

Náung; A coll. word: confusion, disorder, as in *hŭng-hŭng-náung,* in great disorder.

Náung: A coll. word: swelled, puffed, as in *méng náung,* the face bloated.

Nâung, 嫩 Tender; weak; delicate: COM., *sặ-nâung* 細嫩 small; *pé-pé-nâung* 屁屁嫩 very small, delicate.

Né, 餌 A kind of dumpling; cakes; a bait for fish; *met.,* an allurement; to entice: COM., *ngù-né* 魚餌 a bait for fish.

Né: A coll. word, as in *gẹung-né,* near-sighted.

Nê, 二, 弍, 貳, Two; to divide; to repeat; the third also means to help: the first used for the coll. *lâng,* q. v.: COM., *nê-sĕk* 二十 twenty; *nê nguŏk* 二月, the second month; *sặ-nê* 細貳, careful, cautious.

Nê, 膩 Greasy, oily; *gáiu-nê* 垢膩 dirty and greasy.

Ně; A coll. word: inclined, awry: *ně ḳó*, out of perpendicular.

Nék, A coll. word: a very small quantity, as *nék-nék-giang*.

Nék; A coll. euphonic prefix, as in *nék ṇẹuk*, wrinkled: *nék-niák*, to twinkle.

Něng; A coll. word: indurated skin, as *chiū-něng* and *kă-něng*, hard skin on the hands and feet.

Něng; A coll. word used for *něng*, as in *něng-něng*, the mother's milk, the breast.

Néng; A coll. euphonic prefix, as in *néng-náung*, disheveled; *néng-náing*, to walk on tiptoe

Nèng, 能 Power, ability, as in *nèng-gáng* 能幹; to be able, can, may: COM., *cài-nèng* 才能 talent, genius; *bók-nèng*, 不能 unable, cannot.

Nèng, 乳 Read *ŭ;* used for the coll. *nèng;* milk: *siăh nèng* 食乳 to drink or suck milk; *ngù-nèng* 牛乳 cow's milk; *ngù-nèng-iù* 牛乳油 butter; *dáung-nèng* 斷乳 to wean; *nèng-nă* 乳奶 or *nèng-mă* 乳嬤 a wet-nurse.

Nèng, 認 To recognize; to acknowledge: COM., *nêng-cŏi* 認罪 to confess guilt; *nêng-dâng* 認鄭 to confess an error.

Nèng: A coll. euphonic prefix, as in *nêng-náing,* to chant or read over.

Nêng: A coll. word: as in *nêng-gă,* I, we, us.

Nèng, 仈 A coll. character; a man, a person; human: *gáuk-nèng* 各仈 or *nèng-nèng* 仈仈 everybody; *nguāi nèng* 我仈 we, us; *diê-nèng* 俙仈 who?

Nèng, 儂 Read *nùng;* coll. *nèng,* as in *nèng-gă* 儂家 I, myself, we.

Nèng, 膿 Read *nùng;* coll. *nèng:* pus, suppuration.

Nēu, 鳥 A bird; the 196th radical; in the coll. used for *cēu,* q. v.: COM., *hĭ nēu,* 飛鳥 a flying bird.

Néu: A coll. word; to pinch; to pluck, as leaves or flowers.

Nĕu: A coll. word, as in *nĕu-nĕu,* drowsy, half-conscious.

Néuk, 胸, 肭, used in the coll. in the sense of weakness, to fall as in a fit: *chiòng-néuk* 墙胭 a wall sinking and ready to fall.

Nĕung: A coll. word: the opposite of *gĭng,* or *hŭng;* slack, as a rope; slowly, leisurely as *nĕung sĭŏh buó,* wait a little.

Nĭ: A coll. word, as in *nĭ-nĭ* or *ą̊-nĭ*, sticky, adhesive.

Nĭ: A coll. euphonic prefix, as in *nĭ-nĭ nṳ̆-nṳ̆*, dilapidated.

Nĭ: A coll. euphonic prefix, as in *nĭ-nō̤*, the mincing, elegant gait of a lady.

Nì, 呢, A final interrogative particle; in the coll. used for woolens, broadcloth, etc.: *dăng ciŏng cŏ̤ nì,* 伶將做呢 now how shall we manage it?

Nì: A coll. euphonic prefix, as in *nì-nâ*, to plaster; *nì-nùi*, to knead, as dough.

Niă: A coll. word, as in *niă-nó̤i*, a little; *niă-nó̤i-giāng*, a very little, a mite.

Niă, 惹 To stir up, to provoke; COM., *niă-sĕṳ* 惹事, to make trouble; *niă nèng sĕu-ké* 惹仈受氣, to provoke one to anger.

Niá, 尿 Read *niêu;* coll. *niá,* as in *niá-hù* 尿壺, a urinal.

Niáh: A coll. word: suddenly alarmed, startled; *niáh buáng tiĕng-gèng,* jumped half as high as the sky with alarm!

Niăh, 拿 Read *nā;* coll. *niăh:* to seize, to arrest; to manipulate: in a *met.,* sense, to avail of; *niăh diŏh* 拿著 caught; *niăh să* 拿痧 to manipulate one having the colic: COLL., *mò niăh ĭ ài* (spoken *mò- niăh-ài*) no way of doing it; impossible!

Niák: A coll. word: to give the wink; flashing, as in *nék-nék niák-niák.*

Niāng: A coll. word: to combine, to bring together; *niāng siŏh- dŏi* to unite in one; *niāng lā có,* to do both at once.

Niáng: A coll. word, as in *niák-niáng,* flashes of lightning.

Niáng: A coll. word: *niáng-kī-lì,* to blaze up, as a house on fire.

Niĕ: A coll. word, as in *niĕ-ngṍi,* a little, a small quantity.

Niè, 伲 Read *nī* (you); used for the coll. *niè:* a final particle, meaning nearly, about; also used in the terms for children and son-in-law: *tō̤-mō̤-niè* 討拇伲 or *ió̤k-lió̤k-niè* 約略伲 about, or somewhat so; *giăng-niè,* 仔伲 one's chilhren; *niè-sái* 伲婿 a son-in-law.

Niè: A coll. word; as in *niè-giăng,* children; *niè-giăng-gō̤* boys; *niè-giăng tòng,* a youth, a stripling.

Niék, 聶 To incline the ear; to whisper; a surname.

Niék, 攝 To collect as in *siŭ-niék* 收攝; *niék gĕk* 攝挾 to carry away under the arm; *met.*, to pilfer.

Niék, 鑷 Pincers, tweezers; to pull out; used for *giék* in the coll. q. v.: COLL., *giék-niék* 揭鑷 pincers, nippers.

Niék, 廿 Read *ĭk* in the dictionaries; coll. *niék*: a contraction of *nê-sĕk*, 廿 (二十) twenty; *niék-gāu* 廿九, twenty-nine.

Niék, 揑. 捏 To collect, or work up with the fingers; *met.*, to fabricate, as in *nūi niék* 扭揑; COLL., *niék lā uá* 揑喇話 to forge a story.

Niĕng, 拈, 捻 The 2nd read *niék*; coll. *niĕng*: to take in the hand as in *niĕng chū* 拈手; COLL., *tău-niĕng* 偷拈 to purloin.

Niêng 649

Nièng, 染 To dye; to taint; *diòng-niēng* 傳染 contagious, infectious.

Nièng, 年 A year; age: COM., *nièng-nièng,* 年年 yearly: COLL., *kó̤-nièng-màng* 去年明 last year; *co̤-nièng* 做年, to keep the new year.

Nièng, 黏 粘, Paste; to stick up; viscid; *met.,* to be attached to or intimate with a person.

Nièng, 廿 Read *ĭk;* in the *Báik-ĭng,* read *nièng,* twenty; in the coll. used for *niék* and *nĭk* (twenty), q. v.

Nièng, 念 To consider, to think of; to ponder; to repeat memoriter: in the coll. read *náing,* q. v.: COM., *sṳ̆-nièng* 思念, to think of; *yé-nièng* 記念, to remember: COLL., *nièng-tàu* 念頭 thoughts, purposes.

650   Nĭk

Nièu, 饒 To spare, to acquit; to forgive as in *nièu-séu* 饒恕.

Nièu, 尿 Urine; used for *niă* in the coll. q. v.: COLL., *nà-nièu* 放尿 to urinate.

Nĭh: A coll. euphonic prefix, as in *nĭh-nŏh*, to mix with the fingers; *nĭh-niăh* to seize.

Nĭk, 日 The sun; a day, days; time; COM. *nĭk-tàu* 日頭 the sun; *nĭk-éung* 日用 for daily use; *Nĭk-buŏng* 日本 Japan.

Nĭk, 匿 To elude search; to conceal; clandestine; in the coll. to put into, to press full: *nĭk-mìng* 匿名 anonymous: COM., *còng-nĭk* 藏匿 to secrete; *nĭk ciēng-tàu*, to stuff pillows.

Nĭk, 溺 To sink, to drown one's self; to stifle; *met.*, sunk in vice, as in *tìng-nĭk* 沉溺: *nĭk nṳ̌* 溺女 infanticide.

Nïk, 廿 Read ĭk; used for the coll. nĭk, a corruption of nê-sĕk, twenty: for similar uses of this character see niék and niéng.

Nĭng: A coll. euphonic prefix, as in nĭng-niĕng to take.

Nĭng: A coll. euphonic prefix, nīng-niĕng, to dye; nīng-niāng, to mix, to mingle.

Nìng, 寧 甯 Rest, repose; to bring or wish peace to; to prefer, rather; kŏng-nìng 康寧 peace, tranquility; nìng-nguóng 寧願 I prefer, I would rather; the second is a surname.

Nìng, 仁 Read ìng; coll. nìng: the kernel; the pupil of the eye; hŏk-tò-nìng 核桃仁, walnut meat; mĕk-ciŭ-nìng 目睭仁 the pupil, the eyeball.

Niŏ, 嫋 Read niĕu; used in the

Báik-ĭng, for the coll. *niŏ:* the mincing gait of a lady, as in *nĭ-niŏ-niŏ*.

Niŏh, 葉 Read *iĕk*; coll. *niŏh:* a leaf. the leaves of plants; *dà-niŏh* 茶葉 the tea leaf; *lŏh niŏh* 落葉 to shed leaves.

Niŏh, 箬 Read *iŏk*, used for the coll. *niŏh*, as in *niŏh-uâi*, how many? *niŏh-sạ* 箬價 how much or many? *săng-niŏh-iông*, 生箬樣 in what way?

Niōng, 軟 Moving softly, as muffled wheels; soft, weak; yielding: COM., *niōng-iŏk* 軟弱 weak, feeble; *huò-niōng* 和軟 peaceable: COLL., *niōng-ngê*, "limber ears" the contracted form of the 163rd and 170th radicals.

Niòng, 娘 A young lady, Miss; a mother; ladies: in the coll. read *nòng*, q. v.: COM., *niòng-*

Niù 653

nā 娘奶 a mother: COLL., cṳ̆-niòng 諸娘 a woman.

Nióng, 讓 Read iông; coll. niòng: to yield, to give place to; sŏng-niông 相讓 mutual concession; niông-ói 讓位 to yield a place or office.

Niŭ: A coll. word: shriveled, puckered: niŭ kǒ wrinkled.

Niū 扭 To turn with the hand, to twist; twisted, contorted; met., to fabricate as in niū-niĕk 扭揑 trumped up.

Niū, 紐 To knot; to bind; in the coll. used for niù q. v.: COM., niū-huă 紐花 to make flowers.

Niū, 鈕 The knob of a seal; a button as in niū-káiu, 鈕釦.

Niù, 紐 Read niū; coll. niù: to twist as the top of a bag to knot it; to grapple closely, as in play or a fight. niù lāu 紐

了 twisted and knotted.

Nó, 怒 Anger, ire, passion; vigor; mettle; COM., *hūng-nó* 忿怒 or *nó-ké* 怒氣 anger, passion.

Nọ̄, 娜 Agreeable, affable; elegant, a lady's gait as in *niĕu-nọ̄*.

Nọ̄, 惱 Annoyed, angered; to feel irritated, resentful; COM., *ọ̄-nọ̄* 懊惱 vexed; *huàng-nọ̄* 煩惱 troubled, disquieted.

Nọ̄, 腦, 𦝼 The brain; soft, as marrow: COM., *nọ̄-ciòng* 腦漿 or *tàu-nọ̄* 頭腦 the brain; COLL., *mọ̀-tàu mọ̀-nọ̄* 無頭無腦, "no head for," confused.

Nọ̀, 那 How? what? much; to rest, peaceful; a euphonic particle at the end of a sentence: also read *nā*, q. v.

Nọ̀, 挪, 按 To rub between the hands: to transfer; to embezzle; in the coll. meaning how, why, wherefore: *chŏ-nọ̀* 搓挪 to "round by rubbing"; *met.*, to settle an affair: COLL., *nṳ nọ̀-nọ́h mạ-hiĕu-dék*, how do you not understand!

Nọ̀, 懦, 愞 Infirm in purpose, timid, weak, cowardly: COM., *nọ̀-iók* 懦弱 weak, feeble.

Nọ́h, 毛 Used for the coll. *nọ́h*: a thing, matter; articles; things carried in procession; *mò nọ́h* 毛毛 nothing; *sié-nọ́h* 世毛 what thing? what? *cŭ-nọ́h* 諸毛 everything; *nọ̀-nọ́h* 那毛 why? how is it that?

Nọ́h: A coll. word, as in *nọ́h-sọ́h-nŭk*, three days ago; *nọ́h-áu-nŭk*, three days hence.

Nọ́h: A coll. word: to finger; *nọ́h sèu*, to mix evenly with the fingers, as ingredients.

Nōi, 餒 Destitute of food, famished; COM., nōi-cé 餒志 or cé nōi 志餒 depressed, discouraged.

Nói: A coll. word: to hide, to secrete: nói chiū-uōng-diē, to hide in one's sleeve.

Nói, 塊 Read dói, coll. nói, as in muāng-nói, everywhere; mò-nói cāu, no way of escape.

Nói: A coll. word, probably a contraction of niā-nói, as mâing niā-nói, (or mâing nái kó) don't go just yet.

Nôi, 內 Within, inside, in; that which is within; privy, personal; domestic, private; COM., nôi-dê, 內地, the Inner Land, China; nôi-gôh, 內閣, the Privy Council; bók câi nôi 不在內, extra; nôi nguôi 內外 inside and outside; nôi-ìng 內

人 my wife; *nŏi-sĭng* 內心 the heart, mind.

Nŏk, 諾, 喏, An answer of approbation; an assent: COM., *nŏk-ìòng* 諾然 pleased, assenting.

Nōng, 曩 Before, in former times; *nōng-nĭk* 曩日 a former day, lately.

Nōng, 暖 Read *nuāng*; coll. *nōng*: warm, mild, as the weather; *tiĕng nōng* 天暖, the weather is mild.

Nōng, 煖 Read *nuāng*; coll. *nōng*: to warm, to heat over: *nōng-guŏ* 煖鍋 a heater to warm food in.

Nóng: A coll. word: moist, damp, humid, as in *nóng-ké*, dampness; *nóng-tiĕng*, a humid atmosphere; *diōng-nóng*, to become damp.

Nòng, 囊 A bag; a purse; *met.*,

property: COM., *pùi-nòng* 皮囊 a leathern sack.

Nòng, 郎 Read *lòng*; coll. *nòng*, as in *nòng-má* 郎罷 a father; *nòng-má-giāng*, 郎罷仔 father and child.

Nòng, 娘 Read *niòng*; coll. *nòng*, as in *nòng-nā̤* 娘奶 a mother; *nòng-nā̤-giāng*, 娘奶仔 mother and child.

Nông, 閏 To intercalate, as a month: COM., *nông nguŏk* 閏月 a month intercalated: COLL., *ngô nièng lâng-diōng nông* 五年二轉閏, in five years two intercalary months.

Nông, 輭 Read *éng*: used in the *Báik-ĭng* for the coll. *nông*: flexible, but tenacious; met., slow, dilatory; *pì-nông* 疲輭 procrastinating.

Nū, 努 To exert one's self strenuously, to strive; a desperate effort; COM., *nṳ̄-lĭk* 努力, to strive for.

Nù, 奴 A slave, an abject; slavish; used in Foochow for I, as in polite phrase or by inferiors: COM., *nù-bŭk* 奴僕 a bondman; *nù-lâ* 奴隸 abject slave: *nù-bê* 奴婢 male and female slaves; COLL., *nù-gáuk-nḙng* 奴各伩 we all, all of us.

Nù, 傲 Great strength; to exert one's self: *nù-lĭk* 傲力 to put forth one's utmost strength.

Nṳ̄, 女 A female, a woman; a daughter, an unmarried girl; the 38th radical: COM., *hó-nṳ̄* 婦女 women; *nṳ̄-cṳ̄* 女子 a daughter, a maiden; *dĭk-nṳ̄* 姪女 a niece; *sŏng-nṳ̄* 孫女 a grand-daughter.

Nṳ̄, 汝, 你, 女 The second a personal pronoun, thou, you; thy thine, your, yours; *nṳ̄-muòng* 汝們 you all: COM., *nṳ̄ ngō* (or *nguāi*) 汝我 you and I: COLL., *nṳ̄-nèng* 汝仅 you, ye; *nṳ̄ gì* 汝其 yours.

Nuá: A coll. word: turned to one side, deflected, twisted as in *nuá-nuá*.

Nuāng, 暖 The genial warmth of the sun, as in *nĭk nuāng* 日暖; in the coll. read *nōng,* q. v.

Nuāng, 煖 The warmth of fire; agreeable, as a gentle fire; *met.,* warm, friendly, as the feelings; *huò nuāng kọ̆* 和煖去 thawed, warmed up.

Nṳ̆k, 肉 The meat of animals; the pulp or meat of fruits and nuts; fat, fleshy; the 130th radical, contracted in composition: *dṳ̆-nṳ̆k* 猪肉 pork; *iòng-nṳ̆k* 羊肉 mutton; *nṳ̆k-sĭng* 肉身 the body.

Nŭng: A coll. word: to delay, to put off; *cái nŭng siŏh-káik-gū,* defer a little longer.

Nūng, 忍 Read *ŭng;* used for the coll. *nŭng:* to endure, to suffer patiently; *nūng-sáng* 忍性 or *nūng-ké* 忍氣 a patient temper.

Nùng, 農 To cultivate the ground; to plant; agriculture: COM., *nùng-hŭ* 農夫 a husbandman.

Nùng, 濃 Thick, as liquids; strong, as infusions or flavors; in the coll. read *nṳ̀ng,* q. v.: *nùng ḋáng* 濃淡 thick and thin; rich and weak.

Nùng, 醲 Used for *nùng* (thick, rich) strong, high-flavored; *nùng-ciŭ* generous wine.

Nuòi, 挼 To rub, to roll with the hand; in the coll. to knead; *met.,* to vex, to annoy: COLL., *nuòi-cặ,* 挼劑 to knead dough.

662　Ngà

Nuôi: A coll. word: a mortise; a socket.

Ng, 伓 A coll. character; used for the strong nasal *ng* which is not referable to the table of initial and final sounds, mostly placed before verbs in the sense of no, not, will not; before adjectives, it answers to *un, dis, in;* between verbs repeated as *có ng có* 做伓做 it answers a question: *ng-sê bô-gōng,* of course, just so.

Ngā, 雅 Elegant, genteel; also plain, simple: COM., *ngā-dé,* 雅緻 elegant; stylish.

Ngà, 牙 The grinders, molars; the teeth, as *ngà-chī* 牙齒, toothed; ivory; a bud; a broker; the 92nd radical: COM., *chiông-ngà* 象牙 ivory; *gūi-cī ngà* 菓子牙 a fruit broker's.

Ngá   663

Ngà, 芽 A germ, a plumule, a bud, a sprout; to bud as in *mèng-ngà* 萌芽; *huák-ngà* 發芽 to sprout.

Ngà, 齖 Irregular teeth: COLL., *ngà-ngā̤* 齖齬 to look sour, crabbed; *ā̤ ngà-ngḙ̄ung nèng* it will disgust people.

Ngà, 衙 A court, an office residence: COM., *ngà-muòng* 衙門 an office, a yamen.

Ngà, 砑 Used for the coll. *ngá*: to polish by rubbing as in *ngá guŏng-guŏng* 砑光光.

Ngā̤: A coll. word; as in *ngā̤ siŏh siăng*, to emit a creaking sound, as a door; *ngā̤-ngā̤-giéu*, a low cry or wail as of a child.

Ngā̤, 睨 To look askance at, as in *pā-ngā̤* 睥睨: in the coll. read *ngâ̤*, q. v.

Ngā̤: A coll. word: to whimper, as a child.

Ngà, 倪 The young and delicate; to glance at; the verge of; to benefit; a surname: *tiĕng-ngà* 天倪 the verge of heaven.

Ngà, 猊 As in *ngà-dô* 猊道 unreasonable, overbearing.

Ngặ, 睨 Read *ngā;* coll. *ngặ,* as in *pā-ngặ* 睥睨 or *ngặ káng* 睨看 to examine closely; *ngặ mặ chók* 睨賣出 inscrutable.

Ngặ, 枝 Read *ciĕ;* used for the coll. *ngặ;* a branch, a twig: *chéu-ngặ* 模枝 branches of a tree.

Ngặ: A coll. word, as in *ngặ-ngặ-giéu,* to cry and sob, as a child.

Ngáh: A coll. word, as in *ngáh-ngáh-giéu,* a creaking sound.

Ngăh: A coll. word, as in *ngĭk-lĭh ngăh-láh,* a rattling, as of tiles or things, shaken by an earthquake.

Ngài 665

Ngáh, 閞 Read *ngiáh;* used in the
 Báik-ĭng for the coll. *ngáh:*
 a harsh, grating sound: also
 pinched, jammed: *chiŭ ngáh*
 手閞 the hand jammed.

Ngài, 捱 Read *ngài;* used for the
 coll. *ngài:* to endure; as *ngài-
 ngài* 捱捱 to bear trouble;
 muŏng ngài ciā quó 莽捱者過
 just bear and get along with
 it; *ngài mặ quó* 捱賣過 can't
 endure it.

Ngài, 齒 Read *chī;* used for the
 coll. *ngài:* the teeth; *ngài-cṳ̆,*
 齒座 the gums; *ngài-tiáng* 齒
 痛 a tooth-ache; *ngài-sáuk* 齒
 刷 a tooth-brush.

Ngài, 呆 Foolish, silly; stupid:
 used for the coll. *ngài,* bad,
 evil, wicked: COLL., *ngài-nĕng*
 呆仈, a bad man; *ngài-áuk* 呆
 惡 wicked; *ngài-miáng* 呆命

a poor lot in life; *ngài-tiĕng* 呆天 bad weather.

Ngài, 厓, 崖 A high bank, cliff, ledge, precipice; the side of a hill: *ngài nyăng* 崖岸 a steep bank; *met.*, a discrepancy.

Ngái, 礙, 碍, To hinder, to obstruct; a hindrance, an obstacle, as in *guăng-ngái* 關礙 or *cū-ngái* 阻礙.

Ngăing, 硬 Hard, solid; stiff, firm; obstinate; *ngăing-sĭng* 硬心 a hard heart, a stubborn will.

Ngák, 齾 To gnaw, to crunch: *ngák-ngák-giéu* 齾齾叫 the sound of gnawing.

Ngāng, 眼 The eye: COM., *ngāng-kuŏ* 眼科, the treatment of eye-diseases; *ngāng-giáng* 眼鏡 spectacles; *ngāng cĭng giáng* 眼睛鏡 the crystalline lens of the eye.

Ngáu 667

Ngàng, 顏 The space between the eyes and eyebrows; a surname; *ngàng-sáik* 顏色 color.

Ngáng, 岸 The banks of a stream; a shore; a high cliff: in the coll. read *ngiáng,* q. v.: *děng ngáng* 登岸 to land.

Ngâng, 雁 A small kind of wild geese; *ngâng-ngò* 雁鵝 a wild goose.

Ngău, 獟 Read *giéu;* used in the *Báik-ĭng* for the coll. *ngău,* a tiger's howl: *ngău-ngău giêu* 獟獟叫 to howl, as dogs and cats.

Ngău, 咬, 嚙, To gnaw, to bite; to chew: *ngău-ngà chiék-chĭ* 咬牙切齒 to gnash the teeth (in deadly hate.)

Ngău: A coll. word: confused, jumbled; gabble, brogue; *ngău-pék,* a perverse temper.

Ngàu, 肴, 餚, Dressed meats, viands; *ciū-ngàu* 酒餚 the viands of a feast; *ngàu-cuâng* 餚饌 delicacies.

Ngàu, 淆 Muddy water; mixed, confused: *ngàu-luâng* 淆亂 in great disorder, as affairs: *hŏng-ngàu* 混淆 turbid; mixed confusedly.

Ngàu, 鰲 Read *nyĕu*: used for the coll. *ngàu*; warped, twisted as in *kiĕu-ngàu* 橈鰲; *ngàu-ngā* 鰲睨 crabbed, obstinate in bearing.

Ngàu: A coll. word; numb, chill with cold; *kă chiū ngàu*, the feet and hands benumbed.

Ngàu, 藕 Read *nyĕu*: the roots of the water-lily: *ngàu-hūng* 藕粉 flour made of lily-root.

Ngáuk, 愕 Surprised, astonished at, as in *cháuk-ngáuk* 錯愕.

Ngê 669

Ngáuk, 蕚 the calyx of a flower, called *huă-ngáuk* 花蕚: in the coll. read *ngŏk*, q. v.

Ngáuk, 鱷, A crocodile, as in *ngáuk-ngṳ̀* 鱷魚.

Ngáuk, 鯢 Read *ngăk*; as in *ngáuk-ngáuk-giéu* 鯢鯢叫 the cackling of geese.

Ngâung, 獃 Read *ngăk* in the dictionaries; used in the *Báik-ing* for the coll. *ngâung*: dull, stupid; foolish, not intelligent: *ngâung-lẹ̆* 獃驢 a stupid ass— a country clown; *ngâung-siōng* 獃想 to think stupidly.

Ngé: A coll. euphonic prefix, as in *ngé-ngô*, to talk indistinctly; to murmur.

Ngé, 耳 Read *ngī*: an ear; a handle as of a cup, pitcher, tub, pail, basket, etc.: *ngé-giāng* 耳仔 an ear; *ngé-lẹng* 耳聾 deaf.

Ngĕ: A coll. word, as in *ngĕ-ngĕ diŏh*, a grum look; grim, sullen.

Ngék, 吸 To draw in the breath to inhale: COM., *hù-ngék* 呼吸 expiration and inspiration; *ngék-lĭk,* 吸力 gravitation.

Ngék, 吃 To eat food: *kēu ngék* 口吃 to eat or drink

Ngék, 級 A gradation: a degree; classed, sorted: *dēng-ngék* 等級 gradation; *chŭ-ngék* 初級 primary grade; *gŏ-dēng ngék* 高等級 higher primary grade.

Ngék, 迄 To come to, to reach; even, till, until; finally, at last; *ngék-gĭng* 迄今, to this time, even till now.

Ngék: A coll. euphonic prefix, as in *ngék-ngák* or *ngék-ngáuk,* the cackling of geese.

Ngêng, 迎 To go out to meet; to

receive in person; as in *chǐng ngêng* 親迎: also read *ngìng*, q. v.

Ngêng: A coll. euphonic prefix, as in *ngêng-ngiêng*, to hold a coroner's inquest.

Ngēu, 偶 A pair, a match; paired; a partner; to unite, as in marriage; to happen accidentally: *puói-ngēu* 配偶 to mate; *ngēu-hăk* 偶合 matched; *ngēu-iòng* 偶然 by chance.

Ngēu, 咬 Read *ngāu*; coll. *ngēu*, as in *ngēu-siĕk* 咬舌 to gnaw the tongue, as criminals do to kill themselves.

Ngēu: A coll. word; to play a fiddle, as in *ngé-ngēu*.

Ngêu, 寓, 厪, To dwell, to sojourn in; a home: COM., *câng-ngêu* 暫寓 to lodge temporarily; *giĕ-ngêu* 寄寓 to lodge at.

Ngêu, 遇 To meet, to fall in with; to happen; whenever: used for the coll. *páung,* q. v.: *ngêu-náng* 遇難 to encounter trouble; *gĭng-ngêu* 境遇 circumstances: COLL., *ngêu diŏh* 遇着 to happen upon.

Ngéung: A coll. word, as in *ā ngéung nèng,* it will startle people.

Ngéung: A coll. word, as in *ā ngài ngéung nèng,* it will provoke people.

Ngĭ: A coll. euphonic prefix, as in *ngĭ-lĭ ngù-lŭ,* to mutter in a low tone.

Ngĭ, 擬 To estimate, to consider, to guess: *ngĭ-ngiê* 擬議 to conjecture and deliberate about.

Ngĭ, 耳. The ear; to perceive; read *ngê,* q. v.: *ngĭ-ùng* 耳聞 reported: COLL., *ngĭ-mŭk sā* 耳

目佊 "ears and eyes are many" —it is sure to be found out.

Ngì, 儀 The usages of society; a rule; etiquette; what is proper: *ngì-ùng* 儀容 deportment; *ngì-ùng* 儀文 outward forms, ceremonies; *lā-ngì* 禮儀 forms, rites.

Ngì, 宜 Fit, suitable, right; what ought to be; used for *ngiè* in the coll. q. v.: *biêng-ngì* 便宜 convenient, cheap; *hăk-ngì* 合宜 suitable.

Ngì, 疑 To doubt, to suspect: COM., *kō-ngì* 可疑 to be suspicious: coll. *ngì-sĭng dâ̤eng* 疑心重 full of doubts.

Ngiă: A coll. word, as in *ngiă-ngiă,* divergent, as roads.

Ngiăh, 額 The forehead, as in *ngiăh-tàu* 額頭; *ngiăh-só* 額數 the full sum.

Ngiák: A coll. word: to cut with shears: *ngiák dọi-dòng,* cut it in two.

Ngiăk: A coll. word: to raise, to lift up the head, as in *ngiăk-kī-tàu; ngiăk gèng,* to raise (the head) high.

Ngiăng: A coll. word: rough, bristling as uncombed hair; *tàu-huók ngiăng-ngiăng,* the hair is bristling.

Ngiáng: A coll. word, as in *ngiáng chók lì,* toppling forward, as a closet, etc.

Ngiàng, 迎 Read *ngìng;* coll. *ngiàng;* to parade, to carry in procession: *ngiàng bù-sák* 迎菩薩 to parade idols; *ngiàng-gă* 迎街 to parade the streets.

Ngiâng, 岸 Read *ngâng;* coll. *ngiâng:* a shore, a bank; the margin of a brook, river or canal: *siòng ngiâng* 上岸 to go ashore, to land.

Ngiê, 艾 Read *ngái*; coll. *ngiê*: mugwort, artemisia; tinder.

Ngiê, 宜 Read *ngì*; coll. *ngiê*, as in *bèng-ngiê* 便宜 cheap, low in price.

Ngiê, 鵝 Read *ngò*; coll. *ngiê*: a goose: *tiĕng-ngiê* 天鵝 wild geese.

Ngiê, 義 Right, proper; equity, righteousness; virtuous; adopted; COM., *ngiê-lī* 義理 rectitude; *nyiê-ing* 義人 a righteous person; *ngiê ŭng* 義勇 patriotic volunteers; *chṳ̄ ngiê* 取義 catch the meaning.

Ngiê, 誼 Suitable, fit, proper; adopted: COM., *ngiê-chĭng* 誼親 related by adoption; *ngiê hĭng-dă* 誼兄弟 adopted brothers.

Ngiê, 議 To consult, to deliberate

upon, as in *ngiê-lâung*, 議論; *ngiê-huò* 議和 to confer with a view to harmony.

Ngiê, 蟻 An ant; a term for insects like the ant: *met.*, the rabble, commonalty: COM., *tèng-ngiê* 蠹蟻 insects; *èng-ngiê* 紅蟻 the common red ant; *ngiê-cĭk* 蟻集 collected as banditti.

Ngiê, 毅 Firm, resolute, decided: as in *ngiê-iòng* 毅然.

Ngiê, 藝 Ability, skill or art in doing; a craft, an occupation: COM., *ū-ngiê* 武藝 military tactics; *chiū-ngiê* 手藝 a handicraft: COLL., *ŏh-ngiê* 學藝 to learn a trade.

Ngiê. 外 Read *nguôi*; coll. *ngiê*: outside; beyond; foreign; relatives of a wife: *ngiê-dāu* 外斗 or *ngiê-dāu-siê*, or *ngiê-*

Ngiëng 677

hióng, outside; *siàng-ngiê* 城外 suburban; *ngiê-gă* 外家 the wife's family.

Ngiĕk: A coll. word: perhaps a corruption of *giĕk*; to take hold with tweezers as in *ngĕk ngiĕk*.

Ngiĕk, 業 An office, occupation, calling, trade; property as in *ngiĕk-sāng* 業產; *gă-ngiĕk* 家業 a family estate; *bĕk-ngiĕk-sĕng* 畢業生 a graduate.

Ngiĕk, 孽 The son of a concubine; an illegitimate child; *met.*, guilt, retribution as in *kiĕng-ngiĕk* 愆孽, or *cŏi-ngiĕk* 罪孽.

Ngiĕng, 研 To grind fine, to pulverize: *met.*, to investigate as in *ngiĕny-géu* 研究: also read *ngiéng* and in the coll. *ngiĕng*.

Ngiĕng, 研 Read *ngiĕng*: coll. *ngiēng*: to grind, to powder;

ngiēng-tùi 研槌 a pestle; *ngiēng-sióh* 研石 a stone roller for smoothing cloth.

Ngiéng, 硯, 研, A Chinese ink-stone: COM., *tù-ngiéng* 土硯 an earthern ink-stone.

Ngiéng, 癮 Read *ŭng*; used for the coll. *ngiéng*: addicted to, besotted: *ă-piéng-ngiéng* 鴉片癮 confirmed in opium-smoking; *ciū-ngiéng* 酒癮 addicted to drinking liquor.

Ngièng, 嚴 Stern; austere; majestic; awe-inspiring; epithet of a father, as in *gă-ngièng* 家嚴; *gái-ngièng* 戒嚴 to guard, also martial law; *ngièng-géng* 嚴禁 to strictly forbid.

Ngièng, 諺 A proverb, common saying as in *ngiêng-ngṳ̄* 諺語.

Ngièng, 驗 To identify, to discover proof; evidence, testimony: COM., *că-ngiêng* 查騐 or *kō-ngiêng* 考騐 to investigate officially; *háu-ngiêng* 效騐 efficacious; *ngiêng huó* 騐貨 to examine goods (for the duty.)

Ngièu, 堯 Earth heaped up; high, eminent in worth: COM., *Ngièu Sóng,* 堯舜 the emperors Yao and Shun, B. C. 2357 and 2255.

Ngièu, 饒 Abundance of food; an overplus; a surname: also read *nièu,* q. v.

Ngĭk, 迎 To resist; rebellious; adverse, as wind or tide, as in *ngĭk-hŭng* 迎風 or *ngĭk-cūi* 迎水; *ngĭk-só* 迎數 to reckon beforehand: COM., *buôi-ngĭk* 悖迎 to rebel against.

Ngĭk, 凝 Read *ngìng:* coll. *ngĭk:* to freeze, to become solid; frozen, stiffened: *ngĭk-dáęng*

凝凍 to cool, as lard, gravy, etc.

Ngĭk: A coll. euphonic prefix, as in *ngĭk-ngĭk ngŏk-ngŏk* to lift the head and look, as birds, turtles, snakes, etc.

Ngìng, 凝 To freeze, to congeal as in *ngìng-giék* 凝結.

Ngìng, 迎 To receive as a guest: also read *ngêng*, and in the coll. *ngiàng*, q. v.: COM., *ngìng-ciék* 迎接 to greet, to receive, as guests; *huăng-ngìng* 歡迎 to welcome.

Ngìng, 垠 Read *ngùng*; coll. *nging*: a bank, a ridge; *chèng-ngìng* 田垠 a ridge along the edge of a field.

Ngìng: A coll. euphonic prefix, as in *ngìng-ngiàng* to parade, to carry in procession, as idols, etc.

Ngiŏh: A coll. word similar to

ngiăk, as in *ngiŏh gèng*, to raise the head high in order to have one's throat examined.

Ngiŏk, 虐 To tyrannize over, to oppress; unfeeling, inhuman: COM., *bộ-ngiŏk* 暴虐 cruel, oppressive; *ngiŏk-dâi* 虐待 to ill-treat.

Ngiōng, 仰 To look upwards, to regard highly; to long for, as in *ngiōng-uông*, 仰望; a surname; in the coll. thin boards for ceilings, as *ngiōng-bēng* 仰板: COM., *ngiōng-muô* 仰慕 to look to with great desire.

Ngiòng, 言 Words, speech; a sentence; conversation, as in *ngiòng-ngṳ̄* 言語; *ngiòng-háing* 言行 words and acts; *kiĕu-ngiòng* 巧言, artful talk; *sĭk ngiòng* 食言 to retract; lit., to eat one's words.

Ngiù, 牛 An ox, a cow: kine; the 93rd radical; in the coll. read *ngù,* q. v.

Ngô, 五, 伍, 〤, Read *ngū;* coll. *ngô:* five: *sĕk-ngô* 十五 fifteen; *ngô-sĕk* 五十 fifty; *bái-ngô* 拜五 Friday.

Ngō̤, 我 The first personal pronoun, I, my, mine, me; we, our, ours, us: in the coll. read *nguāi,* q. v.: *ngō̤ muòng,* 我門 or *ngō̤ dĕng* 我等 we.

Ngô̤: A coll. word, as in *ngô̤-ngô̤-giéu,* railing at one.

Ngò̤. 俄 A moment; in haste, suddenly; COM., *Ngò̤-lò̤-sṳ̆* 俄羅斯 Russia.

Ngò̤, 嗷 A loud cry, a clamor; noise, hubbub: COLL, *ngò̤-ngò̤-giéu* 嗷嗷叫, the clamor of a multitude.

Ngò̤, 敖 To saunter, to ramble:

Ngộ

COLL., *ngộ-iá* 敖夜 to stay up all night. Read *ngộ*: proud, haughty.

Ngộ, 厫 A granary, as in *chŏng-ngộ* 倉厫.

Ngộ, 熬 To boil in water; to simmer: COM., *ngộ tŏng* 熬湯 to make a decoction of; *ngộ iù* 熬油, to try out fat: *ngộ gọ̆* 熬膏 to make jelly.

Ngộ, 遨 Also read *ngộ*: to saunter, to ramble, as in *ngộ-iù* 遨遊 to stroll about.

Ngộ, 蛾 The silkworm moth, called *càng-ngộ* 蠶蛾; moths: also used for quinsy, as in *hèu-ngộ* 喉蛾.

Ngộ, 鵝, 鵝 A goose; in the coll. read *ngiè*, q. v.: *tiĕng-ngộ* 天鵝 a crane: *iā-ngộ* 野鵝 wild geese.

Ngộ, 傲 Proud, arrogant; uncivil

used for *ngō* in the coll. *ngō̤-máng* 傲慢 to treat insolently; *giĕu-ngō̤* 驕傲 or *gŏ-ngō̤* 高傲 proud, haughty.

Ngō̤, 鏊 An iron pan to bake in: COM., *ngō̤-lù* 鏊爐 an oven; *ngō̤ diăng* 鏊鼎 a baking pan, with flat top on which coals are placed.

Ngō̤, 餓 Hungry; starved, famished: COM., *gĭ-ngō̤* 饑餓 to starve.

Ngŏh: A coll. word: to cut, to slice off; also a sound of rubbing, scraping, or rats gnawing, as in *ngŏh-ngŏh-giĕu.*

Ngói, 僞 False, deceitful; not genuine; to deceive.

Ngói, 魏 High eminent, lofty; a surname.

Ngŏk, 岳 A lofty mountain: COM., *ngŏk-hò* 岳父 or *ngŏk-diòng* 岳

丈 (coll. *diòng-nèng* 丈伩) a wife's father; *ngŏk-mū* 岳母, (coll. *diòng-nā̤* 丈奶) a wife's mother.

Ngŏk, 嶽 A high peak; the principal mountains of China.

Ngŏk, 樂 Music; instruments of music; *met.*, the refinements or elegancies of life; also read *lŏk*, and *ngáu: cáuk-ngŏk* 作樂 or *cáiu-ngŏk* 奏樂 to play on instruments.

Ngòng, 昂 Costly, dear in price: *ngòng-gói* 昂貴 dear, exorbitant.

Ngòng: A coll. word, as in *ngòng-ngòng-giéu*, a loud din, a clamor of voices.

Ngŭ: A coll. word, as in *ngŭ-lŭ*, (or *ngù-lŭ*), to mutter in a low tone; *ngĭ-lĭ ngŭ-lŭ*, a hum, a buzz.

Ngū, 五, 伍, 夊, The second is the complex, and the third the contracted form; five; a perfect number denoting all, as virtues, tastes: in the coll. read *ngô*, q. v.: COM., *ngū-gók* 五穀 all kinds of grain: COLL., *ngū hiă* 五罅 scattered in utter confusion.

Ngū, 伍 A file of five soldiers, squads; a company; to associate with; a surname: *dôi-ngū* 隊伍 rank and file, platoons.

Ngū, 午 Time from 11 a. m. to 1 p. m.; noon, midday; COM., *siông-ngū* 上午 and *á-ngū* 下午 (coll. *siông-dáu* and *á-dáu*) forenoon and afternoon: COLL., *dŏng-ngū* 中午 or *ciáng-ngū* 正午 midday, noon.

Ngù 687

Ngū: A coll. word: used in combination with *ng* (not) not very much, imperfectly; *ng-ngū-báik*, not very well acquainted with; *ng-ngū-chiông*, imperfectly resembling.

Ngù, 吳 Loquacious; to boast, to talk largely; a surname.

Ngù, 吾 A personal pronoun; I, my; we, us: *ngù-dēng* 吾等 we, us, we all; *ngù buói* 吾輩 we of this class.

Ngù, 梧 Name of a tree, the wood is used for making lutes; in the coll. an apparatus for righting buildings, as an upright timber, lever and fulcrum: COLL, *ngù chió* 梧厝 to shore up a house; *ngù ciáng* 梧正 to right, to make it erect.

Ngù, 牛 Read *ngiù*; coll. *ngù*: an ox, a cow, oxen, kine: *ngù-*

mō, 牛母 a cow; *ngù-giāng* 牛仔 a calf; *cūi-ngù* 水牛 buffalo; *ngù-nèng* 牛乳 cow's milk; *ngù-nèng-iù*, 牛乳油 butter;

Ngū, 語 To talk; to converse; speech, language; also read *ngê̤u*, COM., *ngiòng-ngū* 言語 and *uā-ngū* 話語 words, talk; *sṳ̆k-ngū-uā* 俗語話 a saying or proverb.

Ngṳ̀, 魚 A fish; fishy; the 195th radical: *tō̤-ngṳ̀* 討魚 to fish, as with nets; *dó̤-ngṳ̀* 蠹魚 a book moth: COLL, *ngṳ̀-gă* 魚膠 fish glue.

Ngṳ̀, 愚 The capacity of a monkey; simple, stupid; rude, uninstructed, unwise; used for I, your humble: *ngṳ̀-mìng* 愚民 the common people: COM., *ngṳ̀-chūng* 愚蠢 dull, ignorant.

Nguā 689

Nguā, 瓦 A tile; pottery; the 98th. radical: in the coll. read *nguá,* q. v.

Nguá, 瓦 Read *nguā;* earthern tiles; *nguá-piéng* 瓦片 pieces of tile; *chió-nguá-dĭng* 厝瓦頂 the tiled roof of a house.

Nguāi, 我 Read *ngō;* COLL., *nguāi:* the first person, I, my mine, me; we, ours, us: *nguāi gì* 我其 mine; *nguāi-gáuk-nêng* 我各伩 we, all of us.

Nguàng, 頑 Simple, stupid; obstinate, mulish: COLL., *nguàng-tàu nguàng-nō̤* 頑頭頑腦 very naughty, full of mischief.

Nguǎng, 玩 Playthings; to toy with, to delight in; to ramble about; *nguǎng-suā* 玩耍 to recreate; *nguǎng ŭk* 玩物 toys.

Ngùi, 危 Hazardous as *ngùi-hiĕng* 危險; dangerous as in

ngùi céng 危症 a dangerous disease; seriously ill, near death.

Ngŭk, 玉 A gem, precious stone; to complete, to perfect; valuable; your, your precious or noble; the 90th. radical; in the coll. read *nguŏh*, q. v.: *ngŭk-tă* 玉體 your precious self.

Ngùng, 銀, 艮, Silver; money; *ngùng-cièng* 銀錢 silver and cash, money; *cūi-ngùng* 水銀 quick silver; *ngùng-ò* 銀河 the milky-way; *ngùng-òng* 銀行 a bank; *giá-ngùng* 下銀 inferior silver.

Nguô, 誤, 悞 To err, to fail; to mislead; in error, misled: COM., *sék-nguô* 失誤 to fail to do; *cháuk-nguô* 錯誤 a mistake, a fault: COLL., *nguô có* 誤做 to do accidentally.

Nguô, 悟 Aware of, discerning: *cẹ̣u-nguô* 自悟 to bethink one's self: COM., *huôi-nguô* 會悟 to apprehend; *nguô séng* 悟性 quickness in understanding.

Nguô, 卧 To rest from work; to go to bed, to sleep: *nguô-bùng* 卧房 a bedroom; *nguô-sék* 卧息 to rest, to repose.

Nguŏk, 玉 Read *ngŭk;* coll. *nguŏk:* gems, precious stones, jade; *nguŏk-sẹ̄* 玉璽 the imperial seal.

Nguŏh, 獄 Read *ngŭk;* coll *nguŏh:* a prison, a jail: *nguŏh-guăng* 獄官 the keeper of a prison.

Nguôi, 外 Outside, foreign, from abroad; besides, moreover; the wife's relatives: in the coll. read *ngiê,* q. v.: COM., *nguôi-miêng* 外面 the exterior; *nguôi-mâu* 外貌 one's appearance;

nguôi-guók 外國 foreign countries; *é-nguói* 意外 unexpectedly; *ī-nguói* 以外 besides; *bài-nguói cŭng-cī* 排外宗旨 policy of exclusion.

Nguôi, 瑁 Tortoise-shell, called *dái-nguôi* 玳瑁; *dái-nguôi mà*, 玳瑁貓 a tortoise shell cat.

Nguŏk, 月 The moon; monthly; *met.*, round like the moon; the 74th radical: COM., *nguŏk sék* 月蝕 an eclipse of the moon: COLL., *nguŏk băh* 月白 a pale bluish color; *nguŏk-dŏh* 月棹 a round table.

Nguòng, 原 A high level space, a plateau; the origin, foundation; primarily; indeed, truly; *nguòng-iù* 原由 the causes of; *nguòng-ciō* 原主 the first owner; *nguòng-ing sĕ ciŏng-gì?* 原因是將其 what is the real cause ? COLL., *nguòng-cā-cā* 原早早 in the beginning.

Nguòng, 源 A spring; source, origin : COM., *nguòng-tàu* 源頭 head-waters.

Nguòng, 元 The origin, the first cause; chief, primary: COM., *nguòng-sṳ̄* 元始 the beginning; *nguòng-ké* 元氣 the vital principle.

Nguŏng, 愿, 原 The first often used for 願 in the sense of vowing; careful, attentive, good, moral; faithful; devout: the second also read *nguòng*, q. v.: COM., *hṳ̄-nguŏng*, 許愿 to make vows, as in distress.

Nguŏng, 願 To hope, to long for; to wish; to vow; a wish; a vow; each, every: COM., *găng-nguóng* 甘願 to consent willingly to; *sĭng găng é nguông*

心甘意願 a willing spirit; sĭng sṳ̆ nguóng 心所願 the heart's desire: COLL., ng nguóng 伓願 unwilling.

Ó, 惡 To hate, to loathe; abominable; to be ashamed: also read ŭ and áuk, q. v.: ó áuk 惡惡 to hate evil; siŭ ó 羞惡, shame-faced: COM., cêng kō̤-ó 盡可惡 very detestable.

Ó, 塢 A dike; barracks; in the coll. a safe place for boats: COLL., sùng-ó 船塢 a dry or wet dock; ó-muōi 塢尾 a ward in the suburbs of Foochow.

Ó, 汙, 污 Foul, muddy, as stagnant water; impure, lewd; to defile, to stain; also read ŭ, q. v., COM., ó-uói 污穢 defiled: páh ó 拍污 morally defiled.

Ô: A coll. word: a share, portion as reserved for one, as in ó ciā ó diŏh lā̤.

Ò 695

Ò, 務 To apply the mind to, to use earnest effort; important, must: used in the coll. books for ô, to have, to be; is, it is; has, have: sḙu-ô 事務 one's business; COM., ô bék 務必 indispensable; ô nguôi 務外 mere show; COLL., ô âing 務限 limited; iā ô-chḙu 也務趣 amusing; ô-dăng-dŏng 務担當 can, is able.

Ô, 霧 Fog, mist: hùng-ô 雲霧 clouds and mist.

Ô, 有 Read iū; used in the coll. ô, to have, to be; yes, I have, I did, it is; forms the past tense, has, have: and, in addition; ô ā mọ̀? ô à are there any? yes: ô bâng 有病 sick; ô-sĭng-sié 有心勢 or ô-dăng-dŏng 有担當 can.

Ǒ, 焖 To cook, to stew: *cák* ǒ 爅焖 to stew up fragments.

Ǒ: A coll. word: hard, difficult; impolitic: *ǒ-cǒ* hard to do; *ciā uâ ǒ gōng* impolitic to say that.

Ō, 襖 An outer garment; *mièng-ō* 棉襖 a cotton-wadded gown or jacket.

Ō, 懊 Vexed, angry; to regret: COM., *ō-nō* 懊惱 vexed: COLL., *ō-nō gì dài* 懊惱其代 a vexatious matter.

Ǒ, 澳, 灣, A bay, an inlet: *Ǒ-muòng* 澳門 Macao: COM., *ǒ-tàu* 澳頭 a busy landing or wharf.

Ǒ, 奧 Deep, remote, as in *chǐng-ǒ* 深奧 abstruse; *ǒ-miéu* 奧妙 mysterious.

Ò, 河 A river, a canal: COM., *tiěng-ò* 天河 the Milky Way; *Uòng-ò* 黃河 the Yellow river; *Ò-nàng* 河南 Honan.

Ŏh: A coll. word: wise, discreet; clever, shrewd: *ŏh ciáh ŏh,* very clever, quick of apprehension.

Ŏh, 學 Read *hŏk;* coll. *ŏh:* to learn; to imitate, as in *ŏh iông* 學樣 to imitate a pattern; *ŏh ngiê* 學藝, to learn a trade.

Ŏh: A coll. word: as, according to: *ŏh-ciŏng-uáng* 學將換 in this manner, this, then.

Ŏh: A coll. word: to tell, to inform against: *kó ŏh,* to go and tell.

Ói, 畏 To fear; to dread: *ói-gêu* 畏懼 fear; *ói nàng gì sĭng* 畏難其心 timid, fearful; *ói-siŭ* 畏羞 (pronounced *ói-chiŭ*) bashful, sensitive to shame.

Ói, 慰 To soothe, to console, to comfort, as in *ăng-ói* 安慰.

Ói, 位 To sit erect, a place, a seat; a trust; right, proper; a numerative of persons, gentlemen: COM., *Săng-ôi Ék-tā* 三位一體 the Trinity; *ôi-dé* 位置 position, authority; *bĕk ôi-chệu* 別位處 another place.

Ôi, 胃, 脂 The stomach; as in *bī-ôi* 脾胃.

Ôi, 爲 For, because; in behalf of; a sign of the passive; also read *ùi*, q. v.: COM., *ĭng-ôi* 因爲 on account of; *ôi-họ* 爲何 why?

Ọi, 欲 Read *ŭk*: to wish for, to desire, as in *ọi dĭh* 欲値.

Ók, 熨 A flat iron containing coals; to iron: also read *ôi*: COM., *ók-dău* 熨斗 a smoothing iron; *ók ĭ-siòng* 熨衣裳 to iron clothes.

Ók, 屋 A house, a dwelling; *ók siá* 屋舍 habitations: *chiò-ók* 厝屋 a house.

Ŏng, 恩 Favor, kindness, grace:

charitable; to favor; to oblige; to love: COM., *séu ŏng* 受恩 to receive favor; *ŏng-ái* 恩愛 love, grace; *ŏng-diĕng* 恩典 or *ŏng-hié* 恩惠 or *ŏng-dĕk* 恩澤 grace, beneficence: *găng-ŏng* 感恩 to feel grateful.

Ŏng, 秧 Also read *iŏng*: the blade of grain, young rice plants as in *ŏng-cūng* 秧種 ready for transplanting.

Ōng, 影 Read *ĭng*: coll. *ōng*: a shadow: *ōng-hié* 影戲 shadowy, *ōng-gá* 影駕 credit, ability.

Óng, 揾, 搵, To dip in the water; to immerse: COM., *óng láng* 揾濕 to wet by dipping.

Óng, 蕹 Read *ŭng* and *ūng*; coll. *óng*, as in *óng-chái* 蕹菜 the name of a vegetable, greens.

Òng, 行 Read *hèng*; coll. *òng*: a

go-down; *dà-òng* 茶行 a tea-hong.

Òng: A coll. word: a long time; *cêng òng*, a very long time; *cī òng* or *cī-māng òng*, thus long!

Òng: A coll. word, as in *săi-òng*, a sandy beach—the same as *săi-hòng*, q. v.: also a name given to a sand bar in a waterway.

Ông, 運 To revolve, to gyrate: the course of nature; a revolution: luck, lot; a horoscope as in *cê-ông* 字運; COM., *ông-dông* 運動 to influence (a person); athletics, exercise; *ông-dông huôi* 運動會 athletic sports; *sì-ông* 時運 times, stated lot.

Ông, 問 To demand, to exact, to search into; to examine a case; *ông-dák* 問答 question and answer.

Pá   701

Ông, 韻, 韵 Sounds rhyming in their tones; a chord, as in *ĭng ông* 音韻; *sĭ-ông* 詩韻 a book of rhyming characters.

Pă, 抛 Read *pău;* coll. *pă,* as in *pă-déng* 抛碇, to drop anchor; *pă-mâeng* 抛絚 to cast a net.

Pă, 脬 Read *pău;* coll. *pă,* as in *lêng-pă* 腎脬 the scrotum; *niéu-pă* the bladder.

Pă: A coll. word, as in *pă á-dāu kó,* to withdraw by a back way, to go around, so as to avoid meeting a person, or to apprehend a thief.

Pă: A coll. word, as in *pă-pă-gūng,* to bubble up as boiling water.

Pá, 帕, 帊 A veil or kerchief: the first (read *máng* or *măk*) means a fillet, as in *tàu-pá* 頭帕 worn by elderly ladies; *chhu-*

pá 手帕 a handkerchief.

Pá, 怕 To fear, to dread; to apprehend: COM., *kŭng-pá* 恐怕 (coll. *hŭng-pá*) to fear lest.

Pá: A coll. word, as in *cūi-pá,* a water-blister.

Pā̰, 睥 Read *bĕ;* used for the coll. *pā̰,* as in *pā̰-ngā̰* 睥睨 or *pā̰-ngā̰,* to look askance at, to scrutinize.

Pā̰, 頰 The jaws, the cheeks, as in *méng-pā̰* 面頰.

Pá, 稗 Read *bái;* used for the coll. *pá:* a noxious weed.

Pà: A coll. word, as in *pà-pà-giéu,* short quick breathing.

Páek, 魄 The animal soul; form; figure, manner; COM., *săng hŭng chék páek* 三魂七魄 the three souls and seven spirits of a man.

Páek, 珀 Amber: COM., *hū-páek*

琥珀 the common term for amber.

Páek, 迫, 逼 Read *páik;* coll. *páek:* to oppress, to harass; *páek-dŭk* 迫逐 to persecute; *cĭng-sìng-siòng gì giòng páek* 精神上其强迫 moral compulsion.

Páeng, 脝 Read *páung;* used for the coll. *páeng;* to swell, to rise as yeast: *páeng duâi* 脝大 light, spongy.

Páh, 拍 To pat, to caress; to beat, to strike; *páh chiŭ* 拍手 or *páh ciŏng* 拍掌 to clap the hands, to applaud.

Páh: A coll. word of wide significance: to be, to become: to beat, to strike; to fight: also as in *páh puái,* broken; *páh giêu* to bring a sedan; *páh-dòng,* lasting, forever; *páh giù,* to play ball; *páh guăng-sĭ*, to accuse before a magistrate; *páh mộ* lost; *páh dáung*, to let fall; to miss, to pass over.

Pāi: A coll. word; low, mean; shabby, seedy; *pāi-giăng*, a vagabond.

Páik, 逼, 偪 To ill-use, to oppress; pressing, urgent: in the coll. read *páek* q. v. and *pék*.

Páik, 追, 廹 To urge, to insist upon; to compel arbitrarily: COM., *páik gêung* 追近 imminent; COLL., *páik miáng* 追命 to oppress one so he commits suicide: *chuŏi páik* 催迫 to dun one.

Pâiu, 阜, 阝 A mound or hill of earth; great, high; complete, abundant; the 170th radical.

Pâiu, 掊 To grasp; to collect, to exact.

Páng 705

Pâiu, 裒 Also read *pèu:* to collect; to reduce; many, numerous.

Păk: A coll. word: to bubble, to rise and overflow, as in *păk-kī-lì,* bubbling up; *păk làu kó,* full and running over.

Păng, 潘 Read *puăng* in the dictionaries: a surname.

Păng: A coll. word: to divide; to equalize, as in *păng-puŏ; păng só* or *păng cái,* to pay debts.

Păng: A coll. word; as in *păng-păng èng áeng,* gallipots, jars of all sizes; met., a medley of things.

Páng, 有 A coll. character; empty, hollow; as in *kĕng-páng* 空有 light, loose-grained: *páng chà* 有柴 porous wood; *páng-gōng* 有講 to chat; *páng-dàng*

有談 chit-chat; aimless talk.

Pàng, 蟚 Small land crabs: COM., *pàng-gì,* (coll. *kì*) 蟚蜞 a small crab found in rice fields.

Pàng, 膨 The abdoman puffed and swollen as in *bók-lō̤ pàng-pàng diòng* 腹老膨膨漲 flatulency.

Pàng, 澎 The noise of dashing waters: COM., *Pàng-hù-dō̤* 澎湖島, the Pescadore Islands off the west coast of Formosa.

Pàng, 評 To discuss the merits of, as in *pàng-lâung;* 評論 to arrange; to revise for publication, as in *piĕ-pàng* 批評.

Pàng, 砰 Read *pĕng;* used for the coll. *pàng;* to roll out cloth; *pàng-siŏh* 砰石 stone cloth-rollers.

Pàng: A coll. word, as in *pàng-*

Páu 707

pàng-kī, to ascend as smoke or dust.

Pàng: A coll. word, as in *pàng-pàng-ciéng*, in a tremor, shivering.

Páu, 抛 To reject, to cast off; in the coll. read *pă*, q. v.: *pău-mièu* 抛錨 to anchor; *pău-ké* 抛棄 to abandon.

Pău, 枹 Read *hŭ*; used for the coll. *pău*: a pomelo.

Páu, 泡 Read *páu* in the dictionaries: a bubble, spoon-drift, spume; in the coll. read *pău*, q. v. Read *bàu*, copious, abundant.

Páu, 炮 To roast in ashes or in a pan; to boil water, as in *páu gŭng-tŏng* 炮滾湯; *páu dà* 炮茶 to boil water for tea.

Páu, 砲, 礮 A cannon, a great-gun; fire-works: COM., *páu-dài*

砲臺 a fort, a battery; *páu gá* 砲架 a gun carriage; *gĭ-guăng páu* 機關砲 a gatling gun; *páu sùng* 砲船 a gun boat.

Páu, 橐 Used for the coll. *páu:* swollen, puffed up as a boil, as in *páu-páu* 橐橐: also read *pau* in the coll.

Pàu, 跑 To run, to gallop; as in *pàu-mā* 跑馬 to ride rapidly; to dispatch: COM., *páu cáng* 跑站 to post, to travel swiftly.

Páu, 泡 Read *páu;* coll. *páu; cūi-páu* 水泡 water bubbles.

Páu, 鮑 Read *páu;* coll. *páu* as in *páu-ngù* 鮑魚 salted fish from Loochow.

Páu, 皰 Read *páu;* coll. *páu* as in *páu-páu* 皰皰 a blister on the skin; *páu báuk* 皰剝 the blister has burst.

Páuk, 撲, 扑 To recline against; to flap, as in *páuk ĭk* 撲翼 to flap the wings; *páuk-mĭĕk* 撲滅 to puff out, as a light; *met.,* in the coll. to suppress or stop, as a quarrel.

Páuk, 樸 Hard, fine-grained wood; plain, unadorned, simple, sincere: COM., *páuk-sĭk* 樸實 plain, rustic, unpolished.

Páuk, 朴 As in *páuk-siĕu* 朴硝 sulphate of soda; Epsom salts.

Páuk, 璞 An unpolished or unwrought gem, as in *páuk-ngŭk* 璞玉

Páung, 蚌 A bivalve; the pearl oyster.

Páung, 傍 Read *bòng* and *báung;* coll. *páung:* to be at, on, or in: *páung cī̆ bĕng* 傍只邊, it is on this side.

Páung, 遇 Read *ngêu;* used for

the coll. *páung:* to meet, to happen on, as in *páung diŏh* 遇着.

Páung: A coll. word, for which 遇 may be used; to run upon, to strike, to bump or knock against.

Pé, 鼻 Read *bĭk;* coll. *pé:* the nose, nasal; *met.,* skill, cleverness; a point, an end: *pé-liòng* 鼻梁 the bridge of the nose; *pé-kĕng* 鼻空 the nostrils.

Pĕ: A coll word, sometimes used for *pĕk,* very, exceedingly: *pĕ-pĕ iĕk,* very hot! piping hot!

Pè: A coll. word, as in *pè-pè siăng,* a broken voice, wanting in clearness.

Péh: A coll. euphonic prefix, as in *péh-páh,* to beat, to strike.

Pék, 匹 A pair, one of a pair; a mate; to match and pair; a classifier of horses and fledgelings: *pék-hŭ* 匹夫 a man without relatives: COM., *pék-puói*, 匹配 to mate, to marry.

Pék, 疋 A classifier of cloths, woolens, and silks; the 103rd radical: COLL., *siŏh pék* 一疋 one piece of cloth.

Pék, 癖 Indigestion, a morbid appetite; one's natural disposition: COM., *pék-é* 癖意 or *pék-séng* 癖性 or *pék-ké* 癖氣 the natural bent or disposition; *pék-áu* 癖拗 a stubborn disposition.

Pék, 璧 Read *biáh* in the coll. q. v.: the 14th zodiacal constellation in Pegasus, and *a* in Andromeda.

Pék, 僻 Mean, vulgar; depraved as in *piĕng-pék* 偏僻.

Pék, 辟 Used for the coll. *piáh*, q. v.

Pék, 碧 A valuable, translucent stone, like prase or jade; *pék hùng* 碧雲, the azure clouds.

Pék, 嗶 Read *bék;* used for the coll. *pék,* as in *pék-ciĕ* 嗶吱 course, twilled, woolen cloth.

Pék: A coll, euphonic prefix, as in *pék-páuk,* to eat, as dogs do; *pék-piák,* to throw or dash out, as water; *pék-puák,* to scatter, to sprinkle on.

Pĕk, 雹 Read *páu:* coll. *pĕk:* hail: *lŏh pĕk* 落雹, to hail.

Pĕk: A coll. word: hot: *pĕk-pĕk-iĕk,* very warm, hot, piping hot —the same as in *pĕ,* q. v.

Pĕng, 烹 To boil, to stew; to decoct: *pĕng dà* 烹茶 to boil water for tea; COM., *pĕng-diêu* 烹調 to cook professionally.

Péng, 聘 To ask, to inquire of; *péng chīng* 聘請 to request

the services of a teacher; to negotiate a marriage; *péng-lā* 聘禮 marriage-presents.

Péng: A coll. euphonic prefix, as in *péng-páng gīng-gōng*, to chat.

Pêng: A coll. euphonic prefix, as in *pêng-piáng*, the slamming of doors; *pêng-páung*, to knock, strike against; *pêng piâng*, to compare two articles.

Pèng: A coll. word, as in *pèng-pēng-kī*, vapor or steam rising; *met.*, growing prosperity.

Pēu, 否 Not so, ought not; at the end of a sentence it makes a negative interrogation; else, whether or not: also read *pī*, q. v.: *kŏ pēu* 可否 will it do or not? *sĕ pēu* 是否 is it so?

Pēu, 剖 To cut in two; to divide; to lay open; to judge: COM., *pēu mìng* 剖明 to state clearly, to make manifest, as one's innocence.

Pèu, 浮 As in *pèu-pèu* 浮浮 light, vain; much: COM., *kĭng-pèu* 輕浮 fickle, unsteady: *hŭ-pèu* 虛浮 void, unreal.

Pī, 悲 Compassion, sympathy; grief as in *pī-siōng* 悲傷; *pī-ăi* 悲哀, to lament; *cû-pī* 慈悲. pity, compassion.

Pĭ: A coll. euphonic prefix, as in *pĭ-puŏ,* to spread out; *pĭ-piĕ* to whittle to a point, as a pencil.

Pī, 痞 In the coll. *pī,* a scab: *dáu pī* 痘痞 scabs of small-pox; *táung pī* 脫痞 to shed a scab.

Pī, 否 To bar the way, to hinder; bad, wicked, as mankind: also read *pĕu,* q. v.

Pī, 譬 Often read *pé:* to compare; a simile, a parable: *pī-ḙu* (coll. *bī-ḙu*) 譬諭 to illustrate by comparison; *pī-ü̇* 譬如 just like, for instance as.

Pī, 鄙 A frontier town; a town of 500 houses; five *pī* towns in one hsien or district; rustic; to despise: *pī-láiu* 鄙陋 vulgar; mean, dilapidated, as a house; COM., *pī-chiéu* 鄙笑 to despise and ridicule; *pī-lêng* 鄙吝 stingy, niggardly.

Pī, 匪 Banditti; *pī-dōng* 匪黨 a band of villains: *tū-pī* 土匪 local banditti; *pī-dù* 匪徒 or *pī-lôi* 匪類 vagabonds.

Pì, 疲 罷 Fatigued, wearied as in *pì-guóng* 疲倦; the 2nd also read *bâ,* q. v.

Pì, 皮 The skin; tanned hides, leather; leathern; furs; bark; to skin; the 107th radical: in the coll. read *puòi,* q. v.

Pî, 肥 Fat, oily, greasy; corpulent; fertile: in the coll. read *bùi*, q. v.

Pì: A coll. word, as in *pì-pì giéu* or *pì-pạ-pạ*, to pant.

Pì: A coll. euphonic prefix, as in *pì-páu*, to run, to scamper.

Piă, 跛 Read *pọ*: coll. *piă*, as in *piă uăi* 跛歪 to tread obliquely; *piă-kă* 跛胶 to tread the foot to one side.

Pià: A coll. word: to shun, to avoid: *pià kọ,* and *pià cāu*, to run away as from creditors, or the police.

Piáh 僻 Read *pék*; coll *piáh* to get out of the way of another: *biĕng piáh*, retired; a by-place; *piáh biĕng,* 僻邊 to step to one side.

Piáh 辟 Read *pék*; used for the coll. *piáh*, as in *piáh sià*, to expel malign influences.

Piăng   717

Piăh: A coll. word as in *tù-piăh*, mud flats; *săi-piăh*, sand flats.

Piăk, 潑 Read *puăk;* used for the coll. *piăk:* to throw from a vessel; *piăk siŏh sĭng* 潑一身 spattered over the whole person.

Piăk: A coll. word, used for *hiák*, as in *piăk lŏh*, to topple over, as a wall: *piăk gŭó kŏ̤*, it fell the other way.

Piăk: A coll. word: to throb: *piăk-piăk diōng*, to throb or palpitate incessantly; *piăk kĭ piăk* a continuous throbbing.

Piăk: A coll. word: to slap: *piăk siŏh siăng*, the sound of slapping or of a thing falling.

Piăng, 拚 Read *biĕng* in the dictionaries; often read *pĭng;* coll *piăng:* to contend, to strive for the mastery, as in *piăng lā siŏ̤, iăng,* 拚喇輸贏.

Piāng: A coll. word, used for *buói:* the back; behind, rear: *piāng-áu*, behind the back; *piāng-cék-gáuk*, the spine.

Piāng, 跛 Read *pǫ*; used for the coll. *piāng,* lame: *piāng-kă* 跛腳 maimed; *piāng cṳ̌* 跛子 a cripple.

Piāng: A coll. word: a numerative of folded vermicelli, as in *miéng siŏh piāng,* one fold of vermicelli.

Piāng: A coll word as in *piāng-piāng-giéu*, a rattling sound.

Piáng: A coll. word analogous to *kiáng:* to unite: *piáng-ging* or *piáng-lęng*, to bring close together.

Piâng: A coll word; to compare as in *bĭ-piâng,* to illustrate; *piâng cī duâi*, as large as this: *piâng ciā iŏng*, after this sort.

Piĕ 批 To revise; to assist; to give an official reply: com., *piĕ pàng* 批評 to criticise, as an essay; *piĕ cūng* 批准 to grant a petition; *piĕ bánk* 批駁 to return a petition ungranted. coll., *dęuk piĕ* 竹批 a ferule; *chuòi piĕ* 摧批 a switch; *piĕ huák* wholesale; *piĕ huák sū*, a wholesale shop.

Piĕ: A coll. word: a letter, as in *piĕ séng* or *piĕ cák*; *piĕ dội*, an envelope; *siā-piĕ, hŭng piĕ* and *giĕ piĕ*, to write, seal and send a letter.

Piĕ 披 Disheveled: *Piĕ tàu sák huák* 披頭撒髮 the hair all disheveled.

Piĕ 剝 To trim, to peel: coll, *piĕ-puòi* 剝皮 pare off the skin; *piĕ bék* to sharpen a pencil.

Piĕ 礮, 砒 An ore of arsenic: com.

piĕ-sŏng 礮霜 arsenic; also called *séng* and *ìng-ngiòng*.

Piék, ノ A stroke from right to left in writing; the 4th radical.

Piék 擎 To tap, to strike lightly; to divide: in the coll. a light bamboo basket to weigh in: com., *piék siă* 擎榭 the rooms at the side of a court in a Chinese house; *chĭng gŭng piék* 秤斤擎 a weighing-basket.

Piék 劈 To pare, to whittle, to sharpen to a point; *piék bék* 劈筆 to sharpen a pencil.

Piĕng 篇 Slips of bamboo anciently used for books; a section; books, publications: com., *ciòng piĕng* 全篇 a whole section.

Piĕng 偏 Inclined; partial, as in *piĕng bèng* 偏迸; *piĕng giéng* 偏見 prejudiced; *piĕng cék* 偏執 opinionated; *piĕng sŭ* 偏私

selfish: COM., *piĕng pék* 偏僻 a perverted will.

Piĕng 編 To arrange materials for a book; to compose; records; books: *piĕng cĭk* 編輯 an editor.

Piĕng 瘺 A paralysis: COM., *piĕng hŭng* 瘺瘋 a palsy.

Piĕng 翩 to fly swiftly: *piĕng-piĕng* 翩翩 flying about.

Piéng 片 A leaf, a fragment: a petal; a section of; the 91st radical: COM., *piéng sì* 片時 a while: *piéng dăng* 片單 visiting cards; *nguá piéng* 瓦片 bits of broken tiles.

Piéng 騙 To take advantage of, to cheat, to lie to: *piéng guŏh* 騙局 a plan to cheat; *kĭ piéng* 欺騙 or *hŭng piéng* 哄騙 to delude, to cheat.

Piéng 遍, 徧 Universal, pervading as in *puō piéng* 普遍; *piéng* hèng gáuk chéu 遍行各處 going all about.

Pięu 飄 A light, easy manner; vain, frivolous: COM., piĕu hṳ̆ 飄虛 empty, not substantial; piĕu liù 飄流 floating about; roving.

Piĕu 漂 As in piĕu liù lâung cṳ̄ 漂流浪子 a dissipated person: also read piéu, q. v.

Piéu 票 A warrant; a note, a bill: chók piéu 出票 to issue a warrant; huăng piéu 番票 Chinese notes; chău piéu 鈔票 a bank-note; iù-piéu 郵票 a postage stamp; gŭng cái piéu 公債票 government bonds; dèu piéu 投票 to vote.

Piéu 漂 To whiten, as in piéu buó 漂布 to bleach cotton cloth; piéu băh 漂白 to bleach: also read piĕu, q. v.

Pĭng 723

Pièu 薸 Duckweed: *pièu mō* 薸姆 large duckweed.

Pièu 瓢 A calabash, a dipper: in the coll. a spoon: com., *pièu gĕng*, (or *bĕng*) 瓢羹 a soup spoon.

Pièu 嫖 Light, trifling; wanton; given to lewdness.

Pĭh: A coll. word: to dart off as rats or pigs, as in *pĭh cāu*.

Pĭh: A coll. word, as in *pĭh muōi* a blunted end, as of a needle.

Pĭk: A coll. euphonic prefix, as in *pĭk pĭăk*, to throb, to palpitate.

Pĭng 拚 To risk, to jeopardize, to peril: also read *biĕng*, and in the coll, *piăng*, q. v.: *pĭng miáng* 拚命 to peril life.

Pĭng: A coll. euphonic prefix, as in *pĭng păng* to apportion, as shares.

Pĭng 品 A class, a grade, a degree; a rule, law, example; to classify, to rank: *sióng pĭng* 上品, superior; *pĭng máu.* 品貌 countenance; *pĭng háing* 品行 actions, conduct; *pĭng gáh* 品格 one's natural ways; character.

Pĭng: A coll. euphonic prefix as *pĭng piāng* or *pĭng dūng piāng* to surge, to roll as waves or water in a vessel; also an unsteady gait.

Pĭng; A coll. euphonic prefix as in *pĭng pòng*, a report as of fire-crackers; bang!

Pìng; A coll. word: equal, balancing; to make level as in *pìng-pàng; pìng-pìng dòng*, of equal lengths.

Pó: A coll. word: a convex bamboo cover for rice steamers called *pó-lọ̄*.

Pŏ 波 As in *pŏ láung* 波浪 waves, billows.

Pŏ 菠 A coarse winter greens, called *pŏ lìng chái* 菠薐菜 the red-rooted greens: also the name of a tree.

Pŏ 坡 A hill, a mound, as in *săng pŏ* 山坡.

Pŏ: A coll. word, as in *pŏ-dò duái ṳ̄*, a heavy rain, rain falling in torrents.

Pŏ 頗 Used for the coll. *puŏ* q. v.: somewhat, a little as in *pŏ pŏ*, 頗頗 doubtful; *pŏ hŏ* 頗好 pretty well, will answer.

Pŏ 破 To rend, to split; broken; to see through a plot; spoiled; injured, as in *pŏ huái* 破壞: in the coll. read *puái* q. v.: *pŏ liĕk* 破裂 riven; *káng pŏ* to see through; *pŏ hié* 破費 to squander: *pŏ cài* 破財, to waste property; *pọ́ sióng,* 破相 maimed.

Póh: A coll. word, as in *póh siŏh siăng,* a sound as of one falling on the ground.

Pọ̈h 粕, In the coll. the fibrous part of fruits, etc. rejected in eating; dregs, grounds.

Pói 吡 Read *pék;* used in the *Báik-ing,* for the coll. *pói:* to spit: *pói lāng* 吡瀇 to expectorate; *pói háik,* 吡血 to spit blood.

Pók, 覆 Read *hók;* coll. *pók:* to invert: *páh pók* 拍覆 to turn over, to upset.

Pók: A coll. word: to bend, to incline as the head or body: *tàu pók giá,* to bow the head.

Pŏk 桲 Read *buŏk;* used in the *Báik-ing* for the coll. *pŏk,* as in *pŏk siŏh siăng* 桲一聲 a sound as of wood when struck

Póng   727

Pŏk 梆 Read *bŏng*; used for the coll. *pŏk* as in *pŏk pŏk* 梆梆, the sound of a watchman's rattle; *pŏk săng pŏk* 梆三梆 to beat three beats.

Pŏk: A coll. word, as in *pŏk-tōng siŏh siăng*, a sound, as of a stone thrown into the water; *pŏk lòng*, a dull, heavy sound.

Pŏng 斛 Also read *bòng*: abundant: COLL., *pŏng ciáh pŏng* 斛隻斛 superabundant, bountiful.

Pōng 丼 A character used in the *Báik-ĭng* for the coll. *pōng*, as in *pōng siŏh siăng* 丼一聲 a sound as of a thing dropped into a well.

Póng 噴 To expel the breath forcibly, to spurt: COM., *póng cūi* 噴水 to spurt water.

Póng 縫 A seam; a crack, a crevice; spaces between the

fingers or toes: *pùng póng* 縫縫 cracks; *sìng lā́ póng*, to seek an occasion; also read *pùng*, q. v.

Pòng 磅 Read *bòng*; coll. *pòng*: as in *pòng pòng giéu* 磅磅叫 a dull, heavy sound.

Pū 醭 Read *páuk*: used in the *Báik-ĭng* for the coll. *pū*: mold; mildew; *cháu pū* 嗅醭 a moldy scent.

Pù 浮 Read *pèu*; coll. *pù*: to float, to drift; raised in relief, as in *pù huă* 浮花 flowers in relief; *pù giò* 浮橋 a floating bridge.

Pù 烰 Read *pèu*; coll. *pù*: to fry in fat; as in *pù biāng* 烰餅 doughnuts.

Puái 破 Read *pó*; coll. *puái*: to break, to rend; spoiled, injured; *páh puái* 拍破 to break; broken; *puái buó* 破布 cotton rags; *puái ngū hiă* 破五罅

much broken; wholly spoiled.

Puái 派, To branch, as a stream; to distribute; to appoint: COM., *puái cék sẹu* 派執事 to appoint to office: COLL., *puái dáu*: or *puái-dŏng-dáu*, midday, noon.

Puái 紽 Raveled silk : in the coll. to part, to divide, as in *puái tàu-huók* 紽頭髮 to part the hair.

Puák 潑 To sprinkle; to throw water about; a shower: used for the coll. *piák*, q. v.: *puák-cūi* 潑水 to irrigate; *uăk puák* 活潑 lively: *ṳ puák diē lì* 雨潑裡梨 the rain beats in.

Puák: A coll. word, as in *puăk-tẹng*, a well-bucket: *puăk-tẹng, sóh*, a well-bucket rope.

Puáng 判 To divide; to judge: to sentence: COM., *puáng-duáng* 判斷 to judge and decide;

puáng áng 判案 to pass judgment on a case.

Puáng 伴 A companion; to keep one company: *puáng bùng mā* 伴房媽 a bride's attendant.

Pŭh: A coll word: as in *pŭh ngài kó*, puffed and spoiled.

Pŭh: A coll. word, as in *pŭh-pŭh*, a noiseless blow.

Pùi: A coll. word: to eject forcibly from the mouth; a sound expressing dislike or contempt.

Pŭng 蠭蜂 Bees; wasps: hornets: COM., *mĭk pŭng* 蜜蜂 the honey bee; *uòng pŭng* 黃蜂 a hornet: *pŭng cĕng* 蜂針 a bee's sting; *pŭng déng* 蜂釘 the sting of a bee.

Pŭng: A coll. word, as in *pŭng cūi*, swill; *pŭng tĕng* a swill pail; *mī pŭng*, rinsings of rice.

Pùng   731

Pūng 捧 To offer, or receive with or hold in, both hands, as in *pūng dà* 捧茶; a handful, a double handful: in the coll., read *pùng*, q. v.

Pūng 紡 Read *hwōng*: used in the *Báik-ing* for the coll. *pūng*, to spin or twist thread with a machine or hand reel called *pūng chiă* 紡車; *pūng mièng sā* 紡綿紗 to twist cotton yarn.

Pùng 帆, 帆, Sails: as in *hŭng-pùng* 風帆; *kău pùng* 閣帆, (or *kău hióng* 閣向) to tack

Pùng 篷, 笭, Mats of bamboo splints, used for sails, boat covers, etc.: COM., *hŭng pùng* 風篷 a sail; *pùng lèu* 篷樓 a mat lodge or hovel; *buó pùng* 布篷 a cloth awning; COLL., *pùng siŏh liāng* 篷一領 one mat.

Pùng 捧 Read *pūng*; coll. *pùng*:

to offer with both hands; to serve up: *pùng buông* 捧飯 to serve up rice.

Pùng: A coll. word; the same as *pŏ*, q. v.: *pùng dò duái ṳ̄*, torrential rain.

Puŏ 鋪 To spread out, to arrange; to lay, as a pavement, as in *puŏ siŏh* 鋪石: COM., *puŏ bēng* 鋪板 bed boards; *puŏ gái* 鋪蓋 bedding: COLL. *puŏ diô* 鋪路 to pave roads; *puŏ bēng bàng* 鋪板柵 to lay a board floor; *páh-puŏ* to arrange the bed boards.

Puŏ 麩 Read *hŭ*; coll. *puŏ* as in *măh puŏ* 麥麩 the bran or husk of wheat.

Puŏ 菠 Read *pŏ*; coll. as in *puŏ-ling-chái*, a coarse winter greens.

Puŏ 浦 A bank, a margin or brink of a lake or river; a creek;

Huăng-sùng-puŏ 番船浦, the anchorage for foreign vessels in the south suburbs of Foochow.

Puŏ 普 Daylight everywhere; COM., *puŏ piéng* 普遍 universally diffused; *puŏ dô* 普度, rites to get souls out of hell.

Puŏ 譜 A list, a record; a register; to arrange; in the coll. rule, system: COM., *cŭk puŏ* 族譜 a clan-genealogy: COLL., *puŏ diô* 譜路 rule, routine; *mò puŏ diô* 無譜路, no system or method.

Puŏ 斧 Read *hŭ*; used for the coll. *puŏ*, as in *puŏ tàu* 斧頭 an ax, a hatchet.

Puŏ 補 Read *buŏ*; coll. *puŏ*: as in *puŏ guá*, a robe with embroidered squares on the front and back, worn before the republic.

Puŏ 鋪 舖 A shop; a ward, a district: the second is used in the coll. as a numerative of Chinese leagues or ten li: COM., *puŏ nọ̆i* 舖內 in the ward; *puó-sèng-ding* 舖前頂 a ward in the suburbs of Foochow.

Puŏ 簿 Read *buŏ* in the dictionaries and often spoken *buŏ*: a register; a book for accounts etc., to record: *nĭk gé puŏ* 日記簿 a diary.

Puŏh 曝 Read *bŭk*; coll *puŏh*: to sun, to dry in the sun; *puŏh iók* 曝弱 wilted in the sun; *puŏh ngàu* 曝𤉸 warped as by solar heat.

Puŏi 肧, 胚 An embryo; anything unfinished; *puŏi páek* 胚魄 native talent; *puŏi páek hŏ̤*, good natural ability.

Puŏi 坏, 坯, A mound; unburnt

pottery; to plaster up a seam or crack; crude, unformed: COM., *cāi puŏi* 紙坏 pasteboard: COLL., *buòi puŏi* 甕坏 to make pasteboard.

Puói 配 The color of liquor; an equal; united; to mate; to unite in marriage; to compare; in the COLL., the condiments of a meal: *bŏk puói* 不配 ill-sorted; *puói dói* 配對 to join, to match; *puói sùng* 配船 to hire a suitable boat, as to transport goods; *puói buŏng* 配飯 condiments for a meal of rice; *puói sĭk* 配食 relishes.

Puòi 茴 Read *huòi*; coll. *puòi* as in *puòi hiŏng* 茴香 fennel, caraway seed.

Puòi 皮 Read *pì*; coll. *puòi*: the skin; a hide; furs; bark; shameless: *puòi hŭ* 皮膚 the skin; *puòi lâung* 皮蛋 preserved ducks eggs, used at feasts.

Fuòi 裴 A long robe; a surname.

Puói 被 Read *bê,* coll. *puòi:* a coverlet a blanket; *puòi dăng* 被單 a sheet, a counterpane.

Puói: A coll. word: to consult; to deliberate; *puói bī,* to consult about; *puói huŏng* a medical consultation.

Puŏk 渤 Read *buŏk:* used for the coll. *puŏk,* scum, froth.

Puóng 汐 Read *sĭk;* used for the coll. *puóng:* the ebbing of the tide; *cūi puóng* 水汐 the tide is ebbing.

Să 沙 Sand, gravel; pebbles; sandy, gritty; in the coll., ready, skillful at: read *săi* in the coll. q. v.: *să mŏk* 沙漠, a sandy desert.

Să 紗, Thin silk, gauze; *câiu să* 綢紗 crepe.

Să 痧 A coll. character: sudden, pains in the bowels, colic; cholera-morbus: *diŏh să* to have the colic.

Să 師, 司 Read *sự*: used for the coll. *să* as in *să-hô* a teacher or professor; a skilled workman.

Sạ 西 The west; western, foreign; in a *met.* sense, that, there; *sạ câung* 西藏 Tibet; *sạ nàng* 西南 and *sạ báęk* 西北 S. W. and N. W.

Sạ 犀 A rhinoceros, called *sạ ngiù* 犀牛.

Sạ 洗 To wash the feet, to clean; to cleanse morally; *sạ méng* 洗面 to wash the face; in the coll., purging, cathartic; to tease; to annoy.

Sạ 洒 To wash, to wipe off; *met.* to

avenge a wrong: also read *suā*.

Sā 璽 The royal signet, the imperial seal: in coll. read *sḝ*, q. v.

Sá 細 Fine, small and delicate; trifling, unimportant; careful: COM., *sá nâung* 細嫩 small in size; *sá-nê* 細貳 careful, cautious; *sá siăng* 細聲 a low voice.

Sạ: A coll. word, similar to the last: young; inferiority in rank; my, our.

Sạ 俰 A coll. character: many, much: *sạ ciēu* 俰少 many and few; *cêng sạ* 盡俰 very many.

Sáe 疏 Also read *sū*, q. v.: a statement to a superior; a plain record; *sáe gé* 疏記 a written prayer, burnt to an idol.

Sáek 摔 Read *siuk*; coll. *sáek*: to strike violently; to knock things

Săi 739

about in anger: *sáek ptái* 摔
破 to dash to pieces; *saek
diêu* 摔穧 to thresh rice.

Sáeng 送 Read *sóng*: coll. *sáeng*:
to send presents, to accompany; to see a guest out; a
present, a gift; *hô sáeng* 護送
to convoy (ships).

Sáeng 宋 Read *sóng*; coll. *sáeng*:
a surname; *sáeng dièu* 宋朝,
the Sung dynasty, A. D. 970-
1280.

Săh: A coll. word; as in *săh siŏh
siăng*, a slight knock, rattling.

Săh: A coll. word; *săh săh*,
seesaw! up and down!

Săi 沙 Read *să*: coll *săi*: sand,
gravel, pebbles; *săi hòng* (or
òng) 沙痕 a sand beach, or bar.

Săi 鯊 Read *să* in the dictionaries: *săi ngù* 鯊魚, the shark.

Săi 師 Read *sṳ*: coll. *săi*: a master, a teacher; an instructor.

Sāi 獅 Read *sṳ̄* in the dictionaries; a lion: COM., *sāi cṳ̄ lèu* 獅子樓 a tower with three lions couchant, in South street, Foochow.

Sāi 私 Read *sṳ̄*; coll. *sāi*, as in *sāi gă dài* 私家代 one's private affair.

Sāi 屎, 屎, Read *chī*; coll. *sāi*: excrement: *sāi-niéu* 屎尿 ordure and urine.

Sāi 駛, 使, Read *sṳ̄*; used for the coll. *sāi*: to order; to commission one; to employ; need, expense: fit: *sāi ĕung* 使用 to expend; an outlay; *sāi chói* 使嘴 a servant; *sāi sáng* 使性 angry; *ā-sāi-dĕk* 㑒使的 it will answer; *ng sāi* 怀使 need not: *sāi giāng* 使仔 an apprentice.

Sáik 741

Sái 使 Read *sṳ̄*; used for the coll. *sái*: a husband: *sái tuàng* 使團 or *gŭng sái tuàng* 公使團 the diplomatic body.

Sái 殺 Also read *sák* q. v.: to clip, to shear; to reduce.

Sài 臍 Read *cṳ̄*; used for the coll. *sài*, as in *bók-sài* 腹臍, the navel.

Sái 祀 Read *sṳ̄*; coll. *sái*: to set up to worship.

Sái 儎 Read *cái*; used for the coll. *sái*: a boat-load: *gūi sái* 幾儎 how many boat-loads?

Sáik 色 The 139th radical; the appearance; color, hue; quality; beauty; lust: COM., *ngăng sáik* 顏色 color; *chāi sáik* 彩色 colors as of a painting; *tói sáik* 退色 faded out: *họ̄ sáik* 好色 lustful.

Sáik 塞 Also read *sái* and in the

coll. *sék*, q. v.: to fill, to stop up; to obstruct; true, sincere; stupid.

Sáik 虱 A louse, as in *sáik mọ* 虱乸; or *mẹk sáik* 木虱, bed-bugs.

Sáik 瑟 A harpsichord; *kìng sáik* 琴瑟 lutes and harps.

Sáik 嗇 The harvest; to be fond of; frugal: *léng sáik* 吝嗇 niggardly.

Sáiu 瘦 Lean, wasted away, as in *sŏi sáiu* 衰瘦.

Sáiu 宵 Read *siéu*; coll. *sáiu*; the twelve animals, used to designate the year of one's birth.

Sák 殺 To kill; also read *sái*, q. v.: *sák chiū* 殺手 an executioner; *áng sák* 暗殺, to assassinate; *áng sák dōng* 暗殺黨, band of assassins.

Sák 煞 To injure; to kill: COM.,

sák ké 煞氣 deadly vapors: COLL., *gáu sák muới* 皎煞尾 finally.

Sák 霎 A passing rain: COM., *sák sì găng* 霎時間 in a moment: *sák-bók-diòng-sì* 霎不傳時 suddenly.

Sák 薩 A religious word; a surname: COM., *bù-sák* 菩薩 a Budhist deity; an idol.

Sák 颯 The sound of wind; sudden: *sŏi sák* 衰颯, growing old.

Săk: A coll. word; to boil in water, to seethe; *băh săk giĕ*, a fowl boiled without sauce.

Săk: A coll. word, as in *gá-săk* (or *gá lăk*) a roach: *săk-mō*, large roaches.

Săng 三叁參川, Three; thrice; the third: COM., *săng gái* 三界 the three worlds; *săng bēng* 三板 a sampan; *săng gák láiu* 三

744   Săng

夾料 a cement of earth, sand and lime. Read *sáng*; to do thrice, to reiterate.

Săng 山 A hill; a mountain; the 46th radical: COM., *săng díng* 山頂 the top of a hill; *săng iòng* 山羊 a goat.

Săng 生 Read *sĕng*; coll. *săng*: to bear, to beget; life; born, birth: *săng-chók-sié* 生出世 born; *sĭng săng* 先生 a teacher, Sir, Mr.: *săng-dék-hŏ* 生的好 beautiful.

Săng 杉 Fir, pine: COM., *săng mŭk* 杉木 or *săng chù* 杉柴 soft pine wood used for buildings and furniture.

Săng 衫 A coat: *ĭ-săng* 衣衫 garments; *dòng-săng* 長衫 the toga.

Săng 珊 Coral: often read *dăng*, q. v.: *săng-hù* 珊瑚 coral.

Sáng 745

Sāng 產,產, To produce, to bear; a birth; an estate: *siéu-sāng* 小產 an abortion; still-born COM., *chók sāng* 出產 the products of a place; *sāng nâng* 產難 death from child-birth; *ngièk-sāng* 業產, property, an estate.

Sāng 傘. An umbrella, as in *ṳ̄ sāng* 雨傘

Sāng 省 Read *sěng*, coll., *sāng*; frugal: *sāng ciek* 省節 or *sāng giêng* 省儉 economical.

Sāng 散 Also read *sáng*: q. v.: a medicinal powder; in the coll, to scatter.

Sáng 散 To scatter; to disband: COM., *sáng cǎ* 散齋 to dismiss school.

Sáng 姓 Read *sěng*: coll. *sáng*: the surname; *báh-sáng* 百姓 hundred surnames, the people.

Sáng 性 Read *sěng*; coll. *sáng*:

the natural disposition; *sáng nái* 性耐 a patient disposition; *sáng gŏng* 性剛 an inflexible temper; *gék sáng* 急性 quick tempered.

Sáng 疝 Griping pains: *sáng ké* 疝氣 stricture in the bladder: *dòng sáng* 腸疝 hernia.

Sáng 汕, Fish sporting in the water; COM., *sáng tàu* 汕頭 Swatow.

Sáng 訕 To rail at; to slander: *sáng chiéu* 訕笑, to mock.

Sàng 晴 Read *cìng*: used in the *Báik-ing* for the coll. *sàng*, the sky clearing up after rain, as in *tiĕng sàng* 天晴 fair weather.

Sáng: A coll. word: to be silent, not to speak; *sâng năh* quiet, of few words.

Său 梢 A twig; slender; a rudder or tiller; sailors, as in *său-*

cṳ 梢子: COM., *sáu gǔng* 梢公 a steersman.

Sāu 稍 A granary; a ration of grain; slowly; slightly: COM., *sāu-sāu* 稍稍 a little.

Sáu 哨 To patrol; a revenue boat to suppress smuggling, as in *sáu sùng* 哨船; *chók sáu hŭk diô* 出哨伏路 to place pickets.

Sáu 嗽, 欶, To cough; a cough; to raise phlegm as in *tàng sáu* 痰嗽: COLL., *kǎeng sáu*, a hacking cough; *gáiu dòng sáu* whooping cough.

Sáu 掃 Read *suā*; coll. *sáu*: to sweep and clean up, as in *sáu chiô* 掃厝 to sweep the house; *sáu chiū* 掃帚 a broom.

Sáuk 刷, 㕞, A brush, a scraper; to brush, to scrape, to scrub; to print: COM., *ă-sáuk* 鞋刷 a shoe-brush; *sáuk-à* 刷鞋 to brush shoes; *éng sáuk gĭ* 印刷機 a printing machine.

Sáuk 率 To take the command of, as in *sáuk liāng* 率領 to lead (troops); *sáuk cĕung* 率衆 to raise a mob against.

Sáuk 蟀 A cricket, as in *sék-sáuk* 蟋蟀,

Sáuk 擱 To smear; to whitewash walls, as in *sáuk biáh* 擱壁; *sáuk hŭi cūi* 擱灰水 to whitewash with lime.

Sáuk 帥 To lead on, to conduct, as in *sáuk sṳ̆* 帥師 to lead troops; also read *sói*, q. v.

Sáung 算, 筭 An abacus, as in *sáung buàng* 算盤; to reckon; to estimate; to scheme as in *sáung dā* 算打 : *dā sáung* 打算 to plan : *sáung só* 算數 to reckon accounts,

Sáung 蒜 Garlic: COM., *sáung tàu* 蒜頭 garlic bulbs.

Sáung 遜 Meek, mild: *sáung iòng* 遜讓 to yield respectfully.

Sáung 喪, 褎 Also read *sŏng*, q. v.: to lose as in *sáung sék* 喪失; *sáung liòng-sĭng* 喪良心 to sear one's conscience: COM., *sáung dāng* 喪胆 terrified, overcome with fear.

Sáung: A coll. word: as in *sáung sĭ*, to kill by strangling.

Sé 四, 肆, 乂, Read *séu*; coll. *sé*: four, the fourth; *met.*, everywhere; *sé ā* 四個 four of certain things; *sé-giè* 四季 the four seasons.

Sé 是 Right, straight; to be, is, am, are; this, that, there, those: *sé nĭk* 是日 that day, then; *bék sé* 必是 certainly: COM., *bók sé* 不是 (coll. *ng sé*) not so, no;

sê hĭ 是非 right and wrong: COLL., *sê ĭ cô* 是伊做 it was he did it, *sê hĭ cĭ sĭng* 是非之心 conscience; the moral sense.

Sé 諟 Anciently used for the last: to be, is; right, proper; to examine.

Sé 寺, 鬭, An official residence; a Budhist monastery, as in *băh-tăk-sé* 白塔寺 White Pagoda monastery in Foochow.

Sé 侍 To receive the orders of a superior: *hŭk sé* 服侍 to wait on.

Sé 恃 To lean upon, to rely on: *hô sé* 怙恃 parents.

Sé 視, 眎, To see, to inspect; to regard and compare: COM., *gĕung sé* 近視, near sighted; *kĭng sé* 輕視 to slight, to skimp; *sé-hŏk guăng* 視學官 an inspector of schools.

Sék 751

Sĕ 示,示 To show, to declare; an edict: *gó sĕ* 告示 a proclamation; *sĕ ŭi* 示威 to overawe.

Sĕ 氏 A family, a clan; a sect; the 83rd radical.

Sẹ̆ 梳 Read *sŭ* in the dictionaries; coll. *sẹ̆*: a comb, as in *tàu sẹ̆* 頭梳; *sẹ̆ tàu sā méng* 梳頭洗面 to comb the hair and wash the face.

Sẹ̆ 璽 Read *sā*: coll. *sẹ̆*, as in *nguŏh sẹ̆* 玉璽 the imperial seal.

Sẹ̆: A coll. word: to impose on by fraud as in *ngài huó sẹ̆ nẹ̆ng*; *kéuk nẹ̆ng sẹ̆*, to be swindled by persons.

Séh: A coll. euphonic prefix, as in *séh-sóh* to suck.

Sék 惜 To pity; to be careful of: *sék guŏng-ĭng* 惜光陰 careful of time: COM., *kŏ sék* 可惜 alas! *ái-sék* 愛惜 to love, to regard.

Sék 息 A rest; to obstruct; usury, profits: COM., *lê sék* 利息 interest; gain, benefit; *chók sék* 出息 to make profit; *séng sék* 信息 the news; *ăng sék* 安息 to rest.

Sék 媳 Used for the coll. *sĭng*, q. v.: COM., *sék hô* 媳婦 (coll. *sĭng mô*), a daughter-in law.

Sék 濕, 溼 The second is an erroneous form: damp, humid; *hŭng sék* 瘋濕 rheumatism: COM., *sék ké* 濕氣 dampness.

Sék 隰, Low marshy land, as in *sék dé* 隰地.

Sék 失 To lose, to mislay; to omit; to miss the road: to forget; a failure: COM., *sék cūi* 失水 damaged by water, as goods: *sék lā* 失禮 I have failed in politeness; *ciáng sék sék gāng* 失感 to lose interest in a person: *sék bái* 失敗 to fail utterly.

Sék 室 A house, a family as in *gă sék* 家室: COM., *dà sék* 茶室 tea houses.

Sék 釋 As in *sék gáu* 釋敎 Budhism.

Sék 錫 An alloy; pewter of lead and tin; *sék ké* 錫器 a pewter teapot; *sék bŏh* 錫箔 pewter foil.

Sék 識 To know, to learn; to be acquainted with: COM., *dĭ sék* 知識 knowledge, understanding, discretion.

Sék 昔 Dried meats; formerly, as in *sék sì* 昔時.

Sék 飾, To paint, to gloss over: to adorn, as in *siŭ sék* 修飾: COM., *siū sék*, (coll. *chiŭ sék*) 首飾 head-ornaments.

Sék 蟋 A cricket, as in *sék sáuk* 蟋蟀.

Sék 蝕 Also read *sĭk*: to corrode: to encroach on, to eclipse, as in nĭk sĕk 日蝕, a solar eclipse; nguŏh sĕk 月蝕 a lunar eclipse.

Sék 螫 Also read siá: to sting, to poison: a virulent poison, as in sĭng sék 辛螫 malignant.

Sék 式 A form or shape, fashion, style of, as in iông sék 樣式; hăk sék 合式 suitable; cheap.

Sék 塞 Read sáik, to stop tightly as in sék gĭng 塞緊; sék diĕ 塞裡 stuff it in.

Sĕk 十,拾 Ten; wholly; complete; perfect: COM., sĕk ciòng 十全 entire; sĕk bók ciòng 十不全 very defective; sĕk hŭng 十分 the whole; very, exceedingly; sĕk cê gá 十字架 the Cross; sĕk cê gŭng 十字軍 Red Cross Society; sĕk cê gă 十字街 a cross street.

Sĕk: A coll. word: to shake, to agitate; met., to experience (toil or hardship): *muôi sĕk guó*, have not yet passed the ordeal.

Sĕng 生 To bear, to produce; to live; to cause to grow; living; born, birth; the 100th radical: read *săng* and *chăng*, in the coll. q. v.: *sĕng ngiĕk* 生業 a calling, an employment: COM., *hŏk-sĕng* 學生 a pupil, scholar; *siĕng-sĕng* 先生 a teacher; *sĕng-é* 生意 trade.

Sĕng 甥 A sister's children, as in *ngiê sĕng* 外甥 or *ngiê sĕng nṳ̆* 外甥女 nephews and nieces.

Sĕng 笙 A musical instrument: COM., *sĕng, siŭ, gŭ, ngŏk,* 笙、簫、鼓、樂, the organ, flageolet, drum, etc.

Sĕng 先 Read *siĕng*: coll. *sĕng*: before, first; previous; *sĕng gáu* 先至 to arrive first.

Sĕng 叅 Ginseng, as in *ing sĕng*

人蔘; *hāi sĕng* 海蔘 beche-de-mer.

Sĕng 森 The Pride of India; thickly wooded: *sĕng ngièng* 森嚴 majestic, stern.

Sēng 省 To diminish, to lessen; frugal; a province: also read *sĭng*, and in the coll. *sāng* q. v.: COM., *sĕk báik sēng* 十八省 the 18 provinces of China proper: *Hók-gióng sēng* 福建省 Fukien Province.

Séng 信 Sincere; truthful; faith; a letter, as in *piĕ séng* 批信; a seal, as in *éng séng* 印信: COM., *séng sĭk* 信實 sincere; *séng Iá-Sŭ* 信耶穌 to believe in Jesus; *séng sĕk* 信息 the news; *sĕk séng* 失信 to forfeit confidence: *nŏi séng* 內信 the enclosed letter; *mā séng dĕk guó*, 賣信的過 can't believe it,

Séng 勝 To conquer, to win; superior: also read *sing*, q. v.: *dáik séng* 得勝 victorious.

Séng 聖, 圣, Perfect, sacred, holy; sage: *séng ìng* 聖人 The Sage, Confucius; *séng-ìng mièu* 聖人廟 a Confucian Temple, *Séng-Sìng* 聖神, *Séng-Gìng*, 聖經 and *Séng-nĭk* 聖日 the Holy Spirit, the Bible and the Sabbath.

Séng 姓 A surname; a patronymic: in the coll. *sáng* q. v.: *séng sê* 姓氏 a surname, as of a sept: COM., *gói séng* 貴姓, (what is) your honorable surname?

Séng 性, In the coll. read *sáng*: q. v.: the natural disposition, as in *séng cìng* 性情; *pek séng* 癖性, one's natural temper; *séng mêng* 性命 life; *buōng séng* 本性 nature, character.

Sèng 前 Read *cièng*; used for the

coll. *sèng* : before ; in front of ; formerly : *cái sèng* 在前 before, then ; *sèng gŭi nìk* 前幾日 a few days ago.

Sêng 盛 Abundant ; prosperous ; a surname used in complimentary phrases: also read *sing* q. v.

Sêng 甚 Social delights ; very, extremely.

Sêng 腎 The kidneys, as in *nội sêng* 內腎 ; one of the five viscera.

Sêng 乘 A numerative of chariots ; also read *sìng*, q. v.

Sêng 剩 A remainder ; leavings in which sense *diông* is the coll. equivalent.

Sêng 慎 To be careful ; still, quiet : *sêng dẹ̆ung* 慎重 circumspect : COM., *gĭng sêng* 謹慎 careful.

Sḙng 雙, 双 A pair, two ; *sḙng hĭ*

雙喜 the character *hī* 喜 written double, 囍 as on bridal chairs, etc.; *sĕng săng* 雙生 twins: *sĕng buói* 雙倍 two-fold.

Sĕng 鬆 Read *sŭng*; coll. *sĕng*: not strict, easy, relaxed, loose, as in *buŏh dék sĕng* 縛的鬆 tied loosely; *sĭng iā sĕng* 心野鬆 the mind very easy about it.

Sĕu 搜 揝 To search as the police do; to investigate: *sĕu chĕk* 搜賊 to search a thief; *sĕu cŏng* 搜賍 to search for stolen goods.

Sĕu: A coll word: to mix, as water with flour to make dough; *sĕu tŭ-cióng*, to make mortar.

Sĕu 叟, An old man, a senior; Sire!

Sĕu 溲 To urinate; as in *sĕu biĕng* 溲便.

Séu 秀 Gay, splendid; to flourish; elegant; beautiful as a landscape; *séu máiu* 秀茂 green and charming, as fields; *chĭng séu* 清秀 finely chiseled, as the features.

Séu 繡, 绣 To embroider flowers, as in *séu huă* 繡花: COM., *séu buō* 繡補 to darn.

Séu 獸 A beast, a hairy brute: COM., *k'ing séu* 禽獸 birds and beasts; *iă séu* 野獸 wild beasts.

Séu: A coll. word: the nest of a bird; a lair: *èng ngiê séu*, an ants' nest.

Séu 宿 The stars: also read *séuk*, q. v.: COM., *nê sĕk báik séu* 二十八宿 the 28 zodiacal constellations; *séu miăng láung* 宿命論 fatalism.

Séu 首 To confess a crime; to acknowledge: also read *siŭ*, q. v.: COM., *chók séu* 出首 to inform against.

Sêu: A coll. word, frequently: habitually, as in *sèu-sèu-cŏ̤,* to do constantly.

Sèu: A coll. word: pure; uniform; smaller: *sèu sèu buô,* even, regular, steps; *sèu niă-ngi* a little smaller.

Sêu 壽 Age, longevity; *dòng sêu* 長壽 aged; *sêu só* 壽數 length of life; *bái sêu* 拜壽 to congratulate one on his birthday: *sêu ĭ* 壽衣 grave clothes; *sêu bēng* 壽板 coffin boards; *gŏ̤ sêu* 高壽 what is your age?

Sêu 受 To receive; a form of the passive, to suffer; a charge, a trust: *bók gāng sêu* 不敢受, I dare not accept it; *sêu siŏng* 受傷 injured, bruised; *sêu ké* 受氣 to become angry; *sêu cói* 受罪 or *sêu hìng* 受刑 to be punished; *sêu kū* 受苦 to suffer: COLL., *séu nèng ciek cié* 受伩節制 to be subject to another's control.

Séu 授 To give, to communicate: *séu séu* 受授 receiving and giving.

Séu 袖, 裏 The sleeve, the cuff: the 1st used for the coll. *uōng* and the second read *êu* q. v.: *līng séu, (liāng séu)* 領袖 "collar and sleeve"— a chief, one who commands; *séu chiū bòng guāng* 袖手旁觀 to fold the hands and look on.

Séu 思 To be anxious; to have pure intentions; also read *sṳ̆*, q. v.: COM., *é-séu* 意思 thoughts, intentions.

Séu 恕 Benevolent, indulgent; to excuse others; sympathizing: *ngièu séu* 饒恕 to excuse; *kuāng séu* 寬恕 lenient.

Séu 庶 A multitude, the people; all, as in *séu ŭk* 庶物 all things; nearly, about so.

Séu 試 To use; to experiment; a test: used for the coll. *ché* and *sé*, q. v.: *séu ngiêng* 試驗 an inquiry or examination.

Séu 使 A messenger; an agent: also read *sṳ̄* and in the coll. *sái*, q. v.: *chŏk séu* 出使, an envoy; *séu ciā* 使者 one sent; also used for angels.

Séu 四 肆 乂, Four; everywhere; the second is the complex, and the third the abreviated form: in the coll. read *sé*, q. v.: *séu huŏng* 四方 or *séu chệu* 四處 everywhere; *séu cṳ̆* 四書 the Four Books.

Séu 肆 To expand; great, large; reckless, a shop, a market as in *ché séu* 市肆; *huŏng-séu* 放

肆 profligate; *séu ngiòng* 肆言 an unbridled tongue.

Séu 賜, 錫 To confer, to bestow; a favor, a benefit: *siōng séu* 賞賜 a reward.

Séu: A coll. word, as in *tèng séu*, eaten by insects.

Séu 士 A learned man, a scholar; *séu, nùng, gŭng, siŏng,* 士農工商, literati, husbandmen, artizans, merchants.

Séu 仕 To act as a magistrate: an officer: *chók séu* 出仕 to assume office.

Séu 食飼飤 To rear, to nourish; food, provisions: also read *sĭk*, q. v.

Séu 伺 To wait upon, as in *séu háiu* 伺候.

Séu 嗣 To adopt; to inherit; heirs; hereafter, as in *séu háiu* 嗣後; *háiu séu* 後嗣 descendants.

Sëu 祀 To sacrifice to gods, devils, or departed spirits; a year: in the coll. read *sái: nguòng sëu* 元祀 the first year of a reign.

Sëu 樹, 树, 尌 A tree, plants in general; to plant, to set up: *sëu cṳ̄* 樹子 the heir apparent of a feudatory; *sëu lìng* 樹林 a grove, a forest; *sëu mŭk* 樹木, trees.

Sëu 豎 竖 To erect; to establish.

Sëu 嶼, 㠘 An island; detached hills near a shore; *gū láung sëu* 鼓浪嶼 the Island of Kulang-su, near Amoy.

Sëu 似 佀 Like, similar: *siŏng-sëu* 相似 to resemble each other.

Sëu 俟 竢 To wait; until; expecting.

Sëu 事 An affair; a matter; business, occupation; to serve; to obey: *cĕk sëu* 執事 a manager; a deacon; gă séu 家事 domestic affairs; dáung séu 當事 to regard as important: ng cié séu 怀際事 a very trifling amount.

Séu 序 A preface, as in séu tàu 序頭; chéu séu 次序 seriatim.

Séu 叙, 敍, 敘, To converse, as in séu dàng 叙談; ngié séu 議叙 to deliberate about (rewards).

Séuk 宿 A lodging place; to sojourn; former, old; moldy, musty, as food: also read séu, q. v.: COLL., séuk siŏh buŏ 宿一晡 to stay a night; gié séuk siá 寄宿舍 a dormitory.

Séuk 肅 Respectful, reverential; fear, caution, severe, majestic; ngièng séuk 嚴肅 awe inspiring. Read séu: pure, clear; reverential.

Séuk 淑 Good, excellent, virtuous,

Sêung 767

as in *séuk ìng* 淑人 a virtuous man.

Séuk 叔 Also read *céuk*, q. v.: an uncle; a father's younger brother; *séuk dìk* 叔姪 uncles and nephews: *lŏ séuk* 老叔 a father's old friend.

Séuk 粟 Grain, rice in the husk; rent in kind; tithes: *tù séuk* 鋤粟 produce of public fields paid as tax: COLL., *ĕng séuk huă* 鶯粟花, the poppy.

Séuk: A coll word: to become old, aged; mature, as grain; *săng dék séuk*, old looking.

Sêung 訟 To demand justice; legal strife; to sing, to chant: *sêung sù* 訟詞 an indictment; *téng sêung* 聽訟 to hear a case.

Sêung 誦 To hum, to recite over; to dispute, to culminate; *buói sêung* 背誦 to say memoriter.

Sê̤ṳng 頌 The countenance; easy, free, public; to laud, as in *sê̤ṳng cáng* 頌贊.

Sê̤ṳng 䘰 A coll. word: to put on clothes, as in *sê̤ṳng ĭ siòng* 䘰衣裳; *mò̤ nó̤h sê̤ṳng* 毛乜䘰 nothing to wear.

Sĭ 司 A commissioner, a manager; to control, to supervise; a township: also called *sṳ̆* and in the coll. *să*, q. v.: *tì huák sĭ* 持法司 the judicial commissioner; *páh guăng sĭ* 打官司 to go to law.

Sĭ 尸 A corpse; an effigy; *sĭ ôi* 尸位 a sinecure.

Sĭ 屍 A dead body: *sĭng sĭ* 身屍 or *sī sĭ* 死屍 or *sĭ-siū* 屍首 a corpse: *ngiêng sĭ* 驗屍 to hold an inquest.

Sĭ 鳲 The wood pigeon called *sĭ kiŭ* 鳲鳩 or *băng kiŭ* 班鳩.

Sĭ 絲 Silk; silken; fine, minute; a hundreth part, as of a cash; *tŭ sĭ* 土絲 native silk; *sĭ miêng* 綿絲 silk batting; *sĭ hò mò dâng* 絲毫毛鄭 not the least error.

Sĭ 詩 Poetry; an ode, a poem, a hymn: *sĭ gĭng* 詩經 the Book of Odes: *sĭ cŭ* 詩書 the classics.

Sī 死 Read *sŭ*; coll. *sī*: to die; death; deadly; dangerous; pale, ghastly: *sī sĭng* 死心 with intense desire; *sī lâi* 死賴 to involve one by suicide; *cháik sī* 慚死 death from fear or chagrin; *sī hìng* 死刑 death penalty.

Sī: A coll. euphonic prefix, as in *sī-sọ* to lock; *sī sạ* to wash.

Sì 時 Time; an hour; a season; an opportunity; to be, is, this; to see, to observe; at the beginning of a sentence, then, at that time; after a verb, as while, during: *séu sì* 四時 the four seasons: *bók dáik sì* 不得時 an unsuitable time: *sì hâiu* 時侯 time; *dŏng sì* 當時 at that time; *sì sék* 時式 or *sì iông* 時樣 or *sì hìng* 時形 the fashion; *sì céng* 時症 a pestilence; *sì káik* 時刻 incessantly; *sì siŏh tàu* 時一頭 one after another, speaking of animals; *sì siŏh ciáh* 時一隻 ditto, of people; *càng sì* 暫時 temporary; *sì găng* 時間 the times; *sì sié* 時勢 or *sì guŏh* 時局 present-day affairs; *sì pàng* 時評 comments on current events; *sì dài* 時代 a generation; *sì ệung* 時用 the present emergency; *sì ệu* 時譽 prestige.

Sì 蒔 Anise or dill: *mùi-sì (lì)* 莓蒔 the water chestnut. Read, *sê* to transplant.

Sìá 771

Sì: A coll. word: gradually, by degrees: *sì siŏh nĭk*, day after day.

Siā 賖 To buy or sell on credit, as in *siā só* 賖數; *siā gì uá* 賖其話 a surmise.

Siā 寫 To write, as in *siā cê* 寫字; to copy, as in *chău siā* 抄寫; *siā piĕ* 寫批 to write a letter.

Siā 捨 To relinquish; to renounce; to give, as in *Ià-Sŭ siā miâng* 耶穌捨命 Jesus gave his life: *siā ké* 捨棄 to waive.

Siā 舍 Also read *siá*, q. v.: to lodge, to dwell.

Siá 舍 A rest; a stage of 30 *lĭ*; a hospice: lodgings: my, as applied to junior relatives: also read *siā* q. v.: *siá dá* 舍弟 my younger brother: *siá ing mièu* 舍人廟 the name of a temple; *siá-há* 舍下 my humble lodgings.

Siá 卸, 卸 To lay aside; to vacate, as an office; in the coll., to sell off as goods: *siá éng* 卸印 to give up an office; *siá giĕng* 卸肩 to put down a load: *siá huó* 卸貨 to sell off goods.

Siá 瀉, 瀉 To drain land; to leak; a diarrhea; to purge: *siá dó* 瀉肚 dysentery; *báng siá* 病瀉 diarrhea; *báng tó-siá* 病吐瀉 cholera.

Sià 邪 Deflected; depraved; corrupting; illegal; illicit, as in *găng sià* 奸邪; *sià-gáu* 邪敎 heretical doctrines; *ké sià găi ciáng* 棄邪歸正 to reform.

Sià 斜 Distorted; aslant, oblique; *nĭk tàu sià* 日頭斜 the sun is declining; *sià ùng buó* 斜紋布 drillings.

Siá 社 The god of a locality, the *lares rustici;* a hamlet of 25 houses; *siá huói* 社會 society in general, an organized society; *siá-gău séng* 社交性 sociability; *siá huói céng cháik* 社會政策 socialism as a political platform; *siá huói ciŏ ngiê* 社會主義 socialism as a theory; *siá huói găi ngék* 社會階級 caste, social rank; *siá huói dōng* 社會黨 socialists.

Siá 射 To shoot with a bow; to cheat: in the coll. read *siŏh* q. v.: *īng siá* 影射 to implicate; *siá ōng dĕng* 射影燈 magic lantern; Read *ĭk* or *dó*: to dislike, to loathe.

Siá 榭 An arbor: a keep; a military school.

Siá 謝 To decline; to resign, as an office; to thank; to excuse one's self; *dŏ siá* 多謝 many thanks; *gāng siá* 感謝 to feel grateful; *siá cŏi* 謝罪 to confess a sin; *siá cióh* 謝借 thanks for the loan: *háng dŏ siá* 漢多謝 to express thanks.

Siáh 剔 Read *hiēng*; used in the *Báik-ĭng* for the coll. *siáh*: to shave with a knife.

Siăh 食 Read *sĭk*; coll. *siăh*: to eat, to drink; to smoke as in *siăh hŏng* 食煙; *siăh buŏng* 食飯 to take a meal; *siăh lĭk* 食力 fatigued; *siăh mặ dă* or *siăh mặ lì* cannot do it.

Siák 鏁 Read *sák*: similar to *tiák*: to blink, to wink; *mĕk siák* (or *tiák*) 目鏁 the eyelashes.

Siăk: A coll. word: to make a rattling sound.

Siăng 聲, 声 Read *sĭng*; coll. *siăng*: a voice, the tones of Chinese words; a word, a sentence: *siăng ĭng* 聲音 a voice, a sound; *miàng siăng* 名聲 reputation.

Siäng: A coll. word: perhaps a corruption of *chăng* 慘; sad, pitiable; ah! alas!

Siáng 線, 綫, Thread of silk, hemp or cotton; a fine cord; a line, beading; a clue, a trace: *hiŏng siáng* 香線 an incense stick; *siáng hiĕ* 線戲 a puppet play; *tọ̆ siáng* 討線 to seek a clue; *siáng siŏh cī* 線一只 a skein of silk; *cọ̆ siáng sóh* 做線索 to be a spy; *bĕk siáng* 扐線 to humbug; *gĭng-siáng* 經線 parallels of longitude; *hói siáng* 緯線 parallels of latitude; *ù siáng diêng* 無線電 wireless, radio.

Siáng 聖 Read *séng*: coll. *siáng*: propitious, efficacious; *mạ siáng* 賣聖 unpropitious.

Siàng 城 Read *sìng*; coll. *siàng*: a walled city; a city wall: *sēng siàng* 省城 the provincial capital: *siŏh cȯ̤ siàng* 一座城 a city.

Siàng 成 Read *sìng*; coll. *siàng*: to finish, to complete; to become; whole, entire; a tenth: *siàng huă* 成花 to close a bargain; *mạ siàng huă* 賣成花 unable to finish the matter; *ng siàng nẹng* 怀成仈 not to be a man, not capable, not honest.

Siàng 賤 Read *ciêng*; cheap, low in price: *siàng siàng* 賤賤 very cheap.

Siĕ 些 A little, few; trifling, unimportant; rather; also word of comparison: *siĕ sṳ̈* 些須 or *siĕ mì* 些微 a trifling amount.

Siĕ 施 A surname; a banner unfurled; to relieve, to bestow in charity; to permit; to use, to add to: in the coll. to scatter, to drop: also read *sié*, q. v.: *siĕ ŏng* 施恩 to bestow favors; *páh siĕ* 拍施 to scatter, as seeds, etc. Read *chiē*: to relax. Read *ê*: to remove; to transfer, to change.

Sié 晞 Read *iĕ*: The course of the sun; met., in the coll. to move by degrees: to move up, as a heavy article.

Sié 施 To give, to relieve: also *siĕ*, q. v.: *sié cá* 施濟 to give in charity; *sié céuk* 施粥 to distribute congee, as in a famine.

Sié 世, 吉 The world, mankind; times, life; hereditary: *sié sié* 世世 forever; *ké sié* 棄世 or *guó sié* 過世 to die; *chok sié* 出世 to be born; *sié sŭk* 世俗

the customs of the world; *sióh sié nęng* 一世仍 to the very end of life; *sié-gĭ* 世紀 century; *sié-gái guăng* 世界觀 the world view; *sié dại* 世代 an age, a generation.

Sié: A coll. word, for which the last is used in coll. books, as in *sié nóh* 世毛 (or *siẹ nóh*) what? what is it? *sié nóh miàng* 世毛名 what is the matter? what name?

Sié 賒 To get on trust; to borrow; *sié siá* 賒赦 to pardon, as criminals.

Sié 勢, 勢 Authority, station; rank, dignity; splendor; strength; virility: *sié lĭk* 勢力 power, influence; *viá sié* 藉勢 to rely on one's station, or influence, to injure others; *sié-lĭk kuŏng* 勢力圈 sphere of influence.

Siê 779

Siê: A coll. word: to add to, to piece out; to connect: to succeed one in a work: *siê tàu*, to piece out the end; *siê lŏh*, to add on to; continuous.

Siè 蛇 A serpent; serpentine; crooked, malicious, treacherous, subtile: *láu siè* 老蛇 snake; *săng siè tàu* 生蛇頭 to have a whitlow. Read *ì*: crooked; to squirm.

Siè 匙 A key; a spoon: *sṓ siè* 鎖匙 a key: *sṓ siè băh-lăh siŏh â* 鎖匙把拉一下 give the key a turn.

Siè 嗜 To delight in, to relish; *siè ciŭ* 嗜酒 addicted to wine; *siè dŭ* 嗜賭 fond of gambling.

Siè 誓 To swear, to take an oath: *huák siè* 發誓 to swear; *siè cṳ̆* 誓書 oath of office; vow.

Siè 逝 To depart, to pass away;

to die ; to void involuntarily ; *diòng siè* 長逝 gone forever.

Siè 豉 Salted eatables, as beans, etc., dried and used as relishes: *siè iù* 豉油 soy.

Siék 緤 To tie, to fasten ; to put in fetters ; a frame to keep a bow in shape.

Siék 絏 Interchanged with the last : bonds, fetters ; to tether, as animals.

Siék 洩, 泄 To leak ; to divulge, as secrets ; to diminish : *láiu siék gĭ-guăng* 漏洩機關, to divulge the whole scheme.

Siék : A coll. word, for which the last may be used; to disappear unaccountably, to spirit away : *kéyk gŭi siék ko̤* 乞鬼洩去 spirited away.

Siék 設 To institute, to found ; to set up ; to suppose ; large ;

Siëk 781

siék lĭk 設立 to establish; *siék ngiĕ ŏh* 設義學 to open a free school; *siék gié* 設計 to form a plot or plan; *siék sṳ* 設使 if, supposing that; *siék huák* 設法 to devise means; *siék siōng* 設想 to imagine, to picture to one's self.

Siék 屑 Pure, clear; diligent; respectful, observant; to reduce, to powder; minute.

Siék 褻 Undress, dishabille: *siék î* 褻衣 in undress, without one's coat on.

Siék: A coll. word, a corruption of *sê-siék*, forty; *siék-huói*, forty years old; *siék ĕk* forty-one; *siék-nê săng* forty-two or three.

Siĕk 舌 The tongue; the clapper of a bell; talkative, wordy; the 135th radical: *siĕk gĕng* 舌耕 "to plough with the tongue"

—to teach; *chói sièk* 嘴舌 the tongue; *gék sièk* 急舌 to stammer; *sièk giāng* 舌仔 the palate.

Sièk 涉 To implicate, as in *guāng sièk* 關涉; *gău sièk* 交涉 to negotiate; negotiations.

Sièk 折, Read *ciék*: to break; to snap in two; to lose in trade, as in *sièk buŏng* 折本; *páh sièk* 拍折 to break in two.

Sièng 仙 An old man who never dies; a fairy: *sièng dăng* 仙丹 the elixir of immortality; *sièng gīng* 仙境 elysium; *báik sièng* 八仙 the eight genii; *Sièng-iu-gáing* 仙遊縣 a district of Hinghwa prefecture.

Sièng 先 To precede; to go first; to begin; previous, formerly; past; late, deceased; in the coll. read *sĕng* and *sĭng*, q. v.;

cĕng sieng 爭先 to strive to be first; sieng sĕng 先生 a teacher; a physician; in case of address, Sir, Mr.; sieng háiu 先後 before and after; sieng dì 先知 a prophet; sieng ìng 先人 ancestors; sieng hō 先父 my late father. Read sieng: to put first.

Sieng 煽 Read sieng; used for the coll. sieng: to fan grain: hŭng sieng 風煽 a fanning mill.

Sieng 鮮 A live or fresh fish; clean, pure; also read sieng and coll. chieng q. v.

Sieng 鮮 Also read sieng, q. v.: few, rare: complete.

Sieng 癬 Tetter, ringworm; scale: used for chiāng in the coll. q. v.

Sieng 閃 To peep out of a door; to flash, as the lightning: sieng dieng 閃電 a flash of lightning.

Sieng 陝 The province of Shensi,

called *Siēng-să* 陝西; *siēng gǎng* 陝甘, the provinces of Shensi and Kansu. Also read *hŭk*: narrow.

Siēng 跣 To walk without shoes; *siēng céuk* 跣足 naked feet.

Siéng 扇 Leaves of a door; a fan, a screen; a section of the frame of a building: *tuàng siéng* 團扇 round fans painted or embroidered; *iák siéng* to use a fan.

Siéng 搧 To fan, to brush off.

Siéng 煽 A fierce fire; to fan a flame; *met.* to stir up sedition.

Siéng 騸 To graft, as in *siéng séu* 騸樹 to graft trees.

Siéng 醃 To salt, to lay in brine: *siéng nŭk* 醃肉 to salt pork.

Sièng 鹽, 盬, Salt; to salt: *sièng ló* 鹽滷 brine; *sièng mī* 鹽米 salt rice; *sièng diòng* 鹽場 salt yards or works.

Sièng 蟬 The cicada or broad locust.

Sièng 禪 To sit and meditate: *sièng sṳ̆* 禪師 a priest, an abbot; *sội sièng* 坐禪 to sit in deep meditation.

Sièng 嬋 Beautiful, graceful, as a woman.

Sièng 蟾 A striped toad, called *sièng dù* 蟾蜍.

Sièng 簷 The eaves: *hŭng sièng háung* 風簷桁 a heavy timber attached to the eaves to strengthen them.

Sièng 暹 As in *sièng-lò guók* 暹羅國 Siam.

Sièng 單 A famous chief of the Huns, called *sièng ṳ̆* 單于 B.C. 25. Also read *dăng*, q. v.

Sièng 善 Good; wise; gentle; great; clever: *sièng dáik* 善德 virtue: *sièng cŭng* 善終 a good end, a peaceful death: *họ siêng* 好善 to delight in doing good: *siêng liòng* 善良 good and gentle: *bók siêng* 不善 vicious, bad.

Siêng 鱔, 鱓 A kind of eel, as in *siêng ngṳ̀* 鱔魚.

Siêng 饍 Provisions, prepared food; delicacies: *cọ siêng* 早饍 breakfast.

Siêu 燒 To burn; to set fire to; to fry, to roast; distilled, as spirits: *siêu hūi* 燒火 to burn in the fire; *siêu nguá* 燒瓦 to burn tiles.

Siêu 蕭 A surname; *siêu iòng* 蕭然 troubled, agitated.

Siêu 簫 A sort of flute as in *siêu guōng* 簫管; *chūi siêu* 吹簫 to blow the flute.

Siêu 蠨 As in *siêu siêu* 蠨蛸 the name applied to several long-legged insects.

Siĕu 787

Siĕu 蛸 A kind of long legged spider: *hāi piĕu siĕu* 海鰾蛸 a cuttle fish.

Siĕu 消 To melt; to diminish, to annul; spent, as time; to digest, as in *siĕu huá* 消化; *siĕu miĕk* 消滅 to exterminate; *siĕu sĕk* 消息 news; *siĕu chèu gă móng* 消愁解悶 to dissipate one's melancholy: *tiŏng siĕu* 暢消 a good market for; *siĕu kiĕng* 消遣 to indulge in pastimes; *siĕu tàu* 消頭 salable; *siĕu dŭk iŏh* 消毒藥 disinfectant.

Siĕu 銷 To fuse, to melt metals; to finish, to exhaust: *siĕu gá* 銷假 to report one's self after a furlough; *siĕu áng* 銷案 to settle a case amicably; *siĕu huó* 銷貨 goods put into circulation; *siĕu họ ping* 銷耗品

luxuries; *siĕu lô* 鎖路 a market for goods; demand.

Siĕu 宵 Night, the night; *nguòng siĕu* 元宵 the full moon of the 1st month, the feast of lanterns (11th to the 15th day); *nguòng siĕu uòng* 元宵丸 feast-of-lanterns balls, made of rice.

Siĕu 硝 Nitre, saltpetre: *páuk siĕu* 朴硝 Epsom salts.

Siĕu: A coll. word, as in *siĕu mái*, small steamed bread cakes.

Siĕu 羞 Read *siū*; coll. *siĕu*, as in *siĕu lặ* 羞恥 shame, ashamed; *mặ hiĕu-dék siĕu lặ* 賣曉的羞恥 shameless, brazen faced.

Siĕu 小 Small; little; petty, mean; my, our; the 42nd radical: *siĕu sĭng* 小心 careful; *siĕu cūi* 小水 urine; *siĕu ĭng* 小人 a mean, unprincipled man;

siéu i 小兒 my son; *siéu gę̆ng* 小工 jobs; *siéu kŏ* 小可 unimportant; *siéu cụ̆ng* 小種 Souchong tea; *lŏ siéu* 老小 a wife.

Siéu 少 Little, few; rarely, seldom; in a slight degree; insufficient; to owe, as in *siéu kiéng* 少欠; also read *siéu*, and in the coll. *ciḕu* q. v.: *dŏ siéu* 多少 how many? *siéu ké* 少氣 miserly, avaricious, narrow minded; *siéu ciớng* 少將 major general.

Siéu 少 Juvenile; a youth: also read *siéu*, q. v.: *lŏ siéu* 老少 the old and young; *éu siéu* 幼少 tender, delicate; *siéu iè* 少爺 a young gentleman.

Siéu 肖 To assimilate, to be like: in the coll. read *sáiu*, q. v.: *bók siéu* 不肖 degenerate, as a son.

Siêu 鞘 A sheath, the scabbard of a sword. Read *său*: a whip.

Siêu 誚 To blame; to ridicule: used for *chiéu* 笑 (to scold), q. v.: *gĭ siêu* 譏誚 to satirize.

Siêu 韶 An ancient musical instrument.

Siêu: A coll. word: to seesaw.

Siêu 召 Used as a surname and name of a place: also read *diêu*, q. v.

Siêu 邵 A surname; high, eminent in virtue and character: *Siêu-ŭ-hŭ* 邵武府 Shao-wu, a department in the N. W. of Fukien.

Siêu 紹 To connect, to tie: *gái siêu* 介紹 an agent or assistant; to introduce. Read *siêu*: slow, dilatory.

Siêu A coll word: to desire greatly: *siêu sẹụng*, fond of dress;

tăng siéu, to regard admiringly.

Sĭk 襲 Hereditary, as in *sié sĭk* 世襲.

Sĭk 什 Various, sundry: *sĭk ŭk* 什物 things, articles; *sĭk ké* 什器 chattels, utensils.

Sĭk 值 To happen, to occur: also read *dĭk* and in the coll. *dĕk* and *dĭh*, q. v.: *gá sĭk* 價值 position, standing.

Sĭk 埴 Adhesive clay.

Sĭk 殖 To plant; to grow; to amass, as riches: *sĭk huó* 殖貨 to amass, greedy of gain; *sĭk mìng dê* 殖民地 a colony; *sĭk mìng cháik* 殖民策 colonization (as a policy).

Sĭk 植 To plant; to transplant, to set out.

Sĭk 夕 The evening, dusk: the last day, as of the year; the 36th radical: *diêu sĭk* 朝夕

morning and evening.

Sĭk 汐 The evening tide, high tide at sunset.

Sĭk 席 A mat to sleep on; a table, a repast: *siék sĭk* 設席 to spread a feast; *iéng sĭk* 宴席 a banquet: *lìng sĭk* 臨席 a soirée, a levee; *chók sĭk* 出席 to take the floor (parliamentary).

Sĭk 蓆 A mat spread to eat on: a meal, a table; rest, quiet; used for the coll. *chiŏh* q. v.

Sĭk 食 To take food, to eat; to drink; to smoke; to retract; to receive; to delude: the 184th radical: also read *séu* and in the coll. *siăh*, q. v.: *ĭng sĭk* 飲食 to drink and eat; *huōi sĭk* 伙食 daily food, provisions. Read *sék*: an eclipse.

Sĭk 石 A stone, a rock; stony, rocky; hard, firm; a dry and liquid measure; a measure of ten *dāu* or pecks; the 112th radical: in the coll. read *siŏh* q. v.

Sĭk 習 Skilled in; use, custom, habit, as in *sĭk guáng* 習慣, fixed as to habit; *sĭk ngiĕk* 習業 a business; *hŏk sĭk* 學習 a learner.

Sĭk 拾 To gather; to dispose in order: also read *sĕk* and used for *kák* in the coll. q. v.: *siŭ sĭk* 收拾 to put in order.

Sĭk 實,寔,实, Real, solid; settled, compact as ground: true, sincere, honest as in *lō̤ sĭk* 老實; *sĭk cái* 實在 truly, really; *dê sĭk* 地實 the ground is settled; *sĭk géu* 實據 good proof: *giĕk sĭk* 結實 to bear fruit: *sĭk hèng* 實行 to carry through, to accomplish; *sĭk ngiĕk tiăng* 實業廳 a commissioner of industry.

Sĭng 身 The body; the trunk: *met.*, the main part of a thing; I, myself, one's self; 158th radical; *sĭng-tā* 身體 the body; *sĭng sié* 身勢 personal bearing; *buŏng sĭng* 本身 one's self; COLL., *sioh sĭng tiáng,* 一身痛 ache all over: *ô sĭng sié* 有身勢 and *mò sĭng sié* 無身勢 can and cannot.

Sĭng 娠 The foetus; to be pregnant; *sĭng hĭ* 娠喜 (or *dái sĭng*) pregnant: *lŏh sĭng* 落娠 abortion; miscarriage, also called *siĕu sāng* 小產 untimely birth.

Sĭng 媳 Read *sék;* used for the coll. *sĭng* as in *sĭng mô* 媳婦 a daughter-in-law, a bride.

Sĭng 心, 忄, 㣺, The physical heart; the mind; the affections; the will; *met.*, the center; the inside of; intention, desire;

Sĭng 795

the 61st radical; *nŏi sĭng* 內心 in the heart, the heart, the mind; *sĭng síng* 心性 the disposition; *sĭng é* 心意 thought, intention; *sĭng-sṳ̆ ngiòng-háing* 心思言行 the thoughts, words and actions; *liòng sĭng* 良心 a good heart, conscience; *sĭng kiéu* 心竅 the mind, intellect; clever, astute; *sĭng hṳ̆* 心虛 timid; *sṳ̆ sĭng* 私心 selfish; *ngáing sĭng* 硬心 a stubborn will; *sĭng ciĕu* 心焦 bashful, distressed in mind; *mò̤-sĭng-sèu* no heart for it; *sĭng lĭ* 心理 inclination, taste predilection.

Sĭng 星 A star, a planet as in *hĕng sĭng* 行星: *ngū sĭng* 五星 the planets, viz., *cūi sĭng* 水星 Mercury; *gĭng sĭng* 金星 Venus, *huō sĭng* 火星 Mars, *mŭk sĭng* 木星 Jupiter, and *tū sĭng* 土星

Saturn; *chék sǐng* 七星 the Pleiades; *sǐng gǐ* 星期 a week; *niák muói sǐng* 閃尾星 a firefly.

Sǐng 勝 To bear; able to assume; worthy of: also read *séng* q. v.

Sǐng 醒 Also read *sīng*: to recover from intoxication; to arouse or bestir one's self; used for the coll. *chāng*, q. v.: *cói sǐng* 醉醒 to recover from a debauch; *sǐng sié* 醒世 to arouse the age.

Sǐng 鋥 Also spoken *chǐng*, rust, tarnish; *sāng sǐng* 生鋥 to rust.

Sǐng 升 A dry measure, formerly made to hold a catty of rice; a Chinese pint; to advance, to rise in office: in the coll. read *cǐng* q. v.: *sǐng tiĕng* 升天 to ascend to heaven.

Sǐng 陞 To ascend, as stairs; promoted in office: *sǐng siông* 陞上 to take a higher seat; *gǒ sĭng* 高陞 to rise in office: *sĭng kī* 陞起 said to raise the poles when entering a sedan.

Sĭng 先 Read *siĕng*: coll. *sĭng*, as in *sĭng săng* 先生 a teacher, Sir; Mr; a physician; *sĭng-săng-nìòng* 先生娘 Lady; Mrs.

Sĭng 辛 Pungent: acrid, bitter; met., grievous, bitter, toilsome: the 160th radical: *sĭng kū* 辛苦 distressed, wearied, fagged.

Sĭng 新 New and fresh as in *sĭng siĕng* 新鮮 the latest, the best; *sĭng lòng* 新郎 and *sĭng ìng* 新人 bridegroom and bride; *sĭng ùng cāi* 新聞紙 a newspaper.

Sĭng 聲, 声, A sound, a noise: a voice, a tone; music; fame, reputation: in the coll. read *siăng* q. v.: *sĭng ké* 聲氣 harmony, congeniality of spirit.

Sĭng 申 To extend; to stretch,

as from fatigue; to reiterate as in *sīng mìng* 申明, to state clearly: *sīng cūi* 申水 a premium on silver.

Sīng 伸 To straighten, to stretch out; to stretch and yawn; *sīng ùng* 伸文 a statement: *sīng uŏng* 伸冤 to redress a wrong.

Sīng 紳 A sash; to gird; those who may wear sashes, the gentry as in *hiŏng sīng* 鄉紳 or *sīng gái* 紳界.

Sīng 省 To examine, to inspect; watchful; a fault; also read *sēng*, q. v.: *sīng chák* 省察 (also spoken *sēng chák*), to examine.

Sīng 沈 A surname: also read *tìng* q. v.

Sīng 審 To investigate, to search into; to discriminste *sīng óng* 審問 a judicial inquiry; *sīng áng* 審案 to try a case: *sīng*

· Sìng 799

puáng 審判 to decide a case.

Sìng 嬸 The wife of a father's younger brother: *mū* and *sīng*, terms by which wives of older and younger brothers call each other respectively.

Sìng 稔 Read *ing*: ripe grain; abundant, as in *sīng nièng* 稔年 an abundant year.

Sìng 辰 A Chinese hour, the twelfth of a day: the hour from 7 to 9 A. M.; times, seasons; the 161st radical: *sì sìng* 時辰 a Chinese hour.

Sìng 晨 Day, dawn; clear, bright: *sìng sĭk* 晨夕 morn and eve; *cō̤ sìng* 早晨 early dawn.

Sìng 成 To finish, to effect; to aid in effecting; good, entire: used for the coll. *siàng* and *chiàng*, q. v., in which sense the latter means to nourish: *sìng-cêu* (coll. *siàng céu*) 成就 effected, done; *sìng dǐng* 成丁 of age, 16 years old.

Sìng 誠 Truthful, sincere, as in *sìng sĭk* 誠實; guileless: as an adverb, really, verily.

Sìng 城 A walled city; a provincial capital; in the coll. read *siàng*, q. v.

Sìng 盛 To receive, to contain in a vessel; perfected, completed; also read *sêng*, q. v., in which sense it is used as a surname.

Sìng 尋,鱘, To seek, to search for; as in *sìng tọ̆* 尋討 to investigate; *sìng mậ diŏh* 尋賣着 can't find it.

Sìng 蠅 A house-fly; *met.*, a busy-body; *bù sìng* the common house-fly.

Sìng 蟳 A species of crab having a round shell.

Sìng 神 Any invisible, spiritual power or cause; a spirit, the human spirit or mind; a God; a genius; term used by some for God, by others for the Spirit: *sìng lìng* 神靈 spiritual, intellectual: *sìng sṳ* 神思 thoughts; *sìng-mìng bù-sák* 神明菩薩 a common term for idols; *sìng-cū-bà* 神主牌 ancestral tablets; *eung sìng* 用神 to give the mind to; *Séng Sìng* 聖神 the Holy Spirit.

Sìng 臣 A servant; a minister of a prince; to serve the state; the 131st radical: *sìng-cū* 臣子 an officer.

Sìng 承 To receive; to accept a trust; to act as deputy, as in *sìng chă* 承差; *sìng nèng* 承認 to acknowledge; *sìng hèng* 承行 a go-between, agent.

Sìng 乘 To multiply; to plan, to regulate: also read séng, q. v.

Siŏ 輸 Read sṳ̆: to lose, to be beaten: siŏ iàng 輸贏 to lose and to win.

Siô: A coll. word: to spread under; siô â-dā̤ to spread below.

Sióh 削 Read siók: coll. sióh: to cut, to mince, to slice up; sióh sióh piéng 削一片 to cut off one slice.

Sióh 射 Read siá; coll. sióh: to shoot an arrow as in sióh ciéng 射箭; to dart, as rays.

Sióh 石 Read sĭk: coll. sióh, a rock; stony, petrified; a dry and liquid measure of about 120 catties, or about 160 lbs. avoirdupois; also a measure of two hù or about 11 dāu 斗; hiék sióh 熻石 a magnet; sióh gŏ 石膏 gypsum; sióh nṳ̆

石女 a barren woman; *băh siŏh* 白石 white granite; *chăng siŏh* 青石 dark granite; *dù-cṳ̆ siŏh* 圖書石 agalmatolite, used for seals, etc.

Siŏh 一 Read *ék;* coll. *siŏh:* the numeral one; the same, alike; as in *siŏh iông* 一件; a, an; the whole: *met.,* sincere, perfect; single, one by one; at once; *siŏh ciáh* 一隻 one, referring to persons or things: *siŏh á* 一下 once, a while; *siŏh dói* 一塊 one piece, one dollar; *siŏh-dék-giăng* 一滴仔 a small quantity; *siŏh sì cĭ găng* 一時之間 a moment; for a brief time.

Siŏh: A coll. word, as in *siŏh màng,* 一明 yesterday; *siŏh-màng-buŏ* 一明晡 last night.

Siŏh: A coll. word: similar to *chiŏh:* to start, to spring, to leap over or forward as in *siŏh quó*.

Siók 削 To cut, to pare, to shave; to despoil, to seize another's territory; a graving tool, an eraser: in the coll. read *siŏh*, q. v.

Siók 雪 Snow; to whiten; to wash clean; to wipe out; to clear one's self; to revenge as in *siók háung bó-siù* 雪恨報仇; *siók tī* 雪恥 to revenge disgrace.

Siók 說 To say, to talk, to discourse about; to unfold a meaning: also read *suói* q. v.: *iĕng siók* 演說 to lecture: *siĕu siók* 小說 a novel; *gă siók* 解說 to explain.

Siŏng 襄 To effect, to accomplish; to animate, to assist: upper, superior: *siŏng cáng* 襄贊 to encourage by praise.

Siŏng 鑲 To inlay, to enchase; to coat, or plate with metal; to set as a gem, etc.; *siŏng bŏ-là* 鑲玻璃 to set glass; *siŏng nguŏh* 鑲玉 to inlay with precious gems.

Siŏng 傷 To wound, to injure; as in *siŏng hâi* 傷害 a wound; grieved as in *siŏng sĭng* 傷心; *siŏng buŏng* 傷本 impairs the capital—to sell so low.

Siŏng 殤 An untimely death, as of one under 19 years of age.

Siŏng 相 To examine, to inspect; reciprocal; often denotes a reflective form of the verb: also called *siŏng*, and in the coll. *sŏng* q. v.: *siŏng sẹu* 相似 similar; *siŏng gẹung* 相近 contiguous: *mò siŏng găng* 無相間 no matter, vain, worthless.

Siŏng 箱 A box, a trunk of leather, wood or bamboo; a casket; *siŏng lęng* 箱籠 a bamboo travelling chest.

Siōng 商, 謫 To consult, to deliberate; to trade; a merchant from abroad as in *káh siōng* 客商; *siŏng gái* 商界 merchants in general; *siŏng tuàng* 商團 associated chambers of commerce; *siŏng biĕu* 商標 a trade mark.

Siōng 上 Also read *sióng*, q. v.: to ascend, to go up; to insert; to advance; to esteem highly; to exalt, to honor.

Siōng 鯗 Dried fish as in *ngṳ̀ siōng* 魚鯗.

Siōng 賞 To give, to an inferior; to grant, as heaven does; to reward; a reward as in *siōng-sé̤ṳ* 賞賜.

Siōng 想 To think; as in *sṳ̆ siŏng*

想思; an idea; *kĕng siōng* 空想 a vain idea; *siōng muô* 想慕 to long for; *siōng kī* 想起 to recollect.

Sióng 相 To assist, to support; a prime minister as in *cāi sióng* 宰相; *ciòng sióng* 將相 an admiral; to choose, to lead; to observe times; palmistry; *káng sióng* 看相 to tell fortunes: also read *siōng* q. v.

Siòng 常 Usual, ordinary; habitual; a rule, a law: *bàng siòng* 平常 common: *ngū siòng* 五常 the five constant virtues; *siòng siòng* 常常 constantly; *hī siòng* 非常 unusual; *ciéu siòng* 照常 as usual, customary; *siòng liê* 常例 a standing regulation.

Siòng 裳 As in *ī-siòng* 衣裳 clothing, the dress, garments.

Siòng 甞,嘗,嚐. To taste, to test

by tasting, as in *ché siòng* 試嘗; *siòng ùng* 嘗聞 I have heard.

Siòng 償 To restore, restitution; to pay, to forfeit one's life as in *siòng miáng* 償命.

Siòng 痒 Also read *iòng*; a sore, an ulcer: also read *iōng* q. v.: *siòng siòng* 痒痒 a tickling sensation.

Siòng 祥 Happiness, felicity, good luck; an omen: *dĭng siòng* 禎祥 excellent; *gék siòng ù é* 吉祥如意 good fortune according to one's wish; *bók siòng* 不祥 unlucky.

Siòng 詳 To examine carefully; to narrate minutely; the details; minutely, as in *siòng-sá* 詳細; *siòng máeng* 詳夢 to interpret a dream. Read *iòng*: false, hypocritical.

Siòng 旋還 To revolve as in *siòng*

lùng 旋輪; to pursue; then, forthwith: in the coll. to creep; to climb, to trail: as in *siòng dìng* 旋藤 a vine: the second also read *huāng* q. v.: *siòng hŭng* 旋風 a whirlwind; *siòng cūi* 旋水 a whirlpool; *siòng có siòng cuòk* 旋做旋輟 to do by fits and starts.

Siông 上, Above, up; on, upon; the top of; ancient; before in time; excellent, the best; noble, exalted; supreme; also read *siōng* q. v.: *siòng hă* 上下 above and below, up and down; *siòng tiĕng* 上天, to go to heaven; *tiĕng siòng* 天上 in the sky; *siòng chiŭ* 上手 formerly; *siòng ngū* 上午 (coll. *siòng dáu*), forenoon; *siòng sié* 上勢 above; *siòng hŭ* 上府, *siòng diŏ* 上路 interior of a province, up-river.

Siông 尙 High, noble; to honor; to esteem; a surname; still, yet, as in *siông chiā* 尙且 nevertheless; probably, perhaps, as in *siông kọ* 尙可; *siông ū cĭng-sìng* 尙武精神 militarism.

Siông 癢 Read *iŏng;* used for the coll. *siông:* to itch: *céng siông* 靜癢 it itches intensely.

Siŭ 收, 収 To take, to receive; to gather, to harvest, as in *siŭ dĕng* 收冬; *siŭ sìng* 收成 a harvest; *siŭ piĕng* 收編 to incorporate (as troops) into an army; *siŭ diŏng* 收轉 to withdraw (a proposal).

Siŭ 讐, 雔, 仇: To oppose; to hate, to dislike; an enemy as in *siŭ dĭk* 仇敵; to recriminate as in *siŭ kẹu* 仇口; the third also means proud, and is sometimes read *giù* in the sense of to unite; a pair, a match; *siù héung* 仇釁 hatred, resentment; *bó siù* 報仇 to take revenge; *siù sê* 仇視, to regard as an enemy.

Siù 售 Also read *siū*, and *sêu*: to sell, to dispose of by sale.

Siù 泅 As in *siù cūi* 泅水 to swim.

Só 數数數, An account; a shop-bill; to count up; a number; destiny, as in *tiĕng-só* 天數 Heaven's decree: also read *sáuk*, q. v. Read *sŭ*; to count; to find fault, to blame: (math) *dói só* 對數 logarithms; *dâi-só* 代數 algebra; *hiĕng só* 現數 coefficient; *buôi só*, 背數 multiple; *dēng só*, 點數 factor; *dăng só, sĕng só*, odd, even numbers; *hăk só*, product; *cūng só*, sum; *siēu só*, decimal; *mêng hông só*, vulgar fraction.

Só 訴愬 To inform, to announce;

a defense; to detract, calumny; the second read *sáuk*, to fear; alarmed; *gó só* 告訴 to relate, to inform.

Só 遡, 溯, 沂, To go against the current; to meet or go against; formerly: *só hùi* 溯回 to go against the stream; *só iù* 溯由 to go with the tide.

Só 塑 To shape; to model in clay; molded: *só chiông* 朔像 to mold images; *tù só mŭk dĕu* 土朔本雕 molded clay and carved wood, as idols; *met.*; stupid, doltish.

Sŏ 素 Plain, unadorned; empty, all gone; the original state; formerly, as in *bìng sŏ* 平素 habitually; *sŏ siòng* 素常 usually; also read *sáuk*.

Sṳ̆ 梭 A shuttle; swift, as a shuttle; *nĭk nguŏk ṳ̀ sṳ̆* 日月

如梭 days and months (pass) like a shuttle. Read *cóng:* the name of a kind of wood.

Sở 唆 To incite, to instigate, as in *tiều sở* 挑唆 to sow discord; *lỏ sở* 囉唆 troublesome, vexatious.

Sở 莎 A triquetrous plant with hairy roots called *hều sở* 喉莎 a sort of cyprus. Read *să*, as in *să giẻ* 莎鷄 a species of cricket.

Sở 搔 To scratch, to scrape with the nails; to set at variance. Read *cuā:* the nails, the claws.

Sở 騷 To rub down a horse: to agitate; sad; grieved, distressed, as in *lỏ sở* 牢騷.

Sở 臊 Rancid, rank: strong, reeking: also read *chở* q. v.

Sở: A coll. word: a sharp, pungent taste; to smart.

Sở: A coll. word: to eat as ducks

and other broad-billed birds do.

Só: A coll. word; to darn; to mend by darning.

Só 嫂 An elder brother's wife as in *hiăng só* 兄嫂; *ĭ-só* 伊嫂 good woman!

Só 掃 To sweep, to brush away; a broom, a besom; to dampen, as one's ardor or hopes: also read *suā* and in the coll., *sáu* q. v.

Só 鎖, 鏁 A lock; to fetter; to frown: *só siè* 鎖匙 a key; *só muòng* 鎖門 to lock a door.

Só: A coll. word: a sort of inter-laced stitching; *só siáng*, silk thread for binding.

Só 燥 Dry, scorched; to dry by the fire, to absorb: *găng só* 乾燥 dry, parched; *gŏ só* 高燥 high and dry, as a locality; *só dă* 燥乾 to dry by absorbing (the moisture).

Só 譟 The noise of a crowd; a disturbance, a hubbub.

Só 躁 To go quickly; *pèu-só* 浮躁 unsteady, fickle.

Sò 槽 Read *cò*: coll *sò*; 槽 a trough; *cūi-sò*, 水槽 an eaves trough; *pŭng-sò*, a swill trough; *mā-sò* 馬槽 a manger.

Sóh 索 Read *sáuk*; coll *sóh*: a rope, a string: *chāu-sóh*, 草索, grass cord; *cĕng-sóh* 棕索, palm coir ropes; *páh sóh*, 拍索 to twist rope.

Sóh 嗽 Read *chéuk*; used in the *Báik-ing* 八音 for the coll *sóh*: to suck, to cup; *sóh nèng*, 嗽仗 to draw out the pus, as a plaster does; *sóh chói*, 嗽嘴 to suck with the mouth; *sóh háik mā-kì*, 嗽血馬蜞 a leech, a blood-sucker; *met.*, one who cheats another out of money.

Sŏh 鐲 Bracelets, anklets; COLL., *chiū sŏh* 手鐲 a bracelet; *kă sŏh* 胶鐲 anklets. Read *cŏk*: small bells, used for army signals.

Sŏh, A coll word, as in *sŏh-nĭk*, day before yesterday; *sŏh-nièng* or *sŏh-nièng-màng*, the year before last.

Sŏi 衰 To fade, as a garment; old, worn out; lean, emaciated; unprosperous; *sŏi-sié* 衰世 a vicious age; *sŏi muô* 衰暮, the evening of life; *sŏi-iŏk*, 衰弱, debilitated; *sŏi-mì* 衰微, failing, wasting away; *sŏi-ôi* 衰位, an unlucky place, as in a game.

Sŏi 蓑 Read *sŏ* in the dictionaries; a rain cloak of bamboo or palm leaves; *sŏi-lĭk* 蓑笠 a rain cloak and hat.

Sŏi 睡 To sleep; to doze, to nod and snooze, as in a chair.

Sói 穗 An ear of corn, a spike of wheat or any grain; elegant, graceful: *sói giék sìk*, 穗結實 the heads have kernels.

Sói 繸 A fringe, a tassel, any bordering of threads: *siáng-sói* 線繸 a thread tassel; *ciŏ sói* 珠繸, a bead fringe.

Sói 祟 Calamities, as in *guái sói* 怪祟 monstrous calamity:

Sói 遂 To follow, to yield; then, forthwith; a canal or sluice for irrigation; *sói-é* 遂意 or *sói nguông* 遂願, according with one's wishes.

Sói 瑞 A stone signet, or sign of authority, given to a feudatory; a sign, a token; auspicious; felicitous as in *siòng sói* 詳瑞.

Sói 燧 A sun-glass; *huŏ sói* 火燧 a match.

Sṍi 帥 A general, a leader; to lead: also read *sáuk*, q. v.: *ciòng sṍi* 將帥 a general; *nguòng sṍi* 元帥 a generalissimo.

Sṍi 坐 Read *cō̤*; coll. *sṍi*: to sit, to be seated; to sit in judgment: *sṍi sṍi* 坐坐 to sit; just sit! *chiāng sṍi* 請坐 please be seated; *sṍi dòng* 坐堂 to sit in judgment; *sṍi că* 坐齋 to be a schoolmaster.

Sók 束 To bind in a bundle; to coerce: *sók siŭ* 束修 or *sók gĭng* 束金 a teacher's stipend; *guāng sók* 管束 to restrain those under one; *iók sók* 約束 to bind by contract.

Sók 速 Quick; quickly as in *sók sók* 速速; hastily: *sók ngŭk* 速玉 hasten your precious steps, and *sók gáung* 速降 descend soon,—terms on cards of invitation: *sók sìng* 速成 quickly accomplished: *sók-gé huák* 速記法 stenography; *sók gé ìng* 速記人 stenographer.

Sók 恤, 卹, 䘏, To feel pity for; sympathy, sorrow for: *tā-sók* 體恤 to pity and assist; *sók guā* 恤寡 to relieve widows; *cīng sók* 賑恤 to give alms to; *ū-sók* 撫恤 to soothe.

Sók 戌 This must be distinguished from *séu* 戍 (to guard frontiers): the 11th of the 12 branches, denoted by a dog; the fall of the year: *sók nguŏk* 戌月 the 9th moon; *sók sì* 戌時 or *sók káik* 戌刻, 7—9, P. M; *sók ciáng* 戌正, 8 P. M.

Sók 抄 Read *sŏ*; used for the coll. *sŏk*: to stroke, to rub gently with the hand: *muŏ sŏk* 摸抄 to soothe by stroking; *sŏk siŏh* á 抄一下 give it a gentle rubbing.

Sŏk: A coll. word: to paint, smear: *sŏk làng*, to paint a blue color.

Sŏng 桑 The mulberry tree; met., peaceful retirement: *sŏng cṳ̄* 桑梓 one's native village; *sŏng ciĕ* 桑枝, and *sŏng băh* 桑白 mulberry twigs and root-bark, used for medicine.

Sŏng 孫 A surname; a grandchild; *sŏng-nṳ̄* 孫女 a granddaughter; *nguói sŏng* 外孫 (coll. *ngiĕ-sĕng sŏng* 外甥孫) a daughter's son; *cĕng-sŏng* 曾孫, *nguòng sŏng* 元孫 and *lài sŏng* 來孫, the three generations after "grandson". Read *sáung*: mild, complaisant.

Sŏng 相 Read *siŏng*; coll. *sŏng:* mutually, reciprocally: by turns; *sŏng-huò* 相和 agreeing,

Sŏng 821

in accord: *sŏng nióng* 相讓 mutually yielding; *sŏng páh* 相拍 to fight; *sŏng siăh* 相食 adhering; welded; *sŏng kiă* 相跨 to strive to get the advantage of each other; *sŏng dĕng* 相同 alike.

Sŏng 商 Read *siöng*: coll. *sŏng*, as in *sŏng liòng* 商量 to consult, to deliberate: *siöng cìng* 商情 prices current; *siöng ciéng* 商戰 competition in trade; *siöng huôi* 商會 chamber of commerce; *siöng buô* 商埠 towns open to trade.

Sŏng 霜 Hoarfrost, rime; frigid: coll: *sŏng-ŭi* 霜威 stern, majestic; *sŏng siók* 霜雪 frost and snow; *lŏh sŏng* 落霜, frosty.

Sŏng 孀 A widow, called *sŏng-hó* 孀婦; *gŭ-sŏng* 孤孀 orphans and widows; a lone widow.

Sŏng 酸 Sour, acid; harsh, irritating; afflicted: sŏng-guŏ 酸果 pickles; sŏng ê 酸味 a sour or acid taste; sŏng-cō gŏ 酸棗膏 a sour date jelly; dèng sŏng liŏh, verdigris.

Sŏng 痠 In pain; aching, as from fatigue: chiū sŏng niōng 手痠軟 the hands aching and weak; COLL., sŏng nē aching as from toil.

Sŏng 朘 Shriveled, as flesh; puckered, contracted; to diminish, to reduce by oppression.

Sŏng 娑, 喪, To mourn for the dead, funereal; mourning, as in sŏng sêu 喪事, a funeral: also read, sáung q. v.: sŏng hŭk, 喪服 mourning dress: chŏk sŏng 出喪 to inter.

Sŏng 宣 To proclaim, to publish by authority; to summon, as

Sōng 823

rulers do; slow: *sŏng diòng* 宣傳 to promulge; *sŏng diêu* 宣召 to summon, as to court.

Sōng: A coll. word: to bolt, to bar a door; to shove a bolt as in *sŏng diē; sŏng gīng,* bolt it fast; *áng sŏng,* a secret bolt.

Sŏng 損 To diminish, to wound; damage, bad luck; the 41st diagram; *sŏng bái* 損敗 ruined; *siŏng sŏng* 傷損 wounded; *sŏng hái* 損害 to injure, hurtful; *sōng céng* 損症 a wasting disease.

Sōng 選 To choose, to elect; as in *sōng gū* 選舉; to cull; to select men for office; a moment; one hundred thousand; timid, apprehenssive: *sōng dĕk* 選擇 to choose; *sōng găng* 選間 or *siêu sōng* 少選 an instant; *gĕng sōng* 揀選 to elect; *sōng ciòng* 選將 to select a leader. Read *sáung*

824 Sóng

言 to reckon: also used for *sáung*, yielding; *sáung nọ* 選懦 weak, vacillating; *sōng gṳ̄ guòng* 選舉權 elective franchise.

Sōng 爽 To admit the light; light, cheerful; easy, comfortable, healthy as in *sōng kuái* 爽快: impetuous; *sōng iók* 爽約 to fail in an engagement; *sōng sék* 爽失 to lose, to miss; *sōng kēu*, 爽口 palatable: *sōng chuói* 爽脆 quick, ready.

Sōng 礎 The stone base or plinth of a pillar: *sōng buàng* 礎盤 the base of a post (under the *téu-ciŏ* 柱珠, or carved plinth).

Sōng 顙 The forehead, the front of the head: *yuōng-sōng* 廣顙 a broad or high forehead.

Sóng 舜 An ancient monarch; called *ngṳ̀-sóng* 虞舜 B.C. 2255; in posthumous titles, it means sage, holy, intelligent: *Sóng dá* 舜帝 or *dá Sóng* 帝舜, the emperor Shun.

Sóng 宋 A surname: to dwell, to reside; dwelling: the name of a famous dynasty A. D. 970—1280; also a shorter one, A. D. 420—477: in the coll. read *sáęng*, q. v.

Sóng 送, 送 To give, to present; to go or send with; to escort; to see a guest out; a gift, a present: in the coll. read *sáęng* q. v.: *sáęng séng buô* 送信簿 a chit book.

Sóng: A coll. word, as in *sóng-sóng*, to do readily as others say; raw, verdant, credulous; *sóng-sóng gŭng ĭ kó*, has verdantly followed him away.

Sòng 甑 Read *cáing:* used for the coll. *sòng:* a wooden rice steamer, called *buông sòng* 飯甑; *chŭi sòng* 炊甑, a steamer with a fixed grate or rack in the bottom.

Sòng: A coll. word: to smart; a pungent, local pain; to cause to smart: *ậ sòng*, it prickles, it smarts; *ậ sòng nẹng*, it will make one smart.

Sông 順 To accord with, to agree to; to obey, to acquiesce, to yield; harmonizing: convenient; at hand; fair, as the wind or tide; flowing, as style; free, easy, as penmanship: *báik sông* 百順, agreeing in every respect; *sông kēu* 順口, palatable; *háu-sông* 孝順, filial: *sông hŭng sông cūi* 順風順水 with wind and tide.

Sŭ 酥 A preparation of curd; butter, as made in the north;

tender, crisp, flaky, as crust: *sŭ ciŭh sŭ* 酥隻酥 very crisp.

Sŭ 穌 甦 To collect grain; to take; to cease, to enjoy ease; to resuscitate, to revive: a resurrection: *Ià-Sŭ* 耶穌 Jesus.

Sŭ, 蘇, 蘓 A surname; a sort of sage or clary; to revive, cheerful; to cease, to rest; to agitate: *Sŭ-ciŭ* 蘇州, Soochow; *Sŭ-Hòng ciŭ* 蘇杭州 Soochow and Hangchow. Read *só*: to meet, to come in conflict with.

Sŭ 鯂 A monastery, a convent, a nunnery.

Sŭ 蔬 A general term for vegetables and edible herbs, as in *sŭ chái*, 蔬菜.

Sŭ 疏, 踈, 跩, 疎, Open, wide apart; sleazy, as cloth; remiss, careless; easy, free, generous; distantly related; to partition, to engrave; to paint; to discard: also read *sáe* and in the coll. *sĕ*: *chĭng sŭ* (or *sĕ*) 親疏 near and distant relationships; *sŭ ké* 疏橐 generous, free, as with money.

Sū 所 A classifier of houses and parcels of ground; the means or cause by which; a relative pronoun, that, which, what, in which sense it precedes the verb and noun; in the coll. read *sĕ*, q. v.: *sū-cái* 所在 a place; *gŭng sū* 公所 a place of public meeting; *ù-sū-bók-dĭ* 無所不知 omniscient; *sū iū* 所有, whatever, all that there is; *sū-ī* 所以 because; *sū-ī-iòng* 所以然 wherefore; *ù-sū-bók-kiĕng* 無所不慇 faulty in all things; *ù-sū-bók-cé*, 無所不志, unrestrained.

Sŭ 829

Sŭ 師 A company, an assemblage; part of an army, troops; to call out and lead troops: a metropolis; a leader; a master, a professor; one skilled in; a patron; a sage; to teach, to imitate; the 7th of the 64 diagrams used in names of gods of wind, rain and thunder; used for the coll. *să* and *săi*, q. v.: *sŭ sĕng*, 師生 teacher and scholar; *uá sŭ* 畫師 an artist; *sŭ ìè* 師爺 an officer's private secretary; *sŭ mŭ* 師母 and *sŭ gŭ* 師姑 a teacher's wife and sister; *uàng-sié sŭ biĕu*, 萬世師表, the pattern of 10,000 ages—i.e. Confucius.

Sŭ 篩 A huge bamboo, used for boats; a sieve: usually read *tăi*, q. v.

Sŭ 螄 A spiral shell or helix, called *lòi sŭ* 螺螄.

Sŭ 獅 A lion; also a dog that whelps two pups; usually read *săi*, q. v.

Sŭ 思 To think, as in *sŭ siōng* 思想 or *sŭ liòng* 思量 to reflect; *sŭ niéng* 思念 to consider, to wish or desire; *sŭ lêu* 思慮 to be anxious; *sĭng sŭ* 心思, one's thoughts; *sĭng sŭ ngiòng hâing* 心思言行 the thoughts, words and actions.

Sŭ 罳 A screen before a door: *pèu-sŭ* 罘罳 a screen before an entrance.

Sŭ 偲 To urge, to excite one's self to duty; to admonish, as friends do. Read *săi*: a large beard.

Sŭ 愢 The mind not decided, unsettled, uncertain: *chiék-chiék sŭ-sŭ* 切切愢愢, to reprove earnestly, as friends do mutually.

Sü 831

Sü 總 A coarse hempen fabric, used as half mourning for distant relatives; flaxen, hempen.

Sü 需 To be stopped by rain; compelled to stop; to doubt, to hesitate: to search for; necessary, required; *gék sü* 急需 needed at once; *sü ẹung* 需用, wanted for use; the 5th of the 64 diagrams, pertaining to water. Read *ụ*: flexible. Read *niōng*: weak, delicate.

Sü 濡 Also read *ụ*: to steep, to immerse; wet, damp; thick, viscid; fresh, glossy; at ease, tranquil; to urinate; enduring; dregs, sediment: *ciěng sü* 沾濡 soaked; *sü ụng* 濡忍 patient; *sü dê* 濡滯 obstructed, flowing slowly.

Sü 胥 Crabs minced and pickled; to help; to expect; mutually, all, altogether; a final particle; to store, to accumulate: *lê sṳ́* 吏胥, a clerk in a yamen, termed *cṳ́ bâing* 書辦 in the coll.

Sṳ́ 糈 Fine rice, offered to the gods; food, rations, a government salary, official income.

Sṳ́ 私 Private as in *sṳ́ â* 私下; selfish; secret, treasonable; contraband; plebeian; to consider, to regard; urine; in the coll. read *săi*, q. v.: *sṳ́ ció* 私鑄 counterfeit coinage; *sṳ́ sùng* 私艖 smuggling-boats; *sṳ́ ṳ̆k* 私慾 lusts; *sṳ́ sĭng* 私心 or *sṳ́ é* 私意 partial, unjust; *sṳ́ bê* 私弊 a private fault.

Sṳ̆ 須 湏 The second form is erroneous, but commonly used: a surname; the beard about the mouth and chin; to expect; must, ought: *bék sṳ̆* 必須 absolutely required; *ù sṳ̄* 無須 needless; *siĕ sṳ̄* 些須, a small amount, a trifle.

Sṳ̄ 鬚 The hair on the chin, the beard; *huă sṳ̄* 花鬚 the stamens of flowers; *làu sṳ̄* 留鬚, to wear a beard; *piĕk sṳ̄* 撇鬚 mustaches, also called *nĕ-piĕk sṳ̄* 弍撇鬚.

Sṳ̄ 輸, To suffer defeat, to be beaten; to exhaust; a present, an offering: in the coll. read *siŏ*, q. v.: *sṳ̄ nák,* 輸納 to pay a tax; *giŏng-sṳ̄* 捐輸 to subscribe to the government.

Sṳ̄ 司, To preside, to rule, to control; an officer, a commissioner; a township: also read *sĭ*, and in the coll. *să*, q. v.

Sṳ̄ 斯 To split with an ax; to rend, to separate; this, that, these, those; forthwith, then; presently, in a moment; literary, genteel; inferior: a euphonic particle.

Sṳ̄ 澌 Also read *sāi*: to immerse; to melt and disappear; dried up: *sṳ̄ miĕk* 澌滅 lost in the water.

Sṳ̄ 撕 Also read *sāi*: to pull apart; to put one on his guard; *tì sṳ̄* 提撕 to point out.

Sṳ̄ 暑 Summer heat; the sun's heat; hot weather: *sṳ̄ ké* 暑氣 solar heat; *biĕ sṳ̄* 避暑 to escape the heat.

Sṳ̄ 曙 Bright, clear; the dawn of day, sunrise; manifest.

Sṳ̄ 署 A public court, an office; to appoint to an office; holding office temporarily; *guăng-sṳ̄* 官署 a yamen; *sṳ̄ éng* 署印 a seal or office held temporarily.

Sṳ̄ 駛, 駛 A horse running; fleet;

promptly, in haste; to sail a vessel: in the coll. read *sāi*, q. v.

Sṳ 使 To order, to command; to commission; use, service: also read *sẹ́u* and in the coll. *sāi*, q. v.: *téng-sṳ* 聽使 to be in waiting.

Sṳ 史 A historian, an annalist; a history, chronicles; *guók sṳ* 國史 archives; *cō sṳ* 左史 and *ểu sṳ* 右史 the two court historians; *ngẹ̄u sṳ* 御史 censors; *sṳ gé* 史記 history.

Sṳ 始 The beginning, origin; to begin; at the commencement of a sentence, it often means then, at that time, it was: *chảung sṳ* 創始 invention; *kī sṳ* 起始 or *nguòng sṳ* 原始, in the beginning. Read *sẹ́u*, to begin, to originate.

Sṳ 黍 Millet; the 202nd radical:

in the coll. read *sẹ̄*: *gáẹk sṳ̄* 角黍 glutinous rice in bamboo leaves, made on the 5th of the 5th moon, in the coll. termed *cáẹng*.

Sṳ̄ 死 To die; the death of the young; dying; pale, deadly; mortal; fearless; urgent; in the coll. read *sī*, q. v.: *sṳ̄ biĕk* 死別 separation by death; *sṳ̄ sĕng iū mĕng* 死生有命 death and life are appointed (by Heaven).

Sṳ̄ 諝 To know; sage, scholarly: *cá sṳ̄* 詐諝 cunning, deceitful.

Sṳ̄ 醑 To clarify spirits.

Sṳ̀ 薯 An esculent root; the yam: *huăng-sṳ̀* 番薯 sweet potatoes; *huăng-sṳ̀ mī* 番薯米 sweet potato, shredded and dried, used by the poor as a substitute for rice.

Sừ 祠 To sacrifice to ancestors in the spring; an ancestral temple; as in *sừ đòng* 祠堂; to get a blessing.

Sừ 詞 To tell the thoughts; a word, a sentence; a writing; an accusation; to request; to accuse: *ùng sừ* 文詞 writings; *dăk sừ* 達詞 a response; *ngū sừ* 語詞 a verb.

Sừ 辭, 辞, Similar to the last; an expression; a part of speech; language; to decline with thanks; to resign, to leave; to send away: *sừ hèng* 辭行 to bid adieu on commencing a journey: *sừ sié* 辭世 to die: *sừ ng giéng* 辭怀見 to decline seeing a visitor; *sừ cĕk* 辭職 to retire from office.

Sừ 殊 To kill, to slay; to exterminate; to distinguish; a sign of the superlative: *sù sáik* 殊色 surpassingly beautiful.

Sù 攴 The 79th radical.

Sù 徐 A surname: grave, serious; dignified, majestic: *sù buó* 徐步 to walk gracefully.

Suā 耍 To play, to sport; to exercise, as in fencing; play, games; in the coll. easy, remiss; bold, swaggering: *iù suā* 遊耍 to ramble about; *nṳ̄ cī muāng suā* 女只滿耍, you are so free and reckless!

Suā 灑, 洒, To scatter, as the wind scatters leaves; to sprinkle; to divide; high; steep, as a bank; alarmed; the 2nd also read *sā*, q. v.

Suā 掃 To clean and sweep; to sweep up; a broom; to interrupt, as one's pleasure, as in *suā héng* 掃興: also read *sọ* and in the coll. *sáu*, q. v.: *dā-suā* 打掃 to sweep.

Suā 掃 Also read *sọ*; to sweep the ground; a dike; a dam made of bamboo and earth.

Suā: A coll. word: the same as *chuá;* a sudden pain; contraction of the limbs.

Suāi: A country brogue, sometimes used for *sāi*, to use, to employ.

Suāng 孿 Usually read *luāng*; to bear twins.

Sŭi 荽 Also read *chŭi*: *hù sŭi* 胡荽 the coriander.

Sūi: A coll. word; also spoken *suói* or *sói* by some: all, the whole lot; *sūi mā*, to sell off all at once.

Sŭi 隨 To follow, to accord with; to permit; according to, as, like, as one may or can; the

17th of the 64 diagrams: *sùi cék* 隨即 immediately; *sùi biêng* 隨便 at convenience; *sùi chệu* 隨處 everywhere; *sùi uòng* 隨員 followers, attaches.

Sùi 隋 A dynasty, A. D. 590—620. Read *dộ:* to fall; scattered; indolent. Read *tiō:* to part a sacrifice.

Sùi 陲 A limit, a boundary: hazardous.

Sùi 垂, 埀, To hand down from ancient times; suspended; almost, near to, as in *sùi lộ* 垂老 near old age; a boundary; *sùi giá* 垂下 or *sùi lọ̆h là* 垂落梨 to droop, as the limbs of trees; *sùi dĭk gì* 垂直其 perpendicular to the plane of the horizon.

Sùi 誰 Who? *sùi ìng* 誰人 what person? whose? whom? *sùi hò* 誰何 what matters it?

Sŭk 841

Sùi: A coll. word: similar to *sì* in the phrase *sì-niă-nọi*; little by little; *sùi-ciēu tiěng* and *sùi-ciēu gēng*, to add and take out gradually.

Sŭk 朮, 术 A glutinous grain; a bitter herb, used as medicine.

Sŭk 秫 As in *sŭk mī* 秫米 a sort of glutinous rice.

Sŭk 述 To follow another; to narrate, to recite; *siŭ sŭk* 修述 to revise a work; *sŭk cĭng hìng* 述情形 report the facts.

Sŭk 術 An art, an artifice; a device; black art, as in *sià sŭk* 邪術; *sŭk sẹu* 術士, a conjurer; *chŏi mièng sŭk* 催眠術 hypnotism.

Sŭk 蜀 A sort of caterpillar; a sacrificial tripod: *bā sŭk* 巴蜀 one of the three states into which China was divided

A. D. 220 ; a name applied to Sz'chuen.

Sŭk 蠋 Also read chéuk: the caterpiller of the sphinx moth, called dĭk sŭk 蠋蠋 and found on pulse.

Sŭk 續 To continue, to join on; following, continuously: lŭk sŭk 陸續 successively, one after another.

Sŭk 贖 To ransom, to redeem; to give security; to atone for by merit; sŭk huòi 贖回 (coll. sŭk diōng lì), to redeem; sŭk cói 贖罪 to atone for sin.

Sŭk 孰, A crop, a harvest.

Sŭk 熟 Ripe, mellow; well cooked; thorough; skilled, experienced; soft, as silk: a crop: sìng sŭk 成熟 ripe; sŭk chiū 熟手 handy; buáng chăng sŭk 半生熟 half-cooked.

Sŭng   843

Sŭk 塾 A domestic school: *gă sŭk* 家塾 or *mùng sŭk* 蒙塾 a private school.

Sŭk 俗 Ordinary, common; vulgar, unpolished, as manners; the laity: *hŭng sŭk* 風俗 or *hiŏng sŭk* 鄉俗 the customs of a place; *sŭk ìng* 俗人 plebeians; *sŭk-ngṳ̄-uá* 俗語話 proverbs.

Sŭk 屬, 属, Attached to, connected with; to belong to; allied; related, of kin; a rank; is, actual; to revise: *guóng sŭk* 眷屬 or *gă sŭk* 家屬 family relatives; *sŭk guók* 屬國 colonies; *chĭng sŭk* 深屬 kindred; *giĕng sŭk* 見屬 to recognize as acquaintances. Read *cĕuk*: to entrust; to collect: respectful.

Sŭng 嵩崧, The central and highest of the five great mountains—in Honan; a lofty moun-

844 Sŭng

tain; elevated, eminent, as a statesman.

Sŭng 鬆 Disheveled hair: confused, disordered; slack, easy; not anxious: in the coll. read *sĕng*, q. v.

Sŭng 詢 To ask about, to inquire; investigation; to deliberate, as in *sŭng-mèu* 詢謀 to plan.

Sŭng 峋 Also read *sùng*: *ling sŭng* 岭嶙 hills rising over hills.

Sŭng 洵 To sob, to weep convulsively: remote, distant; true, faithful.

Sŭng 珣 Also read *sùng*: a gem from Liautung; a utensil.

Sŭng 徇, 狥, Used for the next: all around, pervading; to extend everywhere; to consider in all aspects; to follow, as in *sŭng ngiê* 徇義 to follow right principles.

Sŭng 殉 To bury the living with the dead, as anciently, though rarely done, as in *sŭng-cáung* 殉葬; to follow; to pursue an object immoderately; engrossed in: *sŭng nâng* 殉難 to risk suffering.

Sŭng 筍, 笋, Edible bamboo shoots, as in *déṳk sŭng* 竹筍: a tenon, a dovetail. Read *công* a bamboo sledge. Read *sùng*: a flexible sort of bamboo for making mats.

Sŭng 恂, Also read *sùng*: true, sincere, conscientious; devoted; to exert a good influence: *tĭng sŭng* 忱恂 faithful.

Sŭng 悚 Fearful, agitated: *sŭng iòng* 悚然 on the *qui vive*, excited; *sŭng lék* 悚慄 at once, prompt as in paying or promising.

Sūng 竦 To stand stiffly; respectful; to exalt; excited, agitated as in *sūng dōng* 竦動.

Sūng 聾 To be born deaf, entirely deaf; to excite; to respect; astonished in hearing it, as in *sūng téng* 聳聽.

Sūng 慫 To arouse, to excite, to stimulate, as in *sūng ūng* 慫慂.

Sūng 攫 To hold, to seize; to stretch one's self out; *sūng sĭng* 攫身 to stand erect.

Sūng 瞬 To roll the eyes about; to dart; a glance; *sūng sék* 瞬息 or *ék sūng cĭ găng* 乙瞬之間 in a twinkling, instantly.

Sùng 船,舡 A boat, a junk, a ship; a saucer; the collar of a coat: *dô-sùng* 渡船 a passenger boat; *chiă sùng* 車船 a steamer; *sùng chōng* 船艙 staterooms; *tō̤ sùng* 討船 to hire a boat; *hŭng sùng*

封船 to impress boats; *sùng céng* 船政 arsenal; *sùng ô buô* 船務部 Shipping Board; *mìng sùng,* 民船 boats in general; *chiă sùng giāng* 傳船仔 a launch; *sùng méng,* 船面 the deck; *sùng ó* 船塢 docks; *sùng hô* 船戶 boatmen, sailors; *sùng diōng* 船長, *sùng ciō* 船主 the captain; *sùng gì ŭng liông* 船其容量, or *sùng gì dóng só* 船其頓數 the ship's tonnage.

Sùng 撫 To feel, to stroke; to soothe, to sympathize with.

Sùng 循 To follow a leader; to accord, to comply with; good, easy, docile, as in *sùng liòng* 循良; *sùng lī* 循理 to follow reason; *sùng giĕ dộ gŭ* 循規矩 to obey the rules.

Sùng 馴 A well-trained horse; gentle, obedient, as in *sùng*

hŭk 馴伏; sùng liòng 馴良 gentle, good-natured.

Sùng 紃 A silk tassel; ornaments; a rule, model, pattern: sùng chák 紃察 to examine.

Sùng 純 Pure silk; unmingled; perfect, entire; sùng hâiu 純厚 honest, upright; sùng ciòng 純全 uniform and entire. Read cūng: a fringe, selvage. Read dòng: to tie in a bundle.

Sùng 唇, 脣, The lips.

Sùng 淳 Pure, clear; honest, true: hŭng sŭk sùng hâiu 風俗淳厚, his manners are plain and correct.

Sùng 醇 Rich, generous; good and thick, as syrups; pure, single, as one's motives; magnanimous: sùng hâiu 醇厚 liberal; sùng gīng 醇景 observant.

Sùng 849

Sùng 旬 A decade of days or years; complete, finished; in the coll. to review lessons on the tenth day; siông 上, dǐng 中 and hâ sùng 下旬, the first, second and third decades of a month.

Sùng 荀 Sometimes read sūng: an edible plant; a surname.

Sùng 郇 A feudal state in the Chow Dynasty, now Puchow-fu in southwest Shansi with the adjacent region.

Sùng 巡, 廵, To go on a circuit as in sùng lô 巡邏; to take a tour of inspection; sùng iâ 巡夜 a night watchman; sùng buô 巡捕 special aides of high officers.

Sùng 蕈 An aquatic vegetable or cress.

Sùng 松 The fir or pine tree: sùng báh 松柏 the pine.

Sùng 榕 Read ùng; coll. sùng;

the bastard banian, the Indian fig, called sṳ̆ng chéu 榕模.

Suói 濬 Deep, profound.

Suói 彗 Also read uói: suói sĭng (or uói sĭng) 彗星 a comet, commonly called chēng chiū sĭng 筅彗星.

Suói 稅 Rent; duty on goods; suói-sauk 稅索, suói-cáik 稅責 tariff; suói ngiăh 稅額 the fixed rates of duties, assessment: COM., bó suói 報稅 to report and pay duty; láu suói 漏稅 to smuggle; siŭ suói 收稅 to receive customs; iòng suói 洋稅 customs on imports; suói kié 稅契 to get a deed stamped or registered; céng kāu suói 進口稅 import duty; chók kāu suói 出口稅 export duty; lŏh dê suói 落地稅 terminal duty; éng huā suói 印花稅 stamp tax; guăng-suói

Suói 851

huói-ngiê 關稅會議 Customs' Conference; *suói-ô-guŏh* 稅務局 excise bureau; *siĕu-diòng-suói* 銷塲稅, consumption tax. Read *tuák;* to release. Read *iŏk*, pleased.

Suói 說 Interchanged with the preceding, in the sense of to be pleased; to urge, to incite to; also read *siók* q. v.: *iù suói* 遊說 to go about and incite others.

Suói 帨 A handkerchief hung at the girdle; *gŭng suói* 巾帨 a napkin.

Suói 蛻 The exuviae or skin cast off by snakes, crabs, locusts, etc.

Suói 賽 To recompense; to contest for, as in plays, etc.: *suói dĕng* 賽燈 to show lanterns, as on the 15th of the 1st moon; *suói iàng* 賽贏 to emulate: *dáu suói* 鬥賽 to contest for the victory; *suói huôi* 賽會 an athletic contest, a pageant.

Suói 歲, 歳 A year of one's age; age, years; a harvest; in the coll. read *huói*, q. v.: *suói chẹu* 歲次 the character for the cyclic year; *cáung suói* 壯歲 robust: com., *uâng-uâng suói* 萬萬歲 may His Majesty live forever!

Suói: A coll. word: a seam, as in *siáng suói*; a crack; a furrow; *là siŏh suói*, 犁一遂 to plow a furrow.

Suôi: A coll. word: something on which to found a claim; an antecedent, a precedent.

Suok (This word is interchangeably read *siok*, q. v.)

Suong (This word is interchangeably read *siong*, q. v.)

Tă 他, 它 A personal pronoun; he, she; him, her, it; *tă muòng*

他門 they, them; *tă dék* 他的 his, hers; *tă ìng* 他人 that person, another; *tă nĭk* 他日 another day.

Tă: A coll. word: to row or work a boat out against the wind as in *tă hŭng chók; tă dōng*, to propel against the flood-tide.

Tá 鮓, 蚱, Read *cá;* coll. *tá*: a sort of medusa or sea-blubber: *tá-pùi* 蚱皮, *tá-kă* 蚱胶, and *tá-nòng* 蚱囊 the skin. feet and stomach, of a medusa.

Tặ 體 The body, the whole person; a body of officers; real, essential; decorous, proper; reputable; to carry out another's views or intentions, *tặ nèng é* 體人意; *tặ sók* 體恤 to pity; COM., *ék tặ* 一體 the whole; the same; *nŭk tặ,* 肉體 or *sĭng tặ*

身體 the body; *báik tā* 百體 all the bodily members; *tā tái* 體態 bearing, gait; *buōng tā* 本體 the original form; *tā liông* 體諒 to show consideration for; to make allowance for; *tā miêng* 體面 respectability, honor; *tā gáik* 體格 standard; *táuk tā* 脫體, or *tuák tā*, to recover from an illness.

Tā 替 To substitute; a substitute, as in *tā sǐng* 替身; for, in behalf of, as in *dái tā* 代替: *ù tā* 無替 unchanging, unfailing; *tā giěng* 替肩 to carry a burden for another.

Tā 匲, 楷, The 2nd is unauthorized; thin, flat: in the coll. a drawer, as of a table, or bureau: *tā běk* 楷拔 the knob or brass-piece to pull a drawer by.

Tā 締 Thick, glossy silk; lus-

Tà 855

trous silk; a coat, a pelisse.

Tá 涕, 鮷, To cry, to shed tears; tears; *tá séu* 涕泗 profuse weeping.

Tà 啼, 嗁, To weep, to bewail; to crow, to coo; the cry of birds; to scream as apes and parrots: in the coll. read *tiè*, q. v.

Tà 稊, 稌, Tares, weeds like rice; cockle in rice fields; *tà bái* 稊稗 tares.

Tà 荑 Plants just budding, new sprouts; weeds, tares. Read *i*: to cut grass.

Tà 霽 The sky clearing up, fair weather.

Tà 鷈 A sort of pheasant. Read *i*, as in *i-iù* 鷉鼯 a flying squirrel.

Tà: A coll. word: usual, ordinary, medium; *tà tà siăng*, monotonous; *tà tà bâng*, ailing.

Táe: A coll. word: to push with the feet: to kick off the bed-clothes, as in *táe puôi*.

Táek 劏 A vulgar character used in the *Báik-îng* for the coll. *táek*: to thrust with a knife, to stab: *táek sī* 劏死 to stab to death.

Táek: A coll. word, as in *tàu táek* a kind of two-pronged hairpin worn by country women.

Táeng 瀄 Read *těng*; coll. *táeng*: to be carried away by a flood or freshet; soaked, saturated, as in *cūi guáng iā táeng* 水灌野瀄, as watered pork; *siông táeng* 上瀄, the upper passage leading to Changloh opposite Pagoda Anchorage.

Táeng: A coll. word: idle, dissipated; untrustworthy.

Tăi   857

Táe̤ng: A coll. word: buoy: *pù-táe̤ng* floats, buoys.

Tâe̤ng: A coll. word: to instigate, to edge on; *tâe̤ng siŏh gu̿ó* to instigate by a word; *táe̤ng ne̤ng sŏng-páh*, to edge on persons to fight.

Táh: A coll. word: clean, pure; clean in a moral sense; honest, not making gain of one; all gone, lost or stolen: *táh gáik*, clean; *mạ táh-táh*, sold all out.

Tăi 篩 Read *sṳ*: a sieve; to sift: COM., *mī tăi* 米篩 a rice sifter; *tăi mī* 篩米 to sift rice; *tăi le̤ng* 篩籠 a sieve.

Tăi 擡 To raise, to lift; to draw, to pull, as a ricksha, called *tăi chiă: tăi chòng* 擡牀 a stretcher: coll., *tăi à-liák* 擡鞋軮 slip shod.

Tăi 胎 The womb; pregnancy;

congenital: to begin; to rebel against: in the coll. read *tŏi*, q. v.: COM., *huài tăi* 懷胎 pregnant; *dáik tăi* 得胎 to become pregnant; *tăi-ĭ* 胎衣 the placenta: COLL., *tăi dáung* 胎當 or *tăi ák* 胎押 to mortgage, as to a wealthy man.

Tăi 駘 A jaded horse; a worthless nag: *tăi dáung* 駘蕩 wide, expanding, as said of the opening spring.

Tăi 苔 Moss, lichens; mossy, moss-grown: in the coll. read *tì*, q. v.

Tăi 邰 An ancient feudal state, in central Shensi.

Tăi 梯 A ladder as in *làu-tăi* 樓梯; stairs, steps; *met.*, a means to an end: *chĭng-hùng-tăi* 青雲梯 the azure-cloud-ladder—degree, rank, promotion.

Tái 859

Tăi 台 See *dài:* a surname; name of a star: *săng tăi* 三台 three double stars in Ursa Major; *tăi buói* 台輩 aged, growing old.

Tăi 颱 As in *hŭng tăi* 風颱 a typhoon.

Tāi 噠 Read *dài;* used for the coll. *tāi:* fine, as a voice in speaking another tongue.

Tái 太, 大, Large, very great; too, very, excessive; extensive; a title of honor; smooth and slippery: COM., *tái gĭk* 太極 The Great Extreme, first cause or origin; *tái bìng* 太平 general peace; *tái cṳ̆* 太子 the crown-prince; *tái lŏ* 太老 and *tái nă* 太奶 an officer's father and mother; *tái tái* 太太 (spoken *tài-tái*). an officer's wife, her ladyship; *tái dŏ* 太多 too much;

tái guó 太過 and *bók gĭk* 不及 excessive and insufficient.

Tái 泰 Interchanged with the preceding: great, exalted, honorable; extreme, extravagant; universal; peaceful; the 11th diagram: *guók tái mìng ăng* 國泰民安 the country prospering and the people at peace: COM., *tái săng* 泰山 a famous mountain in Shantung; an idol, the emperor of the world of spirits.

Tái 汰 Slippery; excessive, overflowing, as waters; to wash, to cleanse; *chiă tái* 奢汰 extravagant; lustful.

Tái 態 Form, figure; one's gait, bearing as in *tā̤ tái* 體態; motions; a circumstance, a state.

Tái: A coll. word, used for *téng* as in *tái-diŏ*, to go by road, to travel by land; *muóng tái cià kọ̆,* just let it go, don't quarrel about it!

Tài 刣 Read *cṳ̆ng*; used for the coll. *tài*: to kill; to execute a criminal: *tài tàu* 刣頭 to behead; *tài chĕk* 刣賊 to kill a thief.

Táik 帖 A written scroll; a writing; a note; a copy-slip; fixed, settled: *bái táik* 拜帖 a visiting card; *ciòng táik* 全帖 a card of several folds; *bóng táik* 放帖 to send cards of invitation.

Táik 貼 To give in pledge; to cover over; to paste up or on; to apply as plasters; to supply a deficiency; to help, to assist: COM., *tā̤ táik* 體貼 to carry out another's views: *táik cièng* 貼錢 to pay extra; *táik băh* 貼

白 to post up white paper, as in mourning.

Táik 怗 Quiet, peaceable: submissive: *táik-hŭk* 怗服 to be resigned. Read *ciĕng* as in *ciĕng dé* 怗濧 discordant, as sounds.

Táik 忒 To change, to alter; to doubt, to suspect; *bók táik* 不忒 no mistake; *hộ tiĕng bók táik* 號天不忒 High Heaven errs not.

Táik 慝 Wicked, dissolute; a depraved heart; malicious; to act the hypocrite; sunk in vice: *siŭ táik* 修慝 to reform one's evil ways.

Táing: A coll. word: jutting, protuberant, as in *táing chók li*, bulging out; *met.*, a molding, raised work, as in panels.

Táiu, 透 Read *táu;* coll. *táiu:* a plank, a gang plank, as in *táiu* bēng; as a verb, to manage, as one does with limited means; táiu cià gúo, to pass a time of want.

Ták 塔, 墖, A pagoda, a tower; băh ták 白塔 and siŏh ták 石塔 the White and Stone Pagodas in Foochow; lò (mó) sĭng ták 羅星塔 the marshaled stars' pagoda—the Pagoda Anchorage in the Min.

Ták 塌 Low ground, ground settling; to fall in ruins: COLL., cáuk ták 作塌 or cău ták, to spoil or ruin, to waste things.

Ták 搨 To lay the hand on, to feel; to make a facsimile by transfer; a copy.

Ták: A coll. word, for which the last may be used: to cover, to sheathe; a sheath, as of a pencil; bék ták, a pencil sheath.

864　Tăk

Ták 榻 A long, narrow bedstead, a wooden couch.

Ták 潒 The name of a stream in Shensi.

Ták 撻 To beat, flog, to chastise; swift, rapid.

Ták 闥 A door; a screen; in the coll. movable boards, as in the front of a shop, called *ták-bēng* 闥板.

Ták 怛 Moved, affected; sad, distressed; burdened, as with trials; to pity, to commiserate.

Tăk 疊, 叠, Read *tiĕk*; used for the coll. *tăk*, to pile up or on; *met.*, to multiply, as accusations against one in court: *tăk páu-huā* 疊枹花 to make "the pomelo flower," *i. e.* the open tiling on walls.

Tăk: A coll. word: the sound of water dropping, called *tăk-tăk-hiōng*.

Tăng 865

Tăng 貪 To covet; greedy: ambitious of; in the coll. to praise, to be pleased with one: *tăng cŏng* 貪贓 to desire bribes; *tăng sĭng* 貪心 a covetous disposition, *tăng làng* 貪婪 niggardly; *tăng siăh* 貪食 gluttonous; *tăng bié* fond of going fast.

Tăng 灘 A rapid, a torrent rushing through a rocky pass: *chĭng tăng* 深灘 a deep torrent; *hāi tăng* 海灘, a Wash, an arm of the sea.

Tăng 癱 As in *hŭng tăng* 瘋癱 palsy, paralysis.

Tăng 探 Also read *táng:* to search for; to investigate, to spy out: *tăng téng* 探聽 or *tăng séng* 探信 to obtain news of; *diāng tăng (táng)* 偵探 a spy; *tăng giéng diéng dĕng* 探見電燈 electric torch; *tăng hiĕng* 探險

venturesome; *tăng hiĕng gă* 探險家 explorers.

Tăng 攤 To open, to spread out; a stand or stall on which things are placed for sale called *bà tăng* 排攤; to share, to divide into three shares as in *săng-gū-tăng* 三股攤.

Tăng 撐,撑, To prop, to shore up; to push off, to pole a boat as in *tăng sùng* 撐船; *tăng dô* 撐渡 to pole over a ferry; *met.*, to intrigue for friends: in the coll. read *táng*, q. v.: *tăng céng* 撐進 pole (the boat) ahead.

Tāng 噇 The hum of a full table when eating; craunching, grinding of the teeth.

Tāng 坦 Plain, level; quiet, tranquil; a son-in-law; *tāng iòng* 坦然 gratified; *lêng tāng* 令坦 your son-in-law.

Tāng 祖 To shove up the sleeve, to bare the arm; to disclose; *cō tāng* 左祖 to help one when in the wrong.

Tāng 禫 A sacrifice to the manes of parents at the end of 27 months, termed the three years' mourning.

Tāng 髳 Long hair falling on the forehead or cheeks; also ornamental fringes.

Tāng 醓 Brine, gravy: *tāng häi* 醓醢 preserved delicacies.

Tāng 毯 A hair rug, or bed mat: *cieng-tāng* 氈毯 felted woollen rugs and hair mats.

Táng 撐 Read *tăng*; coll. *táng*: to prop, to support, to raise, as a shutter with a stick, as in *táng kï* 撐起.

Táng 炭 Charred wood, charcoal; coals of any kind: *páng-táng*

有炭 and *dáing táng* 有炭 soft and hard wood coals.

Táng 嘆, 歎, To sigh, to groan; to laud, to admire: COM., *táng ké* 嘆氣, to sigh; a moan, a groan.

Táng: A coll. word: to compete in trade; to get the custom by under-selling another.

Táng: A coll. word: to converse, to discuss as in *téng táng*.

Tàng 覃 To extend, to reach, to arrive at; great, extensive: *tàng ŏng* 覃恩, royal favor.

Tàng 譚 Used for *dàng* (to converse): to discuss, to talk about; to boast: in the coll. to put tentative questions.

Tàng 潭 The name of a river; a placid expanse of water with deep holes; deep, clear water, as in *tàng cūi* 潭水.

Tàng 墰 Also read *cièng* and *sìng*;

Tàng 869

to scorch; to warm, to boil; warm, hot: *met.*, distressed.

Tàng 墰, 壜, A wine jar, as in *ciŭ tàng* 酒壜.

Tàng 曇 Clouds extending over the heavens; the sky overcast as in *tàng tàng* 曇曇.

Tàng 痰 Phlegm: COM., *tàng sáu* 痰嗽 cough with phlegm; *tàng buòng* 痰盆 a spittoon.

Tàng 檀 Read *dàng*; coll. *tàng*: a tough wood fit for axles; sandal wood; *tàng hiŏng chà* 檀香柴 sandal wood for incense.

Tàng 簜 As in *làng tàng*, 籃簜 thin and spread widely; in the coll. large rocks; *làng tàng siŏh* 籃簜石 boulders.

Tàng: A coll. word; as in *tàng táik*, a mischievous fish: *met.*, a troubler, a mischief maker, as in a shop or school.

Tău 偷 Read *tĕu*; coll. *tău*: to steal, to pilfer as in *tău dò* 偷掏; to obtain unfairly; underhand: *tău diō că* 偷躲齋 to play truant from school; *tău cêng guŏng* 偷盡光 has stolen everything; *tău gōng* 偷講 whisper; *tău káng* 偷看 to use a crib in school.

Tāu: A coll. word: to loosen, to disentangle; intelligent, well-informed; to blow the nose, as in *tāu pé*; *tāu tóh,* (or *lóh*) well, not sick; well-informed; *ng tāu tóh*, indisposed; ignorant.

Táu 透 To pass through; through, throughout; to comprehend thoroughly: used for the coll. *táiu*, q. v.: COM., *tĕng táu* 通透 through, permeable; *táu dạ* 透底 to the last, forever.

Táu: A coll. word: to blow strong

or fresh: *hŭng iā táu*, the wind blows very strong.

Táu: A coll. word: to poison; *táu lō̤-chṳ̄* to poison rats.

Táu: A coll. word: to decoy, to kidnap; *táu kó̤ mā̤*, kidnap and sell.

Tàu 頭 Read *tèu*; coll. *tàu*: the head; the first, best, chief; the large end of a thing; the beginning of; a classifier of animals, birds, fish, reptiles: occurs in the names of round things, as in *siŏh tàu* 石頭, a stone; *tàu sĕng* 頭前 in front; *tàu huòi* 頭回 or *tàu bŏng* 頭幫 the first time; *tàu-nō̤* 頭腦 the brains; *tàu gă* 頭家 or *tàu nĕ̤ng* 頭仒 the principal, the head man; *dŏng tàu* 當頭 to be the manager; *guó tàu* 過頭 too much, in excess.

Tàu: A coll. word; for which the last is often used, as in *tàu-săng,* domestic animals.

Táuk 託 To charge with, to intrust to; to commission as in *hó táuk* 付託; to rely on.

Táuk 托 Used erroneously for the last: to take, to carry on the palm: in the coll. read *tŏh,* q. v.: *táuk buàng* 托盤 a tray: *táuk lŏk* 托落 unfavorable as the times.

Táuk 柝 A watchman's rattle; to beat the watches; *gék táuk* 擊柝 to strike the hours.

Táuk 橐 As in *nòng táuk* 囊橐 bags and sacks.

Táuk 驑 A camel, as *táuk dọ̀* 驑駝 (coll. *lŏk dọ̀*).

Táuk 脫 Read *tuák:* to evade, to get rid of: to recover from sickness; *táuk-tā* 脫體 well.

Táung   873

Táuk: A coll. word: to steep, to scald: *táuk dà*, to steep tea; *táuk chók lâiu*, to draw out the strength, as of tea.

Táung 盪 To push a boat on the land: in the coll. to row: also read *dâung*, q. v.: *táung sùng* 盪䑋 to row a boat; *táung céng* 盪進 to row ahead; *táung tói* 盪退 to back water.

Táung 脫 Read *tuák*; coll. *táung* and used for the next: to undress, to take off, as the shoes; *táung mò* 脫毛 to molt; *táung gáuk* 脫骨 to bone, as fowls; *táung káek* 脫殼 to shed the skins.

Táung 裭 Read *tói*; coll. *táung*: to disrobe; *táung ĭ-siòng* 裭衣裳 to undress.

Táung: A coll. word: to put into boiling water; to scald: *táung káh hĕng*, scalded too much.

Tâung: A coll. word: to heat over or warm up food, as in *tâung iĕk*; *tâung dà*, to heat (cold) tea.

Té 窒 Hindered, embarassed; to obstruct; to unravel embroidery.

Té 嚏 To sneeze; sneezing as in *bóng-té* 噴嚏.

Té 懥 Irritated, angry: *hūng-té* 忿懥 greatly enraged.

Té: A coll. euphonic prefix, as in *té-tié*, to shave; *té-tiéu*, to dance; *té-tó*, to vomit.

Tẹ̆: A coll. word: sloping, inclined; to slide, as on a slope: *tẹ̆-tẹ̆*, slanting; *tẹ̆ lŏh lī* to slide down; *tẹ̆ siŏh dọ̆*, slip and catch a fall.

Tẹ̆: A coll. word: to stretch one's self; to lie at full length, as *tẹ̆-dĭk dĭk*, or *tẹ̆-tẹ̆ dĭk*.

Ték 875

Tẹ̆ 鏾, Read *sāng*; used for the coll. *tẹ̆*: to shell off, to scale: *tẹ̆ kí* 鏾起 or *tẹ̆ kó* 鏾去 to shell it off; *diāng-tẹ̆* 鼎鏾 a small shovel for turning things in a pan.

Téh: A coll. euphonic prefix, as in *téh-tiáh*, to strip or tear off or down; *téh tọ̆h*, to bear on the palm of the hand.

Ték 勅, 敕, 勑, A special ordinance; precepts; a charter: the 3d also read *lài*: COM., *ték hŭng* 勅封 a special title; *ték cṳ̆* 勅書 letters-patent; *ték éng* 勅印 to set seal to.

Ték 飭, 飾 To repair, to strengthen; to direct, to command; *tŭng ték* 通飭 a command.

Ték 裼 To push up the sleeves, to bare the arms and breast.

Ték 惕 Regard, respect; grieved;

diligent; *ték-ték* 惕惕 to love; affectionate.

Ték 踢 To kick, as in *ték gióng* 踢毽 to kick the shuttle-cock. Read *chiók*: hurried, alarmed.

Ték 陟 To ascend; promoted; to advance: *ték gáung* 陟降 promotion and degradation.

Ték: A coll. euphonic prefix, as in *ték-taék*, to stab; *ték-táuk*, to commission.

Těk 宅 A dwelling, a residence, as in *gă-těk* 家宅; a grave, as in *ĭng těk* 陰宅: *diêu těk* 兆宅 to divine for a grave: used for the COLL., *tăh*.

Těk 讀 Read *tŭk*; coll. *těk*: to read aloud; to study, as in *těk cṳ̆* 讀書, to recite, to chant: *těk tŭng* 讀通 well read; *těk má lŏh* 讀賣落 a faulty construction; *těk cṳ̆ nêng* 讀書仒 literati.

Těng 蟶 Read *tǐng:* coll. *těng:* a bivalve, the razor-sheath or solen.

Těng: A coll. word: the same as *chāng* or *siāng;* an interjection, alas!

Těng 很 Read *hěng;* coll *těng:* perhaps a corruption of *hěng;* a superlative, very, extremely: *ngài dék těng* 杲的很 very bad.

Těng: A coll. word: prominent, protuberant, probably a corruption of *táing,* q. v.

Téng 聽, 聼, 听, Also read *tǐng;* to hear; to harken, to listen to; quiet, so as to hear; to receive and obey orders: in the coll. read *tiǎng,* q. v.: *téng chǎ* 聽差 a servant; *téng bìng* 聽憑 to accord; *bāu dā téng* 包打聽 a detective; *dā téng* 打聽 to get news of.

Téng 趂, 趁, To follow, to come up behind; to embrace an opportunity, as in *téng ô èng* 趂務閒 or *téng gĭ huói*, 趂機會; *téng cā là* 趂早來 to come early; *téng diô* 趂路 to go by land; Read *lìng*: to pass, to step over.

Téng 疼 A fever; a delicate appetite. Read *cīng*: the same as *cīng* (pustules) q. v.

Téng 賺 Read *guāng*; used for the coll. *téng*: to gain in trade: also read *cuáng* in the coll. q. v.: *téng siăh* 賺食 to earn a living; *téng gĕng cièng* 賺工錢 to earn wages.

Téng: A coll. euphonic prefix, as in *téng-táng*, to raise, as an awning; *téng tŭng táng*, to assume a defiant attitude.

Tèng 沉, Read *tìng*; coll. *tèng*: to

Tĕng   879

sink; sunk; settled, depressed.

Têng: A coll. word: even, equal in size; uniform, as timber; *iā têng*, very uniform.

Têng: A coll. euphonic prefix, as in *têng-táeng* to instigate, to edge on.

Tĕng 通 Read *tŭng;* coll. *tĕng*: pervious; open to, extending through as in *tĕng táu* 通透; understanding, intelligent; translucent, as glass, as in *tĕng lĕng* 通瓏; *tĕng-tĕng quŏng* 通通光 light, clear; *met.*, to know thoroughly as customs, prices; *tĕng tiĕng* 通天 open to the air or sky.

Tĕng: A coll. word, for which the preceding character is used: ought, must: *tĕng ng tĕng*, ought to or not? *tĕng káng* ought to see?—you must not look at it.

880   Tĕu

Tĕng 桶 A square vessel containing six *cǎng*; a tub; a pail, a bucket: COM., *cūi tĕng* 水桶 large water pails; *kă tĕng* 胶桶 a wash tub; *puăk-tĕng* a well-bucket.

Tĕng: A coll. word: perhaps a corruption of *tĕng*, as in *tĕng-siéng*, a door set open, an open window.

Tĕng: A country brogue, as in *tĕng cā*, early, formerly, a while ago.

Tĕng 蟲, 虫 Read *tùng*, coll. *tĕng:* worms; insects in general; *tĕng-ngiê* 蟲蟻 insects.

Tĕng 桐 Read *dùng;* coll. *tĕng:* a tree producing oily seed, called *tĕng chéu* 桐模: *tĕng iù* 桐油 wood oil.

Tĕu 偷, 偸 To steal, to pilfer; careless, disrespectful as in *tĕu* bŏk 偷薄; těu sĕng 偷生 to save one's life dishonorably.

Těu 鍮 An ore like gold, which forms an amalgam with quicksilver; said to come from Persia.

Těu: A coll. word: turned, soured, spoiled: buông těu, the rice is spoiled.

Těu: A coll. word: weak, infirm, debilitated.

Téu: A coll. word: to exchange, to substitute a bad, for a good article; téu dáung, to pawn another article in exchange.

Těu 頭 The head: the chief; the top or front; the end, one end of; the first, the best; a numerative of acts or affairs; as a suffix, it merely makes a dissyllable, or indicates a roundish form like a head; in the coll. read tàu, q. v.

Tĕu 柱 Read *cêu:* coll. *têu:* a post, a pillar, an upright support; *têu ciŏ* 柱珠 a plinth; *siŏh têu* 石柱 a stone pillar.

Tĕuk 縮 Read *sáuk;* used for the coll. *tĕuk;* to retract, to withdraw; *tĕuk dōi* 縮短 to shorten itself; *tĕuk cāu* 縮走 to recede.

Tĭ 黐 To attach; glutinous; viscous; also read *liĕ; tĭ niĕng* 黐黏 sticking; *tĭ tĭ* 黐黐 sticky, pasty.

Tĭ 蜘 Read *dī* in the dictionaries: a spider; COM., *tĭ-tṳ̆* 蜘蛛 a spider of a web-weaving sort: coll., *tĭ-tṳ̆ măng* 蜘蛛脝 a spider's web.

Tĭ: A coll. word: to appropriate, to pilfer, as in *lŭ-tĭ.*

Tĭ: A coll. euphonic prefix, as in *tĭ-tuă,* to pull, to drag; *tĭ-tiĕu,* to pick out as a splinter; *tĭ-tŏi,* to plane.

Tĭ 聎, 耻, To blush, to feel ashamed; humbled, chagrined: *guók tĭ,* 國聎 national disgrace.

Tĭ: A coll. euphonic prefix, as in *tĭ-tiĕ* to rend; *tĭ-tẹ̆* to scale or shell off;

Tĭ 持 To grasp; to keep; to manage; *bā-tĭ* 把持 to control; *hù-tĭ* 扶持 to aid.

Tĭ 提 To lift in the hand; to hold: to help; to patronize: *tĭ-dók* 提督 a major general; *cūi sŭ tĭ-dók* 水師提督 an Admiral; *tĭ kìng* 提琴 a violin.

Tĭ 堤 A bank, a levee; to guard, to prepare against.

Tĭ 隄 Interchanged with the last: a fence, a ridge, a barrier; to dike off: *tĭ huòng* 隄防 a barrier against floods.

Tĭ 醍 Pure, clear liquor; the essential oil of milk; elaine,

Tì 踟 Irresolute, undecided.

Tì 苔 Read *tăi*; coll. *tì*: moss, lichen: *chăng tì* 青苔 rock moss.

Tì 鮧 Read *tăi*; used for the coll. *tì*, as in *ŭng-tì-giè* 鰮鮧鮭, and *tì-hŏk-giè* 鮧核鮭 small salted sea-fish.

Tì: A coll. word, as in *siŏh bì-tì* a bunch, as of grapes.

Tì: A coll. euphonic prefix, as in *tì-tài*, to kill! ; *tì-tiè*, to cry; *tì-tièu*, to select, to cull out.

Tiáh 拆 Read *cháik*; used for the coll. *tiáh*; to tear in pieces; to remove; *met.*, to abase, to disgrace: to pull down a house, as in *tiáh chió* 拆厝; *tiáh kŭi* 拆開 to open, as a package.

Tiák 獺 The otter: com., *săng tiák* 山獺, a beaver; *hāi tiák* 海獺 a seal; *tiák săi* a flat fish.

Tiáng 885

Tiák: A coll. word: to wink, as in *páh tiák; měk tiák*, the eyelashes.

Tiăng 聽 Read *téng*: coll. *tiăng*: to listen; to understand; to obey: *ng tiăng giéng* 怀聽見 did not hear; *hō̤ tiăng* 好聽 pleasant to hear; *tiăng chói* 聽嘴 to obey orders.

Tiăng 廳 Read *tĭng*: a hall, a drawing room; a political division, smaller than a *hū*.

Tiāng 㨂 Read *diēng*: to push with the hand; *tiāng dō̤* 㨂倒 to push over; *tiāng láek*, to decline and get rid of.

Tiáng 痛 Read *tóng*: coll. *tiáng*: to ache: a pain, an ache; *tàu tiáng* 頭痛 a headache.

Tiáng 愛 Read *ái*; used for the coll. *tiáng*, to love, to take delight in; love, regard; *hō̤*

886 Tiè

- *tiáng* 好愛 lovely, amiable.
Tiàng 程 A road, a journey as in *diô tiàng* 路程; rules, regulations, as *ciŏng tiàng* 章程; met., a task; a course of duty: also read *tìng* q. v.; used as a surname.
Tiĕ: A coll. word: to tear, to rend, to pull apart.
Tié, 剃, 鬀 To shave: COM., *tié tàu* 剃頭 to shave the head: *tié dŏ* 剃刀 a razor.
Tié 薙 Interchanged with the last: to shave. Read *tá*, to root out grass and weeds: underbrush. Read *dê* as in *sĭng dê*, the magnolia purpurea.
Tié: A coll. word: to follow on: *tié chiū có*, to do while one's hand is in; *tié nęng siäng*, to repeat after one: *tié cṳ̆ lâu*, to skip (part of a book).
Tiè 啼 Read *tá*; coll. *tiè:* to cry,

as in *tiè mà* 啼嘛 to weep; to mourn for: *tiè mà chiéu* 啼嘛笑 to smile amid tears.

Tiék 鐵, 鉄 Iron, called *háik gĭng* 黑金 the black metal; made of iron; firm, decided; hard, unfeeling: *tiék ké* 鐵器 iron utensils; *iòng tiék* 洋鐵 sheet tin; *tiék sĭk* 鐵實 in very sooth, positively.

Tiék 徹 Pervious; to penetrate; all, throughout, as in *tiék iá* 徹夜 all night; intelligent; to cultivate: *tŭng tiék* 通徹 to discern clearly.

Tiék 撤 To send away, to remove; as in *tiék ké̤* 撤去; *tiék hùi* 撤回 to recall, as an officer.

Tiék 澈 Read *diĕk*; pure and limpid as water; *dèng tiék* 澄澈 pure-minded.

Tiĕk: A coll word; lean, emaciated from disease; *tiĕk lò* the consumption.

Tiĕng 天, 靝 The heaven, sky, air; a day, a season; the ages; the weather; Providence; Heaven: in the coll. with *dê* 地 (earth) gives an emphatic form to a phrase as in *tiĕng bàng dê bàng*, 天平地平 very level; very correct; *tiĕng bàng dê gèng* 天平地高 very high or lofty; *tiĕng bàng* 天棚 an awning; *tiĕng bàng* 天秤 scales; balance; *tiĕng cài* 天才 talent, genius; *tiĕng cṳ̆* 天資 natural gift; *tiĕng chŏng* 天窗 dormer window; *tiĕng dê gang* 天地間 universal; *tiĕng iĕng* 天演 evolution; *tiĕng iòng* 天然 natural; *tiĕng mêng* 天命 fate; destiny; *tiĕng ò* 天河 Milky Way; *tiĕng séng* 天性 nature, disposition; *tiĕng ùng* dài 天文臺 observatory; tiěng ùng giáng 天文鏡 an astronomical telescope.

Tiēng 添 To add to, to increase; additional: gă tiěng 加添 to add more.

Tiēng 忝 Ashamed; disgraced; ù tiēng 無忝 no disgrace.

Tiēng 諂 To flatter as in tiēng mé 諂媚; pleasing to the eye or ear.

Tiēng 悿 Bashful, ashamed; to feel disgraced.

Tiéng: A coll. word: to sew; to patch as in buō-tiéng.

Tièng 恬 Peaceful, still, contented; tièng cēng 恬靜 quiet.

Tièng 鯽, A coll. character: a darkish white pond fish called tièng láung 鯽蛋.

Tièng: A coll. word: to fatten, as fowls; fat, good and solid as meat; also medium, uniform in size, as in *tièng-tièng duái*.

Tiẽu 刁. The orginal form of the character for *dợ* (a knife): wicked, perverse; artful, intriguing; in the coll. read *dièu*, q. v.: *tiẽu hăng* 刁風 depraved manners; *tiẽu màng* 刁蠻 violent, barbarous.

Tiẽu 佻 Weak, young and tender; light and trifling; to assume.

Tiẽu 削 To pare, to scrape, to cut off.

Tiẽu 挑 To carry on the shoulder or end of a stick, as in *tiẽu dáng* 挑擔; to remove a splinter from the hand, as in *tiẽu chié* 挑莿; to stir up; to embroider; a spoon: in the coll read *tièu*, q. v.: *tiẽu sợ* 唆挑 to instigate; *tiẽu dĭng* 挑燈 to carry a lantern at the end of a stick; *tiẽu-ĭng* 挑引, to lead, as in mischief.

Tiĕu 恌 Mournful, sorry; to disesteem.

Tiĕu 窕 Deep, profound; elegant; lady-like.

Tiĕu 糶 To sell grain: COM., *chók tiéu* 出糶 to dispose of grain; *tiéu-mī* 糶米, to sell rice.

Tiéu 跳, 趒, To dance, to hop or skip about, as in *tiéu-tiéu diŏng* 跳跳轉. Read *diéu*: to walk along.

Tièu 挑 Read *tiĕu*; coll. *tièu*: to choose, to select: *tièu sōng* 挑選 to cull out: *tièu gĕng hŭ* 挑工夫 select men of muscle.

Tĭh: A coll. euphonic prefix, as in *tĭh-tŭh*, to pierce, to thrust, as the finger through paper—about as in *dĭh*.

Tĭk 敵 Read *dĭk*; used for the coll. *tĭk*: to control; to manage as family expenses, as in *tĭk gă-*

gié 敵家計; *tĭk mạ kŭi* 敵賣開 unable to meet (expenses); unable to fight (so many).

Tĭk: A coll. word: to comb out straight, to hatchel; to pull out: *tĭk gáuk* to bone, as fish or fowl; *tĭk chók lì*, to extract, as a book from a pile.

Tĭh: A coll. euphonic prefix, as in *tĭk-tăk*, to pile up; *tĭk-tĕk*, to study, *tĭk-tŏk* to fall, as prices.

Tĭng 偵 A spy, a scout, commonly termed *tăng mā* 探馬; to reconnoiter.

Tĭng 廳 A hall, a drawing room; a court: a political division somewhat smaller than a *hū*: commonly read *tiăng*, q. v.

Tĭng 檉 A water-willow having a reddish bark: *tĭng chà* 檉柴 the wood of the same used in cabinet work.

Tĭng 893

Tĭng 汀 Water with level shores; a low bank: a political division in Fukien. Read *tĕng:* unable to gain one's wish.

Tĭng 湛 To imbue, to moisten; also an excess, as of pleasure: also read *dăng: tĭng ŏng* 湛恩, imbued with favor; *tĭng lŏk* 湛樂 excessive delight.

Tĭng 燂 Also read *sĭng:* a portable furnace.

Tĭng 琛 A beautiful stone; a treasure: *tiĕng-tĭng* 天琛 natural curiosities.

Tĭng 砧 A chopping block, an anvil, for which the coll. words are *dĭng* and *dōng,* q. v.

Tĭng 酖 Given to wine, as in *tĭng ŭ ciū* 酖於酒; spirits impregnated with poison.

Tĭng 鴆 A bird that eats snakes: deadly, poisonous; *tĭng ciū* 鴆酒,

poisoned wine; *tĭng dŭk* 鴆毒 a deadly poison.

Tĭng 忱, 誠, 諶, True, sincere, trustworthy; faithful.

Tĭng: A coll. euphonic prefix, as in *tĭng-tăng*, to open out; met. to strut, as a fop; *tĭng-tĕng*, to clean out, as drains; *tĭng tŏng*, to swallow.

Tĭng 挺 To pluck, to pull out; to hold firmly; to enlarge: *tĭng sĕng* born for a special purpose, as Christ, by a miraculous birth.

Tĭng 脡 Jerked meat.

Tĭng 梃 A stick; a staff, a club: *ciế tĭng* 制梃 to brandish a club.

Tĭng 艇 A boat: a long narrow boat, in the coll. *mà-lāng-sùng* 貓覽船; *hĭ tĭng* 飛艇 an aeroplane, an air-ship; *cūi hĭ tĭng* 水飛艇 a hydroplane; *cièng cūi tĭng* 潛水艇 a submarine.

Tīng 895

Tīng 鋌 Iron or copper ore; empty, hollow.

Tīng 頲 A narrow head; strait, upright.

Tīng 圢 Waste land; a dike, a raised footway between fields, also called *chèng chìng* 田塍.

Tīng 頂 Read *dǐng*; coll. *tīng*: to carry on the head as in *tīng tàu* 頂頭; to support on the palm or foot; to be surety for.

Tīng 鼎, 鼑, 鎛, A tripod a caldron; firm, safe, secure, *met.*, the state: the 50th diagram; the 206th radical; in the coll. read *diāng*, q. v.: *tīng lĭk* 鼎立 to establish; *tīng cę̆uk* 鼎足 a tripod; *met.*, the Three States, A. D. 170.

Tīng 逞 Confident, presuming; rash; pleased with: *bók tīng* 不逞 displeased; careless.

896   Tìng

Tìng 郢 A district city in the North of Hupeh.

Tìng: A coll. euphonic prefix, as in *tìng tiāng*, to push away; to decline.

Tìng 呈 A statement; to present a petition or statement; usually read *diàng*, q. v.

Tìng 程 The hundreth part of a *cháung* 寸 or inch; a percentage; a rule; a pattern; a limit; an allowance; a road, a journey; also read *tiàng*, q. v.

Tìng 酲 Stupified from liquor, the feelings after a drinking spree.

Tìng, 沉, 沈 To sink; lost, ruined; to quash, as a law case; a lake; muddy, confused; the 2nd also read *zīng* and the 1st read *tèng* in the coll. q. v.: *tìng deụng* 沉重 very sick; *tìng mì* 沉迷

besotted: *tìng nĭk* 沉溺 to secrete; to embezzle; sunk in vice; *tìng lùng* 沉淪 to go to perdition; *tìng hiŏng* 沉香 aloes.

Tìng 停 Read *dìng*; coll. *tìng*: safe, well-arranged; correct; honest: *tìng cêng* 停靜 well-behaved; *tìng dáung* 停當 trustworthy, safe.

Tìng: A coll. word: even, equal, uniform: *dáung tìng*, to jounce even.

Tìng: A coll. euphonic prefix, as in *tìng-tŭng*, to pile up.

Tiŏ 妥 Safe, secure; honest, trusty; all right, as in *tiŏ dáung* 妥當; coll. *tiŏ-dáung nĕng* 妥當仒, a trusty person.

Tiŏ 朶, 朵, Pendent branches; a numerative of flowers; the east and west wings of a temple; *huă tiŏ* 花朶 bouquets.

Tiŏ 刴 Read *dṓ*: to cut fine; to mince, as meat.

Tiŏ 埽 Firm ground; clods.

Tiŏng 張 Read *diòng*; coll. *tiŏng*: a numerative of things spread out, as a chair, a table, paper: *cāi siŏh tiŏng* 紙一張 a sheet of paper; *tiŏng-tiŏng*, every sheet.

Tióng 倀 Also read *diòng*: to wander blindly about; to fall down.

Tióng 悵 As in *tióng uŏng* 悵望 sick at heart from disappointed hopes.

Tióng 暢 The inner feelings developed; joyous, as in *tióng lŏk* 暢樂; *tióng dăk* 暢達 permeating; *tióng dāng* 暢膽 very bold, presumptuous.

Tióng 鬯 Mixed sacrificial wine: *cṳ̄ tióng* 鬯主 one who prepares the libations.

Tiŭ   899

Tióng: A coll. word: to disseminate, to spread reports everywhere, as in *tióng gauk cheṇ*, *(sé-sié* or *chék cheṇ); iòng tióng*, to report.

Tiòng 椽 Interchangeably read *tuòng:* the rafters on which the tiling is laid: COM., *tiòng láiu* 椽料 materials for rafters.

Tiòng 杖 Read *diòng:* a cane, a staff, as in *guāi tiòng* 拐杖 a mourning-staff carried by the eldest son of the deceased.

Tiòng: A coll. word, analogous to *diòng:* to move or pass things; to bear as a message; to stir about, to work.

Tiŭ 抽 To deduct; to reject; to draw out; to levy: *tiŭ giòng* 抽捐 to assess taxes; *tiŭ suói* 抽稅 to levy duty; *cūi tiŭ* 水抽 a bamboo pump.

Tiŭ 瘳 To cure: healed; *kuok cĭk bók tiŭ* 厥疾不瘳 his disease was incurable.

Tiū 丑 The second of the 12 horary characters, from 1 to 3 A. M. as in *tiū sì* 丑時; *tiū ciáng* 丑正 2 A. M.

Tiù 籌 To plan, to devise; a lot; a tally, bamboo slips carried by porters: *tiù cháik* 籌策 a stratagem; *tiù mā* 籌碼 bamboo slips used in gaming, also for small weights; *tiù hĕk* 籌畫 to plan, to scheme; *tiù bê* 籌備 to prepare; preparation.

Tiù 躊 Embarrassed: COM., *tiù tụ̀ bók giók* 躊躇不決 irresolute, unable to decide.

Tó 兔 A rabbit: COM., *iā tó* 野兔 a hare.

Tó 吐 To vomit; to spit out; to disclose; to confess: COM., *báng tó-siá* 病吐瀉 vomiting and purging; the cholera; *tó háik* 吐血 to spit blood, hemorrhage of the lungs; *tó sĭ* 吐絲 to spin silk, as the silkworm does: *buŏh huăng buŏh tó* 剝翻剝吐 the stomach nauseated.

Tŏ 叨 To covet, to long for, as honors; to feel deeply grateful for; *tŏ hók* 叨福 blessed with your favor.

Tŏ 刀 Read *dŏ;* coll. *tŏ;* a classifier of Chinese quires or parcels of paper; *siŏh tŏ* 一刀 a quire or parcel.

Tŏ 拖, 扡, To pull, to drag; to defer, to put off; in the coll. read *tuă* and *tuà,* q. v.: *tŏ lôi* 拖累 involved, as in danger: COM., *tŏ nièng* 拖粘 to stick to; persistent, as in doing or saying.

Tŏ 討 To rule, to manage; to attack enemies; to destroy rebels; to seek, to ask for; used variously in the coll. according to subject: *tọ̄ cọ̈i* 討罪 to punish for crime: *tọ̄ cièng* 討錢 to beg money, to dun; *tọ̄ bó-siù* 討報仇 to seek revenge; *tọ̄ siăh* 討食 to beg food; *tọ̄ děng* 討冬 to beg rice or cash in the 11th month: *tọ̄ ngù* 討魚 to fish, as with a net; *tọ̄ séng* 討信 to ask for news: *tọ̄ chĭng* 討親 to marry a wife; *tọ̄ nê-huŏng* 討二婚 to marry a widow; *tọ̄ láung* 討論 to discuss or consider a subject.

Tọ̄ 橢 Oval; *tọ̄ kuàng* 橢環 elliptical.

Tọ̄: A coll. word used for *pọ̄:* about, somewhat, slightly; *tọ̄ tọ̄* or *tọ̄-mọ̄* just nearly; *tọ̄-mọ̄ ciā sì-háiu,* about this time;

tō-mō báik, slightly acquainted with; *tō-mō niè*, about that.

Tọ́ 套 To enwrap; a wrapper, an envelope; *met.*, a snare, a trap; a classifier of suits and sets: *tŭng tọ́* 通套 of general use: *tọ́ săng* 套衫 and *tọ́ kó* 套褲 an under-coat and over-alls; *à tọ́* 鞋套 wooden shoes, worn in wet weather; *tọ́ ùng* 套文 polite phrases; *kuŏng-tọ́* 誆套 a snare; to entrap one.

Tọ́ 唾 To spit: saliva: *tọ́ hù* 唾壺 a spittoon.

Tọ̀ 桃, 夭, A peach: *guáng tọ̀* 絳桃 a large red peach; *tọ̀ huòng* 桃園 a peach orchard; *hŏk tọ̀* 核桃 walnuts.

Tóh: A coll. word: to pierce through, as in *tóh tẹng táu*.

Tọh, 托 Read *táuk*; coll. *tọh*: to bear, to carry on the palm, as in *tóh chiū* 托手; to shoulder things, as in *tóh giěng tàu dīng* 托肩頭頂.

Tóh: A coll. word: also spoken *lóh* as in *tāu tóh* (or *lóh*) well, not sick; perceiving clearly; *ng tāu tóh*, indisposed; dull, ignorant.

Tŏi 推 Read *chŭi*; coll. *tŏi*: to refuse, to decline, as in *tŏi sù* 推辭; *tŏi dŏ* 推刀 a plane; *tŏi ĭ sǐng-siōng* 推伊身上 charge the blame on him.

Tŏi 胎 Read *tăi*; coll. *tŏi*: the womb: the foetus: *tàu tŏi* 頭胎 the first-born.

Tōi 腿 The thigh; the ham: *sŭ tōi* 蘇腿 Soochow hams; *hūi tōi* 火腿, a cured ham.

Tói 碓 Read *tói*; coll. *tói*: heavy, weighty; dull, captious, vexatious, as in *tói mông* 碓悶; *tói mông dăi* 碓悶代 a troublesome affair.

Tók　905

Tòi: A coll. prefix, as in *tòi-tọi*, a hole, a burrow.

Tói 碓, Analogous to *dói:* to attach a weight, to weight the end of a timber in sawing; sagged, loaded: read *tói* in the coll. q. v.

Tọi 退 To retire, to withdraw; to decline; yielding: *tọi sáik* 退色 to fade; *tọi huŏng* 退婚 to break a betrothal; *tọi huói* 退悔 to regret, to repent; *tọi buó* 退步 to recede; *tọi huá* 退化 to retrograde.

Tọi 褪 To disrobe; to fade and fall, as flowers: in the coll. read *táung,* q. v.

Tọi: A coll. word: a hole, as in *tòi-tọi;* a den, a burrow.

Tók 黜 To blame, to degrade; to expel from office as in *tók tọi* 黜退.

906 Tŏng

Tŏk 綳 Crimson silk; to sew, to stitch; bent, obstructed: also read *kŏk*.

Tŏk 恷 To fear, to dread; fear, terror; to tempt, to entice; *tŏk ték* 恷惕 timorous.

Tŏk 沰 Read *táuk;* coll *tŏk*: to subside, to ebb, as the tide.

Tŏk : A coll. word: to lose flesh, as in *tŏk lùng*, emaciated; *tŏk gá*, the price has fallen.

Tŏng 吞 To swallow, to gulp; to bolt; to usurp: *tŏng piĕng* 吞騙 to defraud: COM., *tŏng gĭng* 吞金 to swallow gold-leaf.

Tŏng 湯 Hot water; soup, broth: *tŏng ké* 湯氣 steam; *gŭng tŏng* 滾湯 boiling water; *tŏng muòng* 湯門 the Hot Water gate of Foochow; *tŏng-diè* 湯池 hot springs. Read *táung*: to rinse in hot water. Read *dáung*: dis-

Tòng 907

solute. Read *siōng:* to flow, as waves.

Tŏng 瞠 To stare at, gaze at: coll., *tŏng: tŏng á dāu* 瞠後斗 gazing backward. Also read *dòng.*

Tŏng 倘, 儻 A reading character: if, should, supposing, perhaps; suddenly, unexpectedly.

Tōng 帑 A treasury, as in *hū-tōng* 府帑; a repository of precious metals: *guók-tōng* 國帑 the national treasury.

Tōng: A coll. word: fat, corpulent.

Tōng 躺 To lie down; sleep.

Tóng 痛 A disease giving pain; a pain, an ache; distressed; to feel pity; very, extremely: in the coll. read, *tiáng* q. v.: *ăi tóng* 哀痛 deeply grieved; *tóng-kŭ* 痛苦 deep grief or sorrow; *tóng īng* 痛飲 to drink to excess.

Tòng 糖, Read *dòng:* coll. *tòng:*

sugar; candy: *tòng-bēng* 糖板 red sugar in cakes: *tòng-gūi* 糖粿 steamed sweet-cake of rice; *tòng uòng* 糖丸 balls of dark sugar; *huă-sĕng-tòng* 花生糖 peanut candy.

Tòng 狆 Read *dòng;* used in the *Báik-ĭng* for coll. *tòng*: between puberty and manhood; half-grown: *niè-giāng tòng* 伲仔狆, a large boy, a stripling.

Tòng: A coll. word: alike, equal in size.

Tóng 鼟 Read *lùng;* used in the *Báik-ĭng* for the coll. *tóng*: *tóng-tóng*, the sound of drums—the same as *dóng*.

Tóng: A coll. word: short and thick, as a person or a stick: *ă báik tóng*, low and thick, stout.

Tŭ 凸 Read *dŏk;* used in the *Báik-ĭng* for the coll. *tŭ*: jut-

ting, projecting; in relief: *tū
náh* 凸凹 projections and depressions.

Tū: A coll. word: analogous to the last: to stretch out, as the hand; to put away, as in a drawer.

Tū 土 Earth, ground, soil; earthy; local, native; a region; lands, patrimony: in the coll. read *tù*, q. v.: *tū-kiŏng* 土腔 a patois: *tū-sāng* 土產 productions of a place; *tū-pī* 土匪 local banditti; *gŭi-tū* 歸土 to die; *tū-ìng* 土人 the natives; *cūi tū* 水土, the climate of a place.

Tù 土 Read *tū*; coll. *tù*: earth; soil, clay, mud: *tù-hūng* 土粉 dust; *tù sǎ-hô* 土師父 a mason; *tù-mà* 土貓 a clay cat, as on roofs; *met.*, a stupid fellow; *ă-piéng tù* 鴉片土 crude opium.

Tŭ 侏 Sometimes read *ciŏ*: a

pigmy; *met.*, low, short: a short pillar in the roof, like a king-post: *tṳ̈-ù* 侏儒 a dwarf.

Tṳ̈ 姝 Read *kṳ* in the dictionaries; beautiful, handsome; a fine scholar; weak, timorous.

Tṳ̈ 株 The trunk of a tree; a numerative of trees: the lowest place; used for the coll. *dâu*, q. v.: *tṳ̈-ù* 株儒 a short pillar or post; a dwarf.

Tṳ̈ 蛛 A spider: *tĭ-tṳ̈* 蜘蛛 a spider that weaves webs; *tĭ-tṳ̈ máng* 蜘蛛幔 a web.

Tṳ̈ 銖 An ancient silver coin equal to 100 grains of millet: farthings, trifles; blunt, dull.

Tṳ̈ 佇, 竚 To stand and wait; to long for, as in *tṳ̈ uóng* 佇瑩.

Tṳ̈ 抒 To strain; to explain; to relieve as the feelings.

Tṳ̈ 杼 A shuttle; long; thin, as a

Tuà 911

wheel; a kind of chestnut. Read *sū;* a water-trough.

Tŭ 杵 A beater: *kêu tŭ* 臼杵 mortar and pestle.

Tŭ 紵絟, A coarse kind of hemp for making cloth; *hĭ tŭ* 絺紵 fine and coarse sorts of hemp.

Tŭ 苧 The grass cloth nettle: in the coll. read *dáe̦,* q. v.

Tŭ 貯 To hoard, to store up; a hoard: used for the coll. *diō* and *diŏh;* q. v.

Tŭ 鋤, 鉏 A hoe, as in *tŭ-tàu* 鋤頭 a mattock; to hoe, to cultivate; used for the coll. *tùi,* q. v.

Tù 躇 Embarrassed, perplexed: also read *dù: tiù-tù* 躊躇 hesitating.

Tuă 拖 Read *tŏ;* coll. *tuă:* to draw, to drag, to pull along.

Tuă 拖 Read *tŏ;* coll. *tuă:* like the last: to defer, to put off;

tuà guó nĭk 拖過日 to put off from day to day; to procrastinate.

Tuák 脫, 脱, Thin; wasted; to reject; to evade; if, perhaps: in the coll. read *táuk* and *táung*, q. v.: *tuák liê* 脫離 to get rid of, to escape. Read *iŏk*: to look fresh and well, as insects which have cast their skins.

Tuáng 彖 A pig running or walking; a hedgehog.

Tuáng 鍛, 煆 To forge, heat and hammer metals; practiced, experienced: *tuáng 'liêng* 鍛煉, skilled in.

Tuàng 團 A globular mass; round; united, harmonious; to surround, to mass together; a numerative of lumps, collections and round things: in the coll. read *diòng* q. v.: *tuàng uòng* 團

圓 circular; united, meeting as a family; *siéu nièng ngié ụng tuàng* 少年義勇團, boy scouts; *tuàng siéng* 團扇, a round frame fan; *tuàng liéng guŏh* 團練局, a drill room; *tuàng giék* 團結, blended; *tuàng-tā* 團體, united to help each other; federation; *tuàng-liéng* 團練, volunteers; *tuàng-tā cĕng-sìng* 團體精神, *esprit de corps*.

Tuàng 慱 Mental labor; grief, sorrow.

Tuàng 摶 To turn with the hand; to roll into a ball; to unite in one.

Tuàng 剬 To mutilate, to cut into pieces, as formerly done with criminals.

Tŭh 揬 Read *tŭk*; coll. *tŭh*: analogous to *dŭh*; to thrust at, to pierce: *met.*, to inform against.

914   Tŭk

Tùi 揰 To strike, to beat, as bells; in the coll. a blow, as with the fist; a classifier of blows: also read *dùi*, q. v.

Tùi 槌, 椎, To beat, to knock; a club; pestle; a bludgeon; the 1st also means to reject; *chà-tùi* 柴槌 a wooden pestle; *gū-tùi* 鼓槌 drumsticks.

Tùi 鍾, 鎚, A steelyard weight, to beat, to pound: *tiék-tùi*, 鐵錘 a hammer.

Tùi 鋤 Read *tụ*; coll. *tùi*: as in *tùi-tàu,* a hoe—same as *tụ-tàu,* q. v.

Tŭk 禿 Bald; blunt; bare, fallen off, as leaves; the bald-pated, as a Budhist priest: *tŭk-tàu-haẹng* 禿頭巷 an alley ending at a wall.

Tŭk: A coll. word: a superlative, very, extremely; *tŭk cóng*, very excellent; *tŭk diū ngài*, very bad indeed!

Tŭk 讀 To read aloud, to recite; to study; a reader; also to select: also read *dáiu* and in the coll. *tĕk*, q. v.

Tŭk 黷 Often read *dŭk:* to soil, to blacken; filthy, stained; to annoy, to insult.

Tŭng 通 To go through, to perceive; to inform; prosperous; learned; current, as *tŭng-hèng* 通行; *bók tŭng* 不通 not thorough, as a scholar; *tŭng-dī* 通知 to inform; *tŭng-tiĕng á* 通天下 the world; *tŭng ĭk* 通入 traffic, intercourse; *tŭng gó* 通告 a proclamation: in the coll. read *tĕng*, q. v.

Tŭng 侗 Also read *dùng:* plain, rude, ignorant: *kŭng tŭng* 倥侗 an ignorant boy.

916   Tūng

Tūng 恫 Also read *dòng:* pained, distressed; moaning from pain.

Tūng 冢 A mound; the summit of a hill; first, the eldest; *tūng cṳ̄* 冢子 the eldest son.

Tūng 塚 A grave, a tomb; sepulchres: *ngiê tūng* 義塚 a public tomb for vagrants; *huŏng tūng* 荒塚, a deserted grave.

Tūng 寵寵 Grace, favor, as in *ŏng tūng* 恩寵; love, affection; to esteem: also read *tŭng*, q. v.: *tūng ái* 寵愛 to love ardently.

Tūng 桶 A tub, a cask; a bucket; in the coll. read *tḙng*, q. v.

Tūng 畽 Also read *cṳ̄ng:* wild land near towns; paths of beasts.

Tūng 統 The origin, beginning: the head, the chief, as in *cṳ̄ng-tūng* 總統 the President; also meaning, the whole; in fine, all: COM., *tūng géung* 統共 the sum total; *tŭng liăng* 統領 a general control.

Tŭng 寵 Grace, favor, as in *ŏng-tŭng* 恩寵; love, tender regard; to prefer; also read, *tūng*, q. v.

Tụng 蟲虫 A general term for insects, and worms: in the coll., read *tèng*, q. v.: *báik tụng* 百蟲, insects in general.

Tụng 重 Read *dụng*; coll. *tụng*: to duplicate, repeated; a classifier of thicknesses; *tụng tăk tụng* 重叠重 to pile up; *tụng ĭk* 重入 add to; increase; *tụng iòng cáik* 重陽節 the Feast of the 9th day of the 9th moon.

Ŭ 圬 To plaster, as walls; stucco; *ŭ ing* 污人 a plasterer, a brick-layer.

Ŭ 杇 A trowel for plastering walls; to daub on mortar.

Ŭ 洿 A pool; muddy, standing

water; deep water: *ŭ-diè* 洿池 a pond; *ŭ nièng* 洿染 to stain, to defile.

Ŭ 污, 汙 Stagnant water; impure, unclean, physically and morally depraved; to insult, to debauch: also read *ó*, q. v.: *ŭ ŭk* 污辱 to insult, to debauch; *ŭ uói* 污穢 filthy, impure; *ŭ ciĕng* 污賤 vile, depraved. Read *uă:* to dig into the ground.

Ŭ 惡 An exclamation of regret, why, how! also read *ó* and *áuk*, q. v.

Ŭ 巫 Read *ù* in the dictionaries: sorcery, magic: *nṳ̄ ŭ* 女巫, a sorceress; *nàng ŭ* 男巫 a wizard.

Ŭ 誣 To invent; to deceive; to slander; *ŭ-niĕk* 誣揑 to trump up; *ŭ lái* 誣賴 to charge unjustly, *ŭ gó* 誣告 to accuse falsely.

Ŭ 烏 Used for the next: a crow,

as in *ŭ-ă* 諉鴉; filial, black, inky; to blacken; an interrogative particle, implying a negative, how? what? *ŭ-iŭ* 烏有 how is there? none, all gone; *ŭ áng* 烏暗 darkness; *ŭ-siŏh săng* 烏石山 Black Rock Hill, Foochow; *ŭ-lŏk-gŭi*, you black imp! a black man, a negro; *ŭ hăk* 烏合 Unorganized gathering, (lit collection of crows ready to disperse when eagle appears).

Ū 於, 嗚 An interjection; to sigh, to lament; ah! alas! the 1st also read *ŭ* q. v.

Ū 迂 Also read *ŭ*: far, distant; wide, spacious; bent, distorted.

Ū 侮, 㑄 To insult, to despise; to ridicule; disrespect: *ŭ-máng* 侮慢 to treat contemptuously.

Ū 儛 Interchanged with the next; to skip, and dance.

Ū 舞 To dance about; to gesture; *ū lùng-dǐng* 舞龍燈 to parade the dragon-lanterns—at new year's time.

Ū 撫, 捬 To soothe, to tranquilize; to stroke with the hand; to control, to manage; to comfort one: *ū-iŏng* 撫養 to nourish, to rear up; *ū-gáu* 撫敎, to nourish and teach.

Ū 拊 Used for the last: to pat; to soothe, to quiet.

Ū 憮 To caress, to soothe, to comfort; *ū iòng* 憮然 Alas for you! Sad! Read *hù*: large, great; proud.

Ū 膴 As in *ū-ū*, fat, good-looking; substantial, fine. Read *ù* and *hù*: meat boned and dried; also, a law, a pattern.

Ū 武 Military, martial; strong, brave; *ū-duáng* 武斷 arbitrary, ùng ū 文武 civil and military; ū-ngiĕ 武藝 military arts; ū cŏng gīng cháh 武裝警察 military police; ū-ĭ-ngàng dà 武彝嚴茶 tea from the Bohea hills.

Ù 鵡 A parrot of a large size, called ĕng-ū 鸚鵡; a species of macaw.

Ù 毋 Interchanged with the next: a prohibitive negative; do not, don't; an interrogative particle; the 80th radical.

Ù 無, 无, Not, none; destitute of, without, wanting: used for the coll. mò, q. v.: COM., ù dĭ 無知 without knowledge, brutish; ù sĭng 無心 unintentional; ù só 無數 countless; ù gó 無故 causeless; ù-huă-guō 無花果 the fig.

Ù 湖 Read hù; coll. ù, a lake: Să-ù 西湖 the west lake in the western suburbs of Foochow.

Ù: A coll. word: a buzzing in the ear, as when diseased: *ù-ù-giéu* it buzzes, it rings.

Ụ̆ 於, 扵, 于, A preposition, a relative particle; in, at, on; by, with, through; at the beginning of a sentence, it means respecting, as to; it often points out an accusative; sometimes makes the passive form of the verb; forms the comparative degree, than, more than; the last also means to go; to talk large; an exclamation, oh! also great, extensive, in which sense read *hŭ*: the 1st also read *ŭ*, q. v.: *ụ̆ sê* 于是, thus; *liĕk ụ̆ cọ̆* 列于左 stated below; *ụ̆ săng* 于山 "Temple Hill", close to the white pagoda in Foochow City.

Ụ̆ 竽 Also read *hŭ*: a kind of

Ū 923

organ, having 36 pipes of different lengths meeting in a bulb.

Ū 乳 The breasts, the nipple; milk; to nurse; used for the coll. nèng, q. v.: COM, ū-mū 乳母 (coll. nèng nā), a wet nurse; ū-hiöng 乳香 olibanum, frankincense.

Ū 予 To give, to grant, to bestow, as in séu ū 賜予, to confer on one; also read ü, q. v.

Ū 宇 The sides of a roof; to cover, as the eaves do; to shelter, as birds; to protect; wide, extensive; the canopy of the heavens; the world.

Ū 愈, 癒 To surpass, to prevail; to advance; to increase; more, better, still more; to cure; convalescent; iū sing ū-ū 憂心愈愈 to lament more and more.

Ū 禹 The name of an insect; to expand; expanded: *Dái ū* 大禹 the founder of the Hsia Dynasty, B. C. 2205.

Ū 羽 Feathers; wings, plumes; quick, flying; the 5th of the 5 musical tones; the 124th radical: *ū lôi* 羽類 birds; *ū mò* 羽毛 camlets.

Ū 與, 与 A class, a company, a band; to consort, to be on good terms; a preposition, with, by, to; conjunction, and, together; a disjunctive when repeated, either, or; as, like, as if; followed by *nìng* 寧 denotes comparison; to give, to grant, to bestow; to concede to, to promise; to permit, to allow; to delay; to employ; sometimes marks the dative before, and a transitive sense after verbs;

925

also read *ù* and *éu* q. v.

Ṳ 雨 Rain: a shower; to come thick and fast as rain; the 173rd radical: *ṳ cūi* 雨水 rain water; *ṳ-ló* 雨露 rain and dew; *há-ṳ* 下雨 (coll. *dáung-ṳ*), to rain; *ṳ náh* 雨凹 rain has slacked. Read *éu* and *ėu*: to rain.

Ṳ 予, 余 As a personal pronoun: I, we, myself, ourselves; the 2nd is a surname: the first also read *ū*, q. v.

Ṳ 愈, 俞 To answer, respond; yes, well, very good, quite so: a surname.

Ṳ̀ 餘 A remnant, residue, surplus: *dŏ ṳ̀* 多餘, or *iū ṳ̀* 有餘 more than enough; *gì ṳ̀* 其餘 overplus; *ṳ̀ â* 餘下 what remains: coll. *ṳ̀-diông* 餘剩 the remnant.

Ṳ̀ 儒 A scholar; the literati: *ṳ*

séu 儒士 scholars; *ù ngā* 儒雅 genteel, elegant; *ù gáu* 儒教 Confucianism.

Ù 如 A conjunction: as, according to; like, as if; if, perhaps; at the beginning of a sentence, means, as to, regards, like as; following adjectives, denotes manner, appearance, also adds emphasis to the meaning: *hò ù* 何如 how is it? *ù guō* 如果 truly, verily; *huāng* (or *dó* 倒) *bók-ù* 反不如, but its nothing like, or as good as.

Ù 孺 Also read *ū*: a surname; an infant, as in *ù cū* 孺子 a child.

Ù 榆 The elm, of which there are some ten varieties: *sōng ù* 桑榆, the mulberry and elm; *met.*, the evening of life, old age.

Ù 渝 To deteriorate; to become muddy, as a stream.

Ụ̈ 臾 A brief time, a moment; *sŭ-ụ̈* 須臾, in a little while. Read *gôi*: a basket to contain grass.

Ụ̈ 與, 歟 A final particle, indicating surprise or admiration; an interrogative or dubitative particle; a sign of the vocative; easy, dignified; the first also read *ụ̄* and *éụ̈*, q. v.

Ụ̈ 輿 The body of a cart; a barrow; to sustain as the earth does; a foundation; a term for the earth; many, numerous.

Ụ̈ 瑜, 瑀 The luster of gems; a beautiful stone; *met.*, virtue, excellence.

Ụ̈ 茹 Also read *ụ̄*: roots intertwisted; tangled; to take, to receive; to eat and drink greedily; to conjecture; pliant, flexible; putrid as herbs: *ụ̈-ngụ̈* 茹魚 putrid fish.

Ù 腴 Rich, fertile: *gŏ-ù* 膏腴 fertile as land.

Ù 諛 To flatter, as in *tiĕng ù* 諂諛: one who flatters, a sycophant.

Ù 譽 To praise, to extol; to eulogize extravagantly: also read *êu,* q. v.

Ù 窬 A small door cut in a large gate; to bore a hole: *chiŏng-ù* 穿窬 to cut through a wall, as thieves do.

Ù 踰, 逾 To pass over; to go beyond; to exceed a limit: *ù nguŏk* 逾月 to pass over the month; *ù-uŏk* 逾越 to overstep; *ù áing* 逾限 to exceed the limit.

Uă 劃 Read *hĕk;* used for the coll. *uă:* to mark or cut with a knife; to cut open; to cut glass: *uă buō* 劃補 to revise or counterfeit, as by changing a word.

Uă 呱 Also read *gŭ:* to cry out, as children do; to babble as a child in play with the hand over the mouth.

Uă 娃 A beautiful woman; a pretty girl. Read *gĭ:* deep sunken as the eyes.

Uă 蛙, 䵷, A frog, green and striped; also wanton sounds: *cĭng-dī uă* 井底蛙, a frog in a well; inexperienced.

Uă 窪, A deep ditch; a puddle; also deep, clear water.

Uā: A coll. word: to turn aside, to call at on one's way: *uā biĕng,* to avoid; *ă̤-uā* to loiter about.

Uá: A coll. word: brisk, flourishing as trade: *uá ciăh uá,* very busy, as a market.

Uâ 話, Words, discourse; language; to talk; to narrate: *gŏng uâ*

講話 to speak; *uâ tàu* 話頭 by-words: *tū-uâ* 土話 or *bàng uâ* 平話 the colloquial; *dṏ uâ* 多話 (coll. *dṏ uâ sṏ*), talkative; *duāi uâ* 大話 bragging; *huòi uâ* 回話 to return a verbal answer.

Uâ 畫, 畵, 圖, To draw, to paint pictures; to map; a picture or drawing, a painting: the 2nd also read *hĕk*, q. v.: *uâ sṳ̌* 畫師 an artist; *dâng uâ* 淡畫 and *chāi uâ* 采畫 ink sketches and colored paintings; *uâ hṏ* 畫號 to sign one's private mark.

Uáh 豁 Read *hŭk*; used in the *Báik-ĭng* for the coll. *uáh*; to grunt, as swine; *uáh-uáh-giĕu* 豁豁吅, to squeal, as pigs; *uà-uáh*, grunting; *met..* a hog, a pig.

Uăh 畫 Read *hĕk*; coll. *uăh*: a line; strokes of the pencil; to line off; *uăh siŏh uăh* 畫一畫 make one stroke; *uăh lā iŏng* 畫喇件 to sketch a pattern of.

Uăi 歪 Awry, askew; crooked; wicked, depraved as in *uăi sià* 歪斜 corrupt; *uăi buáng-bèng* 歪半爿 aslant, on one side, as a house; *uăi tàu uăi nŏ̤* 歪頭歪腦 "wry head and brains"; *met.*, very crooked.

Uăi: A coll. word: a country brogue for *ăi*, as in *uăi-á*, or *uăi-ò*, an exclamation of wonder, astonishment, etc.; *uăi á* a term of intense astonishment.

Uák 窊 To hollow out a cavity in the ground; a deep hollow; large and hollow.

Uák 挖 To excavate; to gouge, to dredge; to scratch or claw the door, as in *uák muòng* 挖門.

Uăk 曰 To say, to declare; to speak

of; called, termed; the 73d radical: also read *uŏk*, q. v.: *dói uăk* 對曰 he answered, saying; *cṳ̄ uăk* 子曰 Confucius said.

Uăk 活 Living, moving; life, motion; lively, active; cheerful; also read *guák*, q. v.: *uăk-miáng* 活命 life; *uăk dóng* 活動 quick, handy; *uăk puák* 活潑 and *uăk tuák* 活脫 vigorous, lively; active quick to perceive; *uăk cé* 活字 a verb; *ká-uăk* 快活, in good health and spirits; in easy circumstances.

Uăk 襪, 袜, Socks, hose; *dăng uăk* 單襪 stockings of a single thickness; *gák uăk* 夾襪, lined hose: *uăk-dái* 襪帶 garters.

Uăng 彎 To draw a bow; to bend; bent, bowed, curved: *uăng-uăng* 彎彎, bent, crooked; *diōng-uăng-tàu* 轉彎頭 the place to turn, the corner; *uăng diē* 彎入 to turn and enter, as a street.

Uăng 灣 A curved shore; a cove, a bay; to anchor, to moor; an anchorage: used for the coll. *uàng*, q. v.: *dài uăng* (coll *Dài-uàng*), 臺灣 Formosa.

Uăng 挽 To draw a bow; to lead, to conduct; to carry in the hand; to restore to a good state as in *uāng huòi* 挽回: *uāng dòi hŭng* 挽頹風 to reform.

Uăng 輓 Similar to the last; to pull, to drag as a carriage or hearse; *uāng lièng* 輓聯 funeral scrolls.

Uăng 晚 Evening, night; *met.*, late in life; late, tardy; used for the coll. *muōng*, q. v.: *uāng huò* 晚禾, the last crop of rice; *uānggŭ* 晚鼓 the evening drum;

uāng gīng 晚景 evening prospect; *met.*, the condition of the aged; *uāng buói* 晚輩, juniors; *uāng cṳ̄* 晚子 the child of old age; *cā uāng* 早晚 morning and evening; *uāng chuăng* 晚餐 supper.

Uāng 挽, 腕 The wrist; to grasp and twist, to wrench; *chiū uāng* 手腕 (coll. *chiū guāng* 手官) the forearm.

Uāng 剜 To pare, to cut off; to scrape.

Uāng 婉, 媫 Docile, obedient; winning; youthful, beautiful; the 2d also read *miēng*, q. v.: *ūi uāng* 委婉 easy, gentle.

Uāng 琬 A scepter of jade or gem, given to princes.

Uāng 碗, 盌, 椀, A bowl, a dish; a bowlful: *uāng chái* 碗菜 dishes of food; *buông uāng* 飯碗 rice bowls.

Uâng 935

Uāng 蔿 Also read *ók*: luxuriant, abundant, flourishing: also used for *uōng* 苑 a pasture, a park.

Uāng 莞 To seem pleased. Read *huàng*, a species of coarse grass for weaving into mats. Read *guāng*, as in *Dùng guāng* 東莞 a district in Kwantung.

Uāng 浣 Read *nguāng* in the dictionaries; to wash, to bathe; a decade of days: *uāng i* 浣衣 to wash one's clothes.

Uāng 綰 To tie, to bind; to hem: bad, evil; also read *guāng*.

Uàng 玩 Read *nguáng*; used for the coll. *uàng*: to ramble: *uàng suā* 玩耍 to recreate.

Uàng 灣 Read *uăng*; coll. *uàng*: a turn, a curve or bend, as in a river; *Dài uàng* 臺灣 Formosa.

Uàng 換, 換, To change; to commute; to barter as in *dọi uàng*

兑換; *uāng ī-siòng* 換衣裳 to change one's dress; *uâng gié* 換季 to change clothes with the seasons.

Uâng 萬, 万, Bees swarming; a myriad, ten thousand; all, many, an indefinite large number; as a superlative, very, wholly, great; *chiĕng-uâng* 千萬 ten millions; *met.*, most positively; *uâng bók kọ̆* 萬不可 positively ought not: *uâng bók dáik ī* 萬不得已 it must be, no help for it.

Uâng 卍 The Indian figure Swastica, called the myriad character.

Ŭh: A coll. word: to rise, to get up, as from the floor.

Ŭi 威 Majesty, official dignity; state, pomp; august, grave; overawing: *ŭi-nyièng* 威嚴

stern and severe: *mò ūi* 無威, has no dignity or sternness, as a teacher.

Ūi 葳 Pendent twigs or branches; a flag: the 5th moon.

Ūi 卉 A general term for plants; *ūi-mŭk* 卉木 herbs and trees, plants.

Ūi 唯 To answer in the affirmative, yes! also read *mì*, q. v.: *ūi-ūi*, 唯唯, aye, aye! yes, yes!

Ūi 虺 A large snake, with a huge head and small neck: also read *huòi: cūi ūi* 水虺 a sea serpent; *hŏk ūi* 蝮虺 an adder.

Ūi 偉 Great, rare; *cŏng ūi* 俊偉 a hero; *gì ūi* 奇偉 curious, remarkable.

Ūi 委 To bend under a burden; to sustain, as an office; to belong to; to reject, as in *ūi cī* 委之; *ūi báing* 委辦 a committee; *ūi dáung* 委當 same as *ciáng dáung* 正當, correct.

Ūi 諉 To involve, to implicate; to shirk the trouble, to entrust as in *ūi táuk* 諉託.

Ùi 桅 The mast of a vessel, as in *ùi găng* 桅杆; *duái ùi* 大桅 the mainmast. Read *gūi*: a yellow wood to dye with; a javelin.

Ùi 爲, 為, To do, to effect; to make; a substantive verb; to cause; to manage; also read *ói*, q. v.: *hèng-ùi* 行爲, to do, acts, doings; *ùi siéng* 爲善 to do good; *ùi hái bók chieng*, 爲害不淺 it will be very injurious.

Ùi 韋 Tanned leather, soft leather; rebellious; a surname; the 178th radical.

Ùi 圍 To enclose; to limit; to besiege; to encircle, as animals in hunting, as in *dā ùi* 打圍;

kuàng-ùi 圜圍 encircling: *báu ùi* 包圍 encircled; *ùi bìng* 圍屏 screens.

Ùi 違 To disobey, to rebel; to transgress rules, as in *ùi huák* 違法 and *ùi liĕ* 違例: perverse, seditious; *ùi buôi* 違背 to turn the back on, to rebel against.

Ùi 闈 The examination hall: *hiŏng ùi* 鄉闈, or *chiŭ ùi* 秋闈 the examination for Kujin; *huôi ùi* 會闈, or *chŭng ùi* 春闈 examination for Chinsz'.

Ŭk 勿 A negative, not, do not: *ŭk-ŭk*, 勿勿, in haste; *hĭ lā ŭk ngiòng* 非禮勿言 do not utter what is impolite or indecorous.

Ŭk 沕 As in *ŭk mŭk* 沕目 abstruse. Read *mĭk*: small, minute recondite; an atom.

Ŭk 物 A thing, a substance; goods merchandise, as in *huó-ŭk* 貨

物; *dóng ŭk* 動物 and *sĕng ŭk* 生物 animate objects, living things; *ìng-ŭk huă-nēu* 人物花鳥 men, flowers and birds; *cī ŭk cē* 指物字 a classifier.

Ŭk: A coll. word: to toss, to pitch things: *ŭk guó chiòng*, to toss over the wall.

Ŭk 欲 Interchanged with the next: to breathe after, to long for; to covet; to love; desires, aims; inclinations; on the point of: used for coll. *ói* q. v.

Ŭk 慾 Inordinate desire; licentious: *ŭk-huŏ* 慾火 raging lust.

Ŭk 浴 To bathe; as in *mŭk ŭk* 沐浴 to cleanse, to purify and correct the mind.

Ŭk 溽 Damp; moist and hot; rich, as food; the name of a stream.

Ŭk 辱 To put to shame, to disgrace, as in *lìng ŭk* 凌辱; *kók*

Ŭk 941

Ŭk 屈辱 to submit to ignominy.

Ŭk 蓐 Grass again springing up; shoots, sprouts; *ŭk siŭ* 蓐收 the harvest of the 7th moon.

Ŭk 褥 A mattress; a cushion; a thick, felt cover: *puói ŭk* 被褥 coverlet and mattress. Read *nǵ*: a child's dress.

Ŭk 鵒 An aquatic bird which knows the time of rain; to dart, as the kingfisher on its prey.

Ŭk 鴝 A species of singing thrush or grackle, as in *gù ŭk* 鴝鵒 or *báik gŏ*.

Ŭk 聿 A writing implement, a pencil; to obey, to follow; to narrate; an initial word: then, accordingly; the 129th radical.

Ŭk 毓 Same as the next: to nurture, to rear; to train a child to virtue; abundant.

Ŭng

Ŭk 育 To bear; to nourish, to bring up; to educate to virtuous habits: *ŭk dáik* 育德 to cultivate virtue.

Ŭk 鬻 Used for the last: to nourish; to sell. COM., *ŭk-chạ nĭk-nŭ* 鬻妻溺女 to sell wives and drown daughters. Read *géuk*: to nourish; young, tender. Read *céuk*: congee, gruel, using only upper half of the character in the coll. q. v.

Ŭng 氲 Vapor; the genial life-giving principles of nature.

Ŭng 溫 A river and district in Honan; warm, tepid; kind, gentle as in *ŭng iù* 溫柔 yielding; *ŭng huò* 溫和 mild, temperate as the weather; *ŭng cṳ́* 溫書 a three days' review; *ŭng sĭk* 溫習 a review of six days' lessons.

Ŭng 943

Ŭng 煜 A smothered fire; a genial warmth; vapor, warm steam. Read *ūng*: to stretch things by heat.

Ŭng 瘟, 瘟 A pestilence, as in *ŭng ŭk* 瘟疫 a plague, distemper. Read *ŭk*: sorrow, sadness.

Ŭng 鱙 As in the coll. *ŭng tì* 鱙鮐 small sea fish; *ŭng tì giè* 鱙鮐鱎 the salted *ŭng-tì*.

Ŭng 翁 Plumage on the neck; a term of honor, a title of respect used in letters; a venerable man, a grey beard; *bĕk-tĕu-ŭng* 白頭翁 a white-headed thrush; an old man; a surname.

Ŭng: A coll. word, as in *ŭng-nóng* or *ŭng-sùng*, dull, stupid: *ngài cièng sāi ặ cêng, ŭng-nóng sī mặ uòng*, bad cash get used up, but dolts never all die off!

Ŭng 塕 Read *ūng*: to sprinkle: *ŭng-dìng* 塕塵 dust.

Ūng

Ūng 刎 As in *ūng sī* 刎死, to commit suicide by cutting the throat.

Ūng 吻 The lips; *met.*, speech, talk: *kĕu ūng* 口吻 one's peculiar talk or meaning.

Ūng 胭 To blend in one; joined, as in *ūng hăk* 胭合 blended harmoniously.

Ūng 殞 Interchanged with the next in the sense of to fall: to perish; *ūng-miĕk* 殞滅, to become extinct, as a family; *ūng-mêng* 殞命 to die.

Ūng 穩 穏 To tread out grain; safe; free from risks, as in *ūng-dáung* 穩當; settled, fixed securely, as in *ăng-ūng* 安穩; trusty, steady, constant, as in *ūng-dẹung* 穩重.

Ūng 媼 Also read *ŭng*: a dame, a term for mother. Read *ŭk* as in *ŭk năk* 媼納 a fat child.

Ūng: A coll. word as in *ūng-dọ̆ piăng,* hump-backed.

Ùng 文 Strokes, lines; spots, bands, striae; colored, ornate; chaste; elegant as in *ùng ngā* 文雅; letters, literature as in *ùng cê* 文字; learned; literary and official or civil; a dispatch; a classifier of coins, as in *ék ùng* 一文; the 67th radical: used for the coll. *muòng,* q. v.: *ùng huák* 文法 grammar; *nguòng ùng* 原文, the original text; *hṳ̆ ùng* 虛文 empty forms; *ùng- dáng,* a superior sort of pomelo. Read *ŏng:* to hide, to gloss over.

Ùng 抆 Also read *ūng:* to rub, to feel; to wipe dry by rubbing: *ùng lôi* 抆淚 to wipe away tears.

Ùng 紋 A pattern in weaving;

marks, seams in wood; the lines on the palms of the hand, as in *chiū ùng* 手紋; *sià-ùng-buó* 斜紋布 cotton drills; *ùng-ngùng* 紋銀 sycee.

Ùng 蚊 A mosquito, a gnat: used for the coll. *hŭng*, q. v.

Ùng 云 To say, to declare; said: *ùng-ùng* 云云 what was spoken of, this and that; etc.; *gŭ ngṳ̄ ùng* 古語云, the old saying is; *ùng òi cê* 云謂字 a verb.

Ùng 芸 A fragrant herb like rue—its leaves keep insects out of mats and books: *ùng chŏng* 芸窗 a library.

Ùng 聞 To hear, as in *téng ùng*; 聽聞 news as in *sĭng ùng* 新聞; to learn by report; to inform; *diòng ùng* 傳聞 to publish a report; tradition; a report as in *hŭng ùng* 風聞; *ngĭ ùng* 耳

聞 reported; *giéng ùng* 見聞 see and hear. Read *óng:* character, fame.

Ŭng 殷 Used for the next: the highest degree of, great, perfect; a name for part of the Shang dynasty B. C. 1401—1137. Read *ūng* as in *ūng-ūng,* abundant.

Ŭng 慇 Sorrowing, depressed in spirit; sorrowful as in *ŭng-ŭng; ŭng-kùng* 慇懃 very carefull, anxiously diligent.

Ŭng 雍, 邕. The 1st is more commonly used; used for the next; harmony of sounds; to assist, to protect; crowded together: *ŭng huò* 雍和 harmonious; *ŭng-céng* 雍正 the Emperor Yung-ching A. D. 1723. Read *éung:* to guard against freshets.

Ŭng 雝 Similar to the last: *ŭng-*

huò 雞和 harmonious, agreeable.

Ụ̄ng 癰 A boil, an abscess; *buói-ụng* 背癰 a carbuncle on the back; *ụng cṳ̄* 癰疽 a deep sluggish ulcer.

Ụ̄ng 饔 Dressed food; an early meal, breakfast: *ụng-chuǎng* 饔飡 breakfast and supper.

Ụ̄ng 允 To permit, to promise; allowed; truly, honestly, sincerely.

Ụ̄ng 尹 To hold, to govern; to advance; faithful; a surname.

Ụ̄ng 忍 To endure; patience, as in *ụng nái* 忍耐; fortitude: used for *nūng* in the coll. q. v.: *ụng ṳ̆k bó siù* 忍辱報仇 to bear disgrace in order to take revenge: *ụng mặ guó* 忍賣過 unable to endure it.

Ụ̄ng 勇 Strong, brave, fearless;

courage; at Foochow used of soldiers from outside places: *ṳ̄ng sèu* 勇士 a hero; *ṳ̄ng gāng* 勇敢 rash: *ṳ̄ng lĭk* 力勇 vigorous.

Ụ̄ng 隱 隱 阭, Small, minute; secret; retired as an officer, as in *ṳ̄ng sèu* 隱士; *ṳ̄ng còng* 隱藏 to secrete; *ṳ̄ng mì* 隱微 abstruse.

Ụ̄ng 檃 The hidden frame work of a roof: *ụ̀ng guák*, machines for straitening and squaring wood.

Ụ̀ng 匀 Equal, even; to divide alike: *ụ̀ng sèu* to apportion equally; *ụ̀ng sāng hóng* 匀三分 to divide into three equal parts.

Ụ̀ng 畇 Land laid out in fields, for cultivation; to till land.

Ụ̀ng 戎 A weapon, arms; soldiers,

as in *ùng bĭng* 戎兵; thou, you.

Ụ̀ng 絨 Fine cloth; sometimes used for woolens; fine silk; velvet: *siĕu ùng* 小絨 flannel; *sià-ùng* 斜絨 kerseymere.

Ụ̀ng 容 Feeling in receiving; to receive kindly; to tolerate: the face as in *ùng-mâu* 容貌; *kuăng-ùng* 寬容 to be lenient; *ùng-ê* 容易 easy, not hard.

Ụ̀ng 榕 The bastard banyan; called *ùng chéu* in the coll. q. v.: *ùng siàng* 榕城 the banyan city, Foochow; *ùng kiŏng* 城腔 the Foochow patois.

Ụ̀ng 蓉 The Hibiscus: *hù-ùng* 芙蓉 hibiscus mutabilis.

Ụ̀ng 茸 Plants growing thick and luxuriantly; collected.

Ụ̀ng 鎔 To smelt, to fuse metals: to cast, to forge; a die for coining: used for the coll. *iòng*, q. v.

Ùng 庸 To employ, as servants; constant, ordinary: ùng-ìng 庸人 a mediocre; ù-ùng 毋庸 unnecessary: dŭng ùng 中庸 The Doctrine of the Mean, one of the Four Books.

Ùng 傭 To hire, to serve for wages; hired; in the following senses read cŭng and cūng in the dictionaries; equal; of the same rank: gă-ùng 家傭 domestics; ùng-gĕng 傭工 engaged as a laborer.

Ùng 融, 蝎 Vapor rising; liquified; harmonising; high and large; intelligent: ùng huò 融和 genial, as temperature.

Uŏ 窠 Read kuŏ in the dictionaries: a hollow place; a nest in a cave, or hollow.

Uŏ 窩 To dwell in a cave: a bird's nest, as in cēu-uŏ 鳥窩; a lonely dwelling; *met.*, a den of thieves, as in *chĕk uŏ* 賊窩; to harbor thieves: used for the coll *uō*.

Uŏ 媧 The Chinese Pandora, called *nṳ̈-uŏ* 媧女.

Uŏ 萵 A kind of vegetable, called *uŏ-sḙ̈u* 萵苣, wild endive; *uŏ bù* 萵瓤 a smooth-skinned gourd.

Uŏ 倭 Japan: also read *uŏi* q. v.: *uŏ-ing* 倭人 the Japanese; *uŏ káiu* 倭寇 Japanese marauders: *uŏ-dák* 倭鍵 pirates from "the eastern sea" who infested the coasts of Fukien at the close of the Ming dynasty.

Uŏ 盂 Read *ṳ̈* in the dictionaries; also read *uŏ*, but commonly *uò*: a basin of wood or metal; a vessel to contain food or liquids.

Uŏ 芋 The taro (arum aquaticum):

uó-nà 芋泥 taro pudding.

Uóh 沃 Read *áuk:* used for the coll. to irrigate; wet, as with rain; *uóh siŏh sĭng* 沃一身 got thoroughly drenched.

Uŏi 倭 Yielding: *uŏi dì*, to come from a distance: also read *uŏ* q. v.

Uŏi 煨 The fire in a chafing dish; to roast in embers, or ashes: *uŏi huōi lẹng* 煨火籠 to cover coals in a hand-stove. Read *ók:* a collection of burning coals.

Uŏi: A coll. word like the preceding: to cover, to secrete; *uŏi tù-diē,* to bury or hide in the ground.

Uŏi 洧 Occurs in the names of several streams: a small branch of the Han in Kai-fêng-fu, Honan.

Uōi 賄 Wealth, riches; to give to others; to bribe, as in *uōi-lô* 賄賂; hush-money.

Uói 噦 A rising of wind or breath; to eructate; wind on the stomach.

Uói 穢 Weeds or plants growing in disorder; unclean as in *ŭ-uói* 汚穢 morally defiled; *săng uói* 荾穢 to weed.

Uói 衞, 衛, To accompany and protect; to defend: *uói dôi* 衞隊 a guard of soldiers; *uói sĕng* 衞生 to protect against disease, sanitary.

Uŏk 兀 High and level at the top; to maim, as a penalty; an interjection, oh! ah!

Uŏk 曰 A euphonic initial particle, to direct the attention; now, now then: usually read *uăk*, q. v.:

Uŏng

Uŏk 粤 An initial particle, to draw the attention to, now, see, observe; in which senses interchanged with the preceding; in, at: *Uŏk hāi guăng* 粤海關 the hoppo of Canton; *uŏk-dŭng* 粤東 the Kwangtung Province.

Uŏk 越 To pass over; to excel; to transgress, as rules, as in *uŏk giĕ* 越規; to publish, as in *uŏk iòng* 越然; a sign of the comparative, more; *uŏk dì uŏk họ* 越遲越好 the later the better; *uŏk cā uŏk họ* 越早越好 the sooner the better; *Uŏk săng* 越山 a hill in Foochow near the North Gate.

Uŏng 寃, 冤, To force one to crouch; to injure, to oppress; to accuse falsely as in *uŏng-kók* 寃屈 or *uŏng-uōng* 寃枉 (coll. *uŏng-gōng* 寃講); *uŏng gă*

冤家 at feud, as brothers; *sing uŏng* 伸冤 to redress a wrong.

Uŏng 尢 Lame, deformed, a hunch-back; short and contorted; the 43 radical.

Uŏng 尪 Interchanged with the last: lame, crooked legs; weak, feeble.

Uŏng 汪 Deep and wide; a lake, a pool; the southern sea; a surname: *uŏng iòng* 汪洋 the vast ocean.

Uŏng 鴦 As in *uŏng-iŏng* 鴛鴦, the mandarin drake and duck, an emblem of conjugal love.

Uŏng: A coll. word, as in *uŏng-hing,* a dizziness, dizzy.

Uŏng 往, 徃 To go, to depart; to send, as a present; formerly, as in *uōng nĭk* 往日; *uōng-gū* 往古 anciently; *lài uōng* 來往 coming and going, both ways;

friendly intercourse; COLL., *uōng-uōng ciŏng-uâng* 往往將換 constantly so.

Uōng 枉 To oppress; bent, crooked; illegal, unjust: *uŏng-uōng* 寃枉 or *uōng kók* 枉屈 to accuse unjustly; *uōng hiè sĭng gĭ* 枉廢辛機 to lose all one's labor.

Uōng 網 A net for fowling or fishing; a net, a web; *met.*, that which binds or restrains, as the law; to involve, to entangle; to wind, as in *uōng sī* 網系 to spin cocoons; *tĭ-tŭ-uōng* 蜘蛛網 a spider's web.

Uōng 苑 A pasture, a paddock; a palace, as in *nô̤i uōng* 內苑; *gŭng uōng* 宮苑 (coll. *gŭng-uōng diē*), 宮苑入 the imperial apartments.

Uōng 遠, 逺 Distant, remote; to regard as distant: also *uóng* q.v.: *uōng gŭ* 遠古 in remote antiquity: *īng uōng* 永遠 eternal, forever: COLL. *uōng uāng* 遠挽 troublesome, difficult.

Uōng 阮 Read *nguāng* in the dictionaries; the name of a hill.

Uōng 袖 Read *séu;* used for the coll. *uōng*, as in *chiū-uōng* 手袖 a sleeve; *uōng-tàu* 袖頭, (or *muōi* 尾) the end of the sleeve; *chiū-uōng lŏh* 手袖絡 sleeve covers.

Uòng 怨 To hate, as in *uòng-hâung* 怨恨 hating; to dislike; an injustice, a wrong; ill-will, malice: *uòng táng* 怨嘆 to murmur at, grumbling. Read *hŭi*: to hoard up.

Uòng 丸 A pellet: a bullet as in *dàng uòng* 彈丸; *met.*, a very small plot of land; a pill as in *iŏh uòng* 藥丸; a classifier of boats and round things.

Uòng 紈 Read *huàng* in the dictionaries: plain, white sarcenet: *uòng siéng* 紈扇 silk fans.

Uòng 亡, 兦, Used for the next, also for *ù* (no, not): lost, gone; destroyed; dead, forgotten; to escape; a fugitive as in *uòng ìng* 亡人; one dead; *uòng guó* 亡過 or *sĭ uòng* 死亡, dead; death.

Uòng 忘 To escape the mind, to forget, as in *uòng gé* 忘記; to disregard: *uòng cìng* 忘情 unfriendly.

Uòng 員 A numerative of round things, as dollars and of officers; round, a round thing; to circulate: *guăng-uòng* 官員 officers, grandees.

Uòng 圓 Round, a circle; a ball, a sphere, a round lump, in which senses analogous to the preceding; to interpret, as dreams as in *uòng móng* 圓夢: in the coll. read *ièng* q. v.: *tuàng uòng* 團圓 a complete circle, as a family; the full moon.

Uòng 完 To finish, to complete; satisfactorily completed: *uòng ciòng* 完全 all completed; *gōng uòng* 講完 done speaking; *uòng cóng* 完竣 finished, as a job: *uòng liòng* 完糧 or *uòng cièng-liòng* 完錢糧 to pay land tax. COLL. *dŭ sāi uòng* 都駛完 all used up.

Uòng 爰 Often read *uóng*: to lead to another subject; an illative word, hence, therefore; at, in, up to; to deduce; to change; sad, lamentable; *uòng-uòng* 爰爰 slowly.

Uòng 援 Also read *uóng*, q. v.: to

Uòng 961

take by the hand; to pull or pluck out; to lead forward; *uòng īng* 援引 to lead on.

Uòng 湲 Water flowing or drawn off; the purling noise of a rapid current.

Uòng 黃 Yellow, a clay color; the imperial color; hurried; the 201st radical: *uòng huák* 黃髮 an old man; *chŏng uòng* 蒼黃 hasty: *uòng dộ* 黃道 the ecliptic: *uòng-ò* 黃河 the Yellow river; *uòng lì* 黃黎 a pine-apple; *uòng-ciĕng-mī* 黃粘米 rice of the late harvest.

Uòng 癀 The jaundice, as in *uòng dāng* 癀瘴; icterus: the term also includes some forms of dropsy.

Uòng 潢 A pool, a lake without an outlet; deep and clear water; the Sira-muren river flowing into the gulf of Chihli. Read *uōng*: to dye paper.

Uòng 輨 The cross-bars in front of a chariot; the thills or shaft; the east and west gates of a yamun or temple, as in *děng uòng-muòng* 東輨門 and *sặ uòng-muòng* 西輨門.

Uòng 王 A king, a sovereign; lords and princes; royal, princely; also read *uóng*: *guók uòng* 國王, a ruler; *Uòng-sĭng-dĭ* 王審知 the chief who subdued the Min country (Fukien).

Uóng 旺 The sun appearing in splendor; flourishing, as in *hĭng-uóng* 興旺; *cáung uóng* 壯旺 strong and lusty; *sŏi-uóng* 衰旺 losing and winning.

Uóng 望 To hope, to expect; a hope or expectation, as in *uóng-tàu* 望頭; *āi uóng* 倚望 to expect confidently; opposite, as the moon in apposition; *sáuk uóng* 朔望 the 1st and 15th of the moon; *mìng uóng* 名望 a good reputation.

Uóng 妄 Disorderly; vain, wild; reckless: sometimes used for *huảng* (all): *ù-uóng* 無妄 the 25th diagram. Read *uòng*; to cease to be.

Uóng 遠 To separate: as in *uóng liê* 遠離 to be free from: also read *uõng*, q. v.: COLL. *ngài nẹng uóng liê* 呆伏遠離, may you be rid of bad people.

expect confidently; opposite, as
the moon in apposition; and
嬲望 the 1st and 15th of
the moon; 有望 yǒu wàng a
good reputation.

Lòng 奀 Disorderly, vain, wild;
reckless; sometimes used for
lòng (all); a word 奀奀 the
verb diagram. Head wrong, to
cease to be.

Cáng 藏 To appear, as in song
佗 逯藏 to be free from; when
mad song, p. v. corr. 佗逯 sǒng
zāng, 佗 奀休逯藏, may you
be rid of bad people.

LIST OF 214 RADICALS.

With their sounds in the Foochow Dialect, and one or more of their leading significations, as found in Kanghi's Dictionary. The sign [1] marks the Radicals mostly used in combination; the contracted forms are always found in combination.

I STROKE.

一 1. *Ék*, one, unity
丨 2. *Gūng*,[1] a stroke
丶 3. *Cū*,[1] a point
丿 4. *Piék*,[1] a left stroke
乙 5. *Ék*, one, curved
亅 6. *Kuók*,[1] hooked

II STROKES

二 7. *Nê*, two
亠 8. *Tèu*,[1] a cover
人 亻 } 9. *Ìng*,[1] man
儿 10. *Ìng*,[1] a man walking

THE RADICALS

入	11.	*Ĭk*, to enter
八	12.	*Báik*, eight
冂	13.	*Hĭng*,[1] a limit
冖	14.	*Mĭk*,[1] to cover
冫	15.	*Bĭng*,[1] ice, cold
几	16.	*Gī*, a table
凵	17.	*Kāng*,[1] a receptacle
刀刂	18.	*Dŏ*,[1] a knife
力	19.	*Lĭk*, strength
勹	20.	*Bău*,[1] to infold
匕	21.	*Bī*,[1] a spoon
匚	22.	*Hŭng*,[1] a chest
匸	23.	*Hī*,[1] to conceal
十	24.	*Sĕk*, ten
卜	25.	*Bŏk*, to divine
卩㔾	26.	*Chiĕk*,[1] a joint, a knot
广	27.	*Háng*,[1] a shelter
厶	28.	*Sŭ*,[1] selfish, deflected
又	29.	*Êu*, moreover

III STROKES.

口	30.	*Kēu*, mouth, orifice
囗	31.	*Ùi*,[1] to inclose

THE RADICALS

土	32.	*Tŭ*, ground, earth
士	33.	*Sẹ̆u*, a scholar
攵	34.	*Cŭng*,[1] to follow
夊	35.	*Sŏi*,[1] to walk slowly
夕	36.	*Sĭk*, evening
大	37.	*Dâi*, large
女	38.	*Nṳ*, female
子	39.	*Cṳ̄*, a child
宀	40.	*Mièng*,[1] a cover
寸	41.	*Cháung*, an inch
小	42.	*Siĕu*, small
尢 兀 尤	} 43.	*Uŏng*,[1] distorted, lame
尸	44.	*Sĭ*, a corpse
屮	45.	*Tiĕk*,[1] a sprout
山	46.	*Săng*, mountain
川 巛	} 47.	*Chiŏng*, a stream
工	48.	*Gŭng*, work
己	49.	*Gī*, one's self

THE RADICALS

巾	50.	Gŭng, a napkin
干	51.	Gǎng, a shield
幺	52.	Iĕu, small
广	53.	Iēng,[1] shelter, roof
廴	54.	Ing,[1] a journey
廾	55.	Gŭng,[1] to join hands
弋	56.	Ik, an arrow
弓	57.	Gŭng, a bow
彑彐	58.	Giĕ,[1] a swine's head
彡	59.	Săng,[1] feathers, hair
彳	60.	Tĕk,[1] a short step

IV STROKES

心忄小	61.	Sĭng, the heart
戈	62.	Kuŏ, a spear
戶	63.	Hô, a door
手扌	64.	Chiŭ, a hand
支	65.	Ciĕ, a branch
攴	66.	Páuk,[1] a blow

THE RADICALS

疋	103.	*Pék*, a roll, a piece
疒	104.	*Chòng*,[1] diseased
癶	105.	*Buák*,[1] to straddle
白	106.	*Bĕk*, white
皮	107.	*Pì*, skin
皿	108.	*Mĭng*, a dish
目 目	109.	*Mŭk*, the eye
矛	110.	*Màu*, a spear
矢	111.	*Chī*, an arrow
石	112.	*Sĭk*, a stone
示 礻	113.	*Sé*, to admonish
禸	114.	*Niū*, print of a claw
禾	115.	*Huò*, grain
穴	116.	*Hiĕk*, a cave
立	117.	*Lĭk*, to stand

VI STROKES

竹	118.	*Dĕuk*, bamboo
米	119.	*Mī*, rice
糸	120.	*Sī*,[1] silk
缶	121.	*Pēu*, crockery

THE RADICALS

网 四 冗	122.	*Uōng*, a net
羊	123.	*Iòng*, a sheep
羽	124.	*Ŭ*, feathers
老	125.	*Lọ̄*, aged
而	126.	*Ì*, and, still
耒	127.	*Lọ̆i*, a plough
耳	128.	*Ngī*, the ear
聿	129.	*Ŭk*, a pencil
肉 月	130.	*Nŭk*, flesh
臣	131.	*Sìng*, a minister
自	132.	*Cĕu*, self, from
至	133.	*Cé*, to extend to
臼	134.	*Kêu*, a mortar
舌	135.	*Siĕk*, the tongue
舛	136.	*Chuāng*, error
舟	137.	*Ciŭ*, a boat
艮	138.	*Gáung*,[1] perverse
色	139.	*Sáik*, color
艸 艹	140.	*Chọ̄*, shrubs

THE RADICALS

火灬	86.	*Huŏ*, fire
爪爫	87.	*Cāu*, claws
父	88.	*Hó*, a father
爻	89.	*Ngàu*,[1] to blend
爿	90.	*Bèng*,[1] a couch
片	91.	*Piéng*, a splinter
牙	92.	*Ngà*, teeth
牛	93.	*Ngiù*, a cow
犬犭	94.	*Kēng*, a dog

V STROKES

玄	95.	*Hièng*, somber
玉王	96.	*Ngŭk*, a gem
瓜	97.	*Guă*, a melon
瓦	98.	*Nguā*, earthen tiles
甘	99.	*Găng*, sweet
生	100.	*Sĕng*, to produce
用	101.	*Ĕung*, to use
田	102.	*Dièng*, a field

THE RADICALS 969

文	67.	*Ùng*, letters
斗	68.	*Dĕu*, a measure
斤	69.	*Gŭng*, a catty
方	70.	*Huŏng*, square
旡无 }	71.	*Ù*,¹ not, wanting
日	72.	*Nĭk*, the sun
曰	73.	*Uăk*, to speak
月	74.	*Nguŏk*, the moon
木	75.	*Mŭk*, wood
欠	76.	*Kiéng*, to owe
止	77.	*Cī*, to stop
歹歺 }	78.	*Dāi*, evil
殳	79.	*Sù*,¹ weapons
毋	80.	*Ù*, do not
比	81.	*Bī*, to compare
毛	82.	*Mò*, hair
氏	83.	*Sé*, a family
气	84.	*Ké*,¹ breath
水氵氺 }	85.	*Cūi*, water

THE RADICALS

虍	141.	*Hù*, a tiger
虫	142.	*Tùng*, reptiles
血	143.	*Hiĕk*, blood
行	144.	*Hèng*, to walk, to do
衣 衤	145.	*Ĭ*, clothing
襾 西	146.	*Să*, to cover, the west

VII STROKES

見	147.	*Giéng*, to see
角	148.	*Gáuk*, a horn
言	149.	*Ngiòng*, words
谷	150.	*Gók*, a valley
豆	151.	*Dầu*, pulse, beans
豕	152.	*Chī*, swine
豸	153.	*Cầi*, reptiles
貝	154.	*Buói*, pearls, precious
赤	155.	*Chék*, flesh color, bright
走	156.	*Cēu*, to run
足	157.	*Céuk*, the foot
身	158.	*Sing*, the body
車	159.	*Gŭ*, a carriage

974   THE RADICALS

辛 160. *Sĭng*, bitter
辰 161. *Sìng*, time
走⸱辶 }162. *Chiŏk*,[1] motion
邑⸱阝 }163. *Ĕk*,[1] a city (placed on the right)
酉 164. *Iŭ*, ripe, spirits
釆 165. *Biĕng*, to separate, to cull
里 166. *Lĭ*, a mile

VIII STROKES

金 167. *Gĭng*, metal, gold
長⸱镸 }168. *Diòng*, long, old
門 169. *Mùŏng*, a door
阜⸱阝 }170. *Páiu*,[1] a mound (placed on the left)
隶 171. *Dâi*,[1] to extend to
隹 172. *Chŭi*,[1] fowls
雨 173. *Ṳ*, rain
青 174. *Chĭng*, green, azure, dark
非 175. *Hĭ*, not, wrong

IX STROKES.

面 176. *Miĕng*, the face

THE RADICALS

革	177.	*Gáik*, skin, hide
韋	178.	*Ùi*, to oppose
韭	179.	*Giū*, leeks
音	180.	*Ĭng*, sound
頁	181.	*Hiĕk*, the head, a leaf
風	182.	*Hŭng*, wind
飛	183.	*Hĭ*, to fly
食	184.	*Sĭk*, to eat
首	185.	*Siū*, the head
香	186.	*Hiŏng*, incense

X STROKES

馬	187.	*Mā*, a horse
骨	188.	*Gáuk*, bones
高	189.	*Gŏ*, high
髟	190.	*Biĕu*,[1] long hair
鬥	191.	*Dáiu*,[1] to quarrel
鬯	192.	*Tióng*, fragrant wine
鬲	193.	*Gáik*, a tripod, urn
鬼	194.	*Gūi*, a demon

XI STROKES.

魚	195.	*Ngù*, fish
鳥	196.	*Nĕu*, a bird.
鹵	197.	*Lū*, salt

THE RADICALS

鹿 198. *Lŭk*, a deer
麥 199. *Mĕk*, wheat
麻 200. *Mà*, hemp

XII STROKES.

黃 201. *Uòng*, yellow
黍 202. *Sṳ*, millet
黑 203. *Háik*, black
黹 204. *Cī*, to sew

XIII STROKES.

黽 205. *Mīng*, a frog
鼎 206. *Tīng*, a tripod, pan
鼓 207. *Gū*, a drum
鼠 208. *Chṳ*, a mouse, rat

XIV STROKES.

鼻 209. *Bĭk*, the nose
齊 210. *Cà*, even, correct

XV STROKES.

齒 211. *Chī*, the teeth

XVI STROKES.

龍 212. *Lùng*, a dragon
龜 213. *Gŭi*, a tortoise

XVII STROKES.

龠 214. *Iŏh*, a pipe, flute